UNEXPECTED INVITATIONS

*Surprises, adventures, and opportunities
in Mennonite ministry*

*To Peter, a co-worker who
shared some of these journeys
with us!*

Angela Erwin

ANGELA REMPEL, WITH ERWIN REMPEL
An autobiography

Cover:
The background, a watercolor painted by Marcia Rempel Weaver in 1994, is based on a quilt that was pieced by her great-grandmother Ida Albrecht (1884 – 1975) of Kingman, Kansas; quilted by her grandmother Magdalene Albrecht (1916-1986) and the women at Bethel Mennonite Church, Fortuna, Missouri. The quilt was first used in the 1950s by Marcia's mother, Angela (Albrecht) Rempel.

After many years of use, some fraying quilt pieces came off, inspiring the painting, which shows the quilt hanging on a cross, as a symbol of Marcia's parents, Angela and Erwin Rempel, leaving the comfort of the familiar to follow God's leading to a new place.

Photo: The Rempel family in 1981, as shown on a prayer card prepared by the Commission on Overseas Mission of the General Conference Mennonite Church.

Unexpected Invitations: Surprises, adventures, and opportunities in Mennonite ministry
Angela Rempel, with Erwin Rempel
An autobiography

Copyright © 2016 by Angela M. Rempel and Erwin H. Rempel

Cover design by Campbell Print Center, 4564 South Valley Pike, Harrisonburg, VA 22801

Text design and layout by Jim L. Friesen

Library of Congress Control Number: 2016920231

International Standard Book Number: 978-0-9979990-0-6

Printed in the United States of America by Mennonite Press, Inc., Newton, Kansas. www.MennonitePress.com

Dedication

To our three children and their spouses:
Marcia Rempel Weaver and John Weaver
Marc and Hannah Gascho Rempel
Carla and Micah Hurst

And to our six grandchildren:
Rachel and Evan Weaver
Madeleine and Katherine Gascho Rempel
Shawna and Jeremiah Hurst

Contents

Foreword

This is a story of the journey of two ordinary people inspired by their love for God and their love for each other. It is also a story of their common call to serve the purposes of God. That call inserted them into uncommon experiences and called forth in them extraordinary commitments that allowed them to make a difference in the lives of those they served. Along the way they created a family and engaged in cross-cultural mission. They became key players in a story filled with pathos, passion, and the pursuit of their desire to be agents of healing and hope in the world.

Erwin and Angela's story begins with their rootedness in communities that were shaped by the immigrant experience of their forebears who searched for a better, freer, more secure existence. This story recounts the intentional decisions Erwin and Angela made to leave the familiar circumstances that were their lot – risking comfort and security for the sake of Christ's kingdom. In pursuit of their call, they travel to all continents, live in several, and everywhere encounter the surprises of God's love and care in whatever circumstances they were called to face.

The story told here is unvarnished and compelling. Through the journeys of the Rempels we observe the fashioning of a legacy that brought blessing into many lives.

I am grateful for the gift of their story. The mission agency of Mennonite Church USA and its predecessor agencies give thanks for their service. I personally celebrate the privilege I had of intersecting with their story for a few years during the first decade of the 21st century.

– Stanley W. Green, Executive Director,
Mennonite Mission Network

Preface

The big Boeing 707 plane flew steadily through the night, non-stop from New York City to famous and beautiful Rio de Janeiro in Brazil. I was on my way, at last, to what I felt God had been preparing for me.

Back in the country church of my childhood in Missouri, through the words of a missionary to India, I first heard God's quiet voice urging me toward serving in overseas mission. That call intensified through my teenage years. In college I met and then married Erwin Rempel, who shared the same interest. We thought the overseas "mission field" lay straight ahead for us as soon as he completed seminary. However, some unexpected invitations came – tempting detours or part of God's training for us?

Now in the darkened aircraft, at age thirty-one, with a husband and two children, I focused on trying to sleep upright and not kick infant Marc sleeping at my feet. Earlier I had felt as though I, a non-swimmer, was jumping into the deep end of a swimming pool. Now excitement and fear, anticipation and curiosity, blended into a calm confidence of trust in God's leading.

This is a story of God at work, weaving together experiences that brought together a shy little country girl and a tall orphan boy into a life of ministry in Mennonite church circles – both in the United States and internationally. The chapters of our lives include living in nine different states and on three continents and too many travels to relate or even count.

Each chapter of life left a permanent imprint on us. Our time in Brazil turned out to be especially momentous. At the far end of life now, we see that our experiences in earlier chapters of life continued like strands into the next chapters to enrich, enable, and strengthen us for new tasks. Several themes run throughout: major unexpected invitations that changed the direction of our lives, changing times and technologies, and navigating through various aspects of Mennonite church life.

We didn't set out with clearly defined goals. We simply sought to follow the Lord's leading, one step at a time. It is humbling and amazing to realize how full and abundant our lives have been. Erwin and I are overwhelmed with gratitude for God's undeserved blessings in our lives.

For our family, interested friends, and fellow travelers on the journey from the General Conference Mennonite Church to Mennonite Church USA, this account reflects our memories of where we came from and some of what we did.

Unless identified differently, upon first reference, the churches and people mentioned were part of the General Conference Mennonite Church or Mennonite Church USA.

"One generation will commend your works to another;
they will tell of your mighty acts."
Psalm 145:4

Angela Rempel 2016

Chapter One
Childhood and Family Backgrounds

Erwin Rempel's Story

Part One
Family Background

Henry Henry Rempel, Erwin's father, had the distinction of being born in Switzerland into a German-speaking Mennonite family whose home was in Russia. That date was April 10, 1895, depending on which calendar is used.

The Rempels were among thousands of Germans, including Mennonites, who settled in colonies in southern Russia beginning in the late 1700s. Their ancestral sojourn prior to that had been in the Netherlands and Prussia. While settled in Prussia, which now is part of Poland, the Mennonites' diligent farming methods caught the eye of Catherine the Great, empress of neighboring Russia. She recruited Mennonite farmers in Prussia to relocate in Russia's recently acquired Ukraine to develop its agricultural potential. In addition to enticing them with land, she offered exemption from military service and the privilege of maintaining German-speaking communities and churches. The first Mennonites moved to southern Russia in 1789 and began establishing several sizeable colonies.

Henry Aron Rempel, (1861-1900), Erwin's grandfather, was a minister in the Mennonite church in the town of Karassan on the Crimean Peninsula. Seeking more Bible knowledge, Henry Aron took his wife, Barbara Matthies Rempel, and two young daughters to Switzerland where he studied at the St. Chrischona Theological Seminary in the Canton of Basel. During Henry Aron's year of study there, his only son, Henry Henry, was born, thus bestowing on him a Swiss birth certificate. We can only conjecture whether or not that document influenced the trajectory of Henry's life.

The family custom was to give the father or mother's first name as a child's middle name. Apparently they really liked the name Henry (Heinrich in the German) so the boy was named Henry Henry Rempel. The proud father wrote a letter on May 20, 1895, to his own mother back in southern Russia. He attempted to reassure her about the baby's well-being. Here are some excerpts from the English translation of that letter written in the old handwritten German gothic script: "The little Heinzi brings us much joy. ... That Heinzi is not suffering from malnutrition is guaranteed by his peaceful sleep, his round cheeks and legs and then (pardon please!) if you mother could see his accomplishments in his diapers, then surely all your motherly doubts and concerns would fade away."

Returning to Russia

The Rempel family moved back to Karassan in the Crimea when Henry Aron completed his studies in Switzerland. Later another daughter joined their family. Henry Aron suffered from some chronic illness and died in 1900 when his son, Henry Henry, was only five years old. The widow and her children moved from Crimea north to Halbstadt, the administrative center of the large Molotschna Mennonite colony where both she and her late husband had been born. Barbara Rempel and her children likely enjoyed a comfortable and secure life in the Mennonite community.

A 1903 photo of a large prosperous Rempel family shows blond-haired eight-year-old Henry sitting among the other children on the ground near the center of the photo. Erwin's great-grandfather, Aron Johannes Rempel, is the elderly man centered in this photograph. Aron Johannes had been a minister at the Gnadenfeld Mennonite Church in the Molotschna colony, probably about the time that there was a major and bitter split resulting in the formation of the Mennonite Brethren Church.

In general, most Mennonites in Russia enjoyed a comfortable life

2

Henry H. Rempel, age 8, with blonde hair, sits with other children on the ground in center front of large Rempel family at Gnadenfeld, Ukraine, 1903. Henry's grandparents, Aron J. and Anna (Goerz) Rempel are seated behind him.

lived separately from the Russian people around them. Some Mennonites became very wealthy on large estates; some did well in business, but many prospered in agriculture. Among the Rempels there were teachers and ministers. In 1915 when Henry was twenty, he was studying at a commercial school in Halbstadt.

The Great War begins

Life changed when World War I began. During the war, from 1916-18, Henry, along with other Mennonite conscientious objectors, served in an alternative service role with the Russian military as a non-combatant in their version of the Red Cross, called "sanitar." Henry didn't leave any written information about that time. Other young men who served in that capacity have written about caring for wounded and dying Russian soldiers on the trains that shuttled them away from the battlefront to hospitals.

The communist revolution in 1917 began a prolonged chaotic and difficult time for the country and especially for the German-speaking Mennonites, who had kept themselves aloof from the rest of the Russian people and culture. The Mennonites suffered repeatedly as several different armies moved back and forth through their villages and farms, requisitioning food and other items – the White Army, German Army, the Bolsheviks, known as the Red Army. Anarchy reigned at times as vicious bandits took not only possessions and food but terrorized the residents with beatings, rape, and brutal murders. Disease added to their plight. Some accounts relate that about a third of the Mennonites died of typhus, which was transmitted from the body lice on the bandits when they invaded, staying in their houses and sleeping in their beds.

Russian and Ukrainian peasants grabbed land from Mennonites, some who had been their employers. Some Mennonites abandoned their belief in biblical non-resistance and banded together in self-defense units. The loss of their farming equipment, animals, and land, plus lack of rain, brought extreme famine. In 1920, Mennonites in the U.S. and Canada

Henry H. Rempel stands at the right behind his widowed mother in this photo of his three sisters, a brother-in-law, and his sister's child; in Russia prior to 1923.

heard about the terrible conditions of Mennonites in Russia. Efforts to send aid from North America resulted in the beginning of Mennonite Central Committee (MCC). The Rempels undoubtedly benefited from MCC help. The communists eventually gained control of Russia in 1922, imposing their godless philosophy and social structures.

Erwin remembers his father saying he too had been seriously ill for a time in Russia. He said his family buried food under the incinerator in the back yard in attempts to hide it from the marauding soldiers and bandits. Erwin wishes he could have asked more questions or remembered more of what his father may have said about life in Russia. Other people have written about the Mennonite experience of Henry's time, moving from the good times of his childhood to the turmoil, terror, and tragedy during his young adult life. Such writings provoke even more questions about what Henry may have experienced and felt.

Immigrating

Many Mennonites, understandably, sought to leave Russia. By then the United States accepted few immigrants from Russia. Thousands of Mennonites migrated to Canada and Latin America. Henry Rempel also sought to leave.

Henry received assurance of support from relatives living in the U.S. An uncle by marriage, William P. Neufeld of Reedley, California, declared that he was capable and willing to support Henry until he could provide for himself. However, Neufeld died before Henry could come. John J. Peters, married to one of

Henry H. Rempel passport photo, 1923.

Henry's cousins and living in Shafter, California, signed a statement, "I will give him a home and provide for him until he can help himself."

In July 1923, Henry obtained a Russian passport in Moscow and a visa to leave the country. Was it because of his Swiss birth certificate that he was among the few Mennonite immigrants the United States accepted in 1923?

Henry was twenty-eight years old when he said a final goodbye to his widowed mother and perhaps only one surviving sister, married by then. Did they have hopes of eventually joining him in North America? Did they encourage or resist his leaving?

With his new passport and other documents, Henry set off for Constantinople. A document declares:

> American Consulate General in Constantinople, Turkey, on September 26, 1923, Henry Rempel, a citizen of Russia, bearer of passport number 4500 dated September 15, 1923, issued by the British Authority in Constantinople prepared a "Declaration of Alien about to depart for the United States No. 3662.

Henry's statement:

> I was born 1895, at Canton Basel, Switzerland. My occupation is clerk and laborer. I last resided at Constantinople, Turkey, for 2 weeks and I intend to go to California to remain for good for the purpose of joining a friend. My references are John J. Peters, Shafter, California.

Henry Rempel apparently traveled by himself and not with other Mennonites. He went to France where on October 27, 1923, he set sail from Cherbourg on the ship *Berengaria* of the Cunard Steamship Company Line, in third cabin. He arrived in the United States on November 2, 1923. He stated, "I was examined by United States immigration officers at Ellis Island, New York, U.S.A."

New life in California

It is likely that Henry traveled to California by train all across the vast country that would be his new home. What were his impressions of America? How was he received? How did he learn English?

After about eight months in Shafter, California, he apparently worked off the cost of his passage to America. Henry then moved to the Los Angeles area where he did a variety of low-skilled jobs over the years. He lived in several different places.

The economy was good when Henry arrived in the U.S. in 1923. Six years later the Great Depression began. Perhaps Henry found it difficult to secure employment. Anti-immigrant prejudices usually increase during times of economic distress. His English undoubtedly had a heavy German accent; however, his English writing was good in both spelling and grammar. He had a keen and curious mind and continued his formal education.

Family letters from Russia

Henry preserved a few letters from his mother, Barbara Matthies Rempel, and other relatives who stayed in Russia. Less than half of these letters have been translated from the old-style German handwriting, which few people now can read. Apparently for a few years after Henry left Russia, conditions improved somewhat. His mother wrote him in December 1927 from Margenau, a village in the Molotschna colony. Among ordinary items pertaining to Christmas activities, she writes, "May you soon begin to feel at home in those great United States or else return to your mother." That was more than four years after he arrived in the U.S. He must have shared with her some struggles he had in his new homeland.

Four years later, in November 1931, when Stalin had come to power, his mother wrote him from Novopol, which appears to be outside of the Ukraine. No explanation is given for why and how she moved. She writes about someone leaving and adds, "many others are leaving or are being taken." She mentions that the men wanted tools for Christmas, which were hard to get, but they hoped for a change for the better. She wrote about renovating a comforter with old wool to send with her grandson Victor [Henry's nephew] who had to leave for Omsk after New Years for an unspecified reason. Omsk is listed as a city in Siberia. Letter writers knew to be very cautious in what they wrote, assuming the Soviets read their written correspondence.

A few months later, February 1932, his mother wrote again from Novopol, "I take you daily before the throne of God. He will not forsake His child. ...We still hope to see each other." She thanked him for a package he sent with fruit, rice, sugar, and a nightgown. One time

Henry had sent her money via a "Swiss friend," which some interpret to mean the Swiss Red Cross.

"Could you perhaps get a better job in Reedley?" Henry's concerned mother wrote him from far away Russia, based on communication she apparently had from others. "Isaac Warkentin always finds work. They even took over another farm."

The Rempels were related to Isaac J. and Kaethe Warkentin in Reedley, California, who had apparently done well. Isaac Warkentin himself wrote to Henry several times, but only a brief letter was translated in 1937. Isaac wanted Henry to subscribe to one or more newspapers or magazines for German Americans, one in German and one in English – "for the German cause."

Barbara Matthies Rempel's last translated letter was dated September 5, 1932. She died unexpectedly a few days later, on September 9, before she had mailed the letter. In her last letter, Henry's mother commented on not feeling well and staying home instead of going to someone's birthday party. She also comments on their "Siberian experience" and the difficulty in growing vegetables due to frost. Why was she in Siberia? When and how had she gone there?

Henry's uncle Herman Rempel wrote in 1934 from Grodowka, apparently in the Ukraine, with details about how difficult life was. "The God-fearing spirit among our people has vanished to quite some extent, and they go along with the world. We wait for the Lord until he comes."

From 1935 to 1955, during the Stalin years, there are no letters preserved from the Rempel family in Russia. In 1955, a letter Henry wrote got through to Russia. Henry's brother-in-law, Peter Wilmsen, responded within days. Peter's wife, who was Henry's sister, had died. The only indication of location is a mention that Peter's daughter had been in the hospital in the Siberian city of Omsk. There are many blank spaces and unanswered questions about what happened to the relatives who stayed in Russia.

Education, citizenship, and a bride

Meanwhile, Henry struggled and progressed in his new life. Like his father and grandfather, Henry had an interest in biblical studies. He

Henry H. Rempel and Elizabeth Eitzen wed on May 17, 1942, in Los Angeles.

received a degree in theology from Los Angeles Baptist Seminary in 1928 and a diploma from the Bible Institute of Los Angeles (BIOLA) in 1933. He took additional studies at the University of California in Los Angeles (UCLA). Henry spent a brief time in Ohio at Bluffton, Pandora, and Lima, for reasons unknown. There is speculation that he may have studied at Bluffton College. However, he never served as a pastor nor developed another career or profession.

Eventually, Henry was ready to fully embrace his new life and new country. He became a naturalized citizen of the U.S. on February 27, 1942. Another big event for Henry in 1942 was his marriage to Elizabeth Anna Eitzen on May 17. He was forty-seven years old and she was sixteen years younger. It had taken nearly twenty years but at last the single man – who bounced around from place to place and job to job – settled down, married, and bought a house in Los Angeles.

Betty, as Henry's wife was known, enjoyed playing piano, had a ready smile, and hearty laugh. She was born in Mountain Lake, Min-

Elizabeth (Eitzen) Rempel, known as Betty.

9

nesota, September 12, 1911. As in the Rempel family, her Eitzen family also included numerous Mennonite preachers. Betty studied at Northwestern Bible Institute in Minneapolis. Her horizons thus expanded, the small tight-knit community of Mountain Lake couldn't keep her.

Betty's oldest brother, David D. Eitzen, was a Mennonite pastor in California. Setting off on an adventure that changed her life, Betty moved to Los Angeles in about 1934 and probably lived with Dave and his wife, Amanda, at first. Betty continued her education, studying at BIOLA. She found a job at the Wilshire Medical Building in Los Angeles – the same place where Henry worked. What kind of jobs they had there isn't known, but most likely they were involved in clerical or custodial work. It isn't known if they met at work or perhaps when Henry attended the Immanuel Mennonite Church on East 79th Street. Betty's brother David Eitzen was pastor there at the time.

Henry and Betty discovered they had much in common. Her ancestors were Mennonites who had also lived in southern Russia, but they had immigrated to the U.S. in a large migration in 1874. Like Henry, she could speak Low German and some High German. Her brother Dave officiated at their wedding. The new couple bought a house at 722 E. 79th Street, a block from the Immanuel Church.

Part Two
Childhood in California from 1944 to 1957

Erwin Henry Rempel was born on August 8, 1944, to Henry and Elizabeth (Eitzen) Rempel, at a suburban hospital in Bell, California. His brother Norman David was born twenty-two months later, and sister Barbara Elizabeth completed the family by the time Erwin was three years old.

The Rempels' small stucco-covered house on East 79th Street in Los Angeles was full of life, music, and laughter. Built in 1926 with 932 square feet, the house had only two bedrooms and one bathroom. Erwin's recollection is that his Uncle Dave and Aunt Amanda Eitzen had owned the house and sold it to his parents for about $3,300.

Henry thrived in his new role as a family man. With an 8mm home

The Rempel family in early 1950s: Erwin, father Henry, Norman, mother Betty, Barbara.

movie camera he recorded scenes from the honeymoon and later of the children too. With his handy-man skills, he made various pieces of backyard playground equipment for his three active children. Erwin recalls fishing trips to the ocean, going to see snow on nearby Mount Baldy, and being reprimanded for not only taking apricots from the neighbor's tree but breaking off a branch in the process.

Henry provided spiritual leadership in the home. He expected his children to behave properly at home and church. Erwin recalls that once he and another boy, the pastor's son, Jerry Burkholder, sat near the front of the church during a Sunday evening service. Typical young boys, they did not pay attention and began to create a disturbance. To Erwin's embarrassment, his daddy walked up and hauled him out for discipline – a spanking, the norm at the time.

Immanuel Mennonite Church

Immanuel was a closely knit congregation made up, mostly, of people of ethnic European Mennonite backgrounds who had moved to the city for employment. The church began in 1910 as a mission station of the General Conference Mennonite Church and had several changes of name and location prior to 1924.

Erwin remembers that his Uncle Dave Eitzen had left his pastoral position at the church and moved to the somewhat rural suburb of Rolling Hills, nearly an hour away. At some point, Harold Burkholder became pastor at Immanuel. He played a role in Erwin's life in key ways through the years.

The neighborhood around Immanuel Church gradually changed as African-Americans moved into the area. The white Mennonites joined the cultural trend of the 1950s, leaving the cities and moving to the suburbs. The congregation built a new church in the Los Angeles suburb of Downey. The Rempels were custodians at the church and eventually they moved as well. They sold their Los Angeles house in 1953 for $9,900 and bought a three-bedroom house in Downey.

The Rempel family enjoyed their new suburban location at 11263 Adenmoor. There were orange groves and open pastures nearby. Erwin recalls planes landing and taking off at the nearby large North American Aviation plant. It eventually became Rockwell International that made the first space capsules. One of the first McDonalds restaurants opened nearby. Erwin remembers eating there for a special occasion.

Even if they hadn't been church custodians, the Rempel family would have gone to church each Sunday morning, Sunday evening, and Wednesday evening. Henry taught a German Sunday school class and served as a deacon.

Although Immanuel Church was a member of the General Conference Mennonite Church, the congregation included a group of people from Mennonite Brethren background. Usually, the General Conference churches baptized by pouring or sprinkling, but the Mennonite Brethren baptized by immersion. The new church building, therefore, had a baptismal tank at the front behind the pulpit. Erwin remembers there was no way to fill the baptismal tank with warm water. So his daddy carried five-gallon pails of warm water down the side aisle to fill the baptismal tank.

Employment

Employment as church custodians seems to have been the main consistent work and income for the Rempel family over the years. Henry's children have noted that their father had only a series of handy-man jobs and no real profession or career. In addition to the challenges of being an immigrant, as previously noted, Henry's young-adult years in Russia spanned the tumult of war, banditry, famine, and disease – conditions that would have hindered developing skills or career.

Their mother did childcare for other people's children. Erwin remembers that his parents did various cleaning jobs, including in medical offices:

> I recall that Daddy worked as a painter at some manufacturing plant not too far from where we lived in Los Angeles. He also worked as a plumber for Verdi Bixel (Angela's mother's cousin – but that part of the story comes years later), whose plumbing business was not too far from where we lived. I remember Daddy doing gardening for others – that is, mowing lawns and caring for plants in the flowerbeds. He also painted houses for others. In that sense, he was self-employed.

Life was good, but with only a series of jobs as manual laborers, finances were always tight and they lived frugally. At some point in his childhood, Erwin recalls the cupboards being quite bare. They weren't sure what they would eat next. Erwin relates two incidents pertaining to the Rempel family finances.

> One day when Momma was cutting Daddy's hair in the kitchen in the house in Downey, I overheard a rather energetic conversation between them. The issue was giving to a missionary couple serving in Kenya. My parents were giving $20 a month (about $177 in 2016 dollars). Momma was crying. Daddy was insisting that they had made a commitment to give this amount and that they should continue to give even though the family finances were tight. That was the only time that I recall Daddy and Momma in a disagreement.

13

Years later, my cousin Stanley Eitzen shared a memory from his student years at Bethel College in North Newton, Kansas, in the early 1950s. Stan received a card with a five-dollar bill from Daddy and Momma. When Stan told his father, David D. Eitzen, about this gift, Uncle Dave thought it was remarkable because Henry and Betty did not have much money and a gift of five dollars (about $46 in 2016 dollars) was a large gift.

Unknown family history

The Rempel children's lack of knowledge about their father's life in Russia may be attributed, in part, to their young age and inability to ask questions and to remember details. On the other hand, perhaps, this description of another immigrant man would apply to Henry. "[He] sought a fresh start in the New World, not for himself, for he knew the limits of his own career, but for them; he wanted his children as unburdened as possible by the past. But in so doing he denied his own personal history to his children, thereby denying them a crucial part of *their* personal histories."[1]

Cancer intrudes

Cancer began an assault on the Rempel family. Erwin's mother, Betty, was diagnosed with breast cancer and underwent a radical mastectomy in 1953 at about age forty-two. Erwin recalls her saying that the cost at the hospital was ten to fourteen dollars a day. She had a follow-up of forty-three X-ray treatments, which, she wrote to her brother Alvin and his wife, Lena, in Montana, didn't make her as sick as she had expected. Chemotherapy wasn't available at that time. She continued to do what she could with her weakened right arm.

From letters preserved and passed along to Lena Eitzen, we have records of these events and how the writers reacted. The following

---

[1]Halberstam, David, *War in a Time of Peace*, 381 – description of Madeleine Albright's father

excerpts from the letters maintain the original wording, spelling, and style.

In late 1955, Erwin's father began experiencing abdominal pain. He was in the hospital over Thanksgiving. Henry wrote to relatives on November 26 about his inability to eat the hospital's Thanksgiving meal. He had lost weight and needed to postpone a surgery. From the following correspondence, perhaps the family already knew the dire diagnosis of pancreatic cancer.

Betty wrote her father and step-mother, D.P. and Sara Eitzen, in Mountain Lake, Minnesota, on December 8:

> The children haven't seen him since Nov. 11. The hospital rules are —no children unless the patient is very critical or has been there a month.... They, of course, are heart-broken when I try to make it plain to them how serious it is. ...we had devotions, and they prayed, but they didn't know how. Then we all had a good cry and then they went to bed. ... If you can possibly make it, please come. Father and Mother, how about you staying all winter with us? I need you.

Parents can't resist such a plea for help. The Eitzens made plans to go to California for Christmas. They drove with Betty's brother Pete and family, who also lived in the Mountain Lake area.

Betty dashed off a quick airmail postcard, with a couple of two-cent stamps, dated December 10, to "Rev. and Mrs. D.P. Eitzen, Mountain Lake, Minnesota," to let the parents know that Henry had come home from the hospital. "He is doing pretty good under the circumstances. He is pretty weak." She adds, "He is very happy for your plans [to come]."

In a letter of January 10, 1956, to Alvin and Lena, Henry wrote that his main discomfort was from taking the pills he had received at a cancer clinic in Dallas, Texas. The Hoxsey Clinic in Dallas drew people from far and near with promises of astounding cancer cures, even for people whose doctors had given up. Some friends from the Immanuel Church had heard of the clinic and paid for Henry and Betty to make a quick trip by plane to Dallas on December 28-31. The visiting grandparents from Minnesota stayed with the children. Erwin remembers his parents returning with lots of pills for each of them to take. Henry and Betty had been told not to expect immediate results and that there could be unpleasant side effects from the pills, called chemical blood therapy. By 1960, the Hoxsey Clinic was banned as a fraud.

After celebrating Christmas with the grandparents and Uncle Pete's family, Henry wrote to Alvin and Lena, "The kids received a TV set, portable size, for Christmas, and you have to pull them away sometimes to have them do their chores." Erwin recalls that few people had television sets then, and church people didn't really approve of television. However, the TV helped the children endure those difficult times. Their parents strictly limited the number of hours the children watched TV.

Betty added more to Henry's letter of January 10, 1956, to Alvin and Lena, including a description of her days:

> When Henry was in the hospital for four weeks, my life consisted of being more on the road than at home. I had and still have a four-hour morning housekeeping job (in connection with baby-sitting a 7-year old boy.) Then I'd dash home, have a bite, leave orders for the kids when they came home from school and then I'd dash off to the hospital. After that I'd go to Huntington Park to clean the doctor's office. In between I'd go to church to see that things were taken care of there. Members of the church have been just wonderful in pitching in to do the work when I couldn't. Then here and there I would babysit evenings. Then Henry came home. That added more work at home tending to him.

A month later, Betty wrote to Alvin and Lena again in a letter mailed February 10, 1956, updating them on Henry's condition. "At present it is rather discouraging. Instead of him getting better, he seems to get worse. He is completely helpless. I got him a hospital bed which makes it easier to raise and lower him." She describes how hard it was to make him comfortable in bed and care for his needs. "He still can't believe that this may be the end for him. Yesterday he said, 'I still can't succumb to cancer.' He has great faith. We still trust the Lord – He knows best."

As evidence of his faith that God would heal him, Henry purchased some new tools. He even talked about buying a new car.

At some point, Henry returned to the hospital. Doctors accurately gave a prognosis of only thirty more days.

"Dear Sweetheart Mine and my darling family," Henry wrote from his hospital bed on February 28, 1956. As if his illness and hospitalization weren't enough for the family to bear, Betty had pneumonia and was in a different hospital. He wrote to her, praying that they both would be made well.

Regarding his hospital stay, Henry wrote, "It pains me that I have to run up the hospital bill here." Someone erroneously had told him that they shouldn't worry about the hospital bills, "...because after our passing, what's left is canceled. The children will not pay." On March 8, he wrote Betty saying he needed to come home to help her with the income tax.

Uncle Dave and Amanda Eitzen lived close enough to assist. Church people also provided a great deal of help. However, the congregation was going through a split at the time. Erwin remembers that people in Group A came to the house to help on certain days, and people in Group B came on different days. Betty and Henry tried not to take sides.

Henry didn't accept that he was not going home again. It was hard for him to get to a telephone. He wrote letters to Betty that became increasingly more difficult to decipher. His last letter to her, on March 12, had a list of miscellaneous small items for her to bring him: paring knife, can opener, Scofield Bible, writing pens and paper, some food items including instant Postum, and a *Popular Mechanics* magazine. He also instructed her to contact a nursery about a plant before the guarantee ended and to get a radio checked and repaired with a new white cord.

Henry was clearly engaged with life's details rather than in thoughts of dying. Betty struggled between having faith and hope and with facing an increasingly apparent reality. She couldn't have received his last letter until after he died.

Erwin remembers his father's death
We received a phone call on Tuesday morning, March 13, 1956, from the John Wesley City Hospital where Daddy had

been for several weeks after his more than a month-long stay at the Los Angeles General Hospital. Daddy was in a coma. Momma arranged for someone to take her to the hospital as she was not feeling well herself, having been hospitalized for pneumonia for a few days during the past week or two. The three of us children went to school. By noon our Uncle Dave came to the school to pick us up and he then told us that Daddy had died that morning.

I recall being asked on the prior Sunday to go along to the hospital to visit Daddy. I was not interested in going at that time...something I regretted later as that would have been my last time to see Daddy.

I did not have a suit to wear to the funeral. I remember going downtown and purchasing a gray suit.

After the funeral, I remember an older lady at the church coming to me and saying something to the effect that I should not cry because we knew that Daddy was with Jesus and that we would see Daddy again someday. In the months that followed, the three of us children were asked to sing at Christian Endeavor meetings occasionally on Sunday evenings. The one song that I recall we sang had words something like this: I have a loving father up in glory land. I don't expect to pass until I shake his hand. And I don't feel at home in the world anymore.

Henry had almost reached his sixty-first birthday when he died. His wife was age forty-five and his children were eight, nine, and eleven.

Living without Daddy

The summer after Henry's death, Betty took Erwin, Norman, and Barbara on a long train trip to visit her Eitzen family. They stopped first in Montana. There they enjoyed the farm and ranch where her brother Alvin Eitzen and his wife, Lena, lived with their adopted son, Howard, who was a year younger than Barbara. Of Betty's three brothers, Alvin was the one she was closest to both in age and temperament.

From the wide-open spaces under the big sky of Montana, Alvin and

Lena drove Betty and the children east to Minnesota. In the Mountain Lake area, where Betty and her siblings were born and raised, her children became better acquainted with their grandfather, D.P. Eitzen. His second wife, Sara, had also come through the crucible of suffering in Russia, although she never talked about it. D.P. Eitzen had served as a German-speaking lay pastor for thirty-three years in the Gospel Mennonite Church in Mountain Lake. That was during the time when P.A. and Elizabeth Penner were sent from that community to serve as the first General Conference missionaries in India.

The children also learned to know their Uncle Pete, Aunt Sue, and their children, who farmed not far from Mountain Lake. Betty, along with Erwin and Norman, spent two weeks at a church camp by Lake Shetek where Betty helped cook for campers. Erwin never forgot the pleasant setting there and years later revisited it for a very special purpose.

Relatives abounded in that Mennonite community around Mountain Lake. But Betty didn't think she could ever again live in that area with the "bickering *frindshaft*" [sic]. There were several branches of Mennonites and large churches in the area. Most Mennonites were involved in agriculture on the fertile, well-watered pleasant plains punctuated with many small lakes. On the return train trip, Betty and the children stopped in Omaha, Nebraska, and Newton, Kansas, where she visited friends. Those places also became significant later in the lives of her children.

What Betty and her children learned and absorbed on that summer trip of 1956 played an important role in some difficult decisions required in the coming year.

Pain and fear

The family returned to their California home in time for the children to begin a new school year in fall 1956. It was hard going back to the empty house. They continued trying to adapt to life without Henry.

Soon after that big trip, Erwin recalls his mother suddenly screaming in intense pain. By late September she wrote to Alvin and Lena and admitted that throughout the summer's travels, she had not felt well because of a cough and chest pains. She had sought medical care while in Minnesota and was told she had a weak heart.

A month later Betty handwrote a ten-page letter to Alvin and Lena with more details:

> I have spent days in bed and sleepless nights due to pain and fear, etc. ... when we came home the pain in the chest, cough and an awful tight feeling around my throat got worse, so bad that the first Sunday morning after we got back, I had a lump on my throat. My conclusion right away was, "cancer of throat." We went to church. Everybody, of course, was happy to see us back. In fact, they had feared that we might stay back there [in Minnesota]. And then, of course, they all expected me to be my old self again. Every time they would ask, "How are you?" I would say, "Pretty good," at the same time thinking of my horrible thought, "throat cancer."

The next morning Betty sought out a doctor who gave her a thorough exam and proclaimed she was a "nervous wreck." He gave her some medications and vitamins to strengthen her heart, and treatments to "quiet down my nerves." Not satisfied about her throat, she went to the surgeon who performed her mastectomy three years previously. He too assured her there was nothing but just a "nervous reaction." Still not satisfied, she went to a cancer clinic in downtown Los Angeles for a complete exam – inside and out. They too said there was no indication of cancer, but she should return for another checkup in six months. That finally gave her a measure of assurance.

But that wasn't all. She continued in her letter, "During all this time I have had some terrible pains in my right arm (the sore one). The pain was so severe that I actually cried. Then one morning I found that my arm was paralyzed – the thumb and part of the next finger were numb – hardly any feeling. When I'd pick up a dish, it would just drop out of my hand." While the pain sometimes subsided, she continued to experience severe pain in various locations – so severe she mentions again that she cried. The doctor called it neuralgia – a nerve pain.

She reported some other problems, including that her voice was so weak she couldn't make herself understood at times. On a more positive note, she writes about each of the three children:

> Erwin is in Jr. High (7th grade) and likes it very much. He has a different teacher for each subject and each one of them is a man teacher. Norman (6th grade) has a lady teacher. He thinks she makes him work too hard. Barbara (4th grade) has a man teacher and she likes him very much.
>
> Norman is so different from Erwin. He always aims to tackle something out of the ordinary. Besides his regular schoolwork, he is taking 'Drama' – acting out skits and plays. To make his living, he is selling Christmas cards in his spare time. He is pretty good at it. He is not afraid to tackle approaching people. Erwin is different that way. Today, just in a few hours Norman sold over $8.00 worth of cards. But then when we have to work at the church, he thinks that is too hard. That is where Erwin shines. He again is not afraid to tackle hard work. Erwin is a big help to me. While I am bothered with my sore arms, he bawls me out when I work too much. Then he says, "You shouldn't do that – better let me do that."
>
> Barbara is more of her own sort. She shines in cleaning up the rooms – kitchen, etc.
>
> People tell me I really have something to be thankful and proud of. And I am. The Lord must have known 12 years ago what I would need at this time. We have a wonderful Father in heaven, who always knows what we have need of.

Betty wrote to her brother Alvin that financially they were doing fine. She received some Social Security checks regularly, payments from the sale of their previous house, the church cleaning salary, plus payments for her occasional babysitting jobs.

Betty's oldest brother, Dave, her closest relative living in the Los Angeles area, had a doctor's degree in psychology from Southern California University. He was teaching psychology of religion at the School of Theology in Claremont, California. His more conservative and less-educated siblings didn't have much in common with him. Those differences were put aside as Dave and his wife, Amanda, accompanied Betty and her children in her difficult journey. By mid-December, Betty could no longer use her arm to handwrite her own letters, so Dave and Amanda wrote to keep the family informed about Betty's condition.

Dave went with Betty to some of her doctor's appointments. He helped decipher medical jargon. While Betty got an X-ray treatment, Dave talked privately with the woman doctor and then wrote to the family:

> She says that the pain in Betty's arm and also the swelling – is all cancer. The numbness she has in her hand and fingers is caused by the presence of the growth in the upper arm which has always bothered her. Then the cough is caused by a growth (cancer) which is pressing on a large nerve which leads to the larynx – this irritates the nerve and causes her to cough and of course, the voice box is affected – therefore the hoarseness. This was quite a shock in a way – and yet this was what we had been fearing for some time. I asked the doctor if she thought the X-ray treatments (on the sternum area) would really help and she said, "Well – it will make her a little more comfortable." More she would not say. So now we have the full story for the present and it looks very dark, doesn't it? We pray that our heavenly father will give strength for the future. Betty looks very sad and I'm sure she feels badly – more so than she allows herself to talk about. I told Betty what the Dr. had told me – so she knows.
>
> We are very anxious about her and the children's future. We are praying, and we know all of you and many others are, that there will be strength to endure – and the grace to say "Not my will be done."

Norman, age ten, also wrote to his Uncle Alvin.

> Since mother can't write, I have to write for her. Mother's arm is so stiff and has so much pain that she can't do anything with it. Barbara has to help her dress. Erwin shifts while she drives the car. I help mother with little jobs. We

three fixed and decorated the Christmas Tree and there are quite a few presents under it. I sure wonder what those packages contain. We sure miss Daddy.

An uncertain future

What would happen to the three children? Should they be divided among Betty's three brothers? Should they go to an orphanage? What were the children themselves thinking? Erwin remembers those days as follows:

> In the months prior to her death, Momma tried to think of how to care for the three of us children after her death. ... She had collected some information on orphanages and I saw some of that literature on her desk. That scared the daylights out of me. I recall lying awake at night frightened by that prospect. As the time passed, Momma met separately with each of the three of us children and asked us where we would like to go when she died. All three of us indicated that we would like to go to live with Uncle Alvin, Aunt Lena, and Howard in Montana.

Alvin and Lena Eitzen offered to take all three of the children to live with them. Dave Eitzen wrote to Alvin and Lena on December 24:

> Thank you for your offer to take the children in case of Betty's Home-going. They had enjoyed their stay there so much. As you say they would miss their friends here – but children do make adjustments rather easily but not without some trauma.

Dave helped his sister prepare necessary legal documents. Amanda went over early in the mornings to get the children ready for school and to help with cleaning and laundry. Fully aware of her condition, Betty reminded Amanda that when Henry died, she had bought a cemetery lot for herself beside his.

When Betty couldn't move her right arm and hold a pen, she stopped writing – for a while. A few weeks later she discovered that using one finger on her left hand, she could peck out one letter at a time on a typewriter. She even typed quite a bit of schoolwork for Erwin in that slow tedious fashion on a manual typewriter

The X-ray treatments slowed the spread of the cancer. Betty experienced some temporary improvements until the end of April.

Their Grandpa D. P. Eitzen wrote, commending the children on how much they helped their mother. He wrote the following about his own experience when he was Erwin's age, giving permission to grieve and indicating that in the bigger picture of life, God is faithful:

> I was 12 years old when my mother died and how it hurt me. I cried, o how I cried, But I am still here yet. It's long ago …Trust the Lord.

Betty still managed to wash clothes in what must have been a wringer washing machine. Barbara, age nine, hung it outside to dry and brought it in. Someone else came to do the ironing, a big project in those days before steam irons, perm press fabrics, and clothes dryers.

Some individuals at the church made sure Betty received the monthly church custodian salary. The children cleaned what they could, but others helped.

"As long as the church is paying for the work the kids are doing, my income is sufficient to cover my expenses," Betty wrote. "But I can't expect the church to continue paying for work that isn't done right." She wondered about applying for "Aid for needy children." And later, "I don't feel right about accepting any financial help from the church as long as we do so little for it, but then again that amount is just what I need to meet all my expenses."

Erwin remembers his mother's death

Momma did not go to the hospital but stayed at home. On the day before she died, I remember going to her bedroom as did each of us children where she said her goodbye to each of us. That was hard for her and for us. If my memory is correct, I think Uncle Dave and Aunt Amanda, as well as Uncle Alvin and Aunt Lena, were there in the room as well.

That night Momma was in considerable pain and I recall her moaning throughout the night. The next day we went to school but for the night we went to the home of our friend Harlan Unrau. The next morning, we went back home. Momma had died during the night.

Betty's suffering ended on June 4, 1957. She was forty-six years old. She was buried next to her husband only fifteen months after his burial. Erwin wasn't yet thirteen, Norman had just turned eleven, and Barbara was nearly ten.

Pastor Albert H. Epp

By the time Betty died, the Immanuel Church had completed its split. The remaining group had a new pastor, young Albert H. Epp from Kansas who had studied at Grace Bible Institute in Omaha, Nebraska, and was doing graduate studies at Fuller Theological Seminary in Pasadena, California. Betty's funeral was his first. The young pastor never forgot the plight of the three children whose parents had both died.

Erwin took a catechism class in preparation for baptism. On their last Sunday in Downey, Erwin was baptized at the Immanuel Church, by immersion. Rev. Harold Burkholder and Rev. Albert Epp officiated. In earlier years, Erwin recalls repeatedly praying to accept Christ, but not being brave enough to go forward when altar calls were given and make a public declaration. At this point, he was more confident in his faith.

Erwin writes:

I remember when Dr. Albert Epp came to our house in Downey shortly after Momma's funeral and just prior to our move to Montana. We gathered as a family including Uncle Dave and Aunt Amanda as well as Howard, Uncle Alvin and Aunt Lena and the three of us children. We were sitting in a circle in the living room. Albert Epp read some scripture and then had a prayer. He then went on to encourage the three of us children to begin to call Uncle Alvin "Dad" and Aunt Lena "Mom." At first it felt a bit awkward. But before long we made the transition and it became a habit that we have had ever since. I am grateful that Albert Epp encouraged us to do that as it marked the reality of that transition.

Early on the morning of June 13, a rented U-Haul trailer, costing $55.00, was loaded with items from the Rempel household in California, including the piano, a small desk, and some bookshelves. It was time for the newly-formed family of six to leave the congested, smoggy Los Angeles area where the climate was mild all year and the horizons were punctuated with silhouettes of tall palm trees waving above the rows of houses. In a 1955 Ford car that pulled the trailer, they headed off to begin a new life on the thinly populated high plains of northeastern Montana where the air was clear, winters were brutally cold, and no trees dotted the distant horizons.

Erwin's Uncle Dave and Aunt Amanda were also moving. They temporarily stayed in the Rempel house on Adenmoor Street and prepared it for sale. After the complicated and time-consuming process of clearing the lien on the Rempel house to pay medical bills, there was little left in the trust established for the children's care.

Memory Lane trip in 2006

On a Memory Lane trip to Los Angeles and Downey in 2006, fifty years after their father's death, the three Rempel siblings, with spouses and some of their children, visited the places important in their childhood. When they visited the Immanuel Church in Downey, who showed up there at the same time, providentially, but Albert Epp. Semi-retired, he kept a supply of Choice Books at the church and distributed them in that area. Albert Epp said that he had prayed regularly for the Rempels through the years. God indeed answered those prayers.

Part Three
Montana Teenager from 1957 to 1962

The full car pulling a full U-Haul trailer took the new family as far as Cedar City, Nevada, for their first night en route to Montana from California. They paid eleven dollars for their motel that night, according to

Lena Eitzen's records. The weather was quite hot. The only way to deal with that in those days before vehicles had air conditioning was to open the car windows. The next travel day was even longer, and again they paid eleven dollars for the night. By the night of June 15, 1957, they safely arrived at their

Howard Eitzen; Barbara, Norman, and Erwin Rempel as they move to Montana in 1957.

new home, the Eitzens' farm in Montana, thus beginning a new chapter in their lives. If the children would have grown up around Los Angeles, their lives would likely have taken very different paths.

Sad as it was for the Rempel children to lose both parents at such young ages, God brought good out of the situation. Lena and Alvin's childlessness provided space for the three Rempels. The Eitzens were the children's legal guardians and didn't adopt them, thus the children kept the Rempel name. By calling their aunt and uncle Mom and Dad, the children distinguished them from their birth parents, Momma and Daddy.

What a wonderful blessing it was for the three orphaned siblings to stay together. What an amazing thing it was for the Eitzens to enlarge their home and hearts to include them. The Eitzen home provided the Rempel children a continuity of family relationships and values, plus church affiliation within the General Conference Mennonite Church.

New home, school, and climate

The sturdy farmhouse Eitzens had built in the late 1940s on the plains of Montana was now full and bursting with life. During the several months before Betty Rempel died, Lena and Alvin Eitzen had begun renovating their house in preparation for doubling the size of their family. By the time all six of them completed their trek from

California, two small new bedrooms on the second floor were nearly finished – one for Barbara and another one for Erwin and Norman to share. The Eitzens' son Howard, age eight, kept his bedroom on the main floor. The main-floor bathroom had a bathtub but no shower. After a day's work on the farm, the grimy farmers used a simple shower in the unfinished basement.

Eitzens lived along a gravel road that served the entire Lustre community as a major link between school, church, and town. Set back from the road by a long lane, their house benefited from a shelterbelt of different kinds of trees and bushes that gave some protection from strong winds and the drifting snow in winter. Several buildings on the yard provided shelter for farm animals and farm equipment. Lena planted a large garden that produced vegetables to can and freeze. Lena's mother, Grandma Baerg, lived in the small old original farmhouse a short distance from the newer and larger house. Electricity had come to that rural community only a few years earlier. They first connected to dial telephone service only the previous Christmastime.

Adapting to new situation

Lena marveled at how quickly the children adapted. She recalled one time on their drive to Montana that Norman cried, obviously missing his Momma. Erwin admits that he cried some, too. Barb remembers very little about that time.

In general, Erwin found it all a big adventure. He greatly enjoyed life on the farm. He was already in the habit of waking early to do his city paper route. In Montana he continued to wake up early. He enjoyed early-morning walks to look at the wheat fields. With all the opportunities to get outside and be active, plus beginning to stretch up to his adult height, Erwin soon slimmed down.

What a contrast this was to living in the Los Angeles area! In Downey, Erwin had been one among 720 students in the seventh grade. In Montana, he was the only student in the eighth grade. The three Rempels and Howard attended a one-room school just across the road from the Eitzens' house, where one teacher taught all nineteen students from grades one through eight. California, the second-largest state by land area at the time, had a population of about ten million; Montana, the third-largest state, had less than one million people. Instead of seeing rows of houses in their neighborhood, here they saw only two houses with the nearest being about a quarter mile away.

From living in a city without animals, in Montana the Rempel children encountered a variety of animals. They played with the Eitzens' small rat terrier dog named Tippy – until he was accidentally run over. About two dozen untamed cats prowled around controlling the mouse population in the barns. Howard had a horse, which the former city kids learned to ride. The Rempel children soon learned how to gather eggs and feed the chickens, pigs, and dairy cows. The boys learned to milk the cows by hand. The cats would come to the milking area, stand up on their back legs, and beg for a squirt of milk. The boys enjoyed accommodating the cats – when Dad Eitzen wasn't looking. Lena designated a garden plot for each of them.

The children looked forward to big snow drifts. Coming from Los Angeles where it didn't even freeze, temperatures of forty degrees below zero sounded amazing. They were so disappointed their first winter in Montana to have only minimal snow and nothing that cold.

The three Rempel children and Howard Eitzen have assigned garden plots on Eitzens' Montana farm.

The Lustre community

The Eitzens eagerly introduced their enlarged family to their church, Bethel Mennonite, which punctuated the open landscape at a corner where two major roads crossed. Their church was one of five Mennonite churches in the area – known as the Lustre community. The Mennonite churches in the area, representing three different Mennonite groups, collaborated to operate Lustre Bible Academy, which later became the Lustre Christian High School. The values and expectations of the community reinforced what the children learned at home and church.

The Lustre community is about one hundred miles west of North Dakota and fifty miles south of Canada. Far-away horizons, unadorned with trees or buildings, meet the edge of the blue sky arching above like the interior of a big bowl. At night the huge sky twinkles with multitudes of stars and sometimes with the dancing northern lights. Straight roads, going either east and west or north and south, frame square-mile sections of land. Erwin seems to have no inner sense of directions, but in Montana, he can confidently talk about going "ten miles north and three miles east."

The Eitzens owned or rented about two thousand acres, a modest-sized farm in that community. More than half of those acres were tillable and planted in annual crops, mostly spring wheat. The arid climate had an annual average of thirteen inches of precipitation. Strip-farming methods – leaving alternating strips of land bare and fallow for a year – attempted to collect enough moisture to produce a crop every other year. The strips also helped slow the nearly constant winds that nibbled away at the layer of good topsoil. The remaining seven hundred acres that weren't suitable for planting provided pasture for the registered purebred Black Angus cattle that Alvin enjoyed raising. When calves grew to about five hundred pounds in weight, he sold them to feeders who fed them until they weighed enough to sell to a slaughterhouse.

Montana's native people

The land was opened to homesteaders in 1917, even though some of it was on an Indian reservation. The Native Americans retained some land, which they often rented to the white farmers. For a while, Alvin Eitzen rented land from a Native American named James Growing Thunder. When the government first parceled out the land, the white settlers expected the native people to somehow automatically change their whole lifestyle and obtain the equipment and techniques to be successful farmers. When that didn't happen, disparaging remarks were made. Many of the native peoples slid into despair, poverty, and alcoholism.

Most of the Mennonites in the Lustre community were of Russian Mennonite heritage and continued using the Low German language. The Eitzens helped organize an annual festival that celebrated their ethnic foods – a Schmeckfest, or tasting festival. People in this Mennonite community didn't associate much with other people, as had been their ancestors' custom in Russia before immigrating in 1874.

Their new parents

The Rempel children's new mom, their Aunt Lena, was born in Montana in 1923. Her pioneer parents had both lost their first spouses to illness. Her father, Henry G. Baerg, with three sons, married a widow with two daughters and formed a new family in the Lustre community. Lena was the younger of two daughters born to the blended family. Lena enjoyed life. She liked to tell jokes and funny stories. She admitted she went to school more for the social life than for the scholastics. For high school, her parents sent her and her sister to stay with relatives in Mountain Lake, Minnesota. If her parents thought Mountain Lake would provide Lena with better prospects for marriage, they were right.

Lena caught the eye of Alvin D. Eitzen, born in 1918 and raised in Mountain Lake. His farmer father was chosen by lot in 1900 to serve as a German-speaking lay pastor in what was then the Gospel Mennonite Church. After high school, Lena went to Freeman Junior Academy in the Mennonite community of Freeman, South Dakota. Alvin went to visit her. Their relationship deepened through letter writing. They were married in September 1943, a year after Alvin's sister, Elizabeth, (Betty) had married Henry Rempel in Los Angeles. Like Lena, Alvin was the youngest in his family. Lena's sociability and levity tempered Alvin's impatient and demanding nature that hid an easily moved soft heart.

The young Eitzen couple began farming in Mountain Lake. While boating on a small Minnesota lake with Lena's sister Susie, the boat overturned. Alvin managed to rescue his young wife, but sadly, Susie drowned. When Alvin and Lena had the opportunity to purchase land in Montana, they moved there. They bought land in the Lustre community a few miles from where most of Lena's family lived and farmed. Lena worked hard alongside Alvin in all aspects of the farm and ranch. When no children came along, they adopted an infant boy, Howard Dean, born in 1948. In 1957, when Lena was almost thirty-four and Alvin nearly thirty-nine, they had the courage and compassion to care for his sister Betty's three orphaned children.

Lena (Baerg) Eitzen dressed for farm work in Montana.

Learning new things

In his excitement about learning more about the farm, Erwin eagerly asked, "Dad, what are we going to do today?" To Erwin's dismay and Alvin's annoyance there seldom was a plan made for the day. Erwin needed to learn that farm work is hard to schedule.

Erwin had acquired a taste for vinegar, pouring generous portions of it on numerous foods. The Eitzens wondered if that might be harmful. Their set of the World Book Encyclopedia did not furnish an answer to that question. To encourage searching for more knowledge in those days before Internet search engines, World Book provided postcards to mail with questions. Erwin used a postcard and wrote asking about vinegar. To his delight, a detailed two-page response came back indicating it is very healthful to use vinegar – plus there are many other good uses of the substance. "Well, but everything in moderation," Dad Eitzen harrumphed.

Other than high school basketball, Erwin didn't follow sports. He always said all the sports genes went to his brother, Norm, who was always curious, studious, and eager to try something new. Barb helped outdoors to some degree, but she mostly stuck to the inside chores. As younger sister, she always enjoyed observing the banter between her two older brothers.

Living far from town

Eitzens went to town once every week or two, either to the east to Wolf Point, about thirty miles from home, or west to Glasgow, a larger town about fifty miles from home. Glasgow had more shops and businesses, but the Eitzens' bank and favorite restaurant were in Wolf Point.

Living so far from town, they had no grocery store close enough to pick up needed items at the last minute. Lena kept a well-stocked pantry at home. In addition to two large freezers in the basement, she had a basement storage room lined with shelves filled with home-canned items and other non-perishable supplies they bought by the case. She didn't need to fear being snowed-in during the winter. When unexpected guests arrived, Lena would go downstairs, collect her thoughts, and pull things from the shelves and freezers to make a nice meal.

Beef, pork, and chicken came from their own farm animals. Erwin fondly remembers butchering hogs at home in a big, day-long event. It was topped off by making tasty cracklings in a big pot that cooked out the lard from small scraps of meat. Periodically they took one of their grass-fed steers to town to be butchered and packaged into frozen meal-size portions of beef.

Lustre Bible Academy

The Rempel children attended Lustre Bible Academy for their high school years. The Academy was the hub of Lustre community life. Thirteen miles of gravel road lay between their home and school. No bus service was available, so they drove their own vehicles. Driving so many miles on unpaved roads quickly wore out family cars. Dad Eitzen bought a new car about every other year.

That small high school out in the middle of nowhere struggled to attract and keep qualified teachers. One teacher, not accustomed to such an arid climate, thought Erwin a bit deranged to delight in rain.

Another teacher believed in sinless perfection for Christians and didn't seem aware of how far he himself was from reaching that elevated state. Most of the teachers, of course, were good and had a sense of calling to teach there.

The only sport at the academy was boys' basketball and all the boys could play on the team. Erwin was captain of the team his senior year, wearing #33, and made the most points. But one year the team lost all its games!

With less than fifty in the whole student body, the students all had opportunities to try everything from music to the school paper and dramas. His pastor, Walter Dirks, talked to Erwin about those school plays – none of them were based on Bible stories. Erwin didn't feel any lack of biblical input. Lustre was a Bible academy, so they had chapel each day, Bible classes, and prayer at the beginning of each class. In addition, they went to church for Sunday morning, Sunday evening, Wednesday evening, and then choir practice on Thursday evening.

Erwin, #33, and Norman, #15, on Lustre Bible Academy basketball team, 1961.

Dad Eitzen directed the mixed choir, plus a men's choir. Youth group met only once a month to play a variety of active games. Youth sponsors provided what little leadership was needed and made sure there was some sort of brief devotional.

Spiritual formation

Erwin's spiritual life was influenced by attending Beacon Bible Camp, a community-sponsored annual church camp, and by the spiritual emphasis week at the high school each year. During that week, a special guest speaker spoke at the academy during the day and at one of the supporting churches in the evening. The blind Mennonite evangelist, J.J. Esau, from Mountain Lake, Minnesota, was one such speaker. Esau traveled alone throughout General Conference Mennonite circles, was well known, and highly respected.

Another formative experience for Erwin took place in about 1958 when a young couple, Fremont and Sara Regier, visited Lustre. They had grown up on farms in Kansas and told about their international work as agricultural missionaries in the Congo[2] and Mexico. Enjoying the farm as he did, that idea intrigued Erwin, and he began to think about following Regiers' example.

Farming in Montana

As with many farmers, the Eitzens were rich in land and equipment, but low on cash. They borrowed from their bank to buy seeds, fertilizer, farm equipment, and farmland. Frugality was a way of life. Mom Eitzen parceled out only a half of a banana or a half piece of chewing gum. Dad Eitzen saved all his old shoes because someday he might need a piece of leather for something.

Farm children learned to drive quite young. Their new younger brother, Howard, was ahead of the Rempels in those skills.

Teenage boys found summer work with farmers in the community. Erwin worked for Henry Rahn, a relative to Mom Eitzen, for four

---

[2]The country name changed several times over the years. For consistency, it is referred to as the Congo.

35

summers. Even though Rahns were their closest neighbors, Erwin spent the weeknights there and only went home on weekends.

Erwin didn't mind doing the summer fallowing. That meant driving the tractor as straight as possible on mile-long strips of bare land to eliminate weeds between the strips of wheat. The tractors he drove at first were small and open – no air conditioned cab with radio and GPS. Dust raised by the tractor and equipment rolled over the driver. Mosquitoes had a captive lunch plate. Fortunately, wind often diminished both dust and biting creatures.

Wheat harvest in August was the highlight of the year in the farming community. The women cooked big noon meals, referred to as dinner on the farm. Some days the women took dinner out to where the men were harvesting. In late afternoon, women took *faspa* out to the field – a light lunch of bologna sandwiches on *zwieback* yeast rolls and some other goodies. After dark, the tired and dusty harvesters headed to the house to clean up, eat supper, and fall into bed for a few hours of sleep before another long day of harvesting.

Most of the years Erwin was in high school, little rain fell and crops were poor. One year Erwin recalls harvesting only fifteen to sixteen bushels of wheat per acre with their Oliver combine that had a fourteen-foot header. The next year, 1961, they only got one and a half bushels per acre. The forty-bushel bin on the combine didn't fill up very fast those years. Erwin's usual task was driving a truck. When the 200-bushel farm truck was full, Erwin drove it to their nearby round metal grain-storage bins on their farm. He raised the front of the truck bed so the harvested grain slid down to where an auger pulled it up and dropped it into the top of a 2,000-bushel round grain bin. By storing their grain, farmers could sell it during the winter when prices were higher.

Eitzens bought an Oliver combine for about $4,000 shortly before the Rempels joined them in Montana. Hydraulic technology came into use. Dad Eitzen wasn't yet using chemical fertilizers. Spreading chicken and cow manure sufficed.

The day started early all year long on the farm. Before school, they milked the cows, fed and watered the chickens, and slopped the hogs. Erwin developed a life-long inner clock that always wakes him early and apparently to some degree, so did Norm. After school, the chickens would have produced their egg for the day and the cows needed to be milked again. They carried heavy buckets of milk to the house and poured the milk through a hand-cranked separator. Its spinning disks separated the cream from the milk. Eitzens sold the cream in town. The pigs enjoyed skim milk, along with kitchen scraps and some grain. Mom Eitzen used cream to make butter in a hand-cranked, clear-glass container.

Accepting her life

Mom Eitzen was glad for the extra help with the farm chores, especially since just having extra people in the house made more work for her as well. Only years later did she admit she didn't really like cooking and gardening. Being a practical woman, she adapted and did what was needed. She kept a detailed diary, including anything medical. Perhaps in a different era and setting, she would have studied to be a nurse. But she uncomplainingly fit into the life that was expected in that farming community.

Mom Eitzen made sure photos had identification – even if it meant writing people's names right on the forehead. Her organized filing provided much of the information for this written account.

The Eitzens enjoyed people. They had many acquaintances. They traveled far to attend special events and conferences. They offered overnight accommodations in their home for visiting preachers and missionaries, plus any relatives traveling through.

A high school senior

Erwin graduated in 1962 as salutatorian of his class. Leadership positions came easily to him. He didn't have to campaign to be elected student body president. Neither then nor later in life did he have a politician's mind set.

The closely knit Mennonite community that made its livelihood in the harsh conditions of the high plains could only absorb a few of its children when they grew up. Most of the youth left the community, usually seeking higher education that opened doors to job opportunities in other places. There was no doubt that the Rempel children would follow that path as well.

Back: Erwin, Norman, Barbara, Howard. Front: Lena and Alvin Eitzen, 1964.

During his senior year, the principal called Erwin into his office. Referring to his good grades and abilities, the principal encouraged Erwin to pursue medical studies. To Erwin, the idea of becoming a doctor felt too prideful.

Henry and Betty Rempel had expressed a desire that their children might someday attend either BIOLA or Grace Bible Institute in Omaha, Nebraska. From Montana, there were more connections to Grace, plus it was closer. Erwin decided to go to Grace, followed a year later by Norman, and a couple of years later by Barbara.

Erwin didn't realize that a girl living about 120 miles southeast of Lustre wondered if she would see him at Grace. He didn't remember their first meeting three years earlier.

Angela Albrecht's Story

Part One
Family Background and Infancy

My parents: Erwin A. Albrecht and Magdalene Bixel

My father wanted to farm. His parents, John T. and Ida (Stucky) Albrecht, were barely hanging on to their Kansas farm during the Great Depression of the 1930s with its droughts and dust storms. Still Erwin Albrecht, the second of their seven surviving children, continued to work with his father and brothers on the farm.

Born October 25, 1906, in rural Eakley, Oklahoma, he moved with his family to Kansas in 1919 where he finished high school in 1925 at Pretty Prairie. During his baptism service at First Mennonite Church in Pretty Prairie, he felt God's presence in a special way. Sitting in the church balcony one Sunday morning, he experienced God's call to ministry, but didn't tell anyone. Strangely, though, when his high school class made predictions about the future, his classmates predicted he would be a preacher.

During the so-called Roaring Twenties, plentiful rains produced good crops. The Albrechts bought a farm about twelve miles away, near Kingman. To keep three sons busy, John Albrecht rented additional farmland. Then the Great Depression arrived, along with drought. They couldn't make the payments for cattle and equipment they had borrowed money to purchase. Erwin avoided debt the rest of his life.

Erwin didn't have inner peace about being a farmer. He couldn't forget that call from God to be a pastor. A pastor? No one else in his family had been a pastor even though his family had been Christians for generations. They traced their roots back to Anabaptists in Switzerland in the 1600s. But they were rural people without advanced education. For him, to be a pastor meant he needed more education in biblical studies and theology. He didn't have money to go to college and seminary.

Erwin ignored the call and continued to farm the nearly flat Kansas prairie. He probably enjoyed the new challenges as farming methods transitioned from horse-drawn implements to the new mechanized, motorized equipment. He dated a girl and hoped to marry her – until she came back from a semester in college and told him she was planning to marry someone she met in college. The rejection, along with the discouragement of the Great Depression, resulted in a time he described as a "spiritual decline."

One day Erwin's younger brother Harry told the family that God was calling *him* to be an evangelist. Furthermore, Harry intended to leave home to study for the ministry.

Erwin felt stricken. Had his disobedience led God to abandon him and call his brother Harry instead? Erwin finally shared with his family that he had been resisting God's call to ministry. He was now willing to go to college with Harry.

Setting off for college

It was the Great Depression and they had little money. Erwin and Harry made plans to study at a Methodist school in nearby Winfield, Kansas. Their mother sent along jars of home-canned vegetables and fruits. They drove out the dusty lane, leaving behind the small white-frame farmhouse and the windmill that towered over several sheds. Thus began my father's journey that eventually led him to meet my mother.

Dad as a 30 yr old college graduate

Erwin and Harry earned some money picking up and delivering clothes for dry cleaning. After the first year of school, the brothers took different paths to ministry and went to different schools. Harry detoured through marriage, started a family, and later enrolled at Grace Bible Institute in Omaha, Nebraska.

Erwin transferred to Bethel College in North Newton,

Erwin A. Albrecht, at age 30, 1936.

Kansas. There he experienced one or more severe dust storms that blackened the daytime sky during the Dust Bowl days of the 1930s. He worked on the college cleaning crew and cleaned up dust the wind drove through cracks around the windows and doors. Everything was dusty, including the books in the library. Erwin graduated from Bethel College in 1937.

Leaving Kansas

Pastoral ministry was changing in the General Conference Mennonite Church. Churches wanted pastors with seminary training instead of lay pastors from within the congregation. However, there was no Mennonite seminary yet, so a number of Mennonites studied at Hartford Theological Seminary in Hartford, Connecticut. Apparently Erwin had a seminary scholarship, so he left the flat, dry prairie and headed east to the rolling green hills of Connecticut. That was a significant change for him. In a letter dated September 21, 1938, he wrote his parents about driving from Kansas to start his second year of study at Hartford. He stayed with friends and relatives along the way spending one night in a motel. He spent about twenty dollars total for gas, food, and lodging. He arrived in Hartford in the aftermath of a hurricane.

While a seminary student, Erwin served as a part-time pastor at Westminster Church, a small Congregational church in the rural area of Canterbury east of Hartford. That must have pushed him well beyond his simple Mennonite background.

During seminary, Erwin experienced again the pain of rejection as another romance failed. Shortly after that, he was critically ill with pneumonia.

After Erwin Albrecht's graduation from Hartford Seminary in 1940, he accepted a call to serve a city mission church in Chicago. The Home Mission Board of the General Conference Mennonite Church started the church prior to World War I on Chicago's south side. He began there on September 15, 1940.

"What is a Kansas farm boy doing in this big city?" Erwin must have asked himself as he served at First Mennonite Church at the corner of Seventy-Third Place and S. Laflin Street in Chicago. The city streets laid out in a square grid may have reminded him of the Kansas grid of roads along section lines, yet the people and experiences in the city put him in a different world. The year after he arrived in Chicago, World War II began. As a pastor, he was allotted extra rations of gasoline. That was especially useful when he was asked to drive women to the hospital to give birth while their husbands were away in military service.

How my father met my mother

During the summer of 1941, several young women visited First Mennonite Church on a warm summer evening. They were Mennonites from Bluffton, Ohio. Erwin understood that they were just visiting a sister who worked in Chicago at Moody Bible Institute. After the service, a family in the congregation invited their bachelor pastor and the visiting young women to their home for fellowship.

Petite dark-haired Magdalene Bixel caught Erwin's eye that night. Whether from shyness or uncertainty, he didn't really learn much about her that evening but he seemed to know that she was the one for him. Later he attended a ministerial conference in her hometown in Ohio and asked about Magdalene.

"She worked all summer in Chicago as a waitress in the YWCA," was the reply. By then Magdalene was teaching at Beaverdam, Ohio, not far from Bluffton. Erwin borrowed a car to drive over and see her.

Letters went back and forth between Erwin Albrecht and Magdalene Bixel. Before long, Magdalene agreed to give up her teaching career to join Erwin as his co-worker in ministry. He concluded that the reason God led him, a farmer at heart, to serve that city church was so that he could meet his future wife.

Magdalene Bixel, my mother

Magdalene, whose family called her Mac, was next to the youngest of eight surviving children born to Samuel S. and Ellen Bixel who farmed near Bluffton, Ohio. She was born at home on June 21, 1916. When she was nine years old, her mother died of complications after goiter surgery. Her two oldest sisters helped raise the younger children. Her father didn't remarry until ten years later.

The Bixel farm was diversified with various crops and livestock. They did some early work developing hybrid corn. The Bluffton community was neat and trim, a legacy of its Swiss Mennonite founders. Her father was a lay leader in the nearby Ebenezer Mennonite Church, several miles from the small town of Bluffton.

One Christmas, in response to the story of God sending Jesus Christ as a salvation gift, Magdalene wanted to give herself as a gift to God, accepting Christ as her Savior.

She studied at Bowling Green State University in Ohio to become an elementary school teacher. Even though she lacked one semester of completing her college degree, she could begin

Magdalene Bixel, date unknown.

teaching. She hoped to someday finish her studies and get a degree. She enjoyed teaching second grade because the students already knew how to read and were still young enough to be respectful.

One day in her classroom, a little boy embarrassedly slipped his completed assignment on her desk and mumbled what she understood to be, "You stink." She was dumbfounded and asked him to repeat it. Eventually, she figured out he was trying to say that he had "used ink" – instead of pencil – to do his work.

With travel discouraged during the war and long-distance phone calls only for emergency use, Erwin and Magdalene developed their relationship by writing letters. The nearly ten years' difference in their ages wasn't insurmountable. She also received a letter from her father expressing his concern about Erwin's Christian faith. After all, Erwin had gone to both Bethel College and Hartford Seminary, too liberal for her father's conservative stance.

It isn't clear whether or not they saw each other again until Erwin went to Ohio for their wedding on June 28, 1942. The horrors of a world at war didn't repress their love and hope.

Erwin A. Albrecht and Magdalene Bixel wed on June 28, 1942, Bluffton, Ohio.

After a honeymoon to Niagara Falls, the couple settled into the parsonage a few blocks from First Mennonite Church in Chicago. They joked that the two-story houses were so close together that someone at the end of the block could fill a plate with cookies and pass it through the windows from house to house. During the Albrechts' time, the south side of Chicago was transitioning to an African American community. The church remained there and transitioned with the community. In 2014 the directory of Mennonite Church USA listed it as a member of the Central District Conference with thirty-five members.

The Albrechts' firstborn

My mother suffered a long and painful labor before my birth on June 20, 1944, at the Cook County Hospital in Chicago. They named me Angela Marie, apparently from a character in a book my mother had read. She spent about ten days in the hospital, as was the custom then. That left her too weak, after dismissal, to walk up the front steps of the porch of their home without help.

One church member knew I liked bananas, a rationed product, and gave her portion to her pastor's family. Mother enjoyed dressing me in pink. The one thing I am certain about regarding my parents' aspirations for me is that I would become a follower of Jesus. They had no idea where that path would eventually take me.

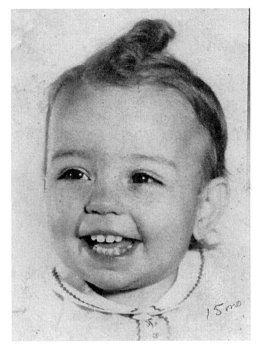

Erwin and Magdalene longed to return to their rural roots. January 1, 1946, they left the soot-filled air of Chicago. They moved to central Missouri to serve a Mennonite church in the country. I was eighteen months old and have no memories of the city where I was born.

Angela Albrecht, 15 months, Chicago, 1945.

Part Two
Missouri Childhood from 1946 to 1956

One bright June morning in 1947 I was sent off to Vacation Bible School. Church was like a second home to this pastor's daughter, and I was too young to wonder why they sent me. Not quite three years old, I wasn't old enough to go to VBS. I didn't realize how special that day would be, the first incident in my life that I remember.

A couple who drove an old black car brought me back home about noon. I entered the house and saw a baby bassinet! I stood on tiptoe and peeked into it. There was my new baby brother, David Alan Albrecht. The doctor had come to the house for the delivery. Mother's sister, Hilda Bixel, who had nurses' training, probably came from Bluffton, Ohio, to help.

Country church, country life

The setting for my childhood in central Missouri was in the country, between the small town of Fortuna, our address, and Versailles, a larger town. Trees edged modest-sized fields on gentle hills. Dad served as pastor for about ten years at the Bethel Mennonite Church. The square white frame church with two bell-less towers was a landmark. Its ten-acre plot included a cemetery and several acres of farmland that lay between the church and the two-story white frame parsonage. Near the house there was a barn, two chicken houses, a pasture, and large garden plots. After living in Chicago, farm-reared Erwin and Magdalene were in their element.

Our chickens provided eggs and meat, cows gave milk, and numerous cats controlled the mice. Tall metal milk cans in the basement kept cream to sell. Large flat cardboard crates of peeping tiny chicks arrived to keep the brooder house supplied. We carefully tended fertilized eggs to sell for hatching more chicks. Dad planted various crops in the field that lay between the church and the house. He fed wheat, corn, and oats he grew to our animals and sold any extra for some income.

Bethel Mennonite Church, Fortuna, Mo., circa 1955.

David Albrecht poses with pets in front of Bethel Church parsonage, the Albrecht family's home from 1946 to 1956.

We didn't have indoor plumbing for the first several years we lived in Missouri. We used a hand pump, in the house, which pulled water from a cistern that collected rainwater from the roof. We used a drafty, stinky, two-hole wooden outhouse. An old Sears Roebuck catalog offered up its glossy pages first as something to look at, and then as a stiff option for toilet paper.

My parents followed society's custom of setting aside Sunday as a special day. We wore our nicest clothes, dressy shoes, and best coats to church. Shopping wasn't an option as most stores weren't open. Sunday was called a "day of rest," but it was a busy day of work for a pastor and for the women who invited guests for a big Sunday dinner.

Preparing for Sunday began on Saturday night when we studied our Sunday school lessons, shined our shoes, and took our weekly bath. Dad brought a large washtub inside, set it close to a gas heater in the dining room, and filled it with warm water. We children bathed first, followed by our parents after we'd gone to bed.

When we children were too old to sleep in our parents' bedroom, we had our own rooms upstairs. The second floor was unheated and the bed was frightfully cold to get into during the winter. On hot summer nights I folded a sheet of paper into pleats and used it as a hand fan before falling asleep.

One day a big strange vehicle and machines showed up in our backyard to drill a well. From our back porch, perhaps thirty feet away, we had a good view of the fascinating process. We joined the trend of having indoor plumbing. Dad crafted cabinets for a modern kitchen and for the bathroom, which had a sink, toilet, and tub – no shower. I was fascinated with the laundry chute in the bathroom closet where we dropped dirty clothes down to a basket sitting near the wringer washing machine in the basement. I don't remember how Mother managed the kitchen prior to having a sink with running water.

Paying the preacher

My father was paid a hundred dollars a month as pastor, but was expected to earn additional income. He painted buildings, helped farmers, and crafted simple cabinets for kitchen and bath. He borrowed farm equipment to plant and harvest crops on the church property.

Erwin Albrecht prepares a sermon in the parsonage office, circa 1953.

Wherever my dad lived, he planted trees and grew strawberries. He also spent many hours in his study on the second floor of the parsonage, pecking out his sermons on a manual typewriter.

I grew up not knowing that statistically we probably were considered poor. Everyone around us lived much the same way we did – making a living on diversified small farms, planting big gardens, and canning and freezing enough to feed the family until the next year's harvest. Women's work was in the home. My mother, like most women in those days, sewed most of the clothes for the children and herself. A common source of fabric was the patterned cotton sacks in which flour and animal feed were sold. The same sack design might show up in one home as pajamas, in another as a dress, and as curtains for someone else. My parents didn't complain about finances and, as far as I knew, were content. What a blessing they gave us in that regard.

Having been shaped by the Great Depression, living frugally was part of my parents very being. That was strongly reinforced by the Mennonite emphasis on simple living and contentment. My parents modeled living within their means, not incurring debt, and taking care of the things we had.

Childhood memories

My childhood memories are of a happy, carefree time. Whatever differences my parents may have had, they settled them without my awareness. They were humble, pleasant people, providing their children with a loving stable home, adequate provisions, and spiritual nurture. They modeled clean living, honesty, responsibility, and keeping one's word. My parents and most of the people I knew didn't use foul language or scream and shout at each other.

We ate together as a family, beginning each meal with prayer. Each day began with family devotions. What a privilege to have been born into a family with a long heritage of committed Christians.

In nice weather, my brother David and I played outside in the grassy yard, on the covered back porch, in the barn, climbed the catalpa trees in the front yard, or explored the back pasture. We happily rode along on the fenders of the small tractor Dad borrowed, unconcerned about the obvious danger.

Erwin Albrecht drives a small tractor with his children, Angela and David, riding along.

"Guess who I'm thinking of" was a favorite game we played on summer mornings as our family sat on the shady west porch. We snapped green beans, shelled peas, cut corn off the cob or removed stems from strawberries. Canning and freezing were messy, hot, and tiring. But at the day's end, Mother was pleased with the rows of gleaming glass canning jars or the boxes ready to freeze. We children accepted that as our way of life during the summers, and usually helped without complaining.

We children enjoyed a small dog. But it was the cats and their playful kittens that captured my attention. My brother David and I spent hours playing with cats. We tried to dress them in doll clothes, which they resisted. About the only time I played much with dolls was with other girls. I actually preferred playing with cats.

Winters brought some snow. We had a sled, but I don't remember any hills big enough to go sledding. Indoors, we played games including Monopoly, checkers, and the card game inelegantly named Old Maid. We didn't play with a deck of cards because, we were taught, the cards contained devilish connotations and were used for gambling.

List of sins

Dancing of any kind was on the unwritten sin list. When my school held a May Day event complete with a Maypole dance, my parents asked that I be excused from the dance part. Instead, I was a princess, sitting on a platform. However, at home Mother let us swoop and sway to classical music played on the phonograph in the front room. Heavy plastic 78 r.p.m. albums could be stacked several high on the record player. The music was often scratchy and the needle sometimes skipped a round or got stuck and kept repeating. We turned the records over to play the second side.

Smoking was also on our list of sins. In those days, before the health hazards of cigarette smoking were widely known, we didn't fuss about people smoking in public places. When Dad came home after a trip by train, his clothes always smelled of smoke. Mother hung them outside to air. People in our churches didn't smoke; nor did my uncles, aunts or cousins, as far as I knew. Alcoholic beverages weren't used either.

Lipstick was frowned upon– at least none of the women we knew in our church wore it. The one tube of lipstick I discovered in my mother's dresser drawer fascinated me. I couldn't imagine when and where she had ever worn lipstick.

One day a new family came to our rural Mennonite church. The wife and mother wore lipstick and sundresses under matching little jackets. Their last name was Groth, not the typical Swiss/German Mennonite names of the others in our church – Garber, Hilty, Welty, Hofstetter, Aeschbacher. But the Groths were welcomed and became life-long active members of the congregation. Mrs. Groth taught me piano for several years.

Christmas in Missouri

Christmas, as it is for most children, was a magical much-anticipated event. We children pored over the Sears Roebuck and Montgomery Ward's special Christmas catalogs, especially the large section featuring children's toys. Mother made a variety of goodies including caramels that we carefully cut into small rectangles and wrapped in waxed paper. By mail, we exchanged goodies and gifts with her family in Ohio.

Colorful Christmas cards arrived in the mailbox from family, friends, and people in the church. We carefully hung the cards with Scotch tape all around the door frames inside the house, a custom I continued into adult years.

David and I would help select items for a Christmas bundle for a faraway child about our own age. We wrapped small items of clothing, a bar of soap, pencils, and a small toy in a bath towel held shut with safety pins. We added a Christmas card to each bundle and a dollar to purchase a Bible in their own language. Mennonite Central Committee sent and distributed the bundles in Europe, still recovering from the extensive damage of World War II. At least once our self-addressed envelope came back from the recipient expressing gratitude.

Dad took us out to a pasture to find and cut down a Christmas tree from among the prickly cedar trees that sprouted in abundance. At home, he put it into a big bucket with dirt. The tree proudly sat in the front room of the house. A white bed sheet carefully covered the ugly bucket giving the impression of a tree with white snow around it.

Our strings of Christmas tree lights had bulbs about the size of a night light four-watt bulb. If one light burned out, all the lights on the string went out. The lights got quite hot and could be a fire hazard. I enjoyed decorating the Christmas tree, arranging the treasured ornaments as artistically as possible. To finish it off, I carefully draped thin silvery aluminum icicles on the branches. I got upset at David when he threw the icicles on in gobs.

As gifts appeared under the tree, excitement built. David and I shook and examined the packages, guessing what was inside. We knew we had to wait until Christmas Eve to open one package as designated by our mother. It would be something to wear to the very special Christmas Eve program at church. Mother usually made me a new dress each Christmas. We opened the other gifts early on Christmas morning. We knew the stories and songs about Santa Claus, but they were just fun stories. Our grandparents, uncles, aunts, and cousins all lived far away. Our little family usually celebrated by ourselves, except for events at church.

The Christmas before I turned twelve, I got a last spurt of interest in dolls, even though I hadn't played much with dolls. Oh, how I wanted the gorgeous doll in an advertisement that showed her with several different outfits. She cost about fifteen dollars, which was a lot of money then. But, my loving parents made sure she showed up under the Christmas tree. I didn't play much with her. But I kept her and her clothes in a box all these years, mainly as a symbol of my parents loving sacrifice for me.

Every Christmas, each of the twenty-six grandchildren on my mother's side received two dollars from Grandpa Bixel. He gave each of his eight adult children one hundred dollars – a substantial amount of money in total. My gift money accumulated and by age eight, I used all sixteen dollars to help buy a bicycle.

First memories of car, phone, and TV

Our first car I remember was a black 1949 Ford. The unusual thing about it was its third headlight in the center of the front grill.

One way to describe cars of my childhood is by what they did not have, a list that grows longer with each new feature added to cars: no automatic transmission, no power brakes or power steering, no power windows, no keyless entry, no seat belts, no shoulder belts, no air bags, no air conditioning, and no cup holders. They certainly didn't have computerized features that alert the driver to drifting out of the lane, cameras that show what is behind the vehicle, GPS maps and navigation, nor hookups for phones and other devices. I'm not sure we even had turn signals or radio in the first car of my memory.

An old-fashioned wooden telephone hung on the wall in our dining room, but I don't remember it being used much. We were quite pleased when it was replaced with a black rotary dial phone that sat on a small phone table. It plugged into a jack along the floor and the handset was attached to the base with a cord. There was no way to misplace that phone.

A couple of brave families in our church bought their first television sets during my childhood in the early 1950s. The first TV that I recall seeing was at the home of someone from our church. They invited us to watch a performance of Handel's *Messiah*. I was mesmerized by the orchestra players and close-ups of various soloists. At another house,

Magdalene Albrecht poses with new dial phone at Bethel Church parsonage, circa 1954.

we watched wrestling. Even that was entertaining then. But many years passed before my parents bought their first TV.

Going to grade school

Kindergarten wasn't an option, so I started first grade at Westview Elementary School, a one-room school about two miles from our house. One teacher taught all the grades and all the subjects. I was the only student in my grade for the three years I went there. My parents must have driven me there in the mornings, but in nice weather, I walked home after school. There were other children to walk with most of the way on the unpaved roads. The road crossed a small creek that had a low concrete bridge without side railings. When we walked across it, I tried not to think of the stories of trolls under bridges who leaped out to grab whoever crossed.

Generally, school was good. The other students' and their families looked much like ours and lived much as we did, although only one other family was Mennonite. A negative note, however, was one boy who waited at the bottom of the slide when girls slid down. He tried to touch us in inappropriate places. To avoid him, instead of saying anything to the teacher, at recess time my girlfriend and I dashed to the girls' outhouse. No boy dared come in there! What a place to spend recess.

We learned and recited the Pledge of Allegiance routinely at school along with raising and lowering the U.S. flag.

The year my brother David started first grade, the one-room country schools consolidated. We both rode a big yellow school bus to the small town of Fortuna. Even there, several grades were together in one room with one teacher. I did grades four through six there. Schoolmates came from two-parent homes and many of them went to some kind of church, but few were Mennonites. Even in the larger school, I don't recall that there were children other than those whose skin was the same color as mine. Sadly, we used the same language of the day when speaking of people of other races, particularly blacks. We didn't realize how pejorative and racist those words were.

Angela practices piano at home, circa 1954.

Developing lifelong skills

My mother often read to us and I learned to enjoy reading. My favorite quiet reading place was in the corner of the front room behind the sofa, set at an angle. The summer after fourth grade, I spent a lot of time back there reading *Eggemeirs Bible Story Book*. That provided me with a life-long knowledge of Bible stories. We did a lot of reading, although I don't remember specific books nor from where we acquired them. We listened to some radio programs including *One Man's Family*, a soap-opera type of serial program.

Living in the country, we couldn't easily play with neighbor children. Sometimes I spent a night at a school friend's house, and returned with her to school the next day. A church friend might come over on Sunday between the morning and evening services.

My third-grade teacher, Mr. Fisher, was also my first piano teacher. My parents bought a big old used piano and nicely refinished it after scraping away layers of different colors. Practicing piano was an excuse to avoid washing dishes. Learning to play a four-part short hymn, such as *Fairest Lord Jesus*, was an important accomplishment on my way to becoming a church pianist. While it wasn't stated, there didn't seem to be any other purpose for learning to play piano than to play in church.

Discipline at home and school

My sixth-grade teacher spanked me in school. Mrs. McDonald was a strict teacher, but a good one. One time she left the room for a few minutes and instructed us not to talk in her absence. But of course, we didn't all remain silent. She returned to a hubbub that cut off as soon as she appeared. When she asked who had talked in her absence, honest little me had to admit that I did. So I was one of those who had to lean over her lap to get a slight spanking.

Spanking was the acceptable and expected mode of discipline in those days, both at home and at school. Parents made it known that if their children were spanked at school, they would give them another spanking at home to reinforce the teacher's discipline.

Usually, just the threat of a spanking was enough to deter me from whatever nefarious activity I contemplated. During one Sunday evening service at church when I was quite small, I played and scooted around on the floor under the pews. In vain Mother asked me to stop. When we got home, feeling guilty, I tried to hide behind the bathroom door. But my parents found me and administered the dreaded spanking.

One hot summer morning, Mother went out to work in the garden. She left instructions that David and I were to clean up the breakfast dishes. He and I goofed off instead, and nothing was cleaned up when she came back. She grabbed a flimsy yardstick, but it broke very quickly, so that spanking didn't amount to much.

Bethel Mennonite Church and beyond

Mother thrived in her role as homemaker and pastor's wife. As was typical in those times, she was known as Mrs. Albrecht, although sometimes as Mrs. Reverend Albrecht. They called my dad Reverend Albrecht. She was expected to be involved in many aspects of church life, but without title or pay. Dad referred to her as his co-worker. They had good relationships with the church people, quietly accompanying them through life's joys and sorrows. Most of the people in the congregation, like my parents, had roots going back to Switzerland. The Bethel Church founders were among Swiss Mennonites based in eastern Ohio in the early 1800s. They moved to Missouri as early as 1866.

We weren't the only Mennonites around. The nearby Mt. Zion Mennonite Church, whose address was that of the small town of Versailles, belonged to what we called the Old Mennonites. Their women wore distinctive dresses and head coverings over their long uncut hair pulled up into a bun. Their men wore "plain coats" without collars or neckties. In our General Conference churches, our clothing reflected a modest version of mainstream American styles. Most women in those days didn't wear slacks or shorts in public anyway. Our women usually cut their hair. For church, they wore hats, gloves, dressy shoes, and long sheer nylon hose with seams up the back of the legs. Our men wore typical suits and ties, as well as a hat. Back then it was unimaginable that eventually our diverse Mennonite churches would be merged into one denomination.

Even though somewhat isolated there in central Missouri, we always felt part of the wider denomination. Dad served in some position in the regional Central District Conference, going to meetings by train. Mother spent hours at a typewriter working on a children's curriculum that was published and used in the churches throughout the General Conference. The summer she did that project was unusually hot. We had electric fans, but no air conditioning. She set up the typewriter in the unfinished basement, the coolest place in the house.

Life revolved around the church. Sunday mornings we always had Sunday school and worship, in that order. Sunday evenings and Wednesday evenings we also had services. We always sat with Mother who made items out of cloth handkerchiefs, gave us little magnetized dogs to play with, and provided a mix of Cheerios and raisins to keep David and me occupied during services. Two weeks of morning Vacation Bible School sessions highlighted the summers.

Spiritual formation

Teachers told us the stories of Jesus, His love for us, His death and resurrection, and that each of us needed to invite Him into our heart in order to go to heaven. When I was about eight or nine years old, I knelt by my bed with my mother one night and prayed to accept Him as my Savior. Whether or not she initiated the conversation, I was willing to do that.

For many years, flannel-graph stories were the state-of-the-art in church visual aids. A wooden easel held a large cardboard piece covered in plain flannel cloth. Teachers placed colorful figures with flannel backing onto the flannel board to illustrate the story. For different background scenes, additional flannel cloths were painted to look like biblical buildings, interiors, and palm-lined landscapes. One memorable flannel-graph story illustrated what happened when we "fed" good or bad to our hearts and minds. We accepted the Bible as God's literal word.

Without invoking any biblical passages about hospitality, my parents certainly demonstrated that art. The lack of nearby hotels and restaurants may have necessitated the custom as much as frugality and fellowship among believers. I've followed their model. Opening our home to overnight guests and sharing meals has been an important and enriching part of life.

Church officials and missionaries often came to Bethel Mennonite Church, the only General Conference Mennonite Church in Missouri. My parents' guest book reads like a who's who in the General Conference. I grew up knowing that we were part of this larger body of Mennonites. That formed an important frame for our life. It continued to do so through contractions, additions, and changes in denominational structures and names.

Overnight visitors were expected to stay at the pastor's home because the parsonage where we lived had a guest room. We enlarged the dining room table for guests and carefully set it with the best tablecloths, dishes, and silverware. Our guests were revered and important people to us and left their imprint on this impressionable young girl.

One memorable guest was the blind Mennonite evangelist, J.J. Esau. While he was staying at our house, my brother and I rearranged some furniture, draping it with sheets and blankets for play. That did not amuse our blind guest.

Missionaries in the 1950s

Missionaries usually devoted their entire career to a country where God had called them to serve. Periodically they spent a year or two on furlough to share with the supporting churches about their ministry. A small periodical, *Missionary News and Notes*, kept people across our denomination informed about mission activities. When missionaries visited in person, we already knew something about them.

People would attend a missionary presentation at church any night of the week. They didn't have TV, nor go to the movies, or dash around to extra-curricular school sports. They certainly had no electronic devices with anything computerized for entertainment or communication. After the singing and the mission message, lights were turned off in the sanctuary. The bright light of a slide projector cast pictures on a white screen unfurled upward to the top of a wobbly three-legged stand. We enjoyed the missionaries' pictures of people dressed in colorful traditional clothes in faraway, exotic places. The last slide was usually a beautiful sunset behind silhouetted palm trees. The mission speakers used that scene to remind us that the time would end for telling other people about God's love. It was urgent to do it now. To make that message even clearer, the closing song often was *Work, for the night is coming.*

One time, Dr. Ella (Garber) Bauman was talking to us children. She had grown up right there in our church. She had done the highly unusual thing for a woman in the 1920s of studying to be a doctor, had married Dr. Harvey Bauman, and together they were medical missionaries in India from 1925 to 1961.

"Perhaps God is calling one of you children to be a missionary too," Dr. Ella said to a group of us children in church.

"Maybe that would be me," a small voice inside of me said.

Many years later it was a special, almost holy, moment for me to personally walk on the Champa mission station in India where the Baumans had lived and to see the medical facilities where they served.

Health issues in the 1950s

Our family enjoyed good health in general. My main health problem was recurring bouts of tonsillitis. When my mother had surgery for some reproductive issues, I had my tonsils removed at the hospital and spent one night in her hospital room before we both were dismissed. I remember the pleasure of being encouraged to eat lots of cold ice cream.

Polio was a dreadful, feared disease during my childhood. Our family was grateful to be spared. When Dr. Jonas Salk discovered a vaccine for polio, we were eager to take it. Tuberculosis was another dreaded disease during the first decade of my life. There was no real cure, so people with tuberculosis were sent away for months to a sanatorium for rest and fresh air. The DPT vaccine became available during my early childhood. But, enduring measles, mumps, and chickenpox was the usual rite of passage through childhood. Both my brother and I had measles and chicken pox, one right after the other. We had to stay in a darkened bedroom when we had measles to avoid harming our eyes. By the time my own children came along, there were vaccinations for measles and mumps, but not yet for chicken pox. Our children all went through rounds of chicken pox.

Visiting our relatives

Following God's call to ministry meant that my parents never lived in their home communities. I had twenty-some cousins on each side of the family but seldom saw them.

Most of my mother's family lived around Bluffton, Ohio, six hundred miles from our central Missouri home. Several girl cousins were within a few years of my own age. Playing with them was special! I always felt a connection with the uncles, aunts, and cousins on the Bixel side, even though I look more like my dad's youngest sister, Luella. The Bixels were short, and I seem to have become the shortest of them all.

Grandpa Bixel died when I was nine. We continued to visit the uncles, aunts, cousins, and step-grandma – notable for driving her car into her 90s. We usually went to Ohio in summer. Playing with my cousins at the swimming pool in Columbus Grove was a highlight. It was more fun to go to a clean swimming pool than to play in the shallow water of a rocky Missouri creek where we had to avoid the green slime of algae on the water and the cow pies on the banks. Hair care was apparently too complicated to easily manage, so we wore rubber swim caps in a vain attempt to keep the hair dry.

Angela and David and some Bixel cousins enjoy the Columbus Grove, Ohio, public swimming pool, 1956.

I vaguely recall riding the train to Ohio, but we usually drove the six hundred miles in one long day. Highways were two-lanes wide and passed through small towns and cities. My folks studied the maps to look for roads that bypassed the larger cities. David and I couldn't understand why Dad preferred to drive around the cities. We wanted to see the bright, blinking city lights, especially after dark.

Four of Dad's siblings and his widowed mother lived near Kingman, Kansas. That was a bit closer to us than Mother's family. We usually drove to Kansas in summer, although I recall one time we went for Christmas.

At the Albrecht farm we swam in the square cement tank where the cattle drank – but it was often edged with slimy green algae. It wasn't as nice as the swimming pool in Ohio. With such limited opportunities to swim, it is no wonder I never learned how. We never went to a swimming pool in Missouri.

Summer visits to Kansas included a watermelon feed at Grandma Albrecht's place. We stood in the yard spitting the big black shiny seeds while juice dribbled down our chins. Dad's youngest brother,

Angela and David with their mother "swim" in the stock tank at Grandma Albrecht's farm in Kansas.

who never married, lived there with Grandma. He kept the diversified farm going after my Grandpa Albrecht had died relatively young from complications after surgery in 1941.

Only occasionally did any of my uncles and aunts come to visit us in Missouri. My parents were usually the ones to travel back to their home communities. Mother kept up with her four sisters with a round robin letter. After my Grandpa Bixel died, I know she was disappointed that she wasn't present when items were distributed from her family home. She treasured the items she did inherit.

Family road trip, 1953

One warm summer Missouri morning I was too excited to sleep. From my second-floor bedroom window, I saw Dad outside in the pre-dawn darkness packing the car. It was the summer of 1953 and I was nine years old. We were setting out on our own family version of the Great American Road Trip, which helped set the stage for my lifetime of travel throughout the United States and around the world. That trip also began a pattern of attending the large conferences of our Mennonite churches. That reinforced the connections to our denomination.

This trip would take us way beyond the familiar terrain and plains of mid-America that we frequently drove from our Missouri home to either Ohio or Kansas. This month-long journey took us to the West Coast. The motivation for the trip was to attend the triennial sessions of the General Conference Mennonite Church held in Portland, Oregon. That was where my Uncle Harry Albrecht was pastor of a Mennonite church. He and Aunt Erma lived there with their four children.

Dad recorded the trip with his new camera that had many complicated settings to calculate and set manually for each picture. Sixty years later, some of those Kodachrome slides he took retained their color and clarity and helped document the many special places we visited.

To begin the trip, we stopped first at Dad's family home in Kansas where Grandma Ida Albrecht joined us for the journey. In his youth, Dad and one or more other young men had driven out west, but for Mother, my brother and me, it was all new.

Most nights we could stay with relatives along the way, but sometimes we needed to sleep in motels. Motels were small, family-run places that often featured a short row of small cabins. When we stayed at a motel, only Grandma and Mother got to sleep in the motel room. Dad worked out a way that he, my brother, and I could sleep in the car to reduce the motel cost. Before signing up for a night at a motel, Mother went inside to inspect the cleanliness, which included lifting the bedcovers to be sure the sheets were clean. We all went in to use the bathroom, even if we had to pay an extra fifty cents.

We mostly made our own meals along the way. There weren't any fast-food restaurant chains back then. I really disliked the powdered milk that Mother made for us to drink and pour on our breakfast cereal. When the sun climbed to mid-day heights, we looked for a nice shade tree where we could park and eat our lunch along the highway.

"Look for a red flying horse," Dad said to us kids as we entered a town whenever the gas gauge was getting low. His only credit card was for Mobile gas, the company with a red flying horse as its symbol. The condition of restrooms in most gas stations was appalling.

Angela, age 9, on the right, experiences the ocean for the first time, with her mother and brother, at Canon Beach, Ore., 1953.

After we crossed high plains and mountains, my first sight of an ocean was at Cannon Beach, set among rugged hills and large rocks on the Oregon coast. We tested the cold Pacific Ocean near the famous Haystack Rock.

For us children, the trip's highlight was the week we spent at Uncle Harry's house in Portland. We enjoyed playing with our four cousins while our parents attended the General Conference sessions. The youngest, Loretta, was my age.

We also took in the wonders of California. In the strange big city of San Francisco, at one point my dad couldn't find his wallet. What panic! And what relief when it was found down between the car seats.

Avoiding Los Angeles, we headed back east, entering barren deserts. After hosting so many missionaries in our home, now it was time to stop and visit some missionaries who served on an Indian reservation in Arizona, Rev and Mrs. Albert Jantzen. We also saw the stunning grandeur of the Grand Canyon. The beautiful turquoise jewelry made by the Native American women caught my eye. I didn't have quite enough money to buy the little ring that I wanted. My grandma dug into her purse and gave me the few extra cents I needed.

Enlarging the family

I noticed that Mother was nauseous in the mornings. Soon after that, she had a miscarriage. So the next time I noticed her nauseous condition, I rightly figured out that she was pregnant again. My sister, LaRita Jean, was born a few months before my twelfth birthday. I remember being at home with David after school when Dad called home to our relatively new dial phone to let us know about our new sister. Mother had gone to a clinic in nearby Versailles for the birth. When it was discovered that the baby was in the breach position, an ambulance was called on standby in case she needed to be taken to a hospital in Jefferson City, about fifty miles away. But she didn't need the ambulance. Because the baby was a girl, I got to help pick out her name.

Once again, my Aunt Hilda Bixel came to help. Mother said she and Dad felt that to obey God's command to be fruitful and multiply, they should have at least three children. People thought that my sister, born when my mother was nearly forty, was an "unexpected blessing." I never doubted that she was planned for and greatly desired. I thought she was the most beautiful baby I'd seen!

Transition time

When Dad completed ten years at the Bethel church, he felt it was time to move on. He contacted someone in the denominational offices in Newton, Kansas, who helped coordinate pastoral placements. While my parents didn't share much about how they determined God's leading to a church in Montana, my sense is that they followed the doors that opened.

The Montana church sent Alvin and Annie Deckert to Missouri with their farm truck to move our things. My parents had requested the measurement of the truck bed ahead of time. They carefully measured all our things to see how much they could take in the truck. A lot of furniture and other items wouldn't fit and were sold at an auction. We sorted through lots of things stored up in the attic, such as school papers, and threw them down from the window for disposal. We couldn't hold tightly to our possessions.

Before moving, we took one last trip to Bluffton, Ohio, to see the Bixel relatives. We included a stop in Chicago at First Mennonite Church where Dad had previously served. We went to the Museum of Science and Industry. At Midway Airport we stood outside the tall chain link fence to watch airplanes land and take off, quite a novelty. We also made a last visit to the relatives in Kansas. Instead of annual visits, several years would pass between visits once we lived in faraway Montana.

60 years later

About sixty years later, I mailed the Bethel Mennonite Church the slide photos Dad had taken of individual church families in the 1950s. The chair of the church historical committee turned out to be Melvin Gerber, a childhood friend of my brother. He wrote:

> "Your family and especially your father, since he worked with my father, has always been one of my heroes. He had such

a combination of humor and insight. We were given an audio tape that he did at the same time of the pictures. He recorded interviews with many of the Bethel families. As I have listened to the interviews it has amazed me how well he knew each person. Every question revealed the important things about the personalities. Quite remarkable. He also made some portable tables for the church. They are still in use and are in good repair because they were so well constructed."

How nice to hear affirmation for my father's ministry. In that context, a solid foundation was laid for the future chapters of my life.

Part Three
Montana Teenager from 1956 to 1962

It was a big move – from rural central Missouri to an even more rural location in eastern Montana. No feelings of anticipation or dread, excitement or fearfulness, linger in my memory. It didn't feel dramatic at the time, apparently. My brother and I accepted the move without

Bethlehem Mennonite Church, Bloomfield, Mont., 2005 aerial view.

hesitation, and I don't recall ever missing Missouri. Baby sister LaRita was only about four months old, David was nine, and I turned twelve that summer of 1956.

Dad's new pastorate, Bethlehem Mennonite Church of Bloomfield, Montana, had 120 members plus another forty children. Dad had been there once, but not the rest of us. So we, including Mom, were wide-eyed as we entered Montana. Soon we passed through the town of Glendive with its shops, medical facilities, and green trees along the Yellowstone River. Climbing upward from the river valley through wide-open plains and hills, another thirty miles took us to an intersection that a small post office designated as Bloomfield: a collection of a few houses, a gas station, grain storage bins, a small white Lutheran church, and nondescript small buildings sitting in a barren valley. Continuing straight on another eight miles to the north, we could see the tall steeple of our new church high on a hill. We then turned east for two miles of gravel road that climbed up to the church and the parsonage. That meant it would be forty long miles to traverse for shopping and medical care in Glendive.

New home in Montana

As in Missouri, here too a ten-acre property included the church, the parsonage, the cemetery, and some acres of farmland. A small barn served as domicile for a cow and some chickens and at times a pig and a calf. Most of the hens resented having their precious eggs removed, so I dreaded being sent out to gather the eggs. My parents again planted a large garden. However, gardening was quite challenging in the short, dry growing season of Montana.

The interior of the one-story white frame parsonage had been redecorated and renovated before our arrival. Mother recalled that when we arrived, men were working on a well and there was no water in the house. We began our Montana chapter temporarily using an outhouse and getting drinking water from a neighbor. The church people warmly welcomed our family. Their generous grocery shower provided us with "96 pounds of sugar, 20 boxes of Jell-O, 30 pounds of cured ham, etc.," according to my mom's records. We also got our first taste of antelope and venison.

Bethlehem Mennonite Church parsonage as it looked when the Albrechts arrived in 1956.

For Mother, who had only known the green summers in Ohio and Missouri, this was a barren contrast. Years later she described her first impressions:

> Around the parsonage there was no grass, just dust when dry and mud when wet. How we missed a tree, let alone the fruit of peaches, pears or apples. Just leaves would have satisfied us, but consoled us in the fact we won't have to rake leaves come autumn. The first spring how I longed to see bulbs come up, roses to watch or anything come through the ground. There was not even a lawn to mow.

My parents did what they could to change that description. They planted trees and evergreen bushes beside the house. Rows of small trees and bushes slowly became a thick shelterbelt softening the impact of cold winds. My parents smoothed and leveled a small patch in the yard and planted it with grass seed for a croquet court. At the front door, an addition of a small entryway and concrete stairs with a nice iron handrail replaced the awkward simple wooden steps.

69

The newly remodeled kitchen had a single-lever kitchen faucet – the first one we'd seen. A visitor to that remote location was surprised, saying he had only ever seen one in Chicago.

The fourth bedroom in our house was reserved for guests. No one back then thought that a house needed more than one bathroom. It had a tub but no shower.

It felt eerie, especially in the dark evening, when Mother sent me to the dimly lit unfinished basement for a jar of canned vegetables or fruit, or something from the freezer. The hallway from the foot of the basement stairs was lined on one side by a dark gray concrete wall of a room-sized cistern filled with dark ominous water. The other side of the hallway opened to the scary furnace with its glowing coals. Dump trucks came periodically to empty a load of black coal down a chute to the supply room behind the furnace. The furthest room in the basement was the brightest and big enough for a ping-pong table or for hanging laundry to dry in bad weather.

Water was always an issue. Whatever water was in the basement cistern we used for all our cooking and cleaning. Before drilling a new well, men came with special willow branches to do witching for water. However, the water they found was a long way down and in the long run, not really usable. Tanker trucks hauled water to the cistern.

From walnut wood Dad had brought from Missouri, he made himself a desk, complete with drawers that file folders fit into and a pull-out shelf for his manual typewriter. Here too, the pastor's office was a small room in the parsonage. He also made a walnut sewing desk for my mom.

Dad made a long cabinet from pine to fit my bedroom. It had three sections: drawers, desk, and enclosed shelves. Later, Dad took off the desk section and LaRita used it. It sported many different colors and designs over the years and eventually returned to my possession.

For the first few years in Montana, I enjoyed having the small northeast corner bedroom to myself. David had his own room too. When LaRita outgrew the crib in my parents' bedroom, she and I shared a double bed. How upset I was whenever she got into my things!

Montana landscape and climate

The church's ten acres was located on the edge of what was called the Retah Table. Our kitchen window looked south across a valley and hills to the distant bluffs of the Yellowstone River beyond Glendive. The open, treeless landscape lay like a slightly rumpled carpet under the horizon-to-horizon span of big blue sky. In late spring there usually was a slight tint of green on the land for a few weeks, but it was never truly green. Large rectangular fields, up to a mile long, had strips of spring wheat alternating with strips of brown dirt kept fallow to conserve moisture for the following year's crop.

Montana is aptly named, "Big Sky Country." Outdoors, I sometimes felt overwhelmed, exposed, and vulnerable under the intense and all-encompassing sky. The wide daytime vista allowed us to watch the billowing clouds of incoming storms. Advancing wind clouds picked up dust to fling around before the first big raindrops fell and pinned the dust back to the ground. Rain was welcome, even if it fell in torrents that carved gullies across the planted fields. Hail was dreaded; it could wipe out a year's worth of work and income in a few minutes. On moonless nights, the vast dark sky filled with stars. We could easily see the Milky Way and constellations. At times, the pastel glowing Northern Lights moved in a slow dance decorating the night sky.

The harsh winters were an adventure for my brother and me – and certainly a much greater adventure for my parents. Temperatures regularly dropped below zero, even to minus forty at times. We didn't know the term "wind chill," but we certainly experienced it. Small man-made lakes and ponds froze deep enough to drive vehicles on the ice. Our church youth went ice-skating each winter. Burning old tires provided light and warmth, even out on the ice. Even though I never learned to balance well on ice skates' thin blades, I wouldn't have missed those events. That is probably when some frostbite left my fingers and toes extra sensitive to cold for the rest of my life.

Winter snows blew without restraint across the open expanses. The main roads were elevated a bit above the level of the fields allowing snow to blow across them unimpeded. The wide deep ditches filled with snow blown in so hard we could walk on top of it. Blizzard winds sculpted big snowdrifts artistically around the house, garage, and shed.

One of our first years there, the drifts were so high that David and I built snow caves and forts in them. Dad had lots of shoveling to do to open the driveway or get to the small barn. He didn't have the benefit of any equipment more than a hand snow shovel. Cancelations of school or church were so rare that I don't recall any. When there wasn't any snow cover, the frequent strong winds carried off the precious top soil, dusting the snowdrifts with a thin layer of dirt.

Only in retrospect do I think about Montana as barren and bleak with harsh weather. At the time, it was simply our family's home.

Bethlehem Mennonite Church

The congregation consisted of people who could trace their family roots back to Mennonites in Europe. Some of them had relatives around Freeman, South Dakota. We hadn't been at the church long when my parents discovered various factions in the congregation. They soon learned who didn't get along with whom. My impression is that these conflicts often related to family issues, inheritance, and land.

A few people in our church were schoolteachers, but most of them were farmers. Their main crop was wheat, planted after spring thaw when the ground was dry enough for the big tractors and planters to work in the fields without being stuck too often. Winter wheat wouldn't have survived the sub-zero winters. Summers were mild with low humidity, long hours of sunlight, and a few quick thunderstorms. Wheat harvest in August was followed closely by the first frost at the end of the month.

Poor crops were common in that semi-arid region of Eastern Montana, which received about thirteen inches of precipitation annually. Prior to our arrival in Montana, there were several years with more rain resulting in better harvests. In the early 1950s, the congregation built a new white church, a landmark visible for miles. Some families built houses in what was then the new ranch style – which meant it was spread out on one floor rather than two. A couple of the women in our church did an amazing job of transforming their yards into beautiful flower gardens. Mom so much enjoyed visiting at those homes.

Dad and Mom made regular pastoral visits with church members in their homes. When they visited in one of the nice new houses, I cleaned up our humbler place so it wouldn't look too bad in contrast when they came home.

The history of the Bethlehem church included the attempted lynching in 1918 during World War I of Pastor John Franz. He was suspect because of his stance on conscientious objection to military participation, along with speaking German. [3]

Grades 6 and 7 in one-room school

Our elementary school teacher in Montana called us Bolsheviks! This was during the Cold War in the late 1950s. Our teacher in the one-room school house had a hard time understanding us Mennonite kids. Some of the parents were descendants of Russian Mennonites. She apparently thought anyone connected to Russia had to be a communist.

For seventh and eighth grades, I was again the only student in my grade in a one-room country school. It was hard to find and keep good teachers in those remote locations. The school provided lodging for the teacher in a small house, called a teacherage, on the school grounds. Outhouses accommodated the students' bathroom needs, and perhaps the teacher's too. David and I often walked to school along a mile of dirt road that descended like a staircase to the south from our house.

One time a family of skunks found shelter under the schoolhouse. Something caused one or more of them to release their stinky spray. We couldn't bear the strong smell. School was dismissed early that day.

Only two news items remain in my memory from the *Weekly Reader* we always got at school during grade school years. One was the announcement about the new Interstate Highway System that President Eisenhower established. That highway system changed America and we ourselves benefited greatly from the wide smooth roads without traffic lights. The second memorable news item was about the founding of Brasília, an amazing new capital city in Brazil. I imagined it built out in the jungle. Years later we got to experience what kind of terrain it really was built in.

---

[3]Gerlof D. Homan, *American Mennonites and the Great War 1914-1918* (Scottdale, Pa. 1994)

When I finished eighth grade, I ranked third in the county schools. My mother made me a new green nylon dress for the countywide eighth-grade graduation ceremony held in Glendive.

Growing spiritually

My spiritual life continued to be nurtured in that Montana community. In addition to Sunday school and worship, there was always a Sunday evening service, a Bible study on Wednesdays and choir practice too. In those days before television was available in the rural communities, and when it was wrong to go to movies and dances, the church was the community center for socializing. Without complaining, we children went to all the church services, sitting with our parents except for Sunday school. By high school, we teens would sit together near the front of the church, girls on one side and boys on the other.

Each summer I attended the nearby interdenominational Eastern Montana Bible Camp. My first year there I made another commitment to Christ. That provided me with the assurance of my salvation that I had lacked until then. The preaching at camp included warnings about hell and the second coming of Christ. It meant a lot to have confidence that I was truly saved and a child of God.

Our catechism class met upstairs in the church in the small room under the steeple to prepare for baptism and church membership. Dad was the instructor and taught us from the Westminster Catechism materials. It began with the question: What is the chief end of man? Answer: Man's chief end is to glorify God, and to enjoy him forever." That is the only thing I remember from catechism studies, and that became my goal and purpose in life – to glorify God.

Baptism Sunday was in early June after my eighth grade. We girls wore new white dresses – or in my case, a new white blouse with a mostly white skirt. We knelt on the floor at the front of the church while a deacon poured water through my dad's hands onto our heads. It was a meaningful experience, but in retrospect, I knew so little about faith and trusting God. Yet, to the best of my understanding, my heart was open to the Lord and His leading.

Somewhere along the way, I learned the main points of our church history – that back in 1525, during the Protestant Reformation in

Europe, there were believers who sought to apply New Testament teachings to daily life. They also believed that each person needs to make an informed decision about accepting Christ. Thus they didn't baptize infants, as did both the Catholic Church and other Protestant reformers at that time. They were first called Anabaptists – rebaptizers. They taught separation of church and state, a radical and political idea at the time. They also sought to put in practice Jesus' words about loving enemies. Several years later a Dutch priest, Menno Simons, converted and became one of the group's leaders. Later the Anabaptists were called Mennonites. They were severely persecuted by both Catholics and other Protestant reformers.

Cross-cultural mission

Bethlehem Mennonite Church strongly supported mission activities near and far. People who had grown up in the congregation had responded to God's call to mission in distant places. One of them was Verney Unruh, who with his wife, Belva, were among some of the first missionaries the General Conference sent to Japan. They returned for their first furlough not long after our own arrival in Montana, and I remember playing with their children.

Not many missionaries and denominational representatives traveled to Montana, but when they did, it was in our house again where they stayed. After all, the parsonage had an extra bedroom set up just for guests. We may have lived far from the centers of our denominational life, but our connections felt strong.

One memorable visitor was the indomitable missionary Martha Burkholder, serving in India. She dressed me in a bright-colored sari, carefully wrapping several yards of exotic fabric around me. What a treat that was! Whenever I would think about what I would do in life, it was always in the context of doing it as a missionary. I wanted to follow God's call.

Our church youth group took a trip to the small towns of Lame Deer and Busby, Montana, where Mennonite missionaries worked and had started several churches on an Indian reservation. The jovial Native American pastoral couple kept us laughing with lots of stories. However, we also learned of the sadness of life on a reservation and the prevalence of alcoholism. That was my first personal experience with cross-cultural mission.

My mom always taught a class of young children during summer Vacation Bible School. Here, as in Missouri, VBS met each weekday morning for two weeks just after public school ended. Prior to the beginning of VBS, Mom brought home the crisp new packets of Herald Press materials. We children helped her sort and punch out the take-home pieces. Once we were high-school age, we girls became teachers' helpers. I learned a lot helping in my mom's classroom.

The only one of my dad's sermons that I remember was when the charismatic movement was beginning in the 1960s. People wondered what was going on. He used Acts 5:38-39 as advice: "If their purpose or activity is of human origin, it will fail. But if it is from God, you will not be able to stop these men; you will only find yourselves fighting against God." (NIV) Except then we still used the King James Version of the Bible, which many considered the only real translation. The recently published Revised Standard Version was unacceptable in our circles at the time because of how one word had been translated: Isaiah 7:14 used "young woman" rather than "virgin."

Visiting relatives

Montana was too far away for any of my mom's family to visit us. Photo records indicate Uncle Frank and Aunt Luella brought along Grandma Albrecht from Kansas to visit us in Montana in 1957. The visits from my dad's brother Harry were more memorable.

One year Dad invited his preacher brother Harry from Portland, Oregon, to give a series of special meetings at church. But at our house, Uncle Harry talked about UFOs and life in outer space. I was captivated! I watched the night sky for any strange lights that might be a passing UFO. I joined a science fiction book club for a while and read some of Isaac Asimov's works. That certainly expanded my world! One time Harry's family, with the three youngest children, came to visit us as well.

Feeding the family

As it had been in Missouri, summer was the time to store up food supplies for the coming winter. David always got to "play" in the cold water at the kitchen sink where the briefly-boiled corn or peas got dunked. They needed quick cooling to stop the cooking process before putting them in the freezer.

For many years, a tiny scar on one of my fingers was a reminder of butchering chickens. Dad would catch about a dozen squawking hens by grabbing their legs with a long stiff wire hook. He ended their lives with a hatchet and hung them by the feet from a clothesline to drain the blood. Meanwhile, we got huge pots of water boiling. We dipped the entire carcass into the hot water, which helped release the feathers. Then we pulled off feathers by the handful. Each naked chicken was held over a flame to burn off the tiny hairs that remained. A scraping with a knife blade finished cleaning the skin. Next was the cutting, which I rather enjoyed. First the legs and wings were cut off and a then a cut across the torso. I learned the hard way to carefully remove the inedible inner stuff.

One of my folks' first major purchases in Montana was a large upright freezer. Later at the same store, Dad bought something for a dollar, which meant he could place one ticket into a drawing for a freezer. And he won! Having already purchased a freezer there, he chose a nice new refrigerator instead. That is the only time we won anything – not surprising since my parents didn't participate in gambling.

Going to high school

High school meant riding a school bus again, from 1958-1962. Richey High School was about fourteen miles away in the small town of the same name. The bus route was a big loop of more than fifty miles. In the mornings, the bus came by our house toward the end of the loop, but then after school, I would be the last one to get off the bus. Sometimes I got off the bus at a point two miles west of our house before the bus headed around the big loop. I often walked home those two miles arriving home before the bus would pass. Sometimes people I knew drove by and offered me a ride. One time I thought I knew the driver of a farm truck only to get up in the cab with him and realize it wasn't that man at all. I was a bit frightened and was grateful he dropped me off safely at home.

In high school, I always felt like I was a mousy little wallflower. I was too short, wore too-thick glasses, and was too quiet. I was keenly aware of my straight pointed nose, overbite, and a receding chin. Boys didn't show interest in me. I was studious and learned easily, almost never having to do any schoolwork at home. In our class of twenty-two, it wasn't hard to become the valedictorian.

I enjoyed music. I wanted to be in the high school band, but my folks couldn't afford to buy a musical instrument. The school owned the cumbersome percussion instruments, so I played those. I bought a pair of drumsticks and practiced at home without a drum. I usually played the snare drum, but sometimes the big bass drum and cymbals. The band mostly played Sousa marches, never any jazz. The dark blue band uniforms trimmed in gold were stiff and uncomfortable to wear.

My singing voice wasn't great, but I enjoyed singing soprano in choirs at church and school. At high school, I sang in some girls' ensembles.

The high school music teacher also taught individual voice and piano lessons during the school day. She had me learn an eight-page recital piece - a sonata by Joseph Haydn.

I had the sonata memorized for a recital. I sat down at the piano in front of the audience and began to play. As I neared the end of the second page, my mind went blank. Without pausing, I started over but still couldn't remember it all. I managed to skip smoothly into the ending part. Apparently only my teacher really knew what I had done. For the processional at high school graduation during my junior year, another girl and I played a piano duet arrangement of *Largo* by Handel. We had to adjust it and repeat some to fit the processional timing. To my embarrassment and her disgust, when it came to the final chord, I loudly hit the wrong notes.

Being in the school dramas would have meant many after-school practices and missing the bus to go home. My folks did let me be the prompter for the plays. That way I only needed to go to the final dress rehearsals and the performances.

The typing classroom had several rows of Royal manual typewriters. I enjoyed typing, even though working with stencils and ink to make the school paper was tedious and messy. My first foray into journalism was writing some pieces for the school paper. I did a brief review of a film about the desert, which I mistitled "Life in the Dessert."

Fortunately, I never needed to use shorthand because I wasn't very good at it. Within a few years, Dictaphones eliminated the need for shorthand anyway.

My senior year I was editor of the high school yearbook. Being an introvert, I worked a lot by myself, not knowing how to lead a team. I took most of the candid black and white photos for the yearbook on my little blue fixed-lens film camera. I also designed the layout.

As if it weren't bad enough to expose my legs wearing shorts for gym class, it was mortifying to take group showers with the other girls. Plus, I was terrible at anything athletic. When square dancing was scheduled for gym class, my folks wrote a note to have me excused because we didn't dance.

Boys' basketball was the only sport at our small high school. I went to some of the games, but I don't recall that my folks ever went. My senior year a girlfriend and I went to the district tournament, spending a night in a hotel by ourselves. Football was introduced my senior year when my brother, David, was a freshman. He joined the team and by his senior year, he was a co-captain.

High school girls had to wear skirts to school – including on cold, windy winter days. It was a public school and reflected the common styles of that era. Those were the days of the can-cans or crinolines – the only fashion I haven't seen come back yet. They were half-slips made of yards of starched ruffled netting that made skirts stand out. I also recall wearing long nylon stockings to high school – before convenient pantyhose came along. By my senior year, the school allowed girls to wear jeans on Fridays.

Preacher's daughter in public high school

Since everyone knew I was a preacher's kid, and I did nothing to dispel their stereotypes, my schoolmates never even asked me to smoke, drink, dance, or go to movies. I had no desire to try those things, anyway.

Later I've realized how my upbringing in my family and church "protected" me. It wasn't hard to make good choices. I wasn't really tempted. I didn't go through a rebellious time, as many teens do. I had a small circle of friends, including non-Mennonites, who shared enough of my values. Riding the bus to and from school significantly limited the amount of time I spent with schoolmates. Miles separated our house from any of my friends.

Not all the teens in my school and church had a lifestyle like mine. One year several girls in the junior class dropped out of school because they "had to get married." It was very awkward one Sunday morning in our church when a teenage fellow stood up nervously in front of the congregation to confess that his girlfriend was pregnant and they were getting married. That was how those situations were handled in those days before birth control pills and legal abortions. Several more years passed before I heard of any unmarried mother keeping her child.

The concept of homosexuality wasn't known to me or even spoken of except from reading about it in the Bible. Drug use wasn't an issue either – just tobacco and alcohol use.

I was too shy to talk about my Christian faith with my classmates, and I felt a bit guilty about that. Over the years after high school, I was surprised when at least three girls in my class reached out to let me know they had accepted Christ at some point.

Politics and religion

"Shadow over the White House!" headlined a Christian magazine during the presidential campaign of 1960. A Catholic, John F. Kennedy, was the Democratic nominee for president. Not only were most people we knew staunch Republicans, but they weren't sure Catholics were truly Christians. Some wondered if the pope might be the anti-Christ and would influence a Catholic president. That remote area of Montana lacked television coverage, so we didn't see the first TV debate between presidential candidates Richard Nixon and Kennedy.

Everyone had white skin in our community and schools. We heard that the famous and talented black singer Marian Anderson wasn't allowed to stay in the Glendive hotel when she gave a performance in town. The percolating unrest of the civil rights movement didn't seem to reach our community. Someone from my high school lost a brother in the early prelude to the war in Vietnam. Everyone was concerned about communism, but it was a far-away threat. Without TV, we got most of our news by radio or printed publications.

Other Mennonites

"She wears a prayer covering even when she goes out to the mailbox!" was the report about a young wife who was part of the Old Mennonite congregation, Red Top Mennonite Church, several miles from Bloomfield.

"She went to Eastern Mennonite College in Virginia," was the reason given, and that was my introduction to a place that would eventually play a large role in our lives.

As in Missouri, we didn't mix much with the Old Mennonite churches – the one near Bloomfield and another one in Glendive. Over the years, the congregations began to work together in some activities, especially at the Eastern Montana Bible Camp. That changed and in the twenty-first century, the dwindling congregations began sharing a pastor.

Talking with a friend

My friend and classmate Carol and I enjoyed talking on the phone. Our phone was on a two-party line and calls were automatically cut off after five minutes. My folks would let us call back only once.

All phones then were still black with a rotary dial and handset attached by a coiled cord: one phone per household. Most of our schoolmates and church people had phone service on a different exchange, which meant an extra charge. We didn't call them unless necessary. My parents made long distance phone calls only when rates were lower in the evenings and on weekends.

Learning to drive

On the gravel roads near our home, Dad tried to teach me to drive. Meeting an oncoming vehicle, I froze and Dad had to relieve me at the steering wheel. Getting the clutch and gas pedals coordinated was daunting, especially starting on an incline. The car we had was a blue Plymouth with a manual three-gear stick shift attached to the side of the steering column. Even though I was already seventeen, I hadn't begged to learn to drive. My folks had to insist. I flunked my first driving test. By the time I was a high school senior, I did have a driver's license. My folks actually let me take their only car and drive to school or youth group events in the evenings or to visit friends.

Youth group meetings

The youth of the church met once a month. The pastor, my dad, was the sponsor. Youth meant ages twelve to thirty! Some of the youth were young married couples with small children.

One memorable youth social was at our house and featured a scavenger hunt. Each carload of youth had a list of items to find in the community, including "something unusual." The most unusual item brought back was a dead skunk. At the end of the evening, my folks talked outside with Janice, a high school student who had brought a new boyfriend to the event. But where was he? They kept talking outside and wondered where he was. We discovered he was locked inside in our bathroom and was banging on the door vainly trying to get help.

Since dancing was off limits, on prom night the churches collaborated to provide an alternative event with a nice banquet for the Christian youth to attend.

Life at home

I continued to be a voracious reader and read most of the books in our small church library, especially the Grace Livingston Hill romance novels. The wholesome dating portrayed by Hill undoubtedly influenced my standards for dating and romance. The Youth for Christ magazine also influenced my understanding of a Christian lifestyle.

My nearsightedness kept getting worse. I had begun wearing glasses at age nine, beginning with bifocals. Ever stronger and thicker lenses were required. There was some talk of getting me contact lenses if I were valedictorian in my class. When I achieved that goal, there was no more talk about contacts, to my disappointment.

By my teenage years, my siblings and I weren't very close, I realized later. David, three years younger than I, was also studious. He was interested in science and made some sort of ham radio from a kit. David and I played some table games together. As brothers do, he teased and pestered me. Once I was so mad at him, I swung my metal lunch box as hard as I could at his head. Fortunately, he ducked!

Twelve years younger than I, little sister LaRita was shy, especially at church. She began first grade when I left home for college, so we don't have many overlapping memories of our childhood years. It was years later before we began to have much in common.

A tall, heavy old piano sat in my bedroom because there wasn't room for it anywhere else in the house. On a typical Sunday afternoon during my high school years, I sat at the piano playing and singing. We had hymnbooks, of course, but even then I didn't find those songs interesting enough musically. My favorites were in the Back to the Bible songbook series with the music from their regular radio programs. Not only did I hone my piano playing ability, but the themes of those songs entered my soul and being. Missionary themes abounded, complete with mournful pleas to "labor unrewarded" where people "die in heathen lands."

Church was a place where youth tested and improved their musical abilities. I began playing piano in church for the evening services on Sundays and Wednesdays. I then figured out how to play the small electronic Hammond organ and eventually played it for the Sunday morning worship services. In our General Conference churches, musical instruments accompanied congregational singing, choirs, and quartets. Most churches had a choir loft to the side or behind the pulpit.

Christmas Eve was my favorite time to play the church organ. The tall Christmas tree with its twinkling lights towered above the organ. I made my own simple arrangements of the traditional Christmas songs for a long prelude. After the program at church, the youth group, in a caravan of several cars, went caroling to church members' homes. We piled out of the warm cars into the sharp cold air and sang two carols plus *We Wish You a Merry Christmas* before loading up again and going to the next place. Houses were far apart and many miles were added to the odometers that night. It was long past midnight before we got home into our own warm beds. That made it a short night before we got up again in the morning to open our gifts and go to church for a Christmas Day service. For special holidays in Montana, someone in the church always invited the pastor's family to join them since we were so far away from any of our own relatives.

Meeting Erwin Rempel

I met the love of my life on Sunday, July 26, 1959. The occasion was the fiftieth wedding anniversary of a couple in our church, Henry and

Lizzie Deckert. The Eitzen family, who lived about a hundred-twenty miles to the northwest, in the Lustre community of Mennonites, had two reasons to attend. First, they knew the Deckert family through family connections. Secondly, Alvin Eitzen needed to talk to my dad about the ordination service for their new pastor, Walter Dirks, at the Bethel Mennonite Church in Lustre. Alvin was one of the church leaders and my dad was one of the pastors in the Northern District conference who worked with pastors' credentials and ordination.

In order to have some quiet time to talk about the ordination service, my folks invited the Eitzen group over to our place after the hubbub of the wedding anniversary at the church. Alvin and Lena had brought along his sister's three orphaned children they had taken into their home: Erwin, Norman, and Barbara. Their adopted son, Howard, and Grandma Baerg were also along. My mom prepared some goodies and sent me out of the kitchen with a pitcher of lemonade to serve. As I approached the handsome Erwin, I was painfully aware of the wart on my right hand. While Erwin admits I didn't make an impression on him then, I knew instinctively that he was the kind of fellow who would be right for me.

Later that fall our family drove up to Lustre for their pastor Dirks' ordination service. It was a rainy day making the unpaved roads dubious. Dad drove furiously on a longer route on paved roads. The last stretch to the church was unpaved and very rough. That jarred loose the car's horn so that it kept on beeping with every bump. It was so embarrassing to drive up to the church a bit late with the horn beeping. Of course, I looked for Erwin. After the service, it was my turn to observe him serving refreshments. I can vaguely recall seeing Erwin one other time when our church youth group went to some event at the Lustre Bible Academy. We were both fifteen. We didn't actually meet and talk with each other until several years later. I'm grateful now that I was never asked out on a date by any of the guys in my high school.

Employment options

Opportunities for teenage girls to earn some money were limited in rural Montana. Sometimes parents with young children asked me to babysit. One woman wanted a bit of help with housework. I don't recall that my parents gave us children any allowances. The main source of income for me was cleaning the church – for twenty dollars a month. There was never any expectation that I would give my few earnings to my parents. My savings account didn't grow very fast.

Teenage boys, including my brother David, found summer work on farms. That led David to declare that he didn't want to spend the rest of his life going in circles – round and round the big fields. My dad continued to do some work outside of pastoring, but not as much as in Missouri. He mainly helped with the harvests. My impression is that he was paid a bit better in Montana.

Finishing high school

During the high school years, I learned several important life skills – typing, communications, music, and driving. I didn't go on the senior class trip because it was costly and didn't fit our lifestyle and values. In 1962, as valedictorian of my class of about twenty-two, I prepared a very short little speech that I read nervously at graduation.

Going to college was not a question of if, only where. Both my parents had gone to college as had most of my cousins and the more studious youth in our community. Only a few of the fellows could take over their family farm and there weren't many other job options in rural Montana. A high percentage of youth left the community for higher education. That barren land launched a number of its youth into leadership roles and occupations, including work with Mennonite institutions and agencies that sent them around the world.

I never considered going to a state university. I so much appreciated the spiritual boost of the week of Bible camp each year that I wanted more. During my senior year of high school, I carefully looked at the colleges advertised in the Christian youth

Angela holds valedictorian trophy, graduating from Richey (Mont.) High School, 1962.

magazine to which I subscribed. I picked out about ten schools and wrote them for information. My list included schools from East Coast to West Coast, from our Mennonite schools to various other Christian schools. As packets came in the mail with catalogs and other information, I carefully listed them all on a chart with different columns of information.

At the time, I didn't realize how important the choice of a college would be in setting the direction for the rest of my life. It is probably just as well that teenagers aren't aware of all the significance of the college choice. Better to simply trust that God is leading.

In the end, the choice came down to which college was the most affordable. Grace Bible Institute in Omaha, Nebraska, cost the least with tuition at only ten dollars per credit hour. Classes were in the mornings so students could work part time. My whole first year there cost about $1,000 in total for tuition, board, and room. My parents committed to paying half of the costs. I needed to pay the other half.

Even though I had not been to the campus, Grace didn't feel like a strange place to go. Others from Montana and some of my cousins had gone there. My uncle Harry Albrecht was in one of the first graduating classes. Mennonites had started Grace as a conservative alternative to the perceived liberal slant of the other Mennonite colleges.

In retrospect, my parents may not have been totally supportive of me going to Grace. "You will probably meet and marry a fellow who will become a preacher who moves every three years," one of my parents said. In contrast, my father's pastorates were each nine to ten years long.

Heading off to college

By August 1962, I had packed my things for college into suitcases and a black trunk. But it wasn't going to be just a straight trip from Montana to Omaha – our whole family drove via Ontario, New York, Connecticut, Pennsylvania and Ohio before reaching Omaha. Not only was it another year for the General Conference triennial conference, but also an assembly of Mennonite World Conference. As before, my parents used such trips to enlarge our acquaintance with the wider world.

This trip, my first foray across the border into another country, started with a stop in Manitoba, Canada, to visit a cousin, Gladys, whose husband was a pastor. From there we drove up around north of Lake Ontario. To save money on the long trip, our family tried camping. Dad and my brother, David, age fifteen, set up a tent while Mom tried to cook supper on a little propane gas camp stove. The most memorable night was along a scenic Canadian lakeshore. About the time Mom had supper ready, heavy rain began pounding through the tall trees. Dad and David tried to dig little trenches to drain water away from the tent where we huddled. By morning, the tent was extra heavy, swollen with water, and difficult to fold again to fit into the car. When we reached our hosts for the Mennonite World Conference in Kitchener, Ontario, they graciously allowed us to set up the tent in their yard to let it dry out.

From Ontario we went east to visit the areas Dad had known during his seminary days in Hartford, Connecticut. We drove to the little village where he had been a student pastor at a stately small white church with a tall steeple. We headed next to the big city of New York. What an adventure that was for us kids from the wide-open spaces and rural farmlands. The city both fascinated and repelled me. We toured the United Nations building, walking through the empty General Assembly hall often seen on TV news. At the docks, we took a tour of an elegant French passenger ship getting ready to leave that evening to cross the Atlantic Ocean. We saw the Statue of Liberty only from a distance. Dad pointed out Times Square where as a seminary student he had gone once on New Year's Eve to watch the ball drop to mark the beginning of the next year. We country folks were obviously from out of town, gawking at the skyscrapers. The New Yorkers' faces appeared cold and sad to me as they scurried along the dirty streets. The women wore lots of makeup and looked harsh. Dad did his best to drive us safely through the crowded streets where taxi drivers behind us began honking even before the lights turned green.

From there we headed to Pennsylvania for the General Conference triennial sessions – my third time to attend with my family. During the conference sessions, our family stayed at Camp Men-O-Lan near Quakertown, about an hour's drive from the meeting place in Bethlehem. Not many years later that campground became a special place in our lives. But for my introduction to the camp, our whole family stayed in one of its simple wood-frame cabins with bunk beds. A big canvas curtain divided it so that two families could stay in the one cabin. The tall trees kept it constantly shaded and I missed the openness and sunshine of the Big Sky Country. Sometimes David and I stayed there during the day while our parents went to the conference meetings. David was bold enough to enjoy the camp's swimming pool. I was too shy to go to the pool and just hung around the shadowed cabin. We probably kept little sister LaRita as well. Organized programs for children and youth had not yet been developed during these big assemblies. After a stop to see Mom's family in Bluffton, Ohio, it was on to my destination in Omaha, Nebraska. It wasn't long until my classes would begin at Grace Bible Institute and I would start a new chapter of life.

"Decade of Destiny" was the theme song for Youth for Christ in 1960 when I was at the halfway point of high school. The '60s did indeed become a decade when I made life-changing decisions. Little did anyone know at the time just how much the decade of the 1960s

Albrecht family at Christmas 1962. Angela, David, father Erwin, LaRita, mother Magdalene.

would change the church, society, politics, and the world. However, most of those dramatic changes swirled around my bubble of Christian and Mennonite sub-culture, barely noticed and having minimal impact on us at the time. That bubble was reinforced at Grace Bible Institute. The school felt securely separate from the bustling city surrounding it. Even so, the four years spent there were life changing for this shy country girl.

Montana visit in 2013

My husband and I visited Montana in 2013, more than fifty years after I left for college. The big sky and brown landscape still were awesome. The farming methods had changed so much that summer-fallow strips weren't needed to control erosion and moisture. Farms were fewer but bigger. Guided by GPS, large farm equipment planted wheat in straight long rows. Even the most careful farmer could never have achieved such straight rows when we lived there. The bleak parsonage of my teen years had new siding and was tucked into a sheltering warm embrace of evergreens.

Bethlehem Mennonite Church parsonage in Montana as it looked in 2013.

There were fewer people, fewer churches, and fewer schools. The landscape looked much the same except for taller trees surrounding the church and home sites. The few hardy people who remained found a bond and belonging in their isolated community. They knew everyone for miles around. With a simple click, they connected with the whole world on the internet, but that only supplemented their need and caring for each other.

Chapter Two
College, Courtship, Wedding, Seminary from 1962 to 1968

I spent several days with my Aunt Luella (Albrecht) and Uncle Frank Fotoplos in Omaha before moving into the dorm in August 1962. Uncle Frank pastored a Baptist church on South Tenth Street only a few blocks from Grace Bible Institute. The incoming students at Grace were listed in a school newsletter that I saw at the Fotoplos' home. I carefully pored over that list of new students. Was there any chance that the handsome fellow from Lustre, Montana, was on the list? And what exactly was his last name – Eitzen or something else? I knew his first name was Erwin, spelled the same as my father's name. There was no Erwin Eitzen listed, so I kept going down the alphabetized list. There was indeed an Erwin Rempel listed from Montana!

Grace Bible Institute[4]
The big old white brick building at 1515 South 10th Street in Omaha was my home for all four years of college. The ground level had administrative offices; the lower level had some classrooms and the dining hall. There were two upper floors of girls' dorm rooms. Male students were not permitted in the girls' dorms except once a year during a couple of hours of open house. "Man on the floor," had to be loudly

---

[4]The name changed to Grace College of the Bible in 1979, and to Grace University in 1995.

announced for the rare times any man was present. The same rules applied to the boys' dorm about the presence of any woman. There were about three hundred students enrolled at Grace.

The rules for conduct and attire were strict. Girls always wore dresses or skirts, which had to be long enough to still touch the floor when we kneeled and leaned backward just a bit. If we had a job doing housework, we had to take our slacks along and change when we got to work so as not to be seen wearing slacks on campus. Makeup, earrings, and sleeveless clothing were prohibited. The guys wore ties and sports coats to classes. Modesty seemed to be the underlying principle for the girls and professional attire for the fellows.

Grace Bible Institute (later Grace University) Omaha, Neb., as it appeared when Angela and Erwin were students from 1962 to 1966.

Movies and dancing ranked right along with smoking and drinking as sinful. For the first nine weeks of school, new students were not allowed to date – not a problem for me. But my first roommate got into trouble at some point during the first semester. One day she and her boyfriend were discovered together in a closed prayer room. Grace rules prohibited unmarried couples being alone. She was put on probation, but he was expelled from school because he was a second-year student and should have known better. She quit after that first semester and they got married a short while later.

Each meal in the dining hall had one menu without choices. Meals in the evening and on Sunday noon were served family style with someone designated as the host at the end of the table to pass the serving dishes correctly. The Sunday noon meal was usually ham and sweet potatoes – neither of which I liked.

Finding my first real job

It was assumed that I would get a job in Omaha to pay my half of college costs. My parents managed to pay the other half. During the few days I stayed at her house before the dorm opened, Aunt Luella encouraged this shy country girl to apply for a job in the big city. She had seen a notice in the newspaper that Mutual of Omaha was hiring part-time workers. She drove me over to the big tall Mutual of Omaha insurance building. I had never applied for a job before. It took all the nerve I could muster to just walk into that imposing place and ask about working there.

On the spot I was hired to work twenty hours a week at the minimum wage of $1.15 an hour. Fifteen other female Grace students also found jobs there. After our morning classes, we ate a hurried lunch and piled into one of three pre-arranged taxis to take us to work. We also returned by taxi. My job was to go through little paper cards on trays in a big file with racks that rotated horizontally. I'm not sure I really knew what I was doing. By the end of that first semester, the task was completed and Grace students were all laid off. The next semester, I did housework in private homes, a common job for the girls at Grace.

To get to my housework job, I learned how to ride city buses, transferring from one bus to another in downtown Omaha. Three days a week I worked for a family where the wife and mother of three school-age children suffered from multiple sclerosis. From her wheelchair, she gave me directions for how she wanted the cleaning and some cooking done. She paid me minimum wage plus bus fare. She referred me to a friend who had seven children and needed help with weekly cleaning.

My sophomore year at Grace, I was glad to be called back to Mutual of Omaha. I worked there the rest of my college years.

With those meager earnings, I paid my half of the college costs. I never borrowed money for college. I wasn't aware of any scholarships or grants to apply for, either.

Looking for Erwin Rempel

Soon after school began in the fall of 1962, I spotted Erwin Rempel among the students. When I joined the Grace band – playing the bass drum – I was pleased to note that Erwin was in the band too. He played trumpet and French horn. That provided a chance for us to greet each other with references to Montana. One time we met each other on the stairway in the music hall and chatted a bit more. He says that is the first time I made an impression on him.

Among the contingent of students from Montana were Erwin's high school classmate Rita Kliewer and her older sister, Jean. At Thanksgiving time, I noticed Erwin and the Kliewer sisters in the dining hall with some visiting friends from their high school in Montana. I was dismayed to see an attractive brunette sitting beside Erwin. I assumed she was his girlfriend and thought that was the end of any chance for me.

Driving home in winter

As Christmas approached that first year in college, I was intrigued by the ornate city decorations, especially in the big downtown Brandeis department store. However, I had also first experienced homesickness and was eager to go home for Christmas. There were enough of us students from my part of Montana to fill a car. After our last class before Christmas, we drove straight through the thousand miles to Montana.

When I was back home, it was with a touch of sadness that I realized the truth of the saying that one can never really go home again. I had changed already. My brother was by then a sophomore in high school and LaRita had started first grade. They too had changed.

Christmas was the only time during the school year that most students at Grace went home. It didn't matter what the weather predictions were along the route to Montana, nor that we would drive through one of the longest nights of the year. Safety belts and airbags hadn't been invented yet then either. We didn't look for a public phone to let our parents know how we were doing along the way. The prevailing philosophy then was "No news is good news."

Construction of the new Interstate highway system was in high gear during those years in the 1960s. We often discovered new sections of the double ribbons stretched over the terrain since our previous trip.

Only the men students had their own cars and they did all the driving on those long trips, as I recall. One year the fellow driving a carload of us girls got so tired that he could hardly stay awake. The North Dakota highway was icy at places. Driving was stressful. He nodded off. Jean Kliewer (Isaac) sitting next to him, grabbed the steering wheel to keep us on the road. It was time to stop! But we had very little money among us to pay for motel rooms. We found a cheap room with two beds. The guy sprawled exhausted on one bed and promptly went to sleep. All of us girls, four or five of us, lay crossways on top of the other bed, fully dressed including our winter coats. We didn't tell anyone back at Grace about the incident.

On another trek home to Montana, after a nighttime stop at a filling station along a two-lane highway, probably on the plains of South Dakota, I noticed that the moon had switched its position in the sky. My sense of direction made me think we might be heading back the direction we had just come from. Sure enough, we soon saw a highway sign indicating we were going south rather than north.

Majoring in Bible and music

Everyone at Grace majored in Bible, and for my secondary major I chose music – until I discovered I didn't have enough talent to major in music. I was quite disappointed that I didn't qualify for the select Grace Chorale. The thought of doing a senior recital was terrifying, especially after attending recitals by the truly good music students.

Music theory and conducting classes were helpful. However, for me to compose some music for an assignment was just an academic exercise of putting together a sequence of chords according to music theory rules. No melodies, let alone harmonies, ever came to my mind. After my second year, Grace introduced a new program that combined music and Christian education. That was the right thing for me. It provided a good basis for the next chapters of my life.

We were taught at Grace that church music needed to be of high quality and appeal only to the heart and mind – not at all to any body part that might be tempted to, heaven forbid, move or sway a bit in time to the music. We considered familiar gospel songs as too simplistic. I continued with voice and piano lessons and took one semester of organ lessons. Playing a full-size electronic organ, using both feet on the bass notes and volume pedals, was a problem for someone as short as I am. In order to reach the pedals, I had to sit so far forward on the organ bench that I could lose my balance. I devised ways to keep from sliding off the bench onto the foot pedals.

Each Christmas the music department presented *The Messiah* by Handel. What a thrill shivered through me as live strains of the introduction poured over the audience, followed by the other familiar pieces. For the finale, the audience rose as one and our hearts sang along with the *Hallelujah Chorus*. Later I sang in an expanded choir for *The Messiah* presentation.

At one evening program in the Grace chapel, just as we were singing *How Great Thou Art*, I noticed a flash of lightening. Sure enough, the thunder came rumbling loudly just as we sang, "I hear the rolling thunder..." God provided the sound effects!

Rooming with a cousin

Loretta Albrecht, my only cousin the same age as I, came to Grace for the second semester of my freshman year. She and I roomed together. She had come to Omaha on a Greyhound bus from her home in Portland, Oregon. On the way, her wallet went missing with all of the money for her school fees. People back in Oregon helped her out financially. Some time later, the bus company found the wallet and returned it to her. All the money was still in it!

With her thick long dark hair piled high on her head and dark sparkling eyes, Loretta caught everyone's attention at Grace. She soon began dating. I was still a shy, mousy gal and wondered if I would ever have a date.

My first date

Late in January 1963, the phone in our dormitory hall rang our room's special ring. Loretta answered and came back to say it was for me – and it was a boy. It was Erwin Rempel! He nervously asked me out on a date. To a Grace basketball game. I could hardly believe my ears. My first ever date! The intervening days I was so nervous.

We doubled on that first date with Erwin's roommate, Martin Fast, who had a car. Erwin had dropped band, but I still played the bass drum for the ball game. Instead of the traditional courtesy of the fellow opening the doors for the girl, I opened the doors while Erwin carried the big drum. After the game, of which I don't recall a thing, we stopped for hamburgers at a drive-in hamburger place. Drive-in food places were common in those days before McDonalds. Servers came to the parked car to get the orders. They brought the food on trays that clipped onto the driver-side window. No touching was expected on early dates. No public hand-holding was allowed within sight of the campus and couples were not to be alone in parked cars.

By the end of our freshman year, we had a total of four dates. By the end of our sophomore year, we had a total of only twenty dates – then I stopped counting.

Erwin Rempel and Angela Albrecht attend Valentine Banquet, 1963.

Growing spiritually at Grace

Was my desire to have spiritual nurture, like at summer Bible camp, fulfilled at Grace? To a large extent, yes. The Bible teaching, theological studies, the chapels, challenges to commitment and spiritual growth, fellowship and prayer time with other students all were positive experiences. While I no longer was at the top of the class in grades, I did reasonably well. Writing a ten-page paper was a challenge. My papers had wide margins and were doubled spaced. My tiny rural high school had not prepared me for library research and analytical thinking.

All students had Christian Service assignments that changed each semester to give us variety and opportunities to test our gifts and interests. The worst assignment for me was going door to door on Sunday afternoons to witness and distribute Christian literature. As we rang the doorbell, I'd pray no one would be home. The weekly programs at nursing homes were terribly depressing. Sad, mostly sleeping or unaware, frail elderly people in wheelchairs were parked around us as we sang, read Scripture, and gave devotional messages in the dimly lit, foul-smelling places that passed for elder care in those days. Helping with a children's program at a church was a much better assignment and fit better with the Christian education classes I took.

Testing God's will

"Is God calling me to be a nurse?" The question haunted me. I didn't want to be a nurse. I'm too squeamish to be a nurse. A number of my classmates were in the pre-nursing program and moving on to nurses' training at a nearby hospital. A number of my Bixel cousins were nurses. Was that what I was to do as well? After one special spiritual life service, I went to my room alone and tearfully surrendered to God. Whatever He wanted, I would do, even being a nurse. And never again after that did I ever have the impression that perhaps I should be a nurse. It was a lesson in being willing to do whatever God wanted.

College roommates

The second year, my roommate situation didn't turn out as expected either. My cousin Loretta and I had planned to room together again. Just before school began, she wrote me saying she had met someone special, was getting married, and not returning to Grace. It was awkward that first day back at school when the fellow she had dated earlier came to me and asked when she was coming.

I began my second year with a roommate even shorter than I am. She was or soon got engaged and quit after the first semester. Then came Janet whose back was always out of joint. She taught me how to readjust her spinal column while she lay on her side.

By the end of my second year, I'd had four different roommates. For my third year I chose a close friend, Viola Voth, who married Delbert Regier at the end of the year. Vi was from a Mennonite Brethren church in British Columbia, Canada. She had the unusual situation, for that time, of having a sister who bore a child out of wedlock and raised it as a single mother. The fourth year my roommate was JoAnn Dahlenberg (Loewen) whose father was also a pastor in the General Conference at that time.

The year of our troubles, 1964

My Dad called 1964 "The year of our troubles." That year I turned twenty, my brother David was seventeen, and LaRita was eight years old.

Albrecht family, late summer 1964 in Montana.

In May, my Mom underwent a major mastectomy after discovering a lump in her breast, which was malignant. My parents needed me at home that summer after my second year at Grace to help with the housework during her recovery. The original plan had been that I would help at home anyway that summer. Mom had planned to go back to college and complete the final semester she lacked for a teaching degree. With the prospect of having both David and me in college at the same time, she wanted to have a teaching job to help pay our college bills. If stress contributes to cancer, she was probably feeling quite stressed about the prospect of leaving her Montana home and family for the summer and going back to college in Ohio at Bowling Green State University. Her surgery canceled that plan.

I had committed to doing two weeks of voluntary service teaching Vacation Bible School at Lame Deer, Montana, on the Indian reservation that summer. Even though my help was needed at home, my parents didn't want me to give up doing that. I took a Greyhound bus, by myself, and went to serve in the same area our youth group had visited several years earlier. There was a lot to learn – one thing was that I genuinely loved the little Native American children.

Mom had no follow-up radiation or chemo after her surgery. That may have been because they felt they had gotten all the cancer – she was scraped to the ribcage and looked awful – or because such treatment wasn't really available. She did exercises to regain the use of her arm.

During that summer, Erwin and I saw each other when the touring quartet he sang with came to our Eastern Montana Bible Camp. At the camp, the quartet fellows and the professor who traveled with them helped with music, Bible teaching, preaching, and as counselors for the boys. I was also a counselor that week in a cabin full of girls. Erwin's folks, the Eitzens, drove more than a hundred miles from their home to visit us at the camp. As I got better acquainted with the Eitzens, I especially enjoyed his mom's humor.

At some point, perhaps that summer, my mom made a comment wondering if I was good enough for Erwin. Perhaps the reason I didn't react much to her comment at the time was because I may have felt the same thing.

Second trouble of 1964

My brother David worked that summer for farmer Myron Schultz from our church. David lived with Schultzes during the week, only spending part of the weekends at home. By the end of summer, he had earned enough money to buy himself a motorcycle, a big Harley-Davidson. That would help with the transportation issues when he practiced and played football that fall as a senior at Richey High School, fourteen miles away. Mom wasn't at ease about the motorcycle, but the salesman tried to reassure her saying that when a cycle hits something, the rider is thrown free. Before I left for college, David gave me one short ride on it.

My new school year as a junior at Grace Bible Institute in Omaha was getting underway when early on a Saturday morning, September 19, 1964, I was called from my dorm room to go down to the lounge because my Uncle Frank and Aunt Luella were there. It was unusual for them to visit me at the school and especially at that hour. They told me the sad news that the previous night my brother David had died in an accident with his new motorcycle. What a shock! Plans were quickly made for two of my dad's brothers in Kansas, Lelo and Elmer,

Erwin Albrecht helps his son, David, work on motorcycle, August 1964.

to drive to Omaha and pick up Aunt Luella and me, and drive to Montana for the funeral.

Apparently David had gone off for a ride by himself after supper. A passing motorist came upon the accident scene only about a mile east of my folks' house. The heavy cycle was on top of him. Not knowing who it was, the motorist stopped at the closest house, my parents' home, and told them. They immediately drove their car to the spot. LaRita and I have different memories of what occurred. She was only eight and a half and I hadn't been there. She thought an ambulance was called. I thought my parents said they had gotten him into their car and rushed to the hospital in Glendive, forty miles away, hoping and praying he could be saved. He had a severe head wound – no helmets were required then. The newspaper report from the police indicates that a ridge of gravel on the road caused loss of control, he was thrown off, and the cycle landed on top of him.

The church overflowed for David's funeral. Many of his high school classmates came, weeping at the sight of the open coffin in the church foyer. He had been co-captain of the little football team, and student council president. Even years later, the high school had a display window with his uniform. We prayed that his life and the words spoken at the funeral made some impact on his schoolmates. Aunt Luella sang *Holy, Holy, is what the angels sang* in her full vibrato voice. At the cemetery gravesite, I clutched my Bible as people passed by to greet and sympathize. I felt as though I were the one needing to comfort them. I clung to the words from the Psalms about God being our rock. It meant a lot to me that the Eitzens came for the funeral. By the end of the week, my relatives and I headed back to Nebraska and Kansas – back to my college life and deepening relationship with Erwin.

At the time of his accident, David was like a stranger to me and his death didn't impact me deeply. However, I'm easily touched by incidents of others losing a child. Many years later, in 2013, we visited in Montana after not being there for perhaps thirty-some years. I was caught by surprise when I entered the church and the first memory that flashed through my mind was a vision of David's open casket in the small foyer.

My parents grieved deeply the loss of their only son. His death, however, meant Mom no longer would have two children in college at once, and, therefore, no need to finish her college degree.

Years later, after taking photos of the two items I had that were from David, I sadly discarded the items, pondering on the meaning of a life so brief, without any trace other than fading family photos and a tombstone in the cemetery. I've often wondered what it would have been like had he lived, married, and had children. I was so glad that my parents had a third child, or I would have been left an only child.

Third trouble of 1964

The third "trouble" of 1964 came in December when Mom needed a second mastectomy. She spent Christmas in the hospital in the town of Sydney. It was an unusually snowy year and the snow-covered fields glistened brightly in the sunlight as we drove to visit her in the hospital. The church people treated our family as they did a missionary family each year, preparing thoughtful gifts for each of us.

Dad was coming to the end of nine years as pastor in Montana by then. Perhaps all the troubles were a factor in the decision to move on. Dad accepted a pastorate at Eden Mennonite Church of rural Inola, Oklahoma, in the summer of 1965. It was time for a fresh start in a warmer climate. That Oklahoma congregation also had experienced hostility because of their objection to participation in World War I. Their meeting place had been set on fire twice.[5]

Getting to know Erwin Rempel

During our third year at Grace, Erwin and I saw each other regularly. I was amazed that he was interested in me. He was a student leader in numerous ways, including president of the Student Body Association our junior year, then president of the student missionary association our senior year. Our relationship greatly helped my self-confidence, and I gradually learned to be more outgoing.

---

[5]Gerlof D. Homan, *American Mennonites and the Great War 1914-1918* (Scottdale, Pa. 1994)

We talked about our sense of call to international mission. Our circle of friends included others interested in mission and ministry.

We adhered to the high standards expected at Grace for dating couples. We finally held hands for the first time nearly two years after our first date. Without speaking about it, we knew kissing was reserved for engagement and virginity maintained until the wedding night.

Attending daily chapel

Students were required to attend daily chapel. Seating was assigned – the females on one side and the fellows on the other side of the center aisle. Missionaries frequently spoke in chapel. Many of them were alumni of Grace who had gone to locations around the world. They usually showed slides to illustrate their message, in the same way I'd seen missionary slides since my childhood. While showing a picture of exotically dressed people, lined up in a group, the missionary often told a lengthy conversion story about one or more of the people staring unblinking from the big screen. Without a written script, the missionaries tended to ramble. They inevitably ended with a colorful sunset picture illustrating that time was ending to take the Gospel to the ends of the earth.

My sense of call to mission deepened. Erwin wanted to go to seminary to prepare for teaching in a Bible training program or seminary overseas.

A common theme at Grace was the second coming of Christ. We surely hoped Christ's return wouldn't happen before we were married.

Mennonites at Grace Bible Institute

Grace felt like a Mennonite school to us. More than half the students and faculty were Mennonites. Several of my relatives had attended there. The president, Waldo Harder, had been a General Conference missionary at a Bible school in the Congo until the turmoil of independence there drove out most mission workers.

Grace was started because its founders felt that the General Conference colleges, Bethel in North Newton, Kansas, and Bluffton in Ohio, were too liberal. (My father had graduated from Bethel and my brother, David, had leaned in that direction as well.) Many students came to Grace from the more conservative churches of the General Conference. Of our Mennonite classmates and friends at Grace, the majority eventually left the Mennonite churches. Some Grace graduates who did pastor in General Conference Mennonite churches tended to convince those churches to leave "the Conference." Only a few of our schoolmates continued to serve in the General Conference. Erwin's brother, Norman, followed us at Grace by a year. He eventually went back to Grace to teach psychology. Norm pushed the boundaries. He wanted to make students think.

We were taught to adhere to Grace's conservative theology, based on Scriptural inerrancy. Keeping the strict rules was never interpreted as a means of gaining salvation. Salvation was clearly taught as a gift of God through grace. But anyone truly born again would believe and live like we did. Any others claiming to be Christians who didn't hold to the same views, including details of dispensationalism, were suspect and perhaps not genuinely saved in the first place. Once saved, always saved – eternal security – was taught, although that wasn't part of general Mennonite understandings. Our professors said that Jesus' teachings in the Sermon on the Mount were largely intended for a future millennium kingdom, not for our time. That was a dispensational pre-millennial understanding. Any whiff of the "social gospel" was clearly wrong, for reasons not well understood. While I never understood what neo-orthodoxy was, we were taught to be wary of it.

Grace students considering seminary studies were discouraged from attending Associated Mennonite Biblical Seminary in Elkhart, Indiana, because it was considered liberal. Some of the respected professors at Grace had gone to Dallas Theological Seminary in Texas. That was recommended as a good choice.

Living in a protected bubble

In our bubble of life at Grace, we were only vaguely aware of the turmoil of the 1960s. What we did know about, we viewed negatively. We were holding to patriarchal views as feminism emerged. Those long-haired singers from England, the Beatles, and Elvis Presley were introducing sinful music styles. Rock and roll came right from the demonic rhythms of the African heathen. Hippies and the sexual revolution demonstrated the depravity of the human condition. The Civil Rights movement and Martin Luther King, Jr. were suspected of linkages to communism. As Mennonites, we believed it wasn't right to participate in war; however, we looked askance at people who publicly protested the Vietnam war. Mennonites who wrote articles against the war were considered quite liberal, along with the denominational magazine, *The Mennonite*, which published such articles.

That bubble at Grace was essentially an extension of how we had grown up. I didn't really know anyone personally who struggled with the draft or served in the war. Mennonite young men usually registered as conscientious objectors and, if drafted, did alternative 1-W service in the U.S. or PAX service abroad. Students, such as Erwin, obtained student deferments. Among my relatives, I'm not aware of uncles who served in the military. We don't have family stories of uncles participating in Civilian Public Service or other forms of alternative service during World War II. One of my cousins went to Congo with MCC, which may have been an alternative to military service.

For a couple of brief moments, world events punctured the isolation of those years. During my first semester at Grace in October 1962, we heard about the Cuban missile crisis. Was the world going to be engulfed in a nuclear war? Would that be the end of the world? That crisis passed and we felt secure, becoming oblivious again.

On Nov. 22, 1963, during my second year at Grace, shortly after I arrived for my afternoon of work at Mutual of Omaha, there was an announcement on the office public address system. We heard that President John F. Kennedy had been shot. No further details were given at that time about the seriousness of his injury. About a half hour later, another announcement informed us that he had died. It was one of those stunning national moments when everyone recalls where and how he or she heard the news. I was standing beside a balky folding machine on the second floor of Mutual of Omaha.

For several days at Grace, a TV sat in the main student lounge in the admin building. I was fascinated watching the logistics of live coverage of the events that followed the assassination. How did the TV anchor and technicians juggle reporters in several different locations? There wasn't much emotion or comment about the assassination on the part of the Grace community. After all, we probably hadn't been in favor of a Catholic for president anyway. We hadn't been following the news much during his brief presidency either.

Working during college

Mutual of Omaha provided me with steady work for my last three years at Grace after I was called back early in my sophomore year. I operated a machine that folded insurance policies and stuffed them into envelopes – if it worked right. There were always a few mangled envelopes and policies that the typists needed to redo. The folding machine was noisy, so it was in the same room with rows and rows of clanging keypunch machines. A woman sat at each machine, keying in data that somehow turned into punched holes in stiff cards that made sense when fed into large computers.

Without any financial help from Eitzens or scholarships, Erwin managed to earn enough to pay all his college expenses without borrowing. He had an ideal job for a college student. For three years he worked at a downtown indoor parking lot. He was paid one dollar an hour plus tips for parking and retrieving cars for businessmen and professionals, including lawyers and judges. Because he could study during the slow times in mid-afternoon, he was allowed to work about thirty hours a week rather than the typical twenty-hour limit for a student.

Summer of 1965

The summer between my junior and senior year, I stayed in Omaha with my uncle Frank Fotoplos' family and worked nearly full-time at Mutual of Omaha. Erwin and a couple of other Grace fellows were serving summer pastoral internships in various Mennonite churches of Mountain Lake, Minnesota. Erwin's grandmother and other relatives lived in the area where his mother had grown up.

Erwin and I handwrote letters to each other daily. One day in June as I was walking the few blocks from the bus stop to the Fotoplos' house, I distinctly remember thinking that Erwin might propose marriage. I had peace thinking that I would say yes.

The Fourth of July weekend that summer, several of us girls drove from Omaha to Mountain Lake. One of our classmates, Bernice Pankratz, lived there and hosted us. Erwin showed me the First Mennonite Church where he was serving. Its pastor, Alvin Kleinsasser, was a Grace graduate and had turned to his alma mater to find a summer intern. Erwin introduced me to his grandmother and some other relatives.

Erwin and I drove to a church camp at Lake Shetek, the same place his mother had taken him years earlier. We walked leisurely alongside the lovely lake. In a secluded place as we embraced, I noted how rapidly his heart was beating. Sure enough, he was working up the courage to ask me to marry him. I said "yes!" And we tried our first kiss!

I didn't say a word about it, though, to any of my friends as we drove back to Omaha or to Aunt Luella and Uncle Frank. Later in July, my parents and LaRita came through Omaha as they were moving from Montana to Oklahoma. I joined them and went on to the little town of Chouteau where the church parsonage was. I helped them unpack and settle into a small house with four tiny bedrooms, one that served as Dad's study.

It wasn't until my last day in Oklahoma with my folks that I got up the courage to tell them that Erwin and I were planning to get married

Angela Albrecht stands at edge of Lake Shetek, Minn., just after Erwin Rempel proposed, July 1965.

the next summer. Mom was quite surprised because I hadn't said any-thing earlier. Erwin wrote them an official letter asking for permission to marry me. Of course, they said "Yes!" If Mom still wondered if I was good enough for him, she didn't mention it again.

Announcing our engagement

One Friday evening in September as our senior year began, on a hillside in a park, Erwin slipped an engagement ring on my finger. When I returned to the girls' dorm by check-in time – eleven o'clock on weekends – I asked the leader on our hall to gather the girls in a circle. She lit a candle and passed it around the circle. When the candle came to me, I blew it out indicating our engagement. We were the first couple to become engaged that school year. Several of our friends and classmates also announced engagements that year.

Where and when should we have our wedding? Montana had been home, but my parents lived in Oklahoma by then. How could we arrange a wedding in Montana? Friendly as the folks were at the Eden Mennonite Church in Oklahoma, that wasn't my church. So we settled on getting married in Omaha at the Grace Baptist Church my Uncle Frank pastored. That was the most practical and economical choice. We had attended the church at times and knew some of the people. If we were married the day after graduation, we hoped we could persuade some of our college friends to stay that extra day before they headed home for their own weddings. And our families would only need to make one trip for our graduation and the wedding.

So it was that we set our wedding date for June 4, 1966, the day after our graduation, shortly before we each turned twenty-two. June 4 has other significance: it's the date of Erwin's mother's death in 1957, and the date of my brother David's birth in 1947. I hoped my parents would feel that they were gaining a son again on a June 4.

My practical, frugal side surfaced as I made the wedding plans. Dresses for the two bridesmaids were simple ones they could make for about ten dollars and in a style they could use for other occasions. I found a student who was willing to sew my bridal gown for five dollars. Altogether, with the fabric of satin, organza, and some nice lace, my wedding dress cost about thirty-three dollars. (After I learned to sew,

I was appalled at the poor quality of sewing on my wedding dress.) Mother came to Omaha from Oklahoma during spring break and we arranged for the cake, flowers, and other things.

Unexpected invitation

On warm spring evenings, after supper in the dining hall at Grace, Erwin and I took walks together. We waited to hold hands until we were out of sight of the Grace campus. We were deep in planning for our wedding, for our summer schedule working in Omaha, and for going to seminary. We had decided he would enroll at Dallas Theological Seminary in Texas that fall. We also thought that I would transfer to an accredited college so that I, unlike my mother, could finish what she considered a "real" college degree. It felt more like something to please her than something that I really wanted to do.

One evening as we walked, Erwin had some interesting news for me. A Grace professor, the same Harold Burkholder who had been Erwin's pastor in California and participated in his baptism, had stopped Erwin earlier that day. Dr. Burkholder asked if we would be interested in Erwin doing another summer pastoral internship after we were married. Dr. Burkholder had a request from the Grace Mennonite Church in Lansdale, Pennsylvania.

This unexpected invitation felt like a door God opened for us. We quickly agreed to spend the summer in Pennsylvania. The church there would provide our housing and pay Erwin fifty dollars a week for eleven weeks. With relief, I gave up the idea of further education.

At the time, we didn't realize what a major fork in the road this unexpected opportunity was for us.

Our wedding, June 4, 1966

Graduation came and went in a blur. We were focused on the real event, our wedding the next day! After the wedding rehearsal and a restaurant dinner, Erwin and I, and our college friends, could still sleep in our dorm rooms that final night before the wedding. Saturday, June 4, was warm and muggy. By afternoon, we learned there was a tornado watch for the area. Fortunately, the day remained sunny where we were.

We decorated the ends of the church pews with plastic white doilies folded over plastic flowers! Yes, plastic! Two real bouquets graced the front. Slightly more than one hundred people attended.

A photographer took black and white photos for a total package of fifty dollars. Mom Eitzen took color Polaroid photos that soon faded. More than forty-five years later, I discovered my dad had taken color slides that still showed the bright green of my attendants' dresses. LaRita and my cousin Kathy Fotoplos, both about nine years old, lit the candles. My roommate, JoAnn Dahlenberg (Loewen), was maid of honor, and Carolyn Harder (Voth) was bridesmaid. Erwin's brother Norm was best man, and former roommate Gary Isaac was grooms-man. Howard Eitzen was one of the ushers. Erwin's sister, Barb, who had been a Grace freshman rooming across the hall from me, attended the guest book. Bernice Pankratz was my personal attendant. My piano and organ teacher, Mr. Wischmeier, played the electric organ. John Voth sang a solo. Erwin and I wrote our own wedding vows, something just coming into vogue at the time. He and I sang a duet, *Together with Jesus*. My father officiated and Uncle Frank gave a meditation that included his trademark humor.

Erwin Rempel and Angela Albrecht wed on June 4, 1966, Omaha, Neb.

As was usual for church weddings at the time in our part of the country, we invited everyone to our reception in the church fellowship hall in the basement. We served simple refreshments of cake, punch, ice cream, and nuts. There was no music and certainly no dancing or alcoholic drinks.

As a side note, within five years of our wedding, two of the young women who helped serve at the reception died because of cancer: my cousin Beulah, and friend Rita Kliewer. Shortly after our wedding, Rita married Gary Isaac. After her death, Gary married Rita's sister, Jean, and their lives intersected ours throughout the years.

Our wedding service was recorded on a reel-to-reel tape recorder: and we have never listened to it. With changes in technology, we soon no longer even had the equipment to play the recording. But the marriage has been sound!

Our classmate Annabelle Unruh helped us quickly open the gifts after the reception. I made some quick decisions about a few basic household items to take to Pennsylvania. My folks packed away the other gifts at the home of Waldo and Abby Harder there in Omaha for the rest of the summer. By late afternoon, Erwin and I drove off to the east in the little blue Volkswagen bug Erwin had bought three years earlier. The car was well-decorated and banging cans created a clatter as we drove away.

We had no debts. We had $100 in cash, which had to last until we got to Pennsylvania the next Saturday. We had no credit card. We were in love and we knew God was in control. That was enough!

Coming out of the artificial setting of a strict college structure, we really didn't know each other all that well. We didn't even know if I could cook – the assumed role of a wife. From one day to the next, we left the cocoon of college dorm life and entered adult life as a married couple. We had no time to experience life as single persons.

Honeymoon road trip

Our first night was in a motel about an hour east of Omaha. I was distraught the next morning when Erwin told me with a straight face that a rat had eaten some of the top of the wedding cake we had brought with us. Well, he turned out to be the rat! There went my plans for keeping the cake top to display at our twenty-fifth anniversary. It was also an introduction to his "seefood" diet and love of teasing.

As we traveled, for our noon meals we made sandwiches and ate along the roadside or in parks, a travel pattern we continued for many years. We spent from six to ten dollars a night on motels. We took in Niagara Falls, as had my parents on their honeymoon. The evening by Niagara Falls we splurged in a restaurant, ordering spaghetti, the cheapest item on the menu, for less than two dollars. We headed on to Pennsylvania wanting to avoid paying tolls on the turnpike. We soon learned why there are toll-roads in the east. The other highways are narrow and winding up and down the hills making for slow travel progress.

We had heard about the Pocono Mountains of Pennsylvania. Looking at the map, we knew we should be in the midst of them, but all we saw were some big tree-covered hills. All my life I've thought real mountains were at least 10,000 feet high, snow covered, and rocky.

We were about to be introduced to the world of Mennonites in the East, a new accent, new ways of living, new foods, and new people who became long-time friends.

Arriving in Lansdale, Pennsylvania

On Saturday, June 11, one week after our wedding, we drove up to the parsonage in Lansdale, Pennsylvania, and were warmly met by tall pastor David Whitermore, his wife, Marion, and their three children. They took us to an older two-story white frame "mission house" where we were to live that summer next to the Grace Mennonite Church. Fully furnished, the house had served mission and church workers over the years. At the time, I thought we would never live in such a nice house again.

The kitchen and refrigerator at the mission house was well stocked for us. For our first dinner, I fried some chicken in a new-fangled Teflon non-stick pan. I assured Erwin that food didn't burn in those kinds of pans. Well, I was wrong! Food may not stick, but the chicken did burn. He delights in the picture he took of me in tears by the burned chicken. He ate it, of course!

It may seem unusual that a church in Pennsylvania, one of the larger churches in the Eastern District of the General Conference, looked

A tearful new bride, Angela sits by burned chicken in Lansdale, Pa., June 1966.

for a summer intern at a Bible institute in Omaha. However, an influential former pastor, D. J. Unruh, had been an interim president of Grace Bible Institute. Some of the people at Grace church supported Bluffton College in Ohio. As had been the case when Erwin served in Mountain Lake the previous summer, some people urged him to go to the Mennonite seminary, AMBS, in Indiana instead of to Dallas Theological Seminary. We didn't consider that option and continued on track to Dallas.

Getting acquainted with church people

Church members expected a pastoral visit in their homes. That task was delegated to us – as if this young newcomer couple could represent their church to them in a pastoral way. Erwin arranged three visits per evening. Our social skills improved. We met some really nice and interesting people that way. It was a good introduction to how people lived and worked in a post-agricultural community. Their hospitality on those hot summer evenings included serving tall glasses of iced tea. How we raced for the one bathroom when we got home.

We visited one family who had a window air conditioner because of air-borne allergies. Air conditioners were still a novelty then. We didn't even have a fan during hot spells that summer.

Car troubles

The Whitermores introduced us to the Jersey Shore and historic spots around Philadelphia. Erwin and I drove down to Washington, D.C., toward the end of summer. On the way back, passing through Baltimore, the VW bug sputtered and we barely made it home. We got it repaired, of course, before we packed up and headed west toward seminary in Texas.

The car acted up again the first day of our trip but we made it to our stop in Bluffton, Ohio, where I introduced Erwin to my mother's family. He was amused by all the short Bixel women. We were grateful that my Bixel relatives contributed for the car repairs we had done there. By then, the Bixels' home church, Ebenezer, was no longer part of the General Conference.

On the next leg of our trip, along Highway 30 below South Bend, Indiana, with a loud and terrible noise the car came to a complete stop! We rode into South Bend in the cab of a tow truck, wondering, *"What now?"* The repair would have been major. We decided to buy a new VW bug sold at a discount because it had been damaged by hail. Erwin

The newly-wed Rempels trade for another VW bug in South Bend, Ind., en route from Pennsylvania to Texas.

phoned his dad in Montana. It was wheat harvest, but Alvin Eitzen went to town and arranged a loan at his bank. He wired the money to the car dealer in South Bend. We transferred our possessions to the new car, a lighter shade of blue than the old one, and continued on our way yet the same day.

Going to Dallas, Texas

The small U-Haul trailer we rented in Omaha was about as big as our VW bug. We loaded the trailer with our wedding gifts that had been stored with Omaha friends. After a stop at my parents' home in Oklahoma, it was on to Texas. Erwin enrolled in a four-year program leading to a masters of theology, Th.M.

Dallas was another new world for us: a new culture, a new accent, and a big city for us to navigate. The seminary was interdenominational, strong on the inerrancy of Scripture and dispensational understandings. They accepted only male students. We wives joked that we were working on our Ph.T degree – putting hubby through.

The furnished one-bedroom, second-floor apartment we rented was in an old building beside the library; Campus Apartments, it was called. The floors sagged. The kitchen was so small that the refrigerator sat outside in the entryway. A drop-leaf table partially blocked two doorways. We were so naïve we didn't even realize that our bed didn't actually have a mattress – just a box spring. In the hot Texas weather, our window air conditioner unit ran continuously from about April through October. But, we were paying only thirty-three dollars a month for rent.

Several Mennonite couples we knew from our time at Grace Bible Institute were also in Dallas at the seminary. My former college roommate, Viola Voth, had married Delbert Regier, and they lived in the apartment across the entryway from our apartment. She and I gaily chattered from our open kitchen doors while our poor husbands used earplugs so they could study. With the Regiers, we bought a used automatic washing machine, but no clothes dryer. Erwin and Delbert installed the washing machine on a landing behind the wall to our bathrooms, with hoses running through the wall to connect to the Regiers' bath tub. Until then, I had used mostly wringer-style washing machines.

Finding work in Dallas

Erwin and I needed jobs and never doubted that we would find work. Erwin got part-time work at a small wholesale hosier business run by a Christian family. There Erwin was introduced to Gold Toe socks, the only kind he has worn since then because the seams at the toes don't bother his feet. He cleaned there after classes. During the summer, Erwin worked more hours and restocked shelves in addition to the cleaning. He found restocking shelves terribly repetitive and dull. He knew he could never spend a lifetime doing that kind of job. On his way to work, Erwin drove the same route through downtown Dallas that President Kennedy had taken when he was shot and killed only a few years earlier.

Having worked at an insurance company for most of my college years, the insurance companies in Dallas appealed to me. I bravely went inquiring about a job, hoping I would understand people's strong southern accent. Eventually, I was hired at the same insurance company where Vi Regier worked. It was easy to ride a city bus to its downtown location. Listening to a Dictaphone, controlling the advance with a foot pedal, I typed letters dictated to policyholders. I learned enough from the content of the dictation to move up to a position to do the dictating myself. Finally, my typing and communication skills were useful.

That workplace was an opportunity to learn to know people beyond the Christian bubble in which we spent most of our time. At work we accepted the fact that some people smoked around our table at break time. Only one Hispanic woman was among the all-white staff.

I enjoyed working in downtown Dallas among the tall buildings. Sometimes during lunch break, I took the elevator down from our seventeenth-floor office and browsed in nearby nice large department stores. If I was dressed in my best, I got up the courage to go into Neiman-Marcus, the luxury department store.

Learning to sew

Prior to getting married, when I surveyed my shabby college wardrobe, my then-roommate, JoAnn, told me that if I sewed things myself, I could save half the cost of ready-made clothes. My folks gave us a sewing machine for our wedding gift and I put it to good use. The new double-knit polyester fabric was in vogue and quite easy to sew with. I had learned more than I realized from my mother about sewing.

My full-time job didn't leave me much time for sewing during the week. One Sunday afternoon while I was sewing, Erwin hit his foot on the sewing machine cover that I had set on the floor. We think he fractured his foot. I was chagrined for not having kept Sunday as a day of rest.

Beyond Mennonite Christians

After our strict dress codes and simple Mennonite living, I was in culture shock when I saw how other seminary wives and Christian women dressed – lots of makeup, earrings, and sleeveless dresses. I soon realized that they also had a deep commitment to Christ.

At that time, there weren't any Mennonite churches in Dallas. We attended one of several independent Bible churches. As had been true previously, nearly everyone we encountered was white. We still lived outside of the turbulence of the 1960s to a large degree. However, even in our conservative school settings the use of the new birth control pills was accepted without question.

Changing lifestyles

During our first year of marriage, I got contact lenses, borrowing money from my parents. Influenced by the new freedom of women's styles and makeup, I was eager to use eye makeup. When I tried some mascara, Erwin took one look and wondered what that "gunk" was on my eyelids. So much for using eye makeup. Wearing contacts went well for me. I enjoyed many years of freedom from glasses that steam up in heat or cold, slide down my sweaty nose, and get spotted with rain. It was nice not to be concerned about changing fashions in frames, nor use awkward clip-on sunglasses. I continued to wear contact lenses in many places and activities around the world, much of the time without backup lenses or glasses. I reached my goal of not giving up contacts until age seventy.

With both curiosity and trepidation, Erwin and I first entered a movie theater in Dallas to see a movie produced by the Billy Graham Association. Each showing ended with a local pastor giving the audience an invitation to come forward and talk with someone about accepting Christ. Erwin and I had taken training to be counselors for anyone who might respond. As students back in Omaha, we had attended a Billy Graham crusade and witnessed the astounding response there as people streamed forward while *Just as I Am* was sung. On a smaller scale, people responded to the movie in Dallas. For a time, Erwin and I met regularly with a young couple who came to Christ because of the movie. Erwin and I had so little in common with them, however, that our relationship didn't last long.

Briefly visiting Mexico

The summer after our first seminary year, we drove to the far southern point of Texas to visit our friends, Vi and Delbert Regier, where they were doing a summer project. From there, it was only a short distance to the Mexican border. Erwin and I drove down and crossed the border at Reynosa, our first exposure to what was then considered a third-world country. There was a very distinct difference from one side of the border to the other. The Mexican side was dusty and dilapidated. The dirt streets had big potholes. We felt very uncomfortable there amidst Spanish signs and conversations. We soon headed back to the familiarity of the U.S. That wasn't a very auspicious start for someone called to international mission work.

While we lived in Dallas, it was a convenient distance to visit my family in Oklahoma. Dad continued pastoral work while LaRita completed her grade school and high school there. As before, Mom found fulfillment in her role as an unpaid co-worker with Dad.

Unexpected invitation

During our second year in Dallas, we had another unexpected invitation. Pastor Whitermore in Lansdale, Pennsylvania, surprised us with a phone call about Thanksgiving time. He asked us to move to Pennsylvania to take up pastoring a new congregation that Grace Mennonite Church was starting in the nearby small town of Harleysville. Erwin was halfway through a four-year program at Dallas Seminary after which we had anticipated heading overseas. Should we turn down the invitation? Could this be a delay, a detour, or a change in direction?

Erwin sought counsel from a seminary professor, George W. Peters, from the Mennonite Brethren Church. After Erwin explained the dilemma, Dr. Peters insightfully asked Erwin, "Are you planning on serving with the General Conference?" Erwin told him that we were. "Then I would advise you to *not* graduate from Dallas Seminary."

Although his question and advice surprised us, we've realized that Dr. Peters understood the Mennonite world better than we did at the time. We accepted the invitation to Pennsylvania, trusting that God was directing our path.

At the end of the school year, we packed our VW and headed back east. Erwin shipped his small but growing collection of books to Pennsylvania. Friends took some of our things in their car when they made a trip east a bit later. We avoided using a U-Haul, which in hindsight is a bit amazing.

By June 1, 1968, we arrived in Pennsylvania again to begin a new chapter of our lives.

Chapter Three
Pennsylvania Pastorate from 1968 to 1975

When Erwin and I returned to Pennsylvania on June 1, 1968, Pastor Whitermore and his family greeted us again. They introduced Erwin and me to the recently formed congregation of Indian Valley Mennonite Church in Harleysville. It was a small town about eight miles from the "mother church," Grace Mennonite in Lansdale, where Whitermore was pastor. The vision for a church in Harleysville had begun a few years earlier when Howard J. Habegger was pastor at the Grace church before he and his family went to Colombia as missionaries. Howard had even left a small monetary "deposit" for the birthing of a new congregation. Thus our journey first connected with Howard Habegger.

An unfurnished two-bedroom apartment awaited us in the Mark Twain Apartments, set back off Main Street in Harleysville. In addition to paying Erwin an annual salary of $4,800, the church paid our rent of $135 a month, and utilities. It seemed strange that such a young first-time pastor was paid significantly more than my father who had about thirty-five year's pastoral experience.

The kitchen electric stove and refrigerator were brown, one of the typical earth-toned colors fashionable in the 1960's. There was no dishwasher or microwave. The second bedroom we made into an office. We bought used furniture for most of the apartment. We wanted the living room to look nice for visitors, so we borrowed money to buy new furniture for that room.

Surrounded by charming farm fields, the small village of Harleys-ville straddled the two-lane Sumneytown Pike where it intersected with equally narrow Highway 113. We could buy groceries and some other basic items there, and do our banking. The larger town of Lansdale provided most other necessities. The sprawling Philadelphia metro-politan area thirty-some miles to the south offered an international airport, large hospitals, universities, major league sporting events, and a world-class symphony orchestra.

Indian Valley Mennonite Church

Before our June arrival, the new congregation had begun meeting in January at a township building in a room above the volunteer fire department. Dave Whitermore preached, so the new church started with having worship first so that he could also preach at the Lansdale church. Having the worship service before Sunday school was rather new then.

Because of Erwin's summer internship at the Grace church two years earlier, in 1966, we gladly reconnected with some familiar people and places. The members of Grace Mennonite in Lansdale who lived close to Harleysville made up a significant number of the new congregation, probably about thirty-five of the fifty who attended. Several other fam-ilies from Eden Mennonite in Schwenksville rounded out the group.

Grace Mennonite funded the new church, but already by the next January, the congregation was self-supporting. Within a few months of our arrival, the congregation rented a small old church building, known as the Chapel.

Following my mother's example, I plunged into being a pastor's wife. I was a church pianist, taught Sunday school, helped Erwin make the weekly bulletins, hosted people, visited in homes, and whatever else was needed.

Erwin and I also worked with youth. One winter we took some youth to Word of Life Snow Camp in upstate New York. That was the only time Erwin and I rode snowmobiles or tried skiing. Some of those same young people continued to meet in our apartment for Bible study into their college-age years.

Soon other people joined our new church, including non-Men-

122

Angela and Erwin Rempel stand in front of old chapel where Indian Valley Mennonite Church was meeting in Harleysville, Pa., after his ordination on July 20, 1969.

nonites and new believers. Some of the women worked outside the home. The middle-class occupations of people in the congregation included factory worker, teacher, realtor, banker, and businessman. We were surprised how few people in the area had completed college or had traveled beyond a couple hundred miles of home, usually to the Pocono Mountains or the Jersey Shore. We were all of white European descent.

Norman and Verna Bergey, already retirement age, took this young couple under their wings. (We were only twenty-three years old upon arrival!) They and the other church folks became the spiritual family Jesus refers to for those of us He calls to live and serve Him at a distance from our biological families. We had a lot of growing up and learning ahead of us.

For a church potluck meal, I prepared a cake – from a box mix. The cake didn't turn out and I quickly made something else. Then I observed that in Pennsylvania Dutch country one makes things from scratch. I was so glad that my box-mix cake had flopped! After that experience, I have almost never used a cake mix other than for angel food cake.

Erwin and I both related part-time to the Grace Mennonite Church in Lansdale, helping with Vacation Bible School in particular. At the beginning, Erwin also served as their director of Christian Education. In hindsight, I was the one who had a Christian Ed minor, yet it didn't seem strange that Erwin was asked for that position rather than me.

Erwin and I decided our new little church needed an organ in addition to the piano it had, and the Spiritual Council agreed. I did a couple

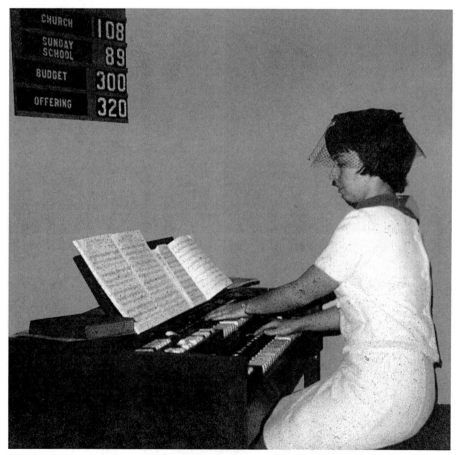

Angela Rempel, organist at Indian Valley Mennonite Church, Harleysville, Pa.

of temporary office jobs until I earned enough money to buy a small electronic organ for about $1,300. We almost always used both the piano and organ to accompany the congregational singing.

At first I was concerned about wearing a hat in church. Some of the church people had recently left the Old Mennonite church where most women still wore head coverings. I was relieved when a woman in our church advised me I didn't need to wear a hat.

First plane trip

It was during our first summer in Pennsylvania, 1968, with shaking knees, fear, and some measure of excitement, that Erwin and I walked down the stairs at the Philadelphia airport to the tarmac. It was our first plane trip. His folks, the Eitzens, were celebrating their twenty-fifth wedding anniversary with a special program and reception at their church in rural Montana – and the whole family was expected to attend. From Pennsylvania, the only way to get there and back in a timely way was to fly. We borrowed about $350 from the bank for our tickets. The first segment of our flight was on a large-size plane to Detroit. There we took a bit smaller plane to the next stop in North Dakota. Then it was onto a still smaller plane to our destination in Wolf Point, Montana. By that time, I relaxed enough to enjoy the view of the terrain below.

Eastern Pennsylvania terrain

Our first springtime in Pennsylvania I was astounded as multitudes of bright flowers pushed out from the ground and bloomed on bushes and trees. Vibrant green covered the rolling hills dotted with farms and trees. What a contrast to the arid landscapes of Montana and the drab concrete and buildings of Omaha and Dallas. Green surrounded us much of the year and became a source of refreshing to my inner being.

I nearly gave up using my sense of directions in Pennsylvania. Narrow roads wound up and down around the hills. One main connector road was aptly named Cowpath Road based on its original use. People there measured distance by driving time rather than by miles.

Seminary and ordination for Erwin

Erwin transferred his seminary credits to Westminster Seminary in Philadelphia and continued his studies. After he completed an M.Div. degree there, he went on for a Th.M. at Eastern Baptist Theological Seminary, which was also in the Philadelphia area. He chose Eastern Seminary (now Palmer Theological Seminary) in order to study under the renowned Carl F.S. Henry. Erwin wrote his master's thesis on the subject of universalism, with Dr. Henry as chief mentor. Erwin painstakingly typed up his master's thesis on an electric typewriter – each page had to be perfect without corrections.

Those seminaries offered broader theological perspectives than the dispensationalism of Grace Bible Institute and Dallas Seminary.

Erwin was ordained on July 20, 1969, a few hours before the first moon landing. After the ordination service and reception, we went to the Bergeys' house to watch the moon landing on their color TV in a living room large enough for all of us. Our folks, both the Eitzens and the Albrechts, had driven to Pennsylvania for that event.

Entering the wider world

The national traumas and events occurring in 1968 motivated us to buy our first TV. It was a small black and white set with one attached antennae that received a few Philadelphia TV stations. It was time to become more aware of the wider world and move beyond our sheltered subculture.

We cast our first political votes during those years. We followed the example set by our parents and the strongly Republican area around us. We voted for Richard Nixon, the Republican nominee who won twice. Nixon went on to become the first U.S. president to resign in disgrace. We voted on big mechanical machines with levers to move for each elected position. The action of pulling a cord to open the voting booth curtain also recorded the votes and reset the levers for the next voter. After that, for the next thirty-six years the places where we voted only used paper ballots. We first saw digital voting machines in Kansas in 2008.

Exploring the area

Without children yet, we were flexible and at the last moment could pack a picnic meal and head out to nearby Green Lake. Movies were still considered less than wholesome entertainment, and TV viewing options were very limited. For entertainment, we sometimes went window-shopping at Plymouth Meeting Mall, rarely buying much. As we had been taught, it wasn't our custom to shop or do other kinds of non-church-related work on Sundays. We discovered that Pennsylvania had "blue laws" actually prohibiting some Sunday shopping and sports.

Visits from out-of-state family or friends motivated us to see the nearby historic sites of the Philadelphia area. Verna Bergey introduced me to riding the train into Philly to go to Wanamaker's department store. She had connections and got us up into the chamber to see the large pipe organ above the Wanamaker's court area. One time with Kenneth and Mary Bauman, missionaries to India at the time, we took the train to Philadelphia to hear the Philadelphia Symphony Orchestra.

Gardening was such a part of our background that we took advantage of offers to make our own garden plots at other people's places. Drawing upon my childhood experience, we sometimes froze extra produce. But also because of my childhood experiences, I wasn't at all interested in the messy process of canning. We never invested in canning equipment. I realized our survival didn't depend on producing and preserving produce.

Using the sewing machine my parents had given, I took opportunities to learn more about sewing. Taking care to be sure things didn't look "homemade," I sewed most of my own clothes – even a winter coat with complicated bound buttonholes. The 1970s styles of bold bright colors and new styles influenced my fashion choices, such as the strange combination of skirt and pants in one piece. A Stretch and Sew class introduced me to sewing with single knit fabrics.

Folly of following fashion

One summer day in 1970, when Erwin was out of town for several days attending a meeting, I went to a large mall looking for a wig. Wigs were promoted as a convenient way to deal with a bad hair day. Satisfied with my wig purchase, I headed home. Only a few miles from our apartment, I noticed the car ahead of me had stopped and was blinking to turn left. I slowed down. In the rearview mirror I saw that the car behind me was coming too fast. Sure enough, my VW and I ended up in the middle of a sandwich. My car had a seat belt that kept me from hitting the windshield but not from banging my head on the dashboard. A gash on my forehead bled. I got out of the car, but I must have looked more seriously injured than I was. Some passersby hurried me into their car and took me to a doctor's office in Harleysville. It took a number of stitches to close the wound.

But then what? I had left the damaged car on the highway and Erwin wasn't around. That is when church family can step in. I contacted Julian and Louise Hagin from church. They took good care of me, and helped with the car and insurance. When Erwin came home the next day, he noticed that my VW wasn't parked in its usual spot. How I hated to tell him it had been totaled! With the insurance payment, we bought another car – a Volkswagen bug, of course.

Beginning a child daycare center

We kept busy with church activities, as well as with involvement in Eastern District Conference and Camp Men-O-Lan. In addition, Erwin was a seminary student for several years. But, I found too much time on my hands.

In 1969, Grace Mennonite explored starting a daycare center in their church facility. More mothers were beginning to work outside the home. There was a growing need for quality childcare in the community. Erwin was on the daycare planning committee.

So who was tapped to be the first director of the daycare center but this under-utilized young pastor's wife. This was certainly an invitation I hadn't expected. With Erwin's strong support, I accepted. I was stretched way beyond my comfort zone, both in preparing for and attempting to carry out that position's duties.

Taking a class at Temple University

My college degree included a Christian Education minor, but I needed additional credits in early childhood education for the new child day care center to be licensed. Without Erwin's encouraging and persistent presence, I would have given up during the complicated process of enrolling in a graduate level summer course at Temple University in Philadelphia. No tests were needed for me to enroll. For several weeks, I rode the commuter train each day into the city and walked several blocks from the train station to the campus. The class was small and all were women of various ethnicities and backgrounds, which opened a new world for me. The class work was easy enough. As a class, we visited various places to observe early childhood education in progress. We needed to find our own way to several such locations in Philly, usually in poor neighborhoods. I nervously walked in run-down parts of the city along sidewalks strewn with trash and feces of unknown origin. I clung to the simple song I had recently been singing with children – *I Will Trust and Not Be Afraid.*

Our class also made trips to Washington D.C., by chartered bus, and by train to New York City to visit what our professor considered quality day care centers. As our class traveled together, I realized that I was seeing my classmates as individuals and not by their ethnicity or skin color.

Beginning a small day care center

With a lot of uncertainty, I helped collect the furniture and equipment to set up a day care center for three to five-year-olds in the basement at Grace Mennonite Church in Lansdale.

We opened in September 1969 with five children and two helpers. The charge was $18 a week per child, which for some poor mothers was too much. Slowly the number of children increased. Each weekend the day care equipment had to be stored away so the space could be used for Sunday school.

An old strict church leader one day came by the daycare center. He caught one little boy running in the church. He tried to spank the child! I boldly spoke up to the old man in defense of the child. Why shouldn't a child run in a church basement day care center? God makes little children to run!

We bought a second VW for me to drive the ten miles to and from the daycare center. That made us a two-bug family for the years I worked at the daycare center.

Much as I tried, I didn't fit that job at the day-care center. My childhood preference for playing with cats rather than dolls and babies could have been a clue. The children's activities bored me. I had some doubts about whether or not I wanted to be a parent, but it was a relief when I became pregnant and could announce that I would resign from the day care center.

The day care center continued to grow after I left. It continues as Rainbow Express. One of the early hopes was that the center would be an outreach for evangelism. Little of that occurred.

In about 2006, I visited Grace Mennonite Church one Sunday. Providentially a young couple joined the church that day, having become Christians because of their child attending the day care center! http://www.rainbowexpress.org/

Increasing our family

When I had my annual physical checkup at age twenty-six, the gynecologist told me I wasn't "an old bag yet," but that it was time for me to have children. I thought perhaps in the next year or two. We had plans to drive across the country the next summer to attend the General Conference triennial sessions in Fresno, California. Our new church would be taken in as a member of the General Conference then.

However, at my next checkup, the doctor discovered I was several months pregnant. Not yet! I wasn't ready for that. The baby was due about the same time as the conference was scheduled in California. I recall being in tears when I told Erwin about the pregnancy. He didn't share my concerns and was delighted.

Erwin and I took Lamaze classes to prepare for a natural childbirth. After years of sedating women for childbirth, the pendulum was swinging back to natural deliveries, and to breastfeeding instead of bottle-feeding.

Labor began close to the due date, but things didn't progress as expected. Dr. McCord talked privately with my husband. Erwin saw the doctor taking measurements on an X-ray. Erwin recalls the doctor's concern as he explained that not only was our baby in a breach position, but my pelvis was too small. I would need to have a C-section, plus my blood type is the rarest, AB negative. Erwin signed the consent forms, and I was wheeled off to the operating room for a C-section delivery.

Just before midnight, little Marcia Angela was born.

Although I spent most of a week in the hospital, nurses got me up as soon as possible. Painful as that was, they knew that was better than staying in bed like my mother had done when I was born.

My mother took her first plane flight, from Oklahoma, to come help with the new baby – their first grandchild. About a week later, my dad and sister, LaRita, drove out to Pennsylvania. My preacher father was there to officiate when we took Marci to church for child dedication.

One day, from her dark eyes that had only a few weeks' experience in looking out at a new world, Marci looked directly into my eyes. I saw another being, a soul, and spirit, holding my gaze, with trust and almost a challenge. In spite of my earlier hesitancy about becoming a parent, it wasn't hard to bond with each of my children.

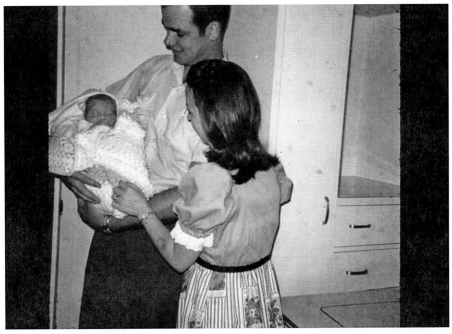

Erwin and Angela Rempel prepare to leave hospital with first child, Marcia, Lansdale, Pa., 1971.

Marci was quite an attraction at our church. She accompanied us to all church events. I don't recall staying home unless she was sick. Her playpen sat in the living room when we hosted the young adult Bible study. Once as a toddler, she put a colander on her head and pushed her way into the home office where Erwin was meeting with the deacons, much to their amusement. She became an out-going friendly little girl, eager to play with other children. It was easy for her to plunge into activities with other children in a church nursery. She amazed her introverted parents.

Life gets messy

My cousin Doris and her husband, Wendell, lived north of us in Allentown, about an hours' drive. He was doing a surgical residency at a hospital there. One early September, Erwin and I went with them to the Jersey Shore taking advantage of the summer-warmed waters and off-season rates. Erwin and Wendell wanted to go deep-sea fishing. As they bought tickets, they were asked if we wanted to go in the pool. We were all so naïve that we thought we needed to take along our swim-suits. When we saw the small boat, we realized there was no swimming pool on that boat. It was a gambling pool to see who got the biggest fish. The little boat steamed out to where we barely saw the shoreline – for the whole day. The gentle waves were enough for Doris and me to be seasick most of the day. The fellows did catch several fish, which Wendell enjoyed frying for our evening meal.

Later after Doris and Wendell had a daughter, we picked up that something strange was going on. We were shocked and dismayed to learn that Wendell was having an affair with a nurse. Doris tried so hard to keep the marriage together, but they divorced – a first in our family. He married the nurse. Eventually, years later Doris also remarried.

Shortly before we left Pennsylvania, Dave and Marion Whiter-mores' marriage also came apart. That was devastating for us. Dave had been an important mentor for Erwin.

We were learning first-hand about some of life's ambiguities and messiness. With the advice of the spiritual council members of our church, Erwin did not perform a marriage ceremony for a couple who wanted to marry again after each had been divorced. Nor did he agree to marry a Christian woman to a professed non-Christian. He found the counseling aspects of pastoral ministry to be quite difficult.

We also learned about mental health issues. Several people we knew in Pennsylvania had "nervous breakdowns" and ongoing struggles. Mennonites had begun a mental health facility nearby. It was one of several initiatives after young Mennonite men did alternative service during World War II in what were sometimes called insane asylums. There was still significant stigma associated with mental health issues, often considered a sinful condition, even demonic.

Among the few non-Mennonite acquaintances we had were Janet and Charles, a young couple who lived in our apartment building. Their daughter was about Marci's age, but Janet was about ten years younger than I. They had some Christian commitment, which apparently was about all that held their fragile, "shotgun" marriage together. Our little girls played together. Charles worked for a telephone company, and Janet didn't have daytime access to a car. I sometimes took her along with me to buy groceries. On hot summer days, her shortest of shorts and skimpy halter tops covered very little of her tall thin stature. What a contrast we made entering the store together. I never said anything to her about her attire.

A number of years later when we visited Harleysville, Janet and Charles came to the church to see us when we spoke there. They had several more children by then and evidenced maturity and Christian commitment.

Traveling in a VW bug

We packed our VW frequently to travel, especially to Oklahoma to see my folks. My sister, LaRita, was a teenager by then. Erwin enjoyed bantering and teasing with her. She called him Meathead, and he called her Dingbat – names which came from the popular TV series *All in the Family*. We didn't realize then how very politically incorrect the show was. It was just a funny show to us.

In summer 1972, we made a big trip to Montana when Marci was just one year old. Her square, folding playpen served as her bed. It traveled in a canvas carrier on top of the VW along with a tent. We learned how much work it is to set up a tent each evening, take it down again in the morning, and stuff everything back into the car to continue the trip.

We had arranged to meet my parents, the Albrechts, and my sister at a campground near the Grand Teton Mountains in Wyoming. By the time Erwin and I arrived at the designated campground, the Albrechts had set up their rented pop-up-tent camper they pulled behind their Ford car. Erwin and I were dismayed that the campground was a parking lot for tents and campers, all lined up side-by-side in rows on a dusty treeless lot. Erwin wasn't about to spend a week "camping" there. We scouted around and found a lovely campground for all of us in a

Erwin and Angela Rempel travel with little Marcia in 1972.

national forest, far from the beaten path. Nestled among trees, close to a small mountain stream, and with views of distant mountains – that was our idea of camping.

Visiting all the states

During the years we lived in Pennsylvania, we made good progress toward eventually traveling in all fifty states. Traveling by plane or train was too expensive, so we took to the highways in our VW bug. We planned family visits and vacation trips to include new states. The car had no air conditioning other than opening the windows. One hot day we bought a block of ice and chipped off pieces to suck on as we rode along. The front seats had seat belts across our laps, which we used, but there were no concerns about how children would be safe in case of an accident. In those days, we held babies on our laps and put children in the back seat without any restraints. We used a simple child seat that loosely hooked over the car's backseat bringing the child high enough to look out. It wouldn't have offered any protection in a collision. We thank God that we had no serious car accidents.

The relatively new Interstate highways were easy to drive; traffic usually wasn't heavy in those days when the population of the U.S. was about 210 million. Food and lodging facilities quickly sprouted at Interstate exits, making travel convenient.

Changing world for women

Being a mother, wife, and volunteer church worker was satisfying and filled my days. The shyness of my younger days receded. Erwin always supported and encouraged me in every endeavor.

The women's liberation movement was spreading throughout society, including the Mennonite churches. Many women reacted negatively to the male gender words in the Bible and in the church. However, I was satisfied with my mother's explanation that those words were gender inclusive. Women of various ages were routinely referred to as "girls." It took me years to become comfortable using the term "woman" rather than "lady."

Some women in the churches felt called to various leadership roles, including pastoring – a role reserved for men at that time. The first woman we met personally who expressed that calling came across to us as being resentful and bitter. Eventually women were ordained and served as pastors.

However, I never felt called to be a pastor. The opportunities I had to serve were well aligned with my interests and abilities. I didn't aspire for more. Over the years there were only a couple of times I noticed restrictions because I was a woman. Once when we spoke at the large Mennonite church in Berne, Indiana, it was made clear that only Erwin could speak from behind the pulpit. One other time, I was quickly informed that I had mistakenly hung up my coat in the men's section of coat racks in a large open foyer of a church in South Dakota.

Changing style of church music

The world of church music also began to change. Ralph Carmichael and Kurt Kaiser, pioneers in contemporary Christian music, introduced new songs with new rhythms. The Jesus Movement of the 1970s inspired more new music. Erwin once heard Carmichael speak and learned of the intense controversy and opposition he faced. Some said the new music was of the devil and came straight from African demon worship. However, I found the new music refreshing and meaningful. Having learned the traditional style of playing piano for four-part hymn singing, I couldn't accurately play the new songs.

The wave of new music enriched our worship. Use of overhead projectors made it easy to project new songs. Unfortunately, that set the stage for what has been called the "worship wars."

Theology and ordinary life

Some of the fine points of theology so important during the years at Grace Bible Institute didn't seem so important when working with real people and their situations. When we graduated from Grace, it felt like we had been taught all the right theology. Sin was carefully defined. It was as if each point fit into its own box on a big spreadsheet, all linked together so that the rows and columns added up. Answers to questions about theology and life were ready to pull out of the right box. It was black and white with few shades of gray. Anyone who arranged the boxes differently was considered already on the "slippery slope to perdition." When Erwin had raised some questions among classmates at Dallas Seminary about eternal security and predestination, they were surprised. Some began praying for him.

Then real life came along. Already at seminary in Dallas we met people who, while making the theological boxes even bolder and larger, arranged the lifestyle boxes differently. In Pennsylvania, fine points of theology didn't relate much to the problems people faced in daily life. Each of the seminaries Erwin attended, while firmly based on the authority of Scripture and the triune God, divided and arranged the boxes differently. We met people in Pennsylvania whose extensive sin list included playing basketball on Sunday afternoons, wearing neckties, and wearing wedding rings. But some of Erwin's professors at Westminster Seminary were smoking pipes and drinking alcoholic beverages.

Erwin soon bumped into another seminary-taught concept that didn't fit well in real life. Erwin recalls:

> I will never forget trying to prepare my first sermon from the Old Testament. I had been trained to use the textual apparatus at the bottom of *Biblia Hebraica* (Old Testament in Hebrew). A seminary rule was to use the original languages to begin the sermon preparation process. I checked out the variant readings and tried my best to be sure I was properly exegeting the biblical text complete with word studies and collateral passages in both the Old and New Testaments. But by Friday, I was drowning in all of the technical stuff of exegesis and I had not yet come up with something to preach. I eventually concluded that the scholarly tasks were best left for the scholars.

Encountering "Old Mennonites"

In Pennsylvania our General Conference churches were known as the "new" Mennonites in contrast to the "old" Mennonites, whose numerous churches surrounded us. I had grown up in communities with Old Mennonite churches, but Erwin hadn't. One young couple coming to our church in Harleysville had been excluded from their Old Mennonite church because they wore wedding rings.

Some younger women in the Old Mennonite churches had cut their hair, and stopped wearing prayer coverings and plain dresses. In pastoral associations, Erwin met most of the pastors of the Franconia Conference, as well as prominent historian John L. Ruth. We participated in tent revival meetings with evangelist George R. Brunk, II. Those experiences helped us to understand and navigate the broader Mennonite world.

Church growth, personal growth

Indian Valley Mennonite Church continued to grow. Erwin used an overhead projector as he preached, turning sermons into teaching sessions. He generally led the whole worship service himself, including the music. That seems to have been typical for pastors at that time, except perhaps for leading singing. Some men in our church who had considerable business administration experience, Norman Bergey, Julian Hagin and Harold Rittenhouse, mentored Erwin's administrative gifts. The growing congregation purchased a plot of four acres on a hill at the edge of town for $19,500 and made plans to build.

Erwin sharpened his administrative abilities in the Eastern District Conference, especially working with Camp Men-O-Lan. We spent much of several summers at the camp. In 1972, little Marci learned to walk there, toddling on the uneven ground.

Continuing the missionary vision

During those years in Pennsylvania, Erwin and I were frequently in touch with the staff of the Commission on Overseas Mission about future international service. We related first to Aron Jantzen, then his brother Lubin, who worked with recruiting overseas workers. Howard Habegger became the executive secretary of COM during those years. Erwin and I flew to Winnipeg, Manitoba, one February to meet with the candidate committee during the annual Council of Commissions meetings. The high snow banks and bitter cold in Winnipeg made quite an impression even on us former Montana residents. As accepted candidates, Erwin and I attended a COM summer missionary seminar in Chicago, and also represented COM at an InterVarsity Urbana conference. Our overseas assignment and beginning of service hadn't yet been determined.

138

Friends from our Bible college days, even classmates who shared our General Conference background, chose to work with interdenominational "faith" mission agencies for overseas service. For Erwin and me, there was never any question but that we would work with COM, the General Conference mission agency.

Angela's parents retire in Newton, Kansas

Dad was about 68 years old when my sister graduated from high school in 1974. By then my folks had completed a positive nine-year pastoral experience at Eden Mennonite Church in Oklahoma and were ready to retire.

The Albrechts moved to Newton, Kansas, where they bought their first house. They had lived in parsonages for more than thirty years. They had saved enough money to pay $20,000 in cash for a two-bedroom house. It had a nice yard, garden, single garage, and a basement with another bedroom, family room, laundry and simple bathroom. They joined First Mennonite Church in Newton. Dad became involved in various kinds of church work, including filling the pulpit in a variety of nearby churches; he thought he was busier than when he was a full-time pastor.

At First Mennonite, Mother coordinated its thirteen women's circles. She found part-time work for a while at a residential facility for troubled youth. But what really helped them most financially was being custodians at the General Conference office headquarters at 722 Main Street. Years later, the staff still would comment on how clean the offices were when my folks worked there. Paid about $8,000 annually as custodians, they earned about double what Dad was ever paid as a pastor. Interest rates were extraordinarily high during those years, and their savings grew. Their first modest splurges were buying a garage door opener and a microwave oven.

Moving to larger house

Our living quarters at Mark Twain Apartments in Pennsylvania were crowded. We began looking at larger living quarters.

In the fall of 1973 we moved a short distance to a double house owned by a young couple in our church, Terry and Wanda (Hagin)

139

Derstine. It had a total of four levels – unfinished basement with the laundry; main floor with kitchen, dining and living room; second floor with two bedrooms and a bathroom, then a semi-finished attic. Once while taking the vacuum cleaner to the basement, I fell down the stairs and cracked some ribs. I've been cautious on stairs ever since.

New church building

When Indian Valley Mennonite's new church building was completed in 1974, we intended to resign and go overseas with COM. However, the church leaders pled with us and COM to delay our leaving. They wanted Erwin to continue pastoral leadership during the first year in the new building.

We did stay for another year and enjoyed the new facility. The new Allen electronic organ with a full foot-pedal board was a challenge for me to play. Erwin had to change his preaching style because the sanctuary didn't accommodate an overhead projector and screen.

Erwin, Marcia and Angela Rempel at the new Indian Valley Mennonite Church building, Harleysville, Pa., 1974.

Erwin finally had an office somewhere other than in one of our bedrooms. He drove to the church office, but didn't change his pattern of rising around four o'clock in the morning and working in the office. One of his first times at the new church office, the local policeman, seeing lights on while it was still dark, came and checked him out.

As soon as the congregation moved into the new building, new families came to church.

Our family grows again

Before we left Pennsylvania, our son, Marcus Erwin, joined the family. Another C-section delivery was scheduled. When Erwin heard that he had a ten-pound son, he was so excited that he hurried to phone the family. I was left to wonder where he was. Again I stayed in the hospital for five to seven days. My mother came from Oklahoma again to help with Marci and the new baby. While Mom was with us, lymphedema flared up in one of her arms because of her radical mastectomies back

Angela Rempel, left, and her mother, Magdalene Albrecht, watch Marcia hold new brother, Marc, Harleysville, Pa., 1975.

in 1964. One night she fainted and was admitted to a hospital. About that same time, I got a breast infection, something that occurred at least once with each child. So for a while, Mom and I were both out of commission.

"I wish Marc would go home," three-and-a half-year-old Marci said about ten days after he was born.

"Where is his home?" I asked her.

"In your tummy!" After that she accepted her little brother.

Preparing for overseas

The spring of 1975 we were leaving Indian Valley church for sure. We had considered opportunities in both Botswana and Brazil. Perhaps in part due to his own missionary experience in South America, the COM executive secretary, Howard Habegger, encouraged us to go to Brazil. He was enthusiastic about the church-planting possibilities along a new trans-Amazon highway planned with new villages and towns at regular intervals. We applied for visas to Brazil and began packing.

We filled eight cardboard-type round barrels to send by airfreight to Brazil, including our small electric appliances and a new 13" black and white TV. Friends from church tucked fabric into the spaces in the barrels so I wouldn't lack for sewing supplies. We had a "garage sale" – a recent invention at the time. Erwin packed his growing book collection into special book bags for the postal service to ship to Brazil.

Sunday, June 1, 1975, seven years after we began the pastorate at Indian Valley Church, we packed two kids into a VW and once again headed west from Pennsylvania. Marc was about three months old and Marci nearly four years old. Saying goodbye to the church people, our friends, was hard for me. I cried much of that afternoon as we drove westward. For months I keenly missed the folks at Indian Valley Church.

Waiting for Brazil visas

The visas for Brazil took much longer to obtain than we expected. We spent most of the next six months living with my folks, who were enjoying an active retirement in Newton, Kansas. Their basement space served our family well, but we ate upstairs with my folks.

During that summer, we spent several weeks in Montana with

Erwin's folks, the Eitzens. Erwin enjoyed helping with the wheat harvest so much that I wondered if we would someday be wheat farmers.

COM arranged speaking engagements for us in a number of churches during the fall. Erwin flew to some more distant places, and we drove as a family to others.

My mom didn't believe in baby proofing the house; just teach the child what not to touch. Sure enough, crawling Marc got into her arrangement of colorful firethorn berries and chewed on some. We called the doctor. He ordered us to give Marc ipecac.

That fall my last grandparent died – Grandma Ida Albrecht. She was ninety-one. She was eager to go on to heaven. Because we were staying with my parents in Kansas at the time, we attended her funeral at the Kingman Mennonite Church. Grandma had prayed regularly for the growing Albrecht family. I felt a sense of loss. Who would pray for the family now?

Some unexpected invitations came for Erwin during that transitional time, perhaps to test our understanding of where God was leading us. One opportunity was to work with church planting in North America. Another was to serve as youth pastor in one of the largest churches. We didn't sense God speaking to us in either of those situations. We kept our eyes on the path leading to Brazil.

Obtaining the Brazil visas

One day we got the awaited news about our visa process, informing us to go to the Brazilian consulate in Los Angeles to get our visas. Los Angeles? We had been dealing with a consulate in New York City. Sometime in October we packed our little car with the two kids and drove west from Kansas to the land of Erwin's birth.

Acquaintances of Erwin's family from long ago provided us a place to stay in Los Angeles. We had time to visit Erwin's uncle and aunt, Dave and Amanda Eitzen, and other relatives. Erwin showed me where he used to live and go to church. We also went to Disneyland, which to me felt so artificial.

When we had arrived at the Brazilian consulate on a Monday morning, they couldn't find anything for us. Told us we should have gone to New York! But with persistence and prayers, eventually they found something and processed us there. We retook medical exams and X-rays. It wasn't until Friday afternoon that we turned in the last of the completed documents. Erwin was scheduled to preach that Sunday at the fall mission festival at the Mennonite church in Pretty Prairie, Kansas. On Saturday Erwin flew from Los Angeles to Wichita. On Monday morning, with trepidation, I packed the VW and kids and drove the big complicated freeways by myself to the airport to meet Erwin's flight from Kansas. When he arrived, I gladly relinquished the driving to him and we all started the long drive back to Kansas.

We managed to include a few of the western states we hadn't seen before such as Nevada and Utah. That completed our being in the forty-eight continental states.

Our visas came through a few weeks later. We scheduled our departure to Brazil for mid-December 1975.

Farewells

We always felt that our parents supported us, indeed, perhaps even considered it an honor to have children serving as missionaries. But what did my folks really think and feel about us taking their only grandchildren so far away?

We flew from Wichita to Allentown, Pennsylvania, to have a farewell and commissioning at Indian Valley Mennonite Church. Indian Valley and Grace Mennonite churches together provided the Commission on Overseas Mission with our financial support. We weren't concerned about the salary and benefits for missionaries. Someone commented that we took a step down by leaving a growing, prosperous church in the U.S. to serve in Brazil. That wasn't an issue for us. We sought to follow where the Lord led.

After the commissioning service, a noisy, small propeller plane carried us out of Allentown into JFK airport in New York City. The children played on the carpeted airport lounge floor while we waited for our overnight flight on TWA[6] to Brazil, departing at 8:30 p.m.

---

[6]Trans World Airlines, bankrupt in 2001 and acquired by American Airlines.

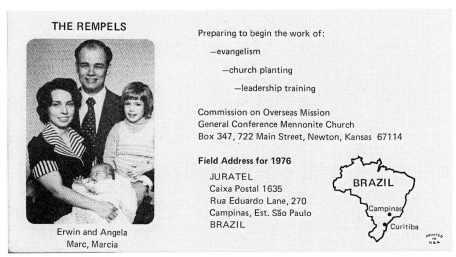

THE REMPELS

Preparing to begin the work of:

—evangelism

—church planting

—leadership training

Commission on Overseas Mission
General Conference Mennonite Church
Box 347, 722 Main Street, Newton, Kansas 67114

Field Address for 1976

JURATEL
Caixa Postal 1635
Rua Eduardo Lane, 270
Campinas, Est. São Paulo
BRAZIL

BRAZIL

Campinas

Curitiba

PRINTED IN USA

Erwin and Angela
Marc, Marcia

Prayercard by the Commission on Overseas Mission sending the Rempel family to Brazil, 1975.

Eleven years after Erwin, as a college student, first wrote to the Commission on Overseas Mission inquiring about overseas mission work, we were finally on our way. At that point, I felt as though I was about to jump off a diving board into the deep end of a swimming pool – and I don't swim!

We couldn't imagine what this next chapter of our lives would be like and how life changing it would become. We looked forward with both some apprehension and much excitement.

Chapter Four
Brazil from 1975 to 1982

Part One
Life and Language School in Campinas

We spent a long night on a four-engine Boeing 707 plane taking us to a new life in Brazil. Ten-month-old Marc slept much better than Erwin and I did as he lay on the floor at our feet. Four-year-old Marci had the seat between us.

This was our introduction to long overnight international flights. We enjoyed the additional amenities for passengers that included blankets, pillows, and small kits with flimsy toothbrushes and minuscule tubes of toothpaste. We chose our dinner items from a colorful menu printed in both English and Portuguese. However, it was very late when our food was served, attractively arranged on trays. Our fitful sleep was interrupted when the cabin lights suddenly blinked on before signs of dawn. The flight attendants handed out warm, moist cloths to freshen ourselves and prepare for breakfast.

Right on schedule, about eight in the morning on Tuesday, December 16, 1975, the big plane came in low over the white sandy beaches of Rio de Janeiro. When the flight crew opened the plane's doors, we got our first sniff of Brazil's warm humid air. This was an abrupt change from winter in the U.S.

The famous city of Rio wasn't our destination, so we stayed on the plane. After a short flight, about 10:30 a.m., we arrived at the Viracopos Airport on the outskirts of the large city of São Paulo. It was near the city of Campinas where we would spend a year learning Portuguese.

147

"Passaporte," a man requested as we waited in line in the airport. Fortunately that word was close enough to English to know that he wanted to see our passports. However, if it hadn't been for the stick figures of men and women on the restroom doors, Marci and I would have gone into the one marked *homens*. To me the word looked similar to our word for women – but it means men. Clearing customs and immigration went smoothly.

Meeting our new "family"

Our new "family" of North American coworkers met us at the airport. Ken and Grace Schwartzentruber, longtime mission workers with Mennonite Board of Missions (MBM), took on a parenting role for us. Gerald and Valetta Kaczor, whom we had known from our days at Grace Bible Institute, also greeted us, along with Carol Fry, the daughter of a pastor we knew in Pennsylvania. She and her Brazilian husband lived in the area. The Schwartzentrubers took us in their well-used VW van, a *combi*, to their home for the noon meal. They enthusiastically introduced us to Brazil.

We were the first missionaries the General Conference Mennonite Church sent to work in Brazil with Portuguese-speaking people. Previous General Conference personnel had related to German-speaking Mennonites, immigrants to Brazil from Russia. However, Mennonite Board of Missions, based in Elkhart, Indiana, had missionaries working in Brazil among Portuguese-speaking people for about twenty years already by the time we arrived. These MBM mission workers didn't fit the stereotypes of the Old Mennonites we'd met before. Most of the missionary women had short hair and didn't wear head coverings. The MBM workers' attire blended with Brazilians' typical Western-style clothes.

The plan from the beginning was that we would work together under the administration of MBM's director for Latin America, Lawrence Greaser. Whether the MBM missionaries in Brazil wondered if this would work or not, they welcomed us warmly and we always felt part of one team. The Associação Evangélica Menonita (AEM) was the organization that included more than twenty Brazilian Mennonite churches, the foreign missionaries, and several bookstores. The Schwartzentrubers' primary ministry was operating a Christian bookstore in Campinas and publishing Anabaptist materials translated into Portuguese.

Within a few weeks of our arrival, we encountered Nelson Litweiler, a retired long-term MBM missionary in Argentina. He and his wife were revisiting South America. After preliminary get-acquainted conversation, he startled Erwin by saying something like, "You will never make it as a missionary here in Brazil." When Nelson had learned that we studied at Grace Bible Institute and Dallas Seminary, he assumed we adhered to the teaching that present-day gifts of the Holy Spirit did not include speaking in tongues. Therefore, he didn't think we could get along with the "charismatic" Mennonite missionaries in Brazil. That was a rather discouraging prediction for us new arrivals! As we became acquainted with our mission colleagues, some indicated they had spoken in tongues during personal devotional time. They didn't insist that others needed to do likewise. We experienced them as warm and genuine Christians.

A modern Brazilian city

Campinas, the city to be our home for a year, was known as one of the nicest cities in Brazil. It was fascinatingly beautiful. Wide sidewalks, laid with small cut stones in various designs, lined the paved streets. Electricity at 110 volts, running water, sewer, and nightly trash pickup all functioned well. Red tile roofs topped off houses built in fascinating designs. Tropical plants with large leaves graced the front yards. Walls enclosed the backyards. Houses were close together, some touching the next house. Decorative metal bars and grates covered windows. Some houses had additional heavy wooden shutters at the windows.

Instead of a central water heater, small electrical heating units that were attached to faucets heated water as it passed through, even in the shower. To avoid getting a shock or worse, a person needed to adjust the heater device before getting wet.

A variety of merchandise filled the shops, both large and small. Large grocery stores looked much as the ones in the U.S. Weekly temporary markets were set up for just one day on specific blocked-off streets where vendors sold colorful fresh produce and equally colorful plastic items. Measurements were in metric units. Having to plunge in and handle things in grams, kilos, liters, and meters is a quick way to learn the metric system. Based only on multiples of ten, it is a simple and sensible system.

New smells soon became familiar – the fragrant frangipani blossoms, coffee beans roasting, bread baking at a corner bakery. Erwin's morning routine included walking to the bakery to buy fresh bread and milk, often with infant Marc jouncing along in a carrier on his back.

During our first weeks in Campinas we stayed in a lovely, upscale, spacious house of an American family, the Junes. Mr. June worked for IBM in Brazil. They worshiped with an international English-speaking congregation. The family had gone to the U.S. for Christmas, so they made their house available to us. Their maid came several times a week to clean. She knew what to do at the house, which was good because she spoke only Portuguese. Mr. June returned in early January. He was a pleasant person, but it did feel a bit strange to be living in his house with him. We were eager to settle into a place of our own.

Learning to live in Brazil

Ken and Grace took us under their wings. They had two daughters away in college and two younger children living with them in Brazil. They taught us a great deal. As I wrote back to friends in the U.S. a few months later:

> It didn't take long to realize how completely dependent we were on the other missionaries. Almost like babies, as they had to help us buy food and to a certain degree show me how to prepare it. They helped us get our proper documents, find our shipment of barrels, and purchase furniture and home furnishings. They helped us find places to live. For five months until we got a car of our own, they took us to church, to shop, to the doctor, and for outings. They are helping us learn how to live in a new culture.

"Drink the water. Eat the lettuce," Grace wisely advised. Our digestive systems went through some unpleasant adapting during the weeks prior to beginning language school. In the end, however, we coped better than some of our language school colleagues who were overly cautious about what they ate and drank. We used basic sensible procedures like filtering our drinking water and washing fresh produce.

Even in the nice house where we first lived, we were introduced to huge flying cockroaches. Various sizes of lizards ran up and down the walls and across the ceiling and floors. Brazilian houses didn't have screened windows. While flies weren't a problem, mosquitoes were. The mosquitoes loved our fresh new blood. Poor little Marc was soon covered in bites. Mosquito netting over his crib helped somewhat. One of Marci's bites became infected. It is good that malaria wasn't a concern in that part of Brazil.

To control mosquitoes at night, we learned how to carefully place a fragile coil of some green smelly mosquito-repelling substance onto a small metal holder. Lit with a match, the coil burned slowly like incense throughout the night.

Christmas arrived within a few days of our arrival in Brazil, so we experienced the first of our eventual ten years' of Christmases in the southern hemisphere. December is summertime there and often very hot. We were amused to see sweating Santas in their bright red heavy suits. Why would their decorations include artificial-looking snow on artificial evergreen trees in a country where few people ever experienced snow?

We learned about Brazilian bureaucracy and paperwork. Ken and Grace steered us through the complicated process of locating and obtaining our eight barrels shipped as unaccompanied airfreight. The barrels ended up in a city about seventy miles away. The list of contents in each barrel had to be translated into Portuguese. However, the customs agent knew English and didn't even use the translated version.

Our home in Campinas

Finding a rental house for the year of language school came down to the last minute. It coincided with the arrival of our barrels, which Ken transported in his faithful old VW *combi*. The house we rented was on the street behind Ken and Grace's house and a few easily walked blocks from language school. God provided in time, but we had spent some anxious moments over it all.

During language school in Campinas, Brazil, 1976, the Rempels lived in the house in the center.

We made our house as homey as we could for the year of language study. The modest three-bedroom house was tightly tucked into a long narrow lot between two other houses. We appreciated the privacy of a high wall around the backyard. Clotheslines took up most of the space in the narrow backyard. A small one-bedroom building at the back of the yard was designed as maid's quarters. It had a tiny bathroom plus hookup for a washing machine. We never hired a live-in maid.

We bought an automatic washing machine, an electric refrigerator, and a gas stove. Most Brazilian kitchen appliances were colored either sky blue or bright red, so I was happy to find white ones. The stove was a typical narrow Brazilian propane gas stove with four burners. It had no pilot light so we used a match to start each burner each time. To control the heat in the small oven, I turned a knob around an unnumbered dial from low to high. The oven thermometer we brought along was essential to determine the approximate temperatures. We purchased replacement bottled-gas containers from trucks that noisily rattled through the streets.

We couldn't simply plug in the electrical items we had brought from the U.S. even though the voltage was 110. Brazilian outlets were made for plugs with three round prongs instead of the two flat ones our electrical things had. Adapters were easily obtained. We were warned that voltage often fluctuated and sensitive electrical items should be plugged into what they called a regulator. Refrigerators had regulators built in that kept them from turning on unless the voltage was adequate. Before the store delivered our new refrigerator, they kept it plugged in for twenty-four hours to be sure it worked. Customers tested each light bulb in sockets at the stores before buying them.

Our house had typical Brazilian floors of either ceramic tile or wooden parquet blocks. Shiny, waxed floors were very important to Brazilian housekeepers. They cleaned the ceramic floors in the bathroom and kitchen with copious amounts of water. That necessitated placing small pedestals under the kitchen appliances to prevent rust. They used a long-handled squeegee (*rodo*) to scrape the water out the door. Then with a dry cloth over the *rodo*, they dried the floor before applying fresh wax. Starting with wax remover, the next week they repeated the process.

Having a maid

We needed someone to help clean the house and take care of the children while Erwin and I studied language. Lacking experience with maids, we were happy to have Grace help us locate someone suitable and orient both her and us. Our first two maids were so young – about thirteen perhaps. Louisa experimented with smoking – just outside our window as we ate lunch. We noticed that powdered milk disappeared faster than we used it, as did other items in the pantry such as raisins and sweets. We figured out that Louisa was taking the powdered milk home for her sister's baby.

The chicken's feet and head always were included when whole chickens were sold. We put those items out for the cat, but were astounded when the maid quickly retrieved them to take home. After that we just sent the chicken head and feet home with her. She also took home a piece of beef fat – after the cat had gnawed on it.

Encountering poverty

Soon after arriving in Brazil, we encountered the troubling issue of poverty. We saw people begging – along the streets, in bus stations, or coming to our front gate.

"Don't give money to beggars," our expatriate mission co-workers and Brazilian teachers at language school told us. Dealing with poverty is a complex issue that we struggled unsuccessfully to resolve for ourselves.

We learned that there are professional beggars who earned more by begging than working a minimum-salary job. A common plea was some variation on the story of needing money to travel to a funeral some distance away. Another frequent plea was to "borrow" money to buy prescription medicine. The person asking waved the supposed prescription paper too rapidly to verify.

About four months after our arrival in Brazil, I wrote:

> At this point, the biggest 'culture shock' is the inner struggle about the extreme poverty that we see. How does one respond? How does one live? About a week ago, I experienced my first real longing for the States. In trying to analyze my feelings a bit, I found that I wanted to live the way we were used to without feeling we were living too well.

Brazil was high on the list of countries with the most disparity between the rich and the poor. While the majority of Brazilians were poor, there was a growing middle class, which included some of the families in Mennonite churches. Among the people we learned to know, poor health and lack of education kept some in desperate circumstances. Personal choices contributed to the poverty of others. Better lifestyle choices, especially by the committed Christians, helped them manage over the years to better their economic situation.

Hurrying to the emergency room

One April afternoon when I returned from language school about five o'clock, the maid gave me a quickly written note from Erwin. It said that he and Grace had taken Marc to the hospital. A curious toddler, Marc had drunk some wax remover the maid left in his reach near the edge of the table. Erwin was home studying and heard Marc coughing. Discovering what happened, Erwin sent the maid to run over to Schwartzentrubers' house on the next street to get Grace. Meanwhile Erwin gave Ipecac to Marc to induce vomiting. Upon hearing the news, Grace phoned a doctor who said to take Marc right to the hospital to have his stomach pumped. She drove over to pick up Marc and Erwin. Marc was getting drowsy and his eyes were rolling. As they reached the hospital, Marc did throw up several times. Just to be sure, they pumped his stomach as well. (Later we learned that inducing vomiting of flammable fluids shouldn't be done.)

At home without a phone or car, I had no way of learning more. I didn't know just where they had taken him. How severe was the situation? Would I ever see my energetic son again? I turned to the Lord in prayer, of course. What joy it was when they returned soon after 6 o'clock with a lively Marc acting as though nothing had happened.

There were many times when Marc's exploring got him into precarious places. I started talking to his guardian angel pleading for help as I rushed to rescue him from some situation or other. He usually had cuts, bumps, and bruises in various stages of healing.

Learning Portuguese

The director at language school welcomed us to a year of suffering. He knew what a challenge it would be for people involved in active ministries in their home country to slow down and babble like babies. We students were probably all at least thirty or more years old.

"Ah, ah, ah. Ee, ee, ee" the language teacher demonstrated with a mouth so large and wide open that we students all gawked. The first several weeks we only worked on basic phonetics, especially vowels. Pronunciation and grammar were drilled into us. Other than the really extroverted students, most of us didn't get a lot of conversational experience. But in the long run, the strong foundation of pronunciation and grammar put us ahead of people who focused on conversation first.

The men went to class in the mornings and the women in the afternoons. Classes varied from individual one-on-one sessions to groups of different sizes.

155

Erwin and Angela Rempel attend Baptist language school, JURATEL, in Campinas, Brazil, 1976.

Marci went to an afternoon preschool with missionary kids and Brazilians. Children learn languages quicker than adults. One time she was behind me getting off a city bus. The bus started to go before she was off. I shouted "Wait!" in English. Once she was safely off, she told me how I should have said it in Portuguese.

The Southern Baptists, who had the largest number of missionaries in Brazil, operated the language school, JURATEL. The instructors were Brazilians. Our Southern Baptist classmates' southern drawl turned vowels into diphthongs. That made it difficult for them to pronounce the short pure Portuguese vowels. The Pentecostal couple had as much trouble learning language as those of us who didn't speak in tongues. The Dutch Reformed couple, born in Holland, amused us with their pithy use of English. The Lutheran couple with four children paid a huge customs charge to import all six of their bicycles. The tall couple from Texas had been told to "bring everything." They did, to the astounding cost of $14,000 for packing, storage, and shipping of their furniture and lovely household goods. And we thought maybe our eight barrels were too much to bring.

Halfway through the year, we had a break in classes. That gave us time for real-life language tests. We loaded our recently-purchased car, a used VW Passat, and bravely headed on our own to the big city of Rio de Janeiro. We found an affordable hotel and managed to order restaurant meals. It was cool season, so the beaches were nearly empty and the water too cool to enjoy. The kids played in the sand with iconic Sugar Loaf Mountain in the background. Erwin managed driving in the crazy Rio traffic while I navigated the Portuguese road signs.

When we first understood a pun in Portuguese, we knew we were really learning the language.

Writing letters

Instead of keeping a journal or diary, I took over our typewriter on Sunday afternoons to write long detailed letters to our parents. Using thin onionskin paper and sheets of carbon paper, I made three copies – one for each of our parents and one for our file. Other than copies of our regular *Rempel Reports* that we sent to our supporting churches, friends, and family, most of our other files disappeared over the years through our several major moves. Erwin's mom faithfully kept our letters, which now provide information for this account of the Brazil chapter of our lives.

We wrote our reports and prayer letters from "the mission field" with the terminology commonly used in our circles at the time. Experiences, sights, sounds, and aspects of the culture that were most different from what we had previously known were the things to write home about. Often it was hard to understand it and not be overly critical.

Airmail letters from the U.S. usually reached us within a few days. Church publications came by ship taking anywhere from a month to six weeks. Telegrams were the quickest way to send and receive messages, but we rarely used those. Phone calls? Way too expensive. Without direct dialing it was complicated to work through an international operator. During our entire time in Brazil, we made or received only a handful of international phone calls, even though direct dialing eventually became available.

About seven months after we left the U.S. taking my parents' only grandchildren to Brazil, my only sibling, LaRita, also left the country. She went to Europe for a year in an MCC exchange program. Her first location was in Switzerland where she worked as a housemaid for a Swiss family with a number of children. She wrote about traveling around Europe and doing things with her host family such as skiing in the Alps. In Brazil, we needed to hire a maid, but my sister went to Europe to work as a maid.

Going to church

In Brazil we continued our habit of attending church services, even in the early months when we couldn't understand the language. Our church attendance was expected and we didn't question that. Before we bought our own car, the Schwartzentrubers transported us on Sundays to the small Mennonite church in Campinas, led by a Brazilian pastor. Ken made headphones connected to a microphone and someone translated the service for us. Sunday school met on Sunday mornings and the worship service was on Sunday evenings. That meant two trips across the city to the church on Sundays. Going to the Wednesday-night service was a step too far for me and I stayed home with the children. A restless toddler and a four-year-old made it hard to get anything out of a service, let alone in a language I couldn't much understand.

When we first met the Brazilian church people, we could only nod, smile, and perhaps give a greeting. Later, when we learned more words, we were too shy and insecure to go to the next level and try conversation.

Assessing our adjustment

By the middle of our first year in Brazil, my mom wrote that people asked how we were adjusting to Brazil. In response I wrote:

> I guess that is a question we ask ourselves, too. In so many ways, life here is similar to what we had before in the U.S., so there aren't a whole lot of adjustments. We have been really quite sheltered yet, always having English-speaking

people around, so we haven't felt isolated. Since the trip here [by plane] went so fast, we don't feel all that far away either. We have a house that we are comfortable in. We now know where and how to buy the necessities. The adjustments to the physical differences are basically not hard because we still live with as much physical comfort as we ever had. The main tensions we face are...about the responsibility of those of us who are rich to the poor.

I observed that generally if the parents adjusted to a new situation the children did too. Marci tended to be either happy or sad. When she was sad, she sucked her thumb. Marc also enjoyed his thumb, plus he twisted his hair and hung onto a flannel blanket. Maybe they were more stressed than we realized at the time.

Other missionaries and churches

During the year of language school, we visited most of the Mennonite missionaries. We learned to travel by bus and train. Peter and Alice Sawatzky in São Paulo introduced us to a Brazilian *favela* – a slum. We walked on rutted hard-packed dirt paths, edged with gullies and puddles of stinky sewage. The path wound around dwellings constructed of whatever odds and ends people could scavenge – wood scraps, tin, cardboard, etc.

We noticed tensions among the missionaries and also in a triangle of MBM missionaries, Brazilian church leaders, and the German Mennonites. The German-speaking Mennonites had emigrated from Russia and settled in rural colonies in southern Brazil as early as the 1920s. They spoke German in their homes and church services. Some moved into the southern city of Curitiba and set up successful businesses. Their churches affiliated with the North American-based General Conference Mennonite or the Mennonite Brethren churches.

The days of setting up mission compounds were past. Missionaries lived among Brazilians. We noticed differing approaches to ministry and missionary lifestyle among various denominations. Mennonite simplicity and frugality reigned in our group, in contrast to how some other missionaries lived.

We learned that even though Brazil was known as a Catholic country, only about ten percent of the people regularly attended a Catholic church, especially in the cities. Rural people were moving in large numbers to cities looking for jobs and education. Unless they had good skills, they often had to live in squatter areas and the *favelas* that dotted the cities. In such difficult situations, the people typically were more open to the good news of Jesus Christ and His love. All Protestants, including Mennonites, were called evangelicals and made up about ten percent of the population. Included in that percentage were the rapidly growing Pentecostal groups.

Politics, economics, history

Brazil was under a military dictatorship when we lived there. People were imprisoned for protests. Yet there were elections and citizens were required to vote. Economically, Brazil focused on exports and placed high tariffs on imported goods. During our first year there, Brazil added a costly exit visa for travel outside the country. To obtain an exit visa, a deposit of about US $1,200 was paid and held by the government for a year without interest. We wrote our families that it would be very difficult for us to make any quick trips back to the U.S., as such visas took as long as six months to obtain. God answered our prayers that there be no death in our immediate families in the U.S. The exit visa requirement didn't last long.

Brazil's increasingly mobile and growing economy required importing oil because almost no oil had been found yet in Brazil. With worldwide interest rates soaring in the latter part of the 1970s, Brazil's foreign debt exploded. Land that had grown the basic rice and beans to feed their people was often planted instead with soybeans and coffee. These were exported so that Brazil could, in turn, import petroleum.

The Portuguese explorer Pedro Cabral had accidentally "discovered" Brazil in April 1500. Other Europeans soon arrived, bringing along their diseases, which decimated the indigenous population. Four times as many African slaves were taken to Brazil than were taken to the U.S., primarily to work on large sugar plantations. In contrast to early settlements in the U.S., the Portuguese settlers were usually men who had come from Europe without a family. They found partners among the indigenous women and Africans. Over the years, the typical Brazilian became a blend of European, African, and indigenous people, with a variety of hair colors and shades of skin color. There didn't appear to be much overt racism, but lighter-skinned people had more prestige and the poorest people often had the darkest skin.

Changing assignment locations

Before we had even departed the U.S. for Brazil, the location of our ministry changed. The original plan had been for us to live and work along the developing Trans-Amazon highway. Then the plan changed to having us work in Curitiba in southern Brazil in the area where German-speaking Mennonites had settled. (In hindsight, that change was good because Erwin and I wouldn't have been a good fit for church planting in the hot, tropical rainforest of the Amazon River area.) The German Mennonites were interested in evangelism and wanted us to help them with church planting in southern Brazil. That was the plan when we began language school.

That changed once again at a strategy conference of the Associação Evangélica Menonita we attended half-way through language school in July. Here are excerpts from a letter sent to supporters in September 1976 describing the change and our impressions gained on a trip to the new location:

> We continue to be flexible. Before we came to Brazil, we expected that after language school we would work in southern Brazil, in or near the city of Curitiba. Instead, we were asked to consider going to a place nearly 1,000 miles from Curitiba – to a new city called Gama in the Federal District.
>
> Most of you have probably heard of Brazil's new capital city, Brasília. It was inaugurated in 1960. It is ultra-modern in its airplane-shaped layout and its architectural designs. Contrary to what most North Americans think, it is not in the middle of the jungle. It is on the high central plains of Brazil, a rather desolate area with scrubby, little, twisted trees covering the ground from one horizon to the other as overgrown sagebrush does in Montana and Wyoming.

The Federal District not only includes Brasília but several planned satellite cities for the poorer people to live in. That is where the bus drivers, road workers, construction workers, maids, filling station attendants, and others, live. Gama is one of those cities with about 127,000 people. A Mennonite congregation is meeting there in a home and there appear to be opportunities for starting Bible studies and hopefully other congregations.

The infrastructure is already developing in Gama. We admired the nice post office, telephone-company building, city hall, hospital, schools, banks, and business and shopping areas. The main streets are paved and have streetlights. Running water is available as well as sewer in most areas. But the housing and most areas have a long way to go in terms of development. Housing will be one of our biggest problems as sixty-two percent of the homes are tiny wooden shacks. About five to eight percent of the permanent houses are privately built, of brick and concrete block, and range from very small to very nice. The rest are government-built houses – quite small and also of brick and concrete. When we made our visit, there were no houses for rent although several were for sale. We, and the Commission on Overseas Mission, prefer to rent.

Preparing to move to Gama

We therefore made plans to move north rather than south after language school. MBM missionaries Betty and Otis Hochstetler lived and worked in Brasília where they operated two Christian bookstores. The Hochstetlers too were most helpful to us in so many ways.

As a family we went to look for a house in Gama. Erwin made one or more trips there himself by bus before finding a suitable rental house.

After he located a house for us to rent, Erwin was on a packed local bus going from Gama back to Brasília, about an hour-long ride. Erwin felt something warm and wet on his back. The drunken man seated behind him had thrown up! When he got to Hochstetlers' house, Betty managed to quickly wash Erwin's jacket. She dried it in a dryer owned by a nearby Presbyterian missionary. Erwin was good to go for his long night on another bus back to Campinas.

We graduated from language school in December 1976, but we still couldn't converse much in Portuguese. We knew we had a lot of language learning yet ahead of us as we tried to put into practice what we had been taught.

We arranged for a professional Brazilian moving company to move our things from Campinas to Gama in January 1977. We packed our VW Passat with the children and drove the 600 miles to our next home.

Part Two
Life in Gama from 1977 to 1980

"I really feel that I am on the 'mission field' here!" I wrote our parents in the first letter from Gama. "Adjusting to life in Gama is going to take some time." We experienced more culture shock moving there than we had a year earlier when we moved from the U.S. to Brazil.

Arriving in Gama

The moving truck slowly navigated the bumpy unpaved streets in Gama. It arrived on schedule in January 1977, ready to unload our things at the house we had rented. Curious neighbors watched the unloading of the moving truck. It was about the size of the wooden shacks they lived in. We were pleased with how well our things fared in the move. The backyard still had some of the homeowner's things, but a man with a horse-drawn two-wheeled cart soon came to haul it away. Another man and children took away the rest in a hand-pulled cart.

At the end of our first week in Gama, our house was still a messy work-in-progress. It was a relief to get into our car, take the paved four-lane divided highway to Brasília, and spend time with our mission co-workers, Otis and Betty Hostetler, and their two children, Dick and Debbie. What a relief to converse in English, away from the mess.

Although it wasn't far, at first walking to and from our Gama house to church was "just about more than enough culture shock for me!" I wrote my sister in late January 1977. The dirt street gave ample evidence by sight and smell of the horse carts that frequently passed through. Swarms of flies hovered over indescribable globs of gook. We dodged mud puddles and gullies carved in the dirt streets by rainy-season downpours. We crossed the street to avoid confronting a drunk. Carefree children played in the street – little boys were often nude or wearing only a shirt while little girls always wore at least a panty. We felt so conspicuous and out of place walking on the street. We found comfortable refuge both in our home and in the house where the church met. It was tempting to isolate ourselves by taking the car instead of walking the few blocks between those locations.

Making a house our home

Brazilians like strong bright colors inside and outside. It took several coats of paint to tame the interior colors of our rented house into the lighter neutral shades we prefer. Ceramic tiles, with various designs and colors, covered the outside front of the house, the short driveway into the carport, the carport walls, most of the floors inside, and the walls in the kitchen and bath. Bedroom and living room floors had nice wooden parquet blocks. A spacious area off the kitchen had a three-section washtub for hand laundry, plus plumbing for an automatic washer. Ceramic tiles lined the floor and walls of that laundry area too. A small bedroom and bath that opened off the laundry area was designed for use by a live-in maid. We set up that room for our overnight guests and my sewing desk. With electricity and indoor plumbing, we had a comfortable living arrangement. It was all very convenient and cozy.

Erwin used the do-it-yourself attitude and skills he observed and learned as a child and youth. He bravely tackled projects – electrical tasks, constructing things with wood or cement, and even making a volleyball net. However, when he picked up a broom to help clean up after a meal with the church people, they were horrified. "No, Pastor," they exclaimed. The young girls took the broom from him. In Brazilian culture an educated man would not do sweeping. That was demeaning work. Illiterate men, however, pushed big brooms cleaning streets.

The owner of our house allowed us to transform the backyard. First, we covered the dirt with smooth clean concrete. Young fellows from the church helped mix cement – by hand on the ground. We put up

The Rempels lived in this Brazilian-style house in Gama from 1977 to 1980.

posts for a clothesline. We made raised flowerbeds along one side of the high wall that enclosed the back yard and soon had a nice variety of ferns and other plants growing.

To our surprise, we discovered a small wading pool buried in a corner of the backyard under the trash. We cleaned and repaired it. We invited several small groups of children and their parents to enjoy it. However, it leaked badly. We eventually filled it with dirt and planted black raspberries. We cleaned up a small shed in the back corner. Erwin made a small swing and hung it for the children.

At the beginning of the rainy season, about November, we started new plants by sticking a branch into the ground. Erwin got a small hand-push lawn mower to cut the little plot of grass in the front yard. The neighborhood children found that quite entertaining and lined the low front wall to watch the big American mowing the yard.

We soon put screening at all the windows because of the flies and mosquitoes. We had been introduced to large flying cockroaches in Campinas, but in Gama they defiantly seemed to take over. We sprayed

165

and squished a lot to begin with. We eventually got them under control, but not before one dropped off the top of a doorframe landing on me just as I passed through. Once, one even dropped down the front of my blouse.

All our electrical items, from large appliances to small lamps, operated on 110 volts, which is what southern Brazil had during our year of language school. But much of Brazil used 220 volts, including Gama. Rather than use a small transformer for each electrical item, we bought one large transformer. An electrician wired it into the house system and all the plug-ins were converted to 110 volts.

When we got the house cleaned, painted, and organized, we found it a delightful place. It was a comfortable home for one of our most challenging, yet satisfying, chapters of our life together. When we eventually left the house, it was in better shape than when we had first rented it.

Becoming suddenly rich

"Que palacio!" (what a palace) one young Brazilian woman exclaimed about our house. By American standards, it was quite small. We realized we were rich – a new feeling for us and hard to get used to. While we had never lacked, we had always lived frugally. Others were rich; we weren't. Here our small house was the nicest one around. Our street had only a few other completed masonry houses, plus some in construction. Most people lived in wooden shacks at the back of their lots, collecting building materials and dreaming of building their own permanent house at the front near the street. No matter how humble the dwelling, the first electrical item people purchased was a television set, evident by a tall outdoor antenna. Next, they purchased a refrigerator, usually displayed in the living room either for show or lack of kitchen space. It was mostly used just for ice and drinks because people retained the habit of shopping nearly daily for any perishable items. We were amazed to learn that they didn't refrigerate eggs, mayonnaise, and butter. Milk, sold in one-liter cartons, was specially processed and kept without refrigeration until opened.

We were the only Americans to live in Gama out of a population estimated at about 127,000 to 150,000. With more than sixty percent of the houses being small wooden structures, reflecting the precarious economic situation of their inhabitants, we expected a lot of beggars would come to our gate. However, we didn't actually have many come. We mostly gave help through the church and to people we knew personally. Word probably circulated that we weren't very generous in giving to strangers.

Keeping busy our first year in Gama

Our first year in Gama, 1977, was quite eventful. There weren't any dull moments. We encountered Brazil's disparities and inequalities. We learned a great deal about Brazil. We managed to get Marci enrolled in school.

People didn't know English, so we had to speak Portuguese. Erwin carefully wrote out his sermons, Bible studies, and prayers in Portuguese. Teenager Lucita checked over it. She helped me as well, but I had fewer public-speaking responsibilities. Our fluency in Portuguese improved rapidly.

The multi-generational household of MariaRosa and Manoel de Souza Sobrinho, founders of the Mennonite church in Gama, Brazil, 1980.

Erwin and Angela Rempel drink a typical cafezinho coffee with Manoel and MariaRosa, Gama, Brazil, 1980.

We worked with the Gama Mennonite Church people to purchase, renovate, and move the congregation into a larger facility. We soon bonded with the people attending the church, especially the family of Manoel and MariaRosa de Souza. They were the church's founding family and hosted the church services in their house. The "regulars" of their four-generation household included their six biological children, her invalid brother, a grandmother, three motherless nieces, and their oldest son's wife and two young children. Other friends and relatives frequently stayed with them too. We learned so much from Manoel and MariaRosa, including an appreciation for Brazilian coffee.

Wherever we visited in homes, even among the poorest, the first thing the hostess did was to heat water for coffee. Erwin already enjoyed coffee, but it didn't take me long to realize that I had to learn to drink coffee too. It wouldn't do to reject this simple, common traditional act of hospitality. I began by sipping the morning-style of coffee made with equal amounts of hot milk and strong sweet coffee. Gradually I learned to drink the typical *cafezinho*, a small cup of strong sweet

168

Maringueth and Erwin Rempel lay concrete blocks around church lot, Gama, Brazil, 1977.

coffee made from finely ground dark-roasted beans. Some Brazilians used instant Nescafé.

Working together with Brazilians in physical, hands-on projects provided us new mission workers with some visible accomplishment. Less visible was what those experiences taught us about language, culture, and relationships.

Visitor in the night

One night only a couple of months after we moved into our Gama house, our sleep was interrupted by a sound at the door. Glad for the metal grates over the windows and door, Erwin cautiously opened a nearly opaque glass portion. He discovered a young man there, panting, gasping, and asking for help. He claimed someone had assaulted him and tried to rob him of his watch. He said someone had tried to kill him. We couldn't understand everything he said, but finally realized that he wanted us to keep his watch and work documents until morning. Erwin says he also asked to leave a gun with us. We agreed

169

to keep the watch and documents but not the gun. He handed us the items through the grates and disappeared into the darkness. We didn't get much more sleep that night. In the morning as we were wondering if the guy would really return, he showed up, quietly took his things and left. It was a weird and scary experience.

A funeral

In May we experienced the first and only death of a member of the congregation while we were in Brazil. The 82-year-old mother of MariaRosa lived with them off and on over the years. She had smoked and picked disagreements with her children until about six years earlier when she too became a Christian and her life changed. She enjoyed good health and she had first seen a doctor only a month earlier. After a Sunday evening worship service, MariaRosa's daughter-in-law, Azenaide, asked me to drive her and the elderly woman to the local hospital emergency room. The woman had severe abdominal pain.

The elderly woman was given a couple of shots and sent to a bone doctor. He said she should sleep on a very firm bed and not on her mattress. Back at their house, Azenaide removed the woman's foam mattress from the bed. That left just wooden slats. A bit stunned, I hurried to our house and got our thick sleeping bags to provide a bit of cushioning for what turned out to be the woman's last night on earth – a very miserable one. MariaRosa was in another hospital at the time because of phlebitis in her legs.

When Manoel went home for his lunch, and saw how poorly his mother-in-law was doing, he left money for the family to take her by taxi to a bigger and better hospital in Brasília. Granddaughter Lucita and another teenage girl from our church, Andrea, took her. The taxi ran out of gas on the way. When they eventually reached the city hospital, medical attention wasn't any too swift there either. She died about three o'clock Monday afternoon, waiting in a wheelchair attended only by Andrea.

In our culture, we take food to the home when someone has died, so I baked a simple cake and took it to the house. I learned that to the Brazilians that was a bit strange. For them, cakes are only for celebrations. Many people streamed to the house and expected to be served something rather than contributing food.

In Brazil, burial has to be within twenty-four hours of death because they don't embalm. Inadvertently, the date of death recorded on the death certificate was Tuesday, a day later than her death had occurred. Her body wasn't released from the hospital in time to be buried within twenty-four hours. In that situation, a body was supposed to be put into cold storage and taken directly to the cemetery for burial. Nevertheless, Betty managed to convince an official that because it was still within twenty-four hours of the wrong date, it wouldn't be illegal for him to release the body to be taken to the church.

A special funeral van brought the body to the church late in the afternoon on Tuesday. The casket cost about ten dollars. It was just a fragile wooden frame covered with plastic, as I recall. MariaRosa got permission to leave the hospital, greatly distressed by her mother's death. About nine in the evening, a brief funeral service began in the church. People wanted a wake that night. Otis had suggested just locking up the church because no one would bother the casket overnight, but that wasn't well received. By eleven in the evening, Erwin and Otis came back to our house for some coffee because they were expected to be at the wake. Erwin only lasted until about one in the morning, but Otis stayed until five o'clock before coming to our place for some sleep.

On Wednesday morning, the Hochstetler's small station wagon carried the casket the short distance from the church to the cemetery for the burial.

Brazil-U.S. politics

We were quite amazed that in less than a year after we left the U.S., someone we had never even heard of was elected president of the U.S. – Jimmy Carter. When we learned that his wife, Rosalyn, was visiting Brazil in early June 1977, I took advantage of the opportunity to see her at the American Embassy in Brasília. The protocols and security fascinated me. She spoke only a few minutes, and her southern accent surprised me. We had never heard either of the Carters speaking because whenever Brazilian TV had broadcast the Carters, we heard only a translator's voice. She shook hands with all of us as we exited. I hadn't expected to get so close to her.

171

At the time of Mrs. Carter's visit, relations with the U.S. were rather cool as the Carter administration focused on human rights issues. Brazil still had a military dictatorship. Brazil wanted to buy a nuclear energy plant from Germany at the time, and that was also controversial.

President Carter visited Brazil later and addressed the Brazilian congress. A young fellow from the Gama church worked as a messenger for a congressman. He figured out a way that we could listen to Carter's speech over the phone. Carter's short presidency came and went during our time in Brazil. We didn't follow much of the political scene in the U.S. during those years.

Making bunk beds

Within the first few months of our arrival in Gama, we had the satisfaction of working with Brazilians in getting a building usable for our church. Soon another hands-on project presented itself for Erwin.

Manoel and MariaRosa were shopping with Erwin one day at a large store where bunk beds caught their eye. Just what they needed for their

Erwin and teenage boys use our backyard to make several bunk beds for church families in Gama, Brazil, 1977.

growing girls – but the beds would cost the equivalent of more than a hundred dollars each, and they would need to buy them on credit, paying a high interest rate. We learned that in their household they had five girls between ages thirteen and twenty sleeping in one small room with three of them in a double bed, and two in a narrow single bed. The youngest girl, age nine, still slept in a crib in her parents' room. She complained that she couldn't stretch out to sleep.

Do-it-yourself Erwin took a good look at the bunk bed we had bought for our own children. He figured it would be simple enough for him to make bunk beds in that style. He worked out an agreement that Manoel would pay for the lumber and materials, and Erwin would make the beds. Young fellows from Manoel's family and the church youth group helped make the beds in our back yard. In one week, they made three sets of bunk beds for the cost of just one in the store. How delighted the girls were to each have a bed to sleep in.

Erwin made bunk beds for several other church families as well.

Visiting in homes

A few months after moving to Gama, Betty Hochstetler accompanied me on my first visit to two different homes. These were people other than Manoel and MariaRosa's middle-class family. We visited Severino's wife who had just given birth to their ninth and last child. She had a C-section delivery and had her tubes tied, a form of birth control easily talked about publicly by women. I wrote on May 1, 1977:

> My culture has been shocked again today, and I am trying to integrate these new experiences into my system. Betty Hochstetler was with me. As we approached the home with the new baby, Betty was commenting on all the positive things she observed out of her numerous years' experience in Brazil.

The same day, Betty took me for my first visit to the widow in our congregation. She had so proudly begged for us to see her dwelling. Betty again pointed out the positives. "That was a good thing for me," I wrote. "By the time we left the second place, I was nearly in tears, as all the negative things hit me first." I had already come to love these two women and it was hard to see their poor living conditions.

One evening later on, Erwin and I together visited the family with the new baby. After writing in some detail about their shabby living conditions and other family members, I noted:

> I had tried to buy some plastic pants for the new baby, but couldn't find the right size for a newborn. I was glad I hadn't given plastic pants when I saw that the baby didn't even have on a diaper!

Lives being changed

It wasn't just tangible physical work results we saw during that first year; we also observed lives changed. We soon learned to know Andrea, a new Christian who attended the Gama church and led the youth group. She worked in Brasília at a child day care center, run by a Baptist church to provide care for children of upper-class people such as congressmen and diplomats. On Andrea's birthday, Betty Hochstetler and I took a cake over to the day care center. Maria, the assistant director of the center, showed us the facility. She told us more about Andrea, who had been her schoolmate. She said that a real transformation had occurred in Andrea. During their school days, Andrea had come to school dressed scantily in dirty clothes, smoking, and cursing. She was such a troublemaker the teachers didn't know what to do with her. Maria, a Christian, hadn't paid much attention to Andrea. They didn't have anything in common.

Unexpectedly Andrea offered Maria a rose and kissed her on both cheeks, as Brazilian women greet each other. Maria was startled and wondered about Andrea's intentions. She cautiously befriended Andrea. We didn't hear when and how Andrea accepted Christ, but Maria said Andrea changed "five-hundred percent."

One day Andrea's mother went to the day care center. Her mother said that at home nothing would suit Andrea; everything and everyone had some defect, except Maria, this Christian woman she worked with. So the mother, a practicing spiritist, wanted to meet this Maria.

By July of that first year, in our newsletter we wrote that several people had made decisions for Christ. One of them was Andrea's mother. Her husband was an alcoholic and a very difficult man to live with. We saw a real change in the woman's life.

Another teenage girl, Dilma, had accepted Christ earlier and had wanted to be baptized the previous September. However, her mother too was a spiritist and refused to allow the baptism. Dilma obediently waited, praying for her mother. In May, Dilma was baptized during the dedication service of our newly-renovated church building. She gave a thrilling testimony, pointing out that God had more than answered her prayers. Not only had her mother now consented to her baptism, but her mother was present along with her ailing alcoholic husband and most of the large family. One of Dilma's sisters had also accepted Christ and was preparing for baptism.

Hosting visitors

Our kitchen table and the small guest bedroom were well used during the years we lived in Gama. As soon as we were settled, our doors were open. One week in July of that first year, I counted serving twenty-eight extra meals at home. I also made some food for an outing with a group of visitors who worked with Mennonite Central Committee in Brazil's northeast. Years later in the U.S., we encountered some of those MCCers in locations varying from east coast to west coast.

The youth from the Gama church were often at our house. They helped Erwin with projects such as mixing cement to make concrete blocks, washing our car, or participating in a Bible study. Teenage girls from church helped me clean or care for our children. Sometimes youth came over just to hang out. We frequently invited them to join us for the noon meal. It was convenient to repeat the same Brazilian menu each time: rice, beans, lettuce salad with tomatoes, a cooked vegetable, and meat. Letters to our parents recount an amazing flow of people through our home. We were glad to be able to relate closely to our new Brazilian friends.

In Brazilian culture the hostess is expected to repeatedly offer more food and for the guest to repeatedly turn it down, only to accept it eventually. However, teenager Paulo had learned that at Americans'

175

tables, he needed to accept something on the first offer, because we Americans didn't repeat it.

It wasn't just Brazilians who visited us. Our roster of visitors over the years included other Mennonite missionaries, traveling North Americans, mission administrators from Newton or Elkhart, and German Mennonites from southern Brazil.

Visit from Erwin's folks

Our most special visitors that first year in Gama were Erwin's folks, Alvin and Lena Eitzen from Montana. We went to the airport in Brasília to meet their flight from Miami early on October 6.

We introduced the Eitzens to many people and places in our area. They went on to visit in Paraguay. That was a special interest because years earlier Dad Eitzen helped raise money to build a road through the Paraguayan Chaco to the Mennonite colonies. There Eitzens communicated in Low German. They marveled that some indigenous people spoke Low German too.

Traveling to the interior

As if our first year in Gama wasn't already overflowing with new experiences, shortly after the Eitzen visit we made a car trip to the interior. We went to the area where MariaRosa and Manoel came from. We took along MariaRosa, a young fellow whose widowed mother had roots in that area, and our two children. We drove along the one paved road that headed north out of the Federal District. Twelve hours of driving brought us to Paraizo do Norte (Paradise of the North) where Erwin participated in a regional conference for ministers. A new small congregation, which met in homes, hosted the event.

Asking for a bathroom, I was shown the back yard with two small buildings. One small building was the toilet. Even I had to duck to enter through the low doorframe. To my surprise, there was only a square hole cut in a wooden floor, my introduction to squat toilets. The other little building was the shower house, made of concrete blocks, where a bunch of cockroaches up in the corner provided an audience for anyone taking a cold shower. Water was drawn up from uncovered hand-dug wells. I was afraid adventuresome Marc would fall into the well.

Women cooked outdoors over fires built between rocks and bricks that supported the cooking pots. Washing dishes was done outside, slopping cold water and suds over the dishes. Food scraps on plates were swished onto the ground where the chickens eagerly plucked up the bits of rice, beans, noodles, etc.

On Sunday of the conference, the highlight was a baptismal service for four teens and a woman. It was the first time Erwin performed an immersion baptism. When I wrote about it to my mother, she wondered how the Brazilians had heard about immersion. Our churches in the U.S. usually baptized inside the sanctuary by pouring. Many of the Brazilian evangelical churches baptized by immersion.

On Monday morning we headed westward into the interior toward the town of Araguecema on the banks of the Araguaia River. The last 200 kilometers were dirt road. When we got there, MariaRosa literally let down her long hair. She was so excited to be seeing familiar people and places that she looked years younger.

Mennonite mission in Brazil began along this Araguaia River in the 1950s. The river was still the focus of village life and its water source when the Rempels visited in 1977.

This was where MariaRosa, at age sixteen, and Manoel, twice her age, began their married life. In the 1950s, this was where the first Mennonite missionaries, led by Howard Hammer, began work in Brazil. Neither MariaRosa nor Manoel were believers at that time. Manoel was the town mayor and granted permission for the Mennonites to establish a mission station on the edge of town. Howard Hammer's untimely and violent death left unanswered questions, but the mission continued. After Manoel suffered political and economic losses, he moved his family to the new capital, Brasilia, in the early 1960s. Mennonite missionaries starting a Christian bookstore in the new city contacted them and held Bible studies in their home. Manoel and MariaRosa became believers.

At the time of our visit to Araguecema, the mission station on the edge of the town was home to an American Mennonite couple, Larry and Annette Eisenbeis from South Dakota, plus some German-speaking Mennonite couples from southern Brazil. The mission station included not only modest sturdy residences for the mission workers, but a church, school, and clinic.

Erwin accepted an invitation to go fishing on the wide Araguaia River, a tributary of the even larger Amazon River. Erwin caught two piranhas, the little fish with sharp teeth that can demolish the flesh of beast or human in short order.

The next day we took a small boat on the same river to the town of Santana where another congregation held a baptism. Erwin will never forget that baptism in the river. Townspeople were up on the riverbank observing everything. What a public witness to one's faith in Christ! People had told us that stingrays lived on the river bottom. In order not to scare the stingrays or step on them, they told Erwin to enter the river slowly, shuffling his feet, so that the stingrays would slither away. If stingrays were stepped on, their long tail would flip up with a terrible poisonous sting, painful and slow to heal. He made sure he followed that advice! While he was praying during the baptism, he felt little nibbles at his toes. He thought uneasily of the piranhas caught in that same river the day before. He didn't take any longer than necessary to perform the baptism and get out of the water. The nibbles were probably just from curious minnows.

We visited other villages, flying with Missionary Aviation Fellowship on a single-engine plane. I'd heard about the careful attention MAF pilots give to the safety and maintenance of those planes, so I wasn't fearful on my first flight on such a small aircraft. The pilot swooped low over a little grassy airstrip a time or two before landing in order to chase off the sheep or goats calmly nibbling grass on it. At the Mennonite church in another village, MariaRosa shared her enthusiastic testimony. Some of her unbelieving relatives were present.

That trip to the interior provided us a glimpse of how mission stations or compounds were set up in earlier years in undeveloped locations. That was a big contrast to how we were living and working in a city.

Describing Gama

From our house on the corner of two unpaved streets, we observed constant movement. Many people of all ages walked past. Women often carried loads balanced on their heads. There were bicycles, motorcycles, horses and carts, occasional cars, and a surprising number of loud trucks. It was a noisy location. People talked loudly, dogs barked at all hours, roosters crowed early in the morning, and radios were played with the volume on high. Amid the cacophony we could hear a parrot squawk. Behind our house we sometimes heard an animated preacher and multiple voices praying aloud at the same time. We appreciated the six-foot-high wall all around our back yard that granted us visual privacy. However, the neighborhood boys sometimes managed to peek over the wall.

Communication

We had no telephone when we arrived in Gama, nor did others in our church. To get in touch with our co-workers Betty and Otis about 25 miles away in Brasília, we would drive to the center of Gama to the phone company building to use a public phone. To get a message to us, Betty contacted someone from Gama who worked in Brasília. Betty gave them the message at work, and when the person returned to Gama, he or she came and told us. What a relief when phones were installed at our house and Manoel's house.

Mail was not delivered to any houses in Gama. We stopped daily at our mail box in the post office in the center of Gama.

Clothing

Brazilians dressed in western-style clothing. The teenage girls often wore jeans, and sometimes shorts, whereas adult women wore skirts. Women wouldn't wear anything sleeveless to church. Adult men didn't usually wear shorts. A man visiting from Germany wore shorts to a Wednesday night service at our church. That was considered quite inappropriate, we learned.

Even poor Brazilians usually dressed in the latest styles. The inexpensive clothing they bought wore out quickly from hand washing on corrugated washboards. Brazilians knew how to get clothes stain-free and sparkling white. Women laid pre-scrubbed wet soapy garments in the sun on any small patch of grass. Few stains resisted the intense sunlight. Even the poorest people stepped out of a dirt-floor shack in a muddy yard wearing spotless white garments. Clothes were draped over fences to dry, even over barbed wire – no clothespins needed.

Keeping clean

Personal cleanliness was important to Brazilians. Daily bathing was expected whether or not hot water was available. Aluminum pots and pans were scrubbed with steel wool and soap until they had a mirror-like finish. The bottoms of some pots even wore out from all the polishing and scrubbing.

Cleanliness in public spaces was another matter: just toss the banana peel over the fence or the eggshells out the window. It was often hard for me to focus on the beauty of the people and nature when there was so much litter scattered around. Periodically, low-paid workers with big brooms and barrels on wheels picked up trash and swept the streets.

Sitting together with Brazilian friends on a park bench one time, I noticed they just dropped their litter on the ground.

"The man will clean it up," was their explanation. Littering was a work program and job security for the poor.

Shopping

Buying things in Gama was an intriguing adventure. Gama was designed with a central area for larger markets, grocery stores and shops. Smaller commercial areas were located in the residential sections. The small shops in the commercial area near our house usually had unrefrigerated wilted produce and limited options of dusty items. Small specialty shops had even less variety – one store sold fabric by the meter, while another little shop sold the needles, thread, or buttons. We visited several small shops to purchase school supplies the children needed. In most stores, one clerk took the money and gave a receipt, then we went to another person to actually receive our purchase after it was wrapped in coarse paper and taped shut. Small bakeries were numerous and we enjoyed purchasing fresh bread for breakfast and again for the evening meal. The bread was best when eaten within a few hours of baking.

A large, covered permanent market in the central part of town had a metal roof, but open sides and a concrete floor. Vendors set up their products and produce in stalls. It was common to see customers leaving with a live chicken hanging by its feet from the handlebar of a bicycle. People wanted fresh meat. They insisted on buying live chickens. Butcher shops in the market had hunks of freshly slaughtered beef hanging in the open air – complete with a swarm of flies. Women and girls carried away their purchases on their heads. Colorful and plentiful fresh vegetables and fruits were available year 'round – new tropical varieties as well as familiar things such as bananas and tomatoes. My favorite aroma at the market was the freshly ground cumin used to flavor black beans served with rice.

Pharmacies were common. Some had names such as *Espirito Santo Pharmacia* – Holy Spirit Pharmacy. People talked with the pharmacist about their medical problems and he offered something for it. That was easier than going to a clinic to see a doctor. If we experienced a recurring sickness for which we had been prescribed an effective antibiotic, we asked the pharmacist for that same antibiotic. He sold it to us without a new prescription from a doctor. Our U.S. doctors were horrified, of course, when they heard that.

Shopping in the city of Brasília was more like shopping in the U.S. A nice Sears store carried items much like in the U.S. Carrefour, a French supermarket chain, had a large store that sold not only groceries but clothing, appliances, and many other products. We bought whole coffee beans and ground them in the store. That delightful aroma filled the car all the way home.

Brazil placed high tariffs on the few things they imported in order to protect and encourage local businesses. Brazil was already a major manufacturing country in South America and exported many items to neighboring countries. Any electrical items, such as fans or sound systems, were very costly, either due to high tariffs or high taxes. Price tags showed only the total price that included taxes.

Taking photos

It was challenging to find film for our cameras in those days long before digital cameras. To make slide sets to show people in the U.S., we needed to take pictures with film made for that purpose. The Kodak film with the best result, Kodachrome, had to be imported. It was very expensive in the local stores. When someone we knew came from the U.S., we asked them to bring several rolls of film for us. Kodachrome was sent to Panama for developing. The less costly Ektachrome film was developed locally, sometimes in only an hour. Over the long haul, Ektachrome slides faded and turned blueish. To economize, sometimes we bought plastic or cardstock frames and mounted the slides ourselves.

A young German-speaking Mennonite from southern Brazil taught Erwin how to develop and print black and white photos. Erwin converted the small back bathroom to a darkroom. We got a second camera to take black and white photos. He made lots of black and white photos of various sizes. Brazil offered so many interesting things to photograph, plus of course, we took pictures of our children and the cats. The cost of film and developing was always an issue, so doing our own developing and printing saved a lot. We shared our photos with the church people.

For our periodic newsletters to supporters in the U.S., Erwin developed and printed dozens of black and white photos that we cut and pasted by hand onto as many as 250 prayer newsletters. Photocopiers couldn't reproduce photos decently. We had a spirit duplicator to make

Erwin Rempel makes copies of teaching materials on a spirit duplicator that printed only in purple, Gama, Brazil.

multiple copies. That involved typing on special stencils and resulted in purple print because of the alcohol-based ink.

Getting around in Brazil

Driving a car on the streets of Gama in the late 1970s had its challenges. Streets were vibrant and full of life. We needed to watch for and avoid many things. That included people on foot who acted as though cars didn't belong on the street; boys playing soccer in the street and piling stones to mark their goal posts; dogs, dead and alive; trash such as tin cans and broken glass; bicycles going with the traffic, across the traffic and against the traffic; taxis stopping to pick up or unload passengers; drunks in the street trying to stop traffic; children throwing rocks and other objects at cars; handmade ridges of dirt and huge stones to serve as speed bumps; deep gullies in dirt streets; abandoned disabled vehicles; disabled vehicles being pushed by a half dozen men; boys carrying styrofoam boxes with cool drinks to sell; men pushing carts with popcorn to sell, boys pushing carts and buying bottles to recycle; one-horse carts hauling people and other items; lovers walking arm in arm oblivious to everything else; bicycles carrying several people with women passengers riding side saddle; vendors on bicycles selling milk, bread, fruits, fish, etc.

Driving at night in Brazil was laden with all the above obstacles but magnified by a perception that turning on the headlights would be rude to oncoming drivers. Even big lumbering buses and trucks drove along darkened roads without lights on. A disabled vehicle, day or night, remained in the roadway, marked by broken tree branches to warn motorists.

At first we were the only ones in the congregation who had a car. Taxis were easy to hail on the major road close to the church. Buses cost much less than taxis, though, and were the usual form of transportation. The high price of gas, about four times as much as it was in the U.S. at the time, made a car trip into Brasília quite costly unless we had a full load. We often rode buses. The typical buses running between the center of Brasília and the various satellite cities were quite an adventure to ride. Private cars and vans pulled up at bus stops to see if anyone preferred to ride in them, for a fee, rather than to wait for a crowded bus. April 18, 1977, I wrote about trying to return to Gama by bus from Brasília:

> When a bus came, it was already full, but a few more people did manage to get on. It was like the jungle – the survival of the fittest. I tried to get in line, but the buses started moving before I got close to the door. Finally after an hour and a half of waiting, I managed to get close enough to the door of a bus, so that the crowd just pushed me in.

Standing bus passengers were usually packed tightly in the aisle. They claimed they couldn't fall over when the buses went around the many traffic circles at speeds that seemed to risk overturning. Whenever I had to stand on a bus at the end of a workday, my nose was about the level of the sweaty armpits of people holding onto the overhead grab bars. My outstretched hand holding onto seat backs made me self-conscious about my engagement and wedding rings. My rings had a modest diamond and a small diamond chip, respectively. I replaced them with a simple narrow gold wedding band similar to what Brazilians wore.

Buses broke down frequently. Their passengers would scramble to squeeze onto another bus. Passengers entered and paid at the front of the bus, but everyone exited at the rear door – quite a feat when the aisle was packed.

We were glad when Executive buses were introduced. After their comfortable seats were filled, the driver didn't stop for any more passengers, so no one had to stand.

About midway between Gama and Brasília an American flag waved above the tall, solid walls that surrounded the residence of the American ambassador. As I understood more about the realities of daily life for Brazilians, that sight reminded me of the ambiguity of being an American. I felt that even more so when I was riding in a tightly-packed bus. From our Brazilian acquaintances, we learned of their "love-hate" relationship with the United States. America was envied and copied, but resented for meddling in Latin America.

Traveling overnight by bus

For long-distance travel, the usual transportation was overnight on a bus. Every passenger had a seat on those buses. For twice the cost, there were special "sleeper" buses with reclining seats. Erwin tried those a few times but felt they were too expensive and beyond the reach of the people we worked with.

As a family, we traveled overnight on buses as well. On one memorable trip, Marc got sick and repeatedly threw up – all over me. When we arrived in the big bus depot in the center of São Paulo early the next morning, Marc and I smelled and looked terrible. That ended our family trips by bus!

Other travel options

Commercial plane travel within Brazil was quite expensive. Our Mennonite co-workers didn't travel by plane, nor did we. Regional railroads had different sizes of tracks, so there was no long-distance passenger rail service. Large highways connected major cities in the southern part of Brazil. But in the rest of the country, there were only a few highways, mostly only two lanes wide. Missionary aviation services such as MAF gave mission workers access to some interior locations on single engine planes.

Driving our Passat

We managed to keep our car, a VW Passat, operating throughout our first term in Brazil. It had neither air conditioning nor radio. We drove it a lot over unpaved roads, which took a real toll on it. Seatbelts weren't an issue, so we squeezed in as many people and kids as we could. We transported all kinds of things tied onto the roof.

Flat tires were common. Since I didn't have the physical strength to manage changing tires, I took at least one of the young fellows from church along when I drove on trips out of town to the church campground. They became proficient tire-changers.

Whenever Erwin used our car on school days, I took the children to school by taxi. Five-year-old Marc decided that he wanted to be a taxi driver when he grew up.

Years later, in 2006 I visited Gama with a work team from our church

Erwin Rempel loads our car with a cabinet he made for someone in Gama, Brazil, 1978.

in Kansas. One evening a slightly drunk man came by the Gama church. When he learned that my family had lived in Gama nearly thirty years earlier, he asked me if we had driven a white car. He remembered, as a boy, seeing us drive that white Passat.

Children playing

Marcia and Marc quickly adapted to life in Gama. They both were extroverts and bilingual. Marc chattered with anyone in either English or Portuguese. Marci was the one to invent things to do, such as play Sunday school with neighbor children. Marc was our entertainer. His blonde hair brought him a lot of unwanted attention.

Our children played with some of the neighborhood children. However, they didn't really know the children right next door. A high concrete wall separated our yards. One day when I was at the kitchen sink where the window faced that wall, I was startled by a loud noise, brighter light, and billowing dust. The ten-year-old boy next door had tried to drive his older sister's car. He crashed it into the wall between our houses. A section of the wall broke. We were grateful that our children hadn't been playing beside it just then. But that provided a literal opening for our children to get acquainted.

Cats appear in many of our family photos. We always seemed to have one or more cats around.

Emergency room visits

In general, the children were healthy but experienced typical upset tummies and colds. In June 1977, one of Marci's colds took a serious turn. She was coughing constantly and wheezing, had a fever and sore throat. After a miserable night trying to sleep with the help of a vaporizer, I phoned Betty in Brasília. I asked for her help since this was a new experience for us. She phoned a pediatrician and was advised that we should take Marci right to the emergency room of the main hospital in Brasília. Marci was soon examined and sent for an injection of adrenalin and a vaporizer treatment. That wasn't enough, and further tests and treatment were ordered. The diagnosis was asthma.

I spent the night with Marci in the hospital, sitting in a straight chair beside her bed in a ward where she had an IV hooked up. Patients

187

needed to supply their own pillows and blankets. Parents needed to be sure the IV was in place and to feed and clean the child. When the medicine began to take effect, I later described how Marci then "began to improve in color and had more spunk – too much. She about drove me up the wall with her questions and demands." She was released the next day and even went to school. Now we knew what caused the wheezing and stuffy nose that she'd had periodically since infancy.

Marc also made a trip to the emergency room. One Wednesday evening in July 1979 after the service at church, we heard him screaming outside. Blood ran over his face. An active two-year-old son of a recent convert had hit Marc in the head with the ragged edge of a tin can. We tried to clean Marc up. We saw that the cut needed stitches. Thankfully, Azenaide, a young mother in our church, went with us to the Gama hospital. With her help, it all went smoothly.

Going to school

We were glad that, in general, missionary children in Brazil didn't go to boarding schools. However, the educational quality of public schools was considered poor. Apparently the teachers missed more days than the students. Without telephones, teachers couldn't even call in to arrange a substitute. Public school itself was free, but children needed to buy a simple uniform, their books, and school supplies. For some poor people, that was a challenge.

Private schools sprang up to accommodate the strong desires of many parents for their children to get a good education. Although it took a while and a lot of help from Betty and others, we got Marci enrolled in Compacto, a private Brazilian school in the central part of Gama. It was only a few minutes from where we lived. It cost US $20 a month, plus supplies and uniforms – one to wear and one to wash. She was younger than the age for their first level class, but she did well there and got good grades. All teaching was done in Portuguese.

I'm not sure how Marci learned to read and write in English because I hadn't spent much time teaching her. We had English children's books at home. Spelling in English was her challenge, as well as for me, because some Portuguese words resemble English words. The Brazilian school year began in February and ended in early December in time for their summer break, which fell over Christmas and New Year's Day.

The second year we were in Gama we enrolled Marc in a preschool. That was more for his socialization than for education. He really struggled the first several weeks. It was so hard to walk away while he was crying loudly. Apparently, when I was out of sight, he settled in fine. We were uneasy with the emphasis on homework for the four-year-olds – assignments to write in cursive. I finally asked the teacher not to give Marc any homework, as that turned out to be

In their school uniforms, Marcia and Marc Rempel leave for school in Gama, Brazil, 1979.

part of his hesitancy in going to school. Teachers told children they needed to learn or else they would have to sweep the streets. But that doesn't mean much to a distraught little kid who just wants his mother.

The next year Marc started kindergarten at Compacto where Marci was. That simplified the daily transportation issue.

We included the children in most church activities, held several nights each week either at the church or by invitation in people's homes. Their bedtimes varied. They seemed to go with that flow amazingly well.

Angela's parents visit for Christmas 1978

I watched my parents, Erwin and Magdalene Albrecht, come down the long stairs from the big plane that had just landed in Brasília. I noticed that they had aged in the three years since we said farewell to them in Kansas. Dad had recently undergone some minor surgery and walked very stiffly. But after all, any 72-year-old would be stiff after such a long flight. My sister, LaRita, age 22, also came. They arrived a few days before Christmas in 1978. They spotted us waving excitedly from the observation deck of the terminal. My folks brought Christmas gifts from themselves and other family members.

They enjoyed attending the Christmas services with us at the Gama church. They met the people we wrote about and they saw for themselves how life was for us. By then, I felt so attached to the church people, that I was actually torn between wanting to spend time with them or my family.

We showed the Albrechts around the Federal District before heading to southern Brazil. We took my mom and dad in our car with the four of us. The car was very full so it was a good thing LaRita was adventuresome enough to fly by herself to Rio de Janeiro ahead of us. We enjoyed driving through lush green countryside and lovely mountains. It was such a change from the wide-open spaces around Brasília. We passed huge old estates in Petropolis, the endless hotels along Rio's beaches, and the lovely homes of all types of architectural designs in São Paulo and Campinas. This was quite a contrast to the modern sameness of Brasília and the wooden shacks and small shabby look-alike houses in Gama. The fast moving heavy traffic in Rio and São Paulo made traffic in Brasília seem tame.

From Brazil, my parents visited the Mennonite colonies in Paraguay, as the Eitzens had done. My folks knew Bob and Myrtle Unruh who lived and worked in Paraguay. Bob was from the Montana church my father had pastored. The Unruhs showed them the agricultural work and experiments they did among the German-speaking Mennonite immigrants who had migrated there beginning in the 1920s, mainly from Canada and Russia. From there my folks headed to Colombia but were delayed for twenty-eight hours passing through Lima, Peru. Somehow they were bumped from their flight. That was a disappointment as that left little time in Colombia with missionaries Gerald and Mary Hope Stucky. Years earlier, the Stuckys were among the first four missionaries the General Conference sent to Colombia. Those four had all stayed with my parents in Chicago while they got their Colombia visas. I was just an infant at the time. To its credit, the airline did reimburse my folks something like $800, which they used to replace their living room carpet.

When they were back home in Kansas, my mother wrote to Erwin's folks in Montana about the trip to South America. My mom commented that Erwin and I both had no problem speaking Portuguese. "Kids [Erwin and Angela] are so devoted and committed to their work in Gama and neighboring Bible classes," she added.

It had been good to visit with my family and to experience the beauty of other parts of Brazil. It was a respite from the constant challenges of walking with people through their pains and sorrows. It felt a bit strange to return to Gama. But after a warm welcoming hug and the double-cheek kisses with the church women, I again felt at home with them.

Another addition to our family

By August 1979, I noticed some familiar changes in my body. We weren't planning for more children. But when we learned I was pregnant, it felt right to us to have a third child. The pregnancy was uncomplicated, but I could tell that I was five years older than previously.

"Are you going to have the baby in Brazil?" people asked. Well, of course! I wouldn't make a trip back to the U.S. to have a baby when Brazilians had a good record of successful births, including C-sections. Our friends were quite pleased that we would have a child born in Brazil. I went to a private doctor in Brasília.

Because I was considered at higher risk – needing a C-section delivery, having a rare blood type and being age 35 – I was sent to the best non-military hospital in Brasília.

I checked into the hospital early on the scheduled morning. After being prepped, the attendant made me hop and skip with her down the hall to the operating room. I struggled to get up on the operating table. A nurse asked me what names we had chosen. As soon as the baby cried, she informed me, *"Carla Cristina nasceu!"* (Carla Cristina is born.) I took a quick blurry look at Carla as she was whisked away to the nursery. It was the custom to have someone stay with the patient in the hospital room. Missionary colleague Margaret Ashley was a nurse by training and came from southern Brazil to be with me in the hospital and help a while at home.

The next day, Carla was brought to my room and not returned to the nursery. Margaret helped immensely. At one point, I remember feeling something tickling in my bed – it was ants. I was released on about the third day, feeling quite weak.

We hoped to hire a full-time live-in house helper for about a month when the baby was born. But that didn't work out and women from church pitched in. It was humbling to have them take home our laundry to wash, some by hand, while I was still too weak to do our own laundry with an automatic washing machine. We hired some teenage girls from church to help with cleaning. Erwin and Marci stepped up and did a lot of the housework too.

Even though Marci wasn't quite nine years old, before Carla's birth she learned a lot about helping at home, including doing laundry. Marc, already five years old, dearly loved his little sister and never seemed to resent her. Marci was a big help with childcare right from the beginning. Later when Carla made quite a mess learning to feed herself, Marci usually opted to give Carla a bath rather than help clean up in the kitchen.

The Rempels enter their home in Gama, Brazil, with baby Carla, 1980.

Carla has indeed been an unexpected blessing in our lives. She was warmly welcomed to our family and church. What a blessing to have had three uncomplicated pregnancies and three healthy babies.

Brazilian health care system

Brazilians were all enrolled in a government-sponsored health care system. That provided basic care, although they often waited in long lines and many delays occurred along the way. In such situations, prayers for healing were important. People often tried traditional remedies, making medicinal "tea" from a variety of plants.

In addition to their work in the government system, some doctors set up private practices. People who could afford it, including us missionaries, generally went to private doctors. Our mission agency reimbursed all our medical expenses. On several occasions, we didn't even have a bill to turn in for reimbursement! We never got bills for our trips to the emergency room with the children and for Carla's birth in the hospital. We asked and made it clear that we weren't in the government system. Apparently they had no system to calculate the cost and bill us.

Shortly after we moved to Gama, MariaRosa's older sister, Rosa, had surgery for a cancerous tumor in the abdomen. As was the custom, she wasn't told she had cancer. The incision wasn't healing well and kept on draining. She had a lot of discomfort, but everyone thought it was part of the disease. Rosa insisted that something was left inside during the surgery. Sure enough, one day she noticed a thread coming out of the incision. A piece of gauze was inside. When it was removed, the incision healed up completely. She lived for many more years.

Periodically we dealt with head lice. A common way to treat lice was to liberally sprinkle Baygon insecticide powder in the hair and wrap something tightly around the hair overnight. By morning the lice were dead. However, their dead eggs remained tightly attached to the hair follicles. It took a fine-tooth comb and nimble fingers to tediously go through the hair by hand pulling off the eggs. Shaving the head was another way to deal with lice, but we didn't resort to that method.

Dental care

Many poorer Brazilians had missing teeth. In general, people went to a dentist only when pain became severe. The offending tooth would be pulled. It wasn't uncommon to see someone with a swollen jaw, suffering in great pain because of an abscessed tooth. However, for a fee, advanced dental procedures were available.

In October of 1979, Erwin went to a dentist in Gama. He needed a root canal and crown. It must have been an office for training dentists. The process was very painful and prolonged. They couldn't get the crown to fit right – repeatedly! As our return to the U.S. approached the following June, he still had "temporary" material and needed to take painkillers. Back in the U.S., in a short time and $600 later it was all done correctly.

Other Mennonites in Brazil

A sizeable group of Holdeman Mennonites from North America had purchased land in Brazil and formed a prosperous farming community. It was about a day's drive from Brasília at Rio Verde in the state then called Mato Grosso. The Mennonite missionaries inquired about holding one of our periodic retreats in their area and worshipping with the Holdemans on a Sunday. They didn't accept us as fellow believers and rejected that idea. However, they said that as individuals they could show us hospitality. Erwin and I took them up on that.

In January 1978, our family made a trip that included an overnight stay with a Holdeman family. They received us warmly and we had a pleasant visit. We learned that when the Holdemans bought the land, it was considered worthless. In a few years they managed to enrich the soil and grow luscious big soybeans plants, much to the amazement of the local Brazilians. We observed their good farming equipment and nice houses. Like pioneers, they grew their own food and didn't have electricity. I wasn't familiar with using kerosene lanterns. When it was time to put out the light, I picked up the glass chimney to blow out the flame. It was hot! I dropped it on the cement floor, and it broke to smithereens.

The Holdemans maintained a distinctive style of clothing, especially the women's dresses and head coverings. They reached out to evangelize Brazilians, particularly through printing and distributing tracts. One tract had the theme of why it was wrong for men to wear neckties.

Erwin was pleased to receive from our hosts a black raspberry plant. We planted it in our backyard in Gama. We soon had a whole row of raspberries growing along our back wall. We gave raspberry starts to other people. The raspberries produced well and I eventually learned to make decent raspberry pies. One Sunday morning as we walked home from church, one of our neighbor boys ran toward us. He agitatedly told us that *other* boys had climbed our back wall and eaten some of the raspberries. We were amused. His face gave evidence that he was one of those boys too!

Part Three
Congregational Life of the Gama Mennonite Church

The people of the *Igreja Evangélica Menonita* of Gama welcomed us warmly when we arrived in January 1977. We bonded with them quickly. We were glad to have the support of experienced mission colleagues Otis and Betty Hochstetler, who lived about an hour away near the center of Brasília. They had worked with the Gama congregation for a number of years in addition to their own assignment with two Christian bookstores. Much as the church people appreciated Betty and Otis, they were glad to have a pastoral couple who lived near them in Gama.

Our stated assignment was evangelism, church planting, and leadership training. Perhaps because of our educational background and pastoral experience, we weren't given much guidance from the mission home office about how to proceed. We saw needs and opportunities and just plunged in.

As it turned out, much of our energy went into leadership training or discipling. We poured our lives into the leaders and youth in our congregation. Several went on to further Bible training.

We also put significant energy into some possibilities for beginning new churches.

Evangelism, less so. The Brazilians were much better at sharing Christ with others than we ever could have done in our still-developing skills in language and culture. Actually, back in the U.S. we had minimal experiences in connecting with non-believers and sharing God's love and salvation with them. Just going to another country didn't change that for us. That realization gives me some measure of feeling guilty and inadequate.

We depended heavily on our mission colleagues and the Brazilian church people as we walked together with them into many new situations. On our own, we were hesitant to reach beyond what had become our new comfort zone. We felt we learned more from the Brazilians than we ever taught them. Our accompanying presence encouraged them in their witness, we trust.

Finding a larger meeting place

When we moved to Gama, the congregation overflowed the living room in the modest house of Manoel and MariaRosa, its founding family. People sat in the hall and in bedrooms. The small bedrooms served as classrooms for Sunday school. The first big task upon our arrival in early 1977 was to obtain another meeting place. With help from the two Mennonite mission agencies in North America – Mennonite Board of Missions (MBM) in Elkhart, Indiana, and the Commission on Overseas Mission (COM) in Newton, Kansas – a house across the street from Manoel and MariaRosa's home was purchased for about $10,000. The local church people contributed their labor and finances for the renovations.

It was one of the government-built houses in that section of Gama, initially available for government employees, such as Manoel, to buy. The houses were look-alike simple structures of concrete block covered with stucco. They had three bedrooms, one bathroom with a shower but not a tub, a living room, and small kitchen. Most home buyers soon added onto their house.

It took a month of hard work to change the house into a church building. Erwin led the project. The youth of the congregation relished bashing and demolishing three interior walls to make space for a sanctuary. They helped with painting. Windows were replaced and electrical wiring repaired. Erwin and others built a concrete block wall around the church lot and covered the dirt yard with concrete. They mixed concrete by hand on the ground. They made all the concrete blocks using a two-piece mold to shape one block at a time. Other missionaries helped too, including a Kansas couple serving with Wycliffe Bible Translators in Brasília. They helped make simple church benches and little stools for the children's classes.

Dedicating the new church building

People came from near and far for the dedication of the renovated building in early May 1977. MBM missionaries Cecil and Margaret Ashley came by bus from São Paulo state. Cecil was the featured special speaker. We understood his Portuguese quite well because he spoke with our same foreign accent. A young Brazilian pastoral couple, Osvaldo and Rivani with their little girl, came from Goiania, only a few hours away by bus. They and the Ashleys all stayed at our place overnight.

Manoel and MariaRosa had the honor of cutting a ribbon for the afternoon dedication service before an estimated 130 to 150 people tried to squeeze inside. Shirtless neighborhood boys peered in through

Erwin Rempel, holding son Marc, stands at the rear with people in front of the Gama church. Marcia is in the front row with other children, 1978.

each of the sanctuary windows. The evening worship service was the climax including a baptism.

A week later, we held the first Sunday school in the new facility. The class I taught, the youngest children, increased from four to twelve to seventeen. Other classes for children and youth also grew.

An active youth group

Being a *crente* – a believer – trying to live a faithful Christian life was a challenge for the youth. They comprised a significant portion of the Gama congregation. The church was the center of their social life, which encouraged their spiritual life and shielded them from some temptations. Youth were involved in the worship services and music. In addition to the regular services at the church on Sunday, Wednesday and Saturday evenings, people frequently invited us to come to their homes for another service. Any teens not taking night classes eagerly went along. Some weeks were so full we hardly had an evening free. Our children were flexible about bedtime, and we often went as a whole family. Erwin used every opportunity for Bible teaching.

Erwin Rempel illustrates a sermon using a chalk board on the wall behind the pulpit of the Gama church, 1977.

Erwin and I were glad that the youth felt free to stop by our house. We often fed them if they were around at mealtime. Erwin involved the fellows in a variety of hands-on projects. He paid them to wash our car so they could earn some money. The girls helped with house cleaning.

Whenever Erwin traveled overnight, MariaRosa sent one of the teenage girls from her household to spend the night with me. In Brazil it was the custom that a woman with small children did not stay home alone overnight. While I didn't experience any nighttime emergency, it was reassuring to know someone was present. In the morning before the children were up, I could leave the house to walk up the street to buy the morning milk and fresh bread.

Introducing the larger world

We enjoyed helping the church youth encounter the larger world. In January 1979, Erwin took a carload of young people to Geração '79, a large youth convention held in the metropolis of São Paulo. What an experience for them to go more than 500 miles from home. They met with 4,000 young people of all denominations for nearly a week. They heard nationally and internationally known speakers such as Luis Palau, Leo Janz, and Billy Graham. The best Christian singing groups in the country were featured along with Evie Tornquist of Sweden. Each day they had intense Bible study in large and small groups. They slept in sleeping bags or on mattresses on the concrete floor of a large convention center. A highlight for our youth was meeting with seventy other Mennonite youth at the convention who had come from other parts of Brazil.

After the convention, Erwin took his carload of youth on a sightseeing tour of São Paulo. They went to the top of the tallest building and ate ice cream in a nice restaurant up there. The youth had never seen the ocean. It was about a two-hour drive from São Paulo, so Erwin took them there as well.

Special challenges

As the years went by, we noticed that a number of the young women remained single. There were few committed Christian young men who would make good husbands. They saw many sad examples of non-Christian men's lifestyles and the devastating impact on their wives and children.

After finishing secondary school, youth wanting more education took special courses to help them pass entrance exams for university or other specialty schools.

Meaningful music and worship

Brazilians enjoy music! We soon purchased a small portable pump organ for the church. The young people were intrigued. They crowded around to watch my fingers moving over the keys on the one short manual while my feet alternated up and down, pumping air to produce the sound. They all wanted to learn to play! Initially, I gave weekly music lessons to more than a dozen youth. But only Wilma, one of Manoel's daughters, stuck with practicing. She had a gift for music and in less than two years she played for congregational singing.

Worship services included a lot of singing. Typically, we began with singing hymns translated from traditional English hymns. They sang the hymns rather slowly, accompanied by the little pump organ. People brought their own small hymnbooks with only the words. After the hymns, we sang more lively and newer songs accompanied by hand clapping and several guitars. Most of those contemporary-style songs were new to me. I assumed Brazilians wrote them. It wasn't until we went back to the U.S. that I realized most of those songs were also translated from the English-speaking world. New contemporary music was sweeping through the Christian world in the 1970s. When Brazilians heard a new song they liked, it didn't take long for someone to play it on the guitar and translate it. Soon others were singing it too. Copyrights were meaningless.

I bought a guitar for myself. With help from mission co-worker Elaine Kauffman and Paulo, a talented teenage son of Manoel and MariaRosa, I learned to play the basic chords.

Paulo, Wilma, and I made a songbook of our favorite songs. My years of studying music theory came to fruition with that project. Paulo played guitar and sang, telling me what chord he was playing on the guitar. On music staff paper, I jotted down the melody notes, the chord letters, and the words. Then I painstakingly figured out the time signature, time values of each note, the key, and filled in rudimentary notes for the left hand to play.

Some of the most meaningful worship I've ever experienced was while playing that simple pump organ, in rhythm with several guitarists, accompanying the congregation's joyful singing. Our children learned the songs. We often heard Marc's strong young voice singing too, right on pitch.

Commotion in church

Erwin had preached for a number of years before we went to Brazil. However, he had to learn new skills in dealing with distractions: dogs in the church, children outside peering in the open windows, children running in and out during the service, late comers loudly calling out a general greeting as they entered, noisy games played in the street outside, a huge moth that he had to kill before proceeding with communion, a noisy toilet that sometimes kept on running, his own children misbehaving (that could happen anywhere!), guitarists tuning or practicing while other people are speaking to the congregation, a

Angela Rempel plays small pump organ at church with teen musicians Wilma and Paulo, 1977.

little girl tinkling on the floor near the pulpit, drunks trying to add their comments, and loud music from the house across the street.

One service coincided with the first significant rain of the rainy season. Shortly after the rain, large yellow ants sprouted wings and flew up from the ground in search of a mate. That particular evening, the ants flew up like a cloud heading to the nearest lights. Our church lights were on, the windows had no screens, so in came the flying ants. Marci did as the other children, catching them and tearing off their wings. Everyone swatted flying ants. I was up front playing the pump organ. Ants settled on me. Some even climbed down the front of my dress! It was hard to keep playing and not deal with those critters. By the next morning, the ants lost their wings and lay on the ground, dying or dead.

Commotion of a different kind occurred at one evening worship service arranged by the youth group. They had invited youth from other churches. Erwin stayed home with the children, nursing a cold. There were some good testimonies from people whose lives changed dramatically when they accepted Christ. When the invited speaker closed his message with a prayer, he launched the group into an emotional, loud, charismatic-style service complete with speaking in tongues.

"Lord, are you still here in all this noise?" I wondered. People wailed, cried, shouted, and prayed aloud. I had never experienced anything like that. We'd heard about this in the fast-growing Pentecostal churches. But, here? In our church?

Three of our youth joined in the emotionalism, but the rest just quietly observed. For me, it felt as if God had left. After the service, I talked with MariaRosa. She also had never been at anything like that. Her feelings and conclusions were much like mine. She even compared it to what goes on in spiritist centers.

Spiritism

Spiritism in Brazil was a pervasive and complex set of religious beliefs practiced by a large percentage of Brazilians. Spiritism apparently blends traditional beliefs of indigenous people, the former African slaves, and Catholicism. At the edges of the roads, especially at intersections, we frequently saw spiritist sacrifices of a few burned candles amid feathers and other trinkets. At beaches, we saw people dressed in long white garments wade out into the surf. They floated flowers and candles on the water to the goddess of the sea. Other forms of spiritism were more intellectual and appealed to people with more education.

Training new church leaders

Several of the young people expressed interest in further biblical study and ministry. We were pleased to see God working in the lives of these potential church leaders. But where should they go to school? The only Mennonite institution in Brazil was ISBIM, in Curitiba about a thousand miles to the south. The school was a joint effort by the German-speaking Mennonites of southern Brazil, although classes were taught in Portuguese. Several of the Gama youth went to ISBIM and received valuable Bible training. They also encountered significant "culture shock" there.

Sharing with women

Often all the women would be talking at once during our Thursday afternoon women's meetings. The church women met weekly

Angela Rempel, 2nd from left, leads weekly women's group in Gama. 1977.

for a time of fellowship, singing, and prayer, usually in MariaRosa's small living room. I shared simple Bible studies or devotionals. Those times together, sharing our concerns and praying for each other, were important and strengthened our spiritual lives.

Attempting to start new churches

Francisca was a young woman married to one of the sons of Otacilia, a woman very faithful in our church even though her husband and sons weren't much interested. Francisca longed for Christian fellowship, but she and her husband lived in Ceilandia, another satellite city some distance away. They had bought a government-built house in a new development. Each lot featured a small house with running water, sewer, and electricity. The expectation was that families would add onto the small house, but at least they began with basic infrastructure.

Once a month, with a carload of women from the Gama church, I drove over for a time of prayer and fellowship with Francisca. The hope was that other women from her neighborhood would join us and that a church would begin in that fast-growing neighborhood. But that didn't happen.

João and Cesarina had moved to Occidental, a new town just outside the Federal District. João worked for the American Embassy in Brasília, spoke English fairly well, and was very musical. She had come from the poor northeastern part of Brazil and stayed home with their three small children. On Sunday afternoons, Erwin and I filled our car with folks from the Gama church and drove to Occidental to hold a worship service in João and Cesarina's home. Some of their new neighbors checked it out.

One woman who visited the group asked, "What are the rules of your church?" The Pentecostal churches she knew all had their own list of prohibitions – so people picked a church with rules they could live with.

João and Cesarina didn't have a car, so sometimes we took them groceries they had bought in the city. When one of their neighbors saw us unloading the groceries, they thought getting free groceries was part of our church life.

Our efforts at planting churches didn't appear to be effective. However, when I visited Gama in 2006, it was exciting to visit several new churches or preaching points in the surrounding area, all begun with Brazilian leadership.

Teaching children

Children of all ages were plentiful in Gama. Most families we knew had six to nine children. Sunday mornings we held Sunday school classes. I often taught the youngest ones with the help of older girls who eventually took over. We also did a yearly weeklong morning Bible school during a break from school. My Christian education classes back at Grace Bible Institute provided me with practical skills. My collection of flannelgraph and other visual aids was useful. A good substitute for glue was a squashed grain of cooked rice. It worked well for any craft project.

Reaching beyond Gama

Initially we devoted all our energy to the work in Gama. But it wasn't long until once again Erwin's administrative abilities surfaced and were

Angela Rempel and Wilma, at the left, teach a children's class at Gama church, 1978.

recognized more widely. He was soon deeply involved in the work of the Brazilian Mennonite church organization known as AEM. He was asked to take the position of its executive secretary. That had always been held by one of the foreign missionaries. He strongly felt that after him, the next executive secretary should be a Brazilian.

He attended many meetings of the AEM board to discuss tedious issues of revising a constitution and by-laws, pastor salary structures, sales and purchases of properties for churches and bookstores, and placements of missionaries and Brazilian pastors. Perhaps one reason he was asked to give leadership is that he represented a fresh and neutral perspective.

Going on retreat

The annual Carnival celebrations in Brazil held many temptations for young people. In addition to the scantily-clad dancers parading with their seductive moves, the drunken revelry and parties promoted an atmosphere that glamorized the "lust of the flesh." The word carnival literally means a festival of the flesh.

To provide wholesome options for the youth, churches planned alternative activities during the long Carnival weekend that preceded Ash Wednesday.

Ever-creative Betty Hochstetler saw the potential of some undeveloped Brazilian farmland owned by an American friend of theirs from Ohio. Russ Yoder had built a one-room cabin and small open shelter that he and his wife used on their infrequent visits to their *fazenda* in Brazil. From where we lived in Gama, it took about two hours by car to get there. By bus it would be about four hours. Twelve miles of rough unpaved road lay beyond the closest bus stop. That was certainly far enough away from the bright city lights and all night partying.

Several times we loaded small cars with youth and food and drove out to the *fazenda* for retreats, not just at Carnival time. The city-raised youth enjoyed the undeveloped open spaces. The 1978 carnival retreat attracted thirty-one youth and several adults. How could a small one-room cabin accommodate that many? It was a challenge!

The weather was good, so most activities were outside. Cooking was the biggest challenge. We cooked on an open-air wood fire and a small

Erwin Rempel, standing, leads a Bible study at a youth retreat, 1978.

two-burner portable propane stove. The fellows slept outside, some on hammocks. The females all slept in the cabin. All the cooking supplies had to be moved at night so mattresses could cover the entire cabin floor. My spot was just inside the door on a sleeping bag. I struggled with enough faith in the Lord to go to sleep on the floor, wondering what might slither in under the door beside me. It is a good thing that I didn't learn until later that someone had killed a tarantula spider in the cabin where we had slept. I can deal with mice better than with large spiders!

After the retreat, I was driving our car behind the other vehicles. Loaded with youth and equipment, it was a challenge to drive on the rough, unpaved road. Suddenly there was a funny noise from the car. No one in the cars ahead of me saw me flash the headlights. It was a flat tire, a common occurrence, especially on that stretch of unpaved road. Because I always made sure to have one young fellow in my car who could help change a tire, I didn't think we had a problem. Then we discovered there were two flat tires! And only one spare tire. Eventually

Erwin drove back looking for us. He took the flat tires several miles to the nearest repair shop. After that, he drove behind me, which was a good thing because the rough road caused another problem. Our car started making funny noises and losing power. Erwin quickly reconnected a hose to the gas tank before all the gas ran out.

Building new retreat facilities

Otis and Betty Hochstetler had been sharing our retreat experiences with their home congregations in the U.S.

"What would it take to develop a campground for your retreats? Our church is looking for special projects for the coming year." This question and offer came from Yellow Creek Mennonite Church, of Goshen, Indiana, Otis's home church. They offered to contribute $7,000 and send a work team to help with construction. Landowner Russ Yoder offered to give one hundred acres of his undeveloped land for the project.

Would this feel like a foreign project without much ownership by the Brazilians? There would be plenty of work for Brazilian church people to do before and after the work team. We prayerfully discussed the pros and cons with Brazilian church people and other missionaries. We accepted the offers and set to work.

Using axes, big hoes, shovels, strong hands and muscles, Erwin and other men and young fellows chopped a kilometer-long entrance road, about a half mile, through the scrubby trees and brush to the designated retreat site. Then they cleared the building site, marked and laid foundations, and dug holes for a well and pit latrines – all by hand. That hard preparation work was done before the work team arrived.

Erwin's task was acquiring the building supplies for the work team. What a challenge! Because of evidence of thieves in the area, they couldn't leave work tools and supplies out there. They managed to hide a few things in the bush.

A construction shop that promised to make and deliver 3,500 concrete blocks had only 900 blocks ready two days before the work team was scheduled to begin. Erwin scurried to other places, having to pay higher prices and delivery fees. He rejected one truckload of concrete blocks. The blocks crumbled and fell apart as they were lifted, by hand, from the truck and placed on the ground.

Self-supporting Mennonite mission workers Lee and Mary Alice Hertzler came from southern Brazil to share their expertise in construction and cooking. The work crew from Yellow Creek Church, seven married couples, was a cheerful group. They worked hard, had a lot of fun, and accomplished a great deal in two weeks. They slept and ate at Russ Yoder's original small cabin, a thirteen-minute drive from the new campsite.

It was quite an experience for the visiting Americans to live for a couple of weeks without electricity and other things we all considered "necessary." Without refrigeration, there was no cold water to drink after working in the hot sun. There was no light to switch on at night; no washing machine to wash their dirty and sweaty work clothes.

All the labor was done by hand, including mixing the cement. The women helped with the construction and did all the laundry by hand. Prayers were answered and there were no serious illnesses or accidents. The experience was very meaningful for the folks from Indiana.

Workteam from Yellow Creek Mennonite Church in Indiana constructs several simple buildings for a retreat center in Brazil, 1979.

209

The work team's two weeks ended on Easter Sunday. The walls and roofs were up for two dormitories, a shower house, two outhouses, and the main building with a kitchen and larger room for meetings and dining. The camp, named *Aconchego Cristão*, (Christian Fellowship) was dedicated that Sunday. A chartered bus brought people from Gama. There were 105 people, along with the work team, who attended a joyous worship service and meal.

There was still a lot of work to do. Our car made many more trips to *Aconchego* loaded with building supplies and energetic youth. One time we discovered a very unhappy anteater down in the pit of an outhouse. It couldn't climb out. Someone slanted a plank down the hole before we all left. The next time we went to the camp, we were glad to see that the anteater was no longer in the hole.

We were ready to plan overnight retreats for various groups.

Using the new retreat facilities

After a regional conference, I wrote the following:

> We'd come a long way from our first retreat group of thirteen young people, packed into two cars, carrying nearly all the food pre-prepared.
>
> Now, most of the sixty people comfortably arrived by chartered bus. Their ages ranged from two to seventy-two. Women and children all slept in bunk beds, and only Erwin slept outside because he wanted to be away from the men who snored. A Brazilian woman and a few others had arrived a day earlier to do the cooking. Water came plentifully by just opening faucets in the shower rooms, kitchen, and at the outdoor washtub. This was the first opportunity for the adults to attend such a retreat and they loved it.
>
> Our campground truly is a place where we can retreat from the rush of life, and feel closer to God and the beauties of nature that He created. The palm trees silhouetted against the night sky made bright by a full moon, the night creatures singing their songs, birds raising their voices in morning praise as the colorful squawking parrots flutter from their

nighttime perches in the palm trees; apparently dead trees suddenly bursting into colorful flowers; new growth at this time of spring – all these help to draw our attention to the Creator who cares more for us than He does for the birds and flowers." *From Rempel Report, September 14, 1979*

Looking back

During the rest of our time in Brazil, *Aconchego Cristão* was truly a place of warm Christian fellowship, as its name meant. Young people and others were challenged and grew spiritually there.

After we left Brazil, we learned that *Aconchego* became somewhat of a white elephant, with dissension among the churches about its use. It was eventually abandoned. When our family visited Brazil in 2005, hardly any evidence of buildings was found in the high grass and overgrowth.

When I visited Brazil in 2006, I met a woman who told me that years earlier as a young person she accepted Christ out at *Aconchego*. That had changed her life.

People of all ages attend the first regional retreat at the new retreat center, July 1979.

Part Four
More Stories of Life in Brazil

One of the couples we met at language school also moved to the Federal District for ministry. They lived in a mission-owned house that fit in with the other large houses in an upscale section of Brasília. From their nice big house, they drove out to various poor areas in the satellite cities for church planting. Contemplating how differently Erwin and I lived and worked, I wrote, "Some missionaries say that their relationship to the people is not based on things and that they can live however they want."

In contrast, some of the Mennonite mission workers felt the struggle of inequality so intensely that they opted to live on a self-support basis. They lived on what they earned in Brazil. The Mennonite mission board usually provided them some support for health care and periodic travel to the U.S.

We never considered either of those extremes. Even when finding a rental house in Gama was difficult, we never thought about living in Brasília and just going out to Gama at times. Had we done so, we would have missed so much. The casual and easy interaction with our church people couldn't have happened much, if at all, had we not lived in their neighborhood, within walking distance. Those years there were the closest we've ever come to what some call "living in community."

Our time in Brazil changed our worldview and political perspectives for the rest of our lives. We realized how rich and privileged we are and that God is at work throughout the world.

A Shooting on the Street

Three shots ring out. A pickup roars away, tires screeching around the corner. An off-duty policeman lies dying in the street in front of his house. Is this the opening scene of a TV crime show?

No, it was late on a Sunday afternoon and the residential street in front of our church was filled with children playing, people visiting and, of course, guys playing soccer. Inside our church, I practiced with a group of young people for special music for the worship service that evening. Playing the pump organ, I concentrated on coordinating with the guitars, a tambourine, and a flute. I hadn't noticed the shots. The young people had. Some thought it sounded like firecrackers.

Hearing the screams and shouts in the street, Andrea ran out of the church to see what happened. Seeing the man lying on the street, she erroneously thought it was her father or brother. She cried uncontrollably. However, it was the 53-year-old man from a house across the street from the church.

Apparently the pickup had stopped in the area where the fellows played soccer. When one of the players objected, the 24-year-old driver, who had been drinking, pulled out a knife. The off-duty policeman approached and identified himself as being with the police. Hearing that, one of the other occupants in the pickup handed a gun to the driver, who promptly shot the policeman three times before speeding away.

Few people in the neighborhood had cars to quickly take the injured man to the hospital. Had I driven to the church that afternoon instead of walking, I'm sure I'd have been asked to use our car for that purpose. The only other person in our congregation to have a car at the time was a young man who drove up just as the shooting occurred. Apparently someone had called to him, but he just stood leaning against his car with arms folded. We are not sure if he didn't understand or refused to help because he didn't want to be involved. Someone farther down the street got a car and they hurried futilely to the nearby hospital.

The next day we visited the widow, left with ten children ages two to twenty-two. She mentioned having called to a young fellow to help, but he wouldn't. Several others commented, and the testimony of our church was damaged.

The assassin was caught the next day. A spoiled "daddy's boy" with a criminal record, his wealthy parents bought his way out of justice. The newspaper account was inaccurate and made it appear as if the shooting was in self-defense rather than a cold-blooded murder. (from *Rempel Report*, October 1978)

Celebrating Christmas in Brazil

Some object stuck out of the window from the driver's side of the VW ahead of us on the four-lane highway. As we passed, we saw it was a five-foot-long tree branch, completely bare. Our Brazilian friends

213

riding with us immediately answered our question as to whatever someone wanted with a dead tree branch other than for firewood. It was to make a Christmas tree!

It was common to make a Christmas tree by wrapping a bare branch in white cotton – to imitate snow, which most had never seen. They put it upright in a container and hung ornaments on it. Artificial trees were quite expensive and spindly. Real evergreen trees were rare.

Christmas in Brazil had many of the same features as Christmas in North America – stores full of toys, decorations in the streets and shops, exchange of names for gift giving, Christmas programs in the schools and churches, and Santa Claus, who was known as *Papai Noel*.

To us the use of candles is an attractive Christmas decoration, but not for the believers in many of the churches. The use of candles, in any form other than to give illumination when the electricity failed, reminded them too much of the rituals of the Catholic Church and spiritism.

Christmas music in church was all familiar. Previous missionaries had translated the carols from English. Public places played all the familiar secular Christmas songs as well.

We found it hard to get into any sort of "Christmas mood" during hot weather. In the southern hemisphere, December is in the midst of the hot summer season. The poinsettias, which grow into large bushes there, don't bloom in December but from May through September. It was too hot to bake Christmas cookies and pies. Those differences helped us focus on the most important fact of Christmas – that Jesus Christ came to earth to be our Savior and Lord. May we never become so taken up with the activities, customs, and emotions of the Christmas season that we forget the true meaning. (adapted from *Rempel Report* December 1978)

Traveling by bus

Erwin attended many meetings that related to the work of AEM, the association of Mennonite churches in Brazil. Most of the AEM directors lived in the southern parts of Brazil. Southern Brazil was highly developed and attracted millions of people seeking comfortable living conditions, employment, and education. It was more economical for

Erwin to take an overnight bus to meetings in the south, than for several others to make the trek up our way.

During trips to and from southern Brazil, the buses stopped at nice stations with snack shops and clean bathrooms. Women sat by the bathroom entrances and handed out toilet paper, for a tip.

Sometimes, while Erwin slept on the bus, someone stole cash from his briefcase on the rack above him. He was embarrassed to have to borrow money at his destination.

Venturing north by bus

Several Mennonite churches were in a remote area well to the north of Brasília. That's where Mennonites began mission work in Brazil. Trips that Erwin took north were quite different from his usual trips to the south. Northbound buses weren't as nice as the buses that headed south, nor were the stopping places as nice.

One time he and mission colleague Bob Gerber went by bus, as usual, to a regional pastors' conference in the north. After a long day of travel, Erwin and Bob arrived at the end of the bus line. It was too late to take a ferry across the wide river to Conceição, where they planned to spend the night. Someone took them across in a small motor boat.

The next day, Erwin and Bob arrived in the small village of Goianorte, the site of the pastors' conference. They were warmly received and shown to their accommodations for the next three nights – a small structure made of thatched palms, a packed-down dirt floor, and hammocks to sleep in. To get water, a bucket attached to a rope over a pulley was lowered between logs placed across the wide opening of a hand-dug well. To remove some of the dirt and sweat accumulating on their bodies in the hot, humid weather, they took a bucket of water into the "shower house." That consisted of three "walls" of palm branches, a short curtain as a door, the open sky for a ceiling, and a dirt floor. Bathers stood on a small wooden board to keep their feet off the wet, muddy floor as they sloshed water from the bucket. Toilet facilities were a path into the brush. Period. Some said that was better than a stinky outhouse.

Erwin felt as though he was in the Wild West. One man carrying a revolver looked in on their meeting, obviously searching for someone. A common subject of conversation was who had recently killed whom.

After the pastors' conference, Erwin and Bob rode in a jeep that broke down before it reached the intersection of unpaved roads where they could get a bus to the main highway. Someone driving a VW bug picked them up. Bob is just as tall as Erwin, but they squeezed into the VW and eventually got to the bus stop. Another man waiting at the bus stop carried equipment for finding gold.

None of the seats were very good on the rickety bus. Some seats stayed permanently forward, others permanently back, and others just rocked back and forth or were crooked. A poor family in tattered clothing got onto the already overcrowded bus. They carried sacks of corn and several live chickens tied by the legs.

Reaching the paved highway, Erwin and Bob caught yet another bus that continued overnight to Brasília. Erwin experienced one of the most miserable nights he ever spent on a bus. It was hot and humid, the seat was too small, and the bus stopped frequently. A family caused a commotion all night with their loud talking. Their children climbed over the seats and up into the luggage racks.

That trip provided an understanding of life in the interior and a new appreciation for the people who lived and worked there. The pastors and lay leaders from the seven Mennonite churches in that region evidenced a good spirit of unity. Their time together at the conference in worship, discussions, and fellowship meant a lot to them.

Baptizing new believers

Several new believers came into the Gama church during the years Erwin and I served there. Riba was a young man who came from the north to stay with his relatives who were part of our Gama church. Riba's nineteen-year-old cousin in Gama talked to him about Christ and brought him to church.

Filozina was seventeen when she married a man older than she. When she moved with him to Gama, she discovered that he had ten children left to him when his first wife deserted him. A woman in our church befriended Filozina, led her to the Lord, and helped her in various ways.

Several other young people, from non-Christian homes, also claimed to accept Christ. However, after a few weeks or months, they disappeared from the church.

A strange religion

There is a strange god in Brazil. The worship of this god is almost constant. People from all levels of society worship this god – from poorest to richest. The places of worship vary from unstructured, informal dirt areas to one of the world's largest meetinghouses. The amount of money spent in the honor and worship of this god could probably feed all the hungry people in Brazil or provide classrooms for the thousands who unsuccessfully seek to study in the few existing universities.

Rivalry is intense among the various branches of this religion, but that rivalry is all forgotten every four years for a month of special worship. Those who can, go to the temple where the pantheon of gods is present. Others watch the special rituals on TV. On as many as seven holy days in that month, the whole country comes to a standstill to worship simultaneously. There is more unity than in a war, more excitement than at carnival, and more devotion than at Christmas or Good Friday. Stores and offices close, classrooms are empty, and the streets are silent for about two hours. If the desired results are achieved during those two hours, the country bursts into an unrestrained spasm of emotionalism. In the exuberance of worship, tremendous quantities of alcoholic beverages are consumed, fingers and faces are permanently disfigured by firecrackers, and some human lives are sacrificed. Hospitals put on additional emergency personnel to handle the results of the excesses of worship. The actual benefits to the individual worshipper are almost non-existent.

What god is this? *Futebo*l, also known as soccer.

Learning generosity

Erwin and I visited with Manoel and MariaRosa one day. We told them about a beggar woman who came to our door earlier that day. They said the same woman had been at their door, too. MariaRosa told us how they related to people in need.

Instead of skepticism about the need, they felt it is necessary to give with the responsibility of the need's validity being on the shoulder of the one asking. They gave as unto the Lord.

Instead of passing by the beggars on the streets and in the markets, they always gave a little, even if only a small coin worth only a penny.

Instead of giving a little out of a plenteous supply, they generously gave from their little. A cup of raw rice wasn't nearly enough to feed the fourteen mouths of her household, so MariaRosa would cheerfully give it to someone who had fewer mouths to feed.

Instead of insisting on repayment of loans, they continued to "loan" knowing it would never be repaid.

Instead of charging small fees to neighbors who used their phone and ran up the phone bill, they would rather get rid of the phone.

As we finished our conversation with Manoel and MariaRosa, I was glad I had given to the beggar woman even though I did not believe all of her story. But MariaRosa had not only given, she had invited the woman to come in, sit down and rest a bit, served her coffee, shared Christ with her, and assured her that it is better to beg than to steal. (adapted from June 1978 *Rempel Report*)

Learning gratitude

It was a Thursday afternoon in November, the same day when Americans celebrated Thanksgiving Day, which wasn't a holiday in Brazil. It was the day for the monthly visit by women from the Gama church to have our usual Thursday women's Bible study and prayer time in the home of Francisca. Francisca lived in another satellite city and looked forward to the monthly Christian fellowship. It was hard for her to attend church.

On that particular day, MariaRosa couldn't go along. I left our little Carla there, as usual, and filled my car with other women. On the return, we could see from a distance a large dark cloud hovering over Gama. It looked like a heavy storm, not uncommon that time of year as the weather transitioned from the dry season to the rainy season.

We encountered moderate rain as we entered Gama. By the time we drove only a few more blocks, the streets were full of water, wind lashed the rain against the car, thunder crackled, and we saw sparks drop from electric wires. The farther I drove, the more water we encountered.

"The water will come into the car. The motor will stop. The gears won't work," I thought anxiously. But the car didn't falter nor take in any water. I managed to drop off several of the women.

A sad sight greeted me when I arrived at MariaRosa's house. Recent remodeling of her house was poorly done. The roofing wasn't nailed down properly. The winds took off or shifted roofing tiles. Water dripped and streamed down in eight rooms of the house. Little Carla was fine, but most of the other older children were about in tears trying to move beds and clothing to dry spots.

The storm ended suddenly. People went out to survey damages. MariaRosa's house seemed to have sustained the most damage. Neighbors, included several who weren't believers, came to see the mess. They heard MariaRosa giving thanks!

"Praise the Lord that I was home and had not gone to Ceilandia leaving only (teenage) Fatima here alone with the three little children. Praise the Lord that Emanuel (a teenage fellow) was here. He climbed

up and got one big piece of roofing back in place over the kitchen. Praise the Lord no one was hurt. Praise the Lord the storm came during the daytime rather than at night."

One neighbor asked, "After all you do to help others, why does God allow this to happen?" MariaRosa told him, "These things happen to all kinds of people, but Christians have the Lord to help them endure difficulties."

I was amazed at all the things she found to be grateful for – it truly was a Thanksgiving Day!

MariaRosa de Souza, 1980.

Part Five
North America Ministry from
June 1980 to June 1981

Preparing for North America Ministry

The usual cycle was for missionaries to spend four years overseas and then one year back in North America for what was referred to as a furlough. But Mennonites reacted to that as being a military term, and in our time they called it North American Assignment (NAA) or later, North America Ministry (NAM). However, it was easier to just call it furlough.

With the comings and goings of other Mennonite missionaries in Brazil, it seemed best to stretch our first term to four and a half years and begin our NAM in June of 1980. Yearlong furloughs, we learned, are very disruptive to life and ministry – planning and packing take about six months, then the year away, plus about another six months to get resettled. Unsurprisingly, some missionaries were opting for a cycle of three years overseas with three months back in North America.

Who would give leadership to the Gama church while we were gone? Where would we store our belongings? Where would we live during NAM? Where would the children go to school? Which churches would we speak in and share about the ministry in Brazil? What kind of vehicle would we use for a year? Where would we be assigned for ministry when we returned to Brazil? So many questions and details.

Erwin worked at the leadership issues together with the leaders of the Brazilian Mennonite churches. A "garage" was built onto the church building to store our things for a year, after which it would be used for a classroom. With mothballs tucked into everything and locks welded to the doors, we stored our things in the newly-built church garage and left them in God's hand. Our small, costlier electrical items we stored in the basement of the Christian bookstore that Otis operated in Brasília. I was at peace about our things, and indeed, nothing was tampered with in our absence.

I had relinquished most of my involvement with church activities when Carla was born in March that year. My star organ student, Wilma, capably played the little pump organ for worship. It is a good thing I didn't realize how seldom I would ever again regularly accompany church singing and how much I would miss doing it.

My birthday that year, June 20, was one of the most tiring days of my life. We were busy from morning to night with packing, moving things to storage, and cleaning the house we had enjoyed for three and a half years. Several times the owner of the house had wanted us to move to another of his properties. Once he wanted to sell the house. We were grateful that we managed to avoid moving until the end of our term.

Flying to USA
Our departure date was set for Monday, June 23. Once again we began extensive travel with a baby about three months old as we had done five years earlier when Marc was an infant. I've concluded that is the best age to travel with an infant because the child still sleeps a lot and doesn't need any supplemental food.

The Varig Airline flight from Brasília to Miami always stopped in the Brazilian city of Manaus. We decided to take advantage of that opportunity to spend most of a day and night in Manaus. That is where two major rivers join to form the mighty Amazon River. We took a boat tour that included seeing where lighter and darker waters of the two rivers meet to flow together for another thousand miles to the Atlantic Ocean. As one would expect of a tropical rainforest, it was hot, humid, and green all around.

The next leg of our flight to Miami didn't depart Manaus until past midnight. But we needed to check out of our hotel and went to the airport in the early evening. At one point, we moved our little family group to another part of the airport. Erwin nearly had a heart attack when a security guard chased us down. The guard held Erwin's small pouch with all of our documents and money. We had left it behind in the airport lounge. Surely God used the guard to help watch over us.

Experiencing reverse culture shock
It's called reverse culture shock – coming back to one's country of origin after living in another country.

Portuguese words first slipped off my tongue whenever I spoke to strangers in the airports and public places. I realized I had actually

221

begun to think in Portuguese. Things looked different, even the American money. Dimes felt incredibly small and hard to handle.

My parents picked us up at the airport in Wichita, Kansas, in what at first looked to us like a boxy limousine. But, no, it was just an average American Ford car, so much larger than the typical car in Brazil.

The American houses painted in basic earth tones and neutral colors looked drab. Wall-to-wall-carpeting, heavy draperies, and fabric-covered upholstered furniture made homes feel heavy and dark – such a contrast to the bright, open, and airy houses in Brazil. To me, American houses looked cluttered with a lot of stuff.

Having lived close to poverty for several years, we calculated that even my parents' modest retirement house and yard was big enough for four Brazilian households, with an average of more than ten people per household. However, the clean streets and neatly trimmed green lawns were a refreshing sight.

Shopping in America again – what a challenge that was at first! Even having shopped in the largest and nicest of Brazil's stores, the first trip to an American supermarket overwhelmed me. Breakfast cereals of all brands, sizes, and flavors filled an entire aisle. Descriptions on hair care products – oatmeal, honey, apple cider, and coconut – made me wonder if I was in the food section. There were so many choices to make for each item on the shopping list. A well-meaning and frugal friend had thrust a handful of discount coupons in my hand. Amidst all the other choices to make, I just couldn't deal with trying to match the right brand and size to a coupon for a few cents off. I stuck them back into my purse.

The children had their own adjustments and amazement. Marc, age five, and Marci, nearly nine, wanted to collect paper cups that had plastic lids with holes for straws, and soft drink cans (a novelty compared to the glass bottles we usually saw in Brazil). They were intrigued by doors that opened automatically at the supermarket.

We were welcomed with a surprising number of hugs. We didn't recall Americans hugging that much before.

"So, what was it like in Brazil?" people asked. Before we could figure out some sort of answer other than a simplistic, "Just fine," they often changed the subject to something more tangible to their own lives. Other than some perfunctory questions, even our family didn't really know how to ask questions about Brazil. We realized that Americans, in general, have little awareness of the broader world while Brazilians usually knew a surprising amount about the U.S.

Putting my feelings into a box

I had so completely taken into my heart some of the Gama church people that I keenly missed them during our time in the U.S. We had shared our lives, our homes, our joys and sorrows. It hurt to consider being reassigned somewhere in the state of São Paulo after furlough rather than returning to Gama. I began to deliberately put my emotions into a box so that I could function. Unfortunately, I think that because of that, I sometimes have found it difficult to really bond again with people other than our family.

My mother's cancer recurs

After sixteen years in remission, my mother's recurrence of cancer hung over our yearlong time in the U.S. She took chemo and then radiation treatments. She often wasn't feeling well. On several long visits to Newton, we stayed in their basement, which accommodated us quite well, although Marci may have used the second bedroom upstairs. But I was always concerned that mom was overworking herself on our behalf. As long as she was up and around and doing things, I wasn't sure how much I should just insist and do. At the end of our year there, however, she had good reports and a good prognosis.

Too busy to rest

The first few weeks back in the U.S. were packed full – medical checkups, dental work, financial matters, and preparing for presentations in churches. We obtained appropriate clothes from second-hand stores, friends, and family, plus a few new items found on sale.

Erwin flew from Kansas out to New Jersey to get a new small Datsun station wagon we bought through a missionary auto service. He drove it back to Kansas alone. We had never had an air-conditioned car up to that point, and didn't want to pay extra for something we didn't think we needed. However, that car came with air conditioning – and we greatly appreciated it in the heat of that summer.

Marc, 5, waits in the Datsun station wagon while Erwin Rempel finishes loading a top carrier, summer 1980.

We thought it had been hot our last day in Brazil as we toured the Amazon. However, the next day in Kansas the heat was worse, although not as humid. We arrived at the beginning of what turned out to be the 1980 summer of record-breaking heat. Daily high temperatures passed one hundred degrees for the rest of June, July and much of August, with an occasional drop into the nineties.

Not only was the weather heating up, so was the 1980 presidential campaign. One of the first things we heard from then-candidate Ronald Reagan was, "Are you better off now than you were four years ago?" That apparently resonated with Americans who had lived through the high inflation and depressed economy of the recent years with Jimmy Carter as president. But to us, having lived among people so much poorer than any of the Americans we knew, that question appalled us. We realized how much our time in Brazil changed our political perspectives. However, we traveled so much that we didn't register to vote in that election.

Visiting a big church

Our first Sunday in the States, we went with my parents to First Mennonite Church in Newton, where they were deeply involved in the congregational life. Attendance there was about 500 – such a contrast to our small fellowship of believers in Brazil. With our young children, we sat in the back. At the end of the service, pastor Epp – the same Albert Epp who participated in Erwin's baptism in Downey, California – asked us to stand as he introduced us to the congregation. It looked like a sea with waves of white and gray turning around to look at us – mostly older people with white hair, white faces, and wearing pale summer clothing. It was so different from the dark hair, brown faces, and brightly colored clothing of Brazilians.

A busy year lay ahead of us. It began with preparing church presentations, visiting family in Kansas, Nebraska, and Montana, and attending conferences during the summer. In the fall, we anticipated living again in Harleysville, Pennsylvania. From January to May we were signed up to audit classes at the Mennonite seminary in Elkhart, Indiana. That would leave a few weeks before our NAM ended and we returned to Brazil. As it turned out, two weddings and a retirement also occurred within our extended family during our year in the U.S. We were glad we could reconnect in significant ways with our families and be present for those important life changes.

Preparing slide sets

Now it was our turn to prepare and show slide sets. We'd had years of watching other missionaries show slides. Before leaving Brazil, I planned, wrote, and took photos for three different sound-slide sets, each about eight minutes long. During those first busy days in Newton, we went to a local studio where a professional radio announcer recorded the narration. The studio added Brazilian background music. When we showed a sound-slide set in a darkened church, I juggled holding a flashlight in one hand to shine it on the printed narration held in the other hand. I could have used yet another hand to advance slides with the narration. I was surprised by the affirmation for my writing and slide sets.

Weddings

My sister, LaRita, was already engaged to Darrel Claassen, who grew up in Newton. He was the third generation Claassen to operate Claassen Hardware and Lumber in Newton. His grandfather had been Mennonite, but his father had married a lovely woman who was Methodist. Darrel grew up in the Methodist church and was active there.

Since our speaking engagements filled up basically all the weekends in the fall, our availability the first weekend in November 1980 determined that as my sister's wedding date. We were all involved in her wedding, except for baby Carla.

Erwin's sister, Barbara, came to see us in Newton soon after we arrived from Brazil. It had been nearly five years since we had seen her. However, we learned we weren't the only reason she had driven down from Omaha where she worked at Grace College of the Bible (formerly Grace Bible Institute). She was rethinking her relationship with a Kansas fellow she dated about a decade earlier as a college student at Grace. She reconnected with him too that weekend in Kansas. They soon announced their engagement and planned a wedding for the Saturday before Easter 1981, in Omaha. We were involved in that wedding as well.

Several times during our year in the U.S., we stopped in Omaha to see Erwin's brother, Norman, and his family. Norman taught at Grace College of the Bible, our alma mater. Liz worked as a nurse. Our children and theirs were fairly close in age and played well together. Norm and Erwin never ran out of things to talk about – both serious and funny.

Attending mission seminar and
General Conference at Estes Park

A few weeks after our arrival in the U.S., we packed the children and our new little station wagon and headed west from my parents' place in Kansas toward the mountains of Colorado. We hoped for cooler temperatures, but it was abnormally hot there too.

At the annual retreat for missionaries, held near Colorado Springs that year, we enjoyed meeting mission workers from various places around the world. The following week we drove on to Estes Park in Colorado for the 1980 triennial session of the General Conference

Erwin Rempel enjoys infant daughter Carla while attending the General Conference triennial sessions at Estes Park, Colorado, 1980. Photo appeared in The Mennonite. *Used by permission.*

Mennonite Church. We entered the registration area where lines of people waited to register. Infant Carla was quite fussy and had drooled all over herself and me. Romaine Sprunger, the wife of the pastor that followed us when we left Indian Valley Mennonite Church five years earlier, greeted us. Like a calming angel, she took Carla so Erwin and I could complete the registration process.

Unbeknown to us, someone took a picture of Erwin enjoying little Carla amid the crowd. The photo was printed in *The Mennonite*. We used that same pose to take photos of Erwin holding each eventual new grandchild.

Visiting in Montana

After those conferences, we headed toward Montana with a stop near Mount Rushmore in South Dakota. Erwin's brother Norm and his family joined us there, much to the little cousins' delight. During several August weeks in Montana with his folks, Erwin enjoyed reconnecting with the farm. The children rode on the combine during wheat harvest. Erwin's former classmates who remained on the farm were doing well. Some of them piloted their own small planes to oversee their large acreages and to make trips to larger cities.

The long drive from Montana to Pennsylvania looked daunting – five long days. However, we stopped in Elkhart, Indiana, to visit with Lawrence Greaser, the Latin America director of Mennonite Board of Missions who administered the Brazil work. We looked at the house in Elkhart where we would live during the last part of our North America Assignment. Then we continued east, eager to settle into a house by ourselves. From the time we had packed up our household in Brazil, we spent ten weeks as nomads, living out of suitcases.

Living in Pennsylvania again

What a delightful home awaited us in Harleysville, where we had lived for the seven years Erwin was pastor at Indian Valley Mennonite Church before we went to Brazil. An older slate-sided two-story twin house was completely furnished for us by the loving hands of folks from the church under the capable direction of Louise and Julian Hagin. Various church people contributed items that amazingly fit together well, including the colors. They did lots of cleaning, repainted the inside, and put down room-size rugs. Everything was there from major pieces of furniture and appliances down to curtains, pictures on the walls, knick-knacks, personal care items, and even pencils and scissors. They collected clothing and toys for the children, filled the cupboards and refrigerator, and welcomed us with much joy and many hugs. We set up our own household again for just our family. Marc and Marci had their own bedrooms. We were so grateful!

Penn View Christian School in Souderton, established by Mennonites, welcomed the children and helped ease their transition to the America school system. Marci was placed in fourth grade without testing. Marc started afternoon kindergarten. A school bus stopped close to our house.

It didn't take long for the Christian influence of the school to make an impact. In Brazil, Marc had said he wanted to be a taxi driver.

But before the end of September, at one supper-table conversation he commented that he wasn't sure anymore that God wanted him to be a taxi driver.

Carla was just old enough during the time we lived there to begin scooting around on the floor. Once while we were upstairs in the bedrooms, she scooted over to the top of the stairs. The next thing I recall was looking down the stairs. I saw a little pink bundle on the floor at the bottom of the straight flight of wooden stairs. What a horrible feeling! We were grateful she didn't show any evidence of injury. Her guardian angel had been on full alert.

At least three men in Pennsylvania had experienced the death of his wife and had remarried by the time we saw them again. All at once, we had to process our own grieving and adapt to the change.

Fall was filled with speaking engagements and went by all too quickly. Ironically, the fall speaking schedule filled up quickly with requests from churches in the middle and western part of the country. Being more agriculturally based, they had the tradition of fall harvest mission festivals. Speaking at some of the Pennsylvania churches didn't get scheduled until spring after we had already moved to Elkhart, Indiana. That added to more travel miles than may have been necessary.

We thoroughly and gratefully enjoyed living in Harleysville again. All too soon it was time to leave that cozy home. Shortly before Christmas, as we had done so many times before, we packed our small car, this time with three children, and headed west from Pennsylvania.

Transitioning at Christmas time

What a Christmas we had with my parents in Newton in 1980. In addition to gifts from our families, the Montana church of my youth chose our family as the one for their gift giving that year. They researched sizes and ages and found appropriate gifts and clothing for each member of the family. Our Christmas trees have never had such a big pile of gifts surrounding them as that year.

En route from Kansas to Elkhart, Indiana, over the New Years' weekend, we stopped in the Chicago area to visit several of my maternal cousins. It had been 20 to 25 years since I had seen some of them. Although most of my maternal cousins grew up in a General Conference Mennonite church, Ebenezer Church near Bluffton, Ohio, none of them we visited were still Mennonites. They were, however, all involved in other churches. By then, Ebenezer Church had withdrawn from the General Conference.

Living in Elkhart, Indiana

To the children's delight, Elkhart had high piles of snow that lasted for weeks. Once again we thanked the Lord that we could move into a fully furnished house. Dale Schumm, whom we met earlier through his work with Mennonite Board of Missions, offered us the use of his home. He and his wife were spending several months in India, where they had once served. Schumms' house was walking distance from Associated Mennonite Biblical Seminary, where Erwin and I audited classes that spring semester of 1981.

Marci and Marc attended Hawthorn Elementary School a few blocks away. As I registered them, I overheard the father of another new student say that his daughter lived with him and his girlfriend. That was a clue this school environment would be quite different than the Christian school they attended in Pennsylvania. Marc was one of only three white children in his class, and Marci was one of five whites. It wasn't long before the children stopped referring to their new classmates by skin color. In Brazil, they were used to classmates who had various shades of skin colors. Marci soon said she liked the school, and a few weeks later, we heard Marc expressing eagerness for Monday.

Brazilian friends in Elkhart

Teo and Suse Penner, German Mennonites from Brazil with whom we had worked closely, were also at the seminary. Marci enjoyed spending time with their two girls. In Brazil the girls had played together speaking Portuguese. But in Elkhart, they only spoke English together. Marci retained some Portuguese during our year in the U.S., but within a few weeks of our arrival, Marc gave up all Portuguese.

Ron and Marlene Daku, whom we met the previous summer at the missionary retreat, were also at seminary preparing to serve in Brazil. They were full of questions for us. Their son and daughter were the same ages as Marc and Carla. Marc and Philip Daku enjoyed playing chess – and they were only five years old.

It was hard to watch as Marci's back was pricked with about sixty different needles. She was tested to determine what triggered her struggles with asthma. The conclusion was that she is allergic to many things. Doctors adjusted her medications and her breathing improved.

Eitzens move to Minnesota

The Eitzens retired from farming and made a major move during our year in the U.S. Erwin went to Montana in March to help them prepare for an auction of their farm equipment and other items. Then Erwin helped load and drive a big U-Haul truck from Montana to Mountain Lake, Minnesota, where the Eitzens had purchased a nice bi-level house. At the time, they had relatives living there including Dad Eitzen's stepmother, his brother Pete and his wife, Mom Eitzen's half-sister Anna Baerg, and other relatives. It was a good location for the Eitzens. They thoroughly enjoyed an active retirement, involved not only with family but also with church and community until health issues arose. We noticed it was at least as cold in Minnesota as in Montana with even more snow.

One disturbing family issue during that time was receiving a letter from Howard Eitzen saying that he no longer wanted to have anything to do with the family. Adopted by Alvin and Lena Eitzen as an infant, Howard was a bit younger than the three Rempel children who joined the family when he was about eight. He was cut from a different cloth, so to speak. He clashed with the Eitzens and the values of the Mennonite community where they lived. His first marriage hadn't worked out. He remarried and had a number of children with his second wife. He was a professional truck driver. Barb hoped he would show up for her wedding, but he disappointed her.

Learning to know more Mennonites

Erwin and I enjoyed the stimulation provided at the seminary. We joined a small group – a K group – that included others who had international experience. Since our previous educational experience had not been in any Mennonite schools, it was good to connect with the broader Mennonite world.

The General Conference churches always had a lot of diversity – that was the idea of having a "general" conference. Rather than focus on confessions of faith and creeds, the ideal was to agree on essentials allowing for diverse opinions on non-essentials. Defining "essentials," however, led to significant differences. Those of us who attended Grace College of the Bible represented a more conservative group. People who went to Bethel and Bluffton colleges and to AMBS leaned toward a more liberal stance.

Erwin and I traveled and spoke in various churches during our time in North America. We related to people across the theological spectrum. Our childhood churches and the ones our relatives attended were on the more conservative side.

At a church near Freeman, South Dakota, Erwin and I shared a table with others for a fellowship meal after our presentation. One man said his wife had gone to Freeman Junior College and that he had attended Bethel College. He then, naturally, asked where we had gone to school. When Erwin said Grace College of the Bible, it grew very quiet around the table. Erwin kept the conversation going on a variety of other subjects.

Later we heard that comments were made such as, "If they went to Grace, how can they be with the General Conference?" The South Dakota people also knew Erwin's folks, the Eitzens, who attended every Northern District conference and were involved in the General Conference as well. They couldn't figure out how the Eitzens had let Erwin go to Grace.

Visiting 50 churches

Even before settling in Pennsylvania in September 1980, we began making what became about 130 presentations in fifty churches as part of our yearlong "assignment" in North America. We tried our newly minted talks, sermons, and slide shows in several Montana churches during August.

We reserved the first September weekend after arriving in Pennsylvania to take the family to the Jersey shore. Then we began itineration in full force. Even before we left Brazil, the fall calendar had been filled.

When we spoke at Indian Valley Mennonite Church, we were pleased to see new people had joined the church we helped begin twelve years earlier. Considering how shy and tongue tied I had been as a child and teen, it was amazing how easily I spoke in front of groups of all sizes. Now I had something to talk about! After a presentation in Ohio that some of my maternal relatives attended, they were surprised that their shy niece could do public speaking.

Erwin preached in Sunday morning worship services. He prepared three basic sermons that he adapted repeatedly. The children began asking him if he was going to give the "cookie" sermon or the "airplane" sermon. They could probably have given those illustrations as well as he did.

Traveling with three kids

I took Carla along when I spoke at women's groups or regional meetings. She flew with me, or us, several times. She was easy to travel with and take into various churches and homes. She was an unusually good baby for all that the year entailed.

While Erwin and I did a few trips by plane, it was typical for us to drive as a whole family to churches near and far. Of the 34,000 miles put on the little Datsun station wagon that year, we calculated that the entire family did about 20,000 of those miles together in the car.

We discovered that it was about as much work to prepare and pack for a short trip as a longer one. I concluded it was easier to take all three children along than to work out all the details of leaving the two older children with other people.

Apparently, we didn't always communicate enough ahead of time with the children. One Friday when Marci came home from school, I tried to hurry her along with packing. She hadn't realized we were going away that weekend.

Sure, the kids fussed in the car. But without being required to be strapped into car seats, they had flexibility in how they played together. Sometimes we put down the back seat in the small station wagon so they had more space. We put luggage into a carrier on top. The car had no built-in system to play music, so we bought a small portable cassette-tape player. The miles passed more quickly listening to narrated children's stories, Bible stories, and lively music.

We made good use of the Interstate highway system. We appreciated the convenience of businesses established near the Interstate. Highly visible big golden arches pointed travelers to food and lodging clustered around McDonald's fast food restaurants. Years later, we learned the negative impact of that convenience.

We often spent nights in a Motel 6. "Home" became wherever we were to sleep for the night – as in "Let's go home" to the motel. Since Erwin doesn't sleep beyond four in the early morning, he would get up, dress quietly, and slip out of the motel to find a nearby truck stop or Denny's restaurant. He would buy coffee and read awhile. He returned to the motel when it was time for the rest of us to awaken, picking up a quart of milk from a convenience store. After the kids spilled Cheerios and milk on the bed several times, we decided it was better to pay for breakfasts at McDonalds.

Some of our travel was during the winter. One snowy day we waited for an accident to be cleared away. Ours was the first car allowed to proceed. The falling snow had covered all the road markings, and we couldn't see where to drive. We pulled off at the first exit and let others blaze the trail. Another time we encountered a couple hundred miles of icy Interstate highway. Tension was high as we saw other cars in the ditch. We thanked God when we made it safely to our destination.

Our visit to the central Missouri church where I spent my childhood was especially meaningful for me. Touring the church and parsonage brought to mind many long-forgotten past events.

Teaching Marc table manners

We ate and slept in many different homes. Several times at a nicely prepared dinner table five-year-old Marc embarrassed us by pointing out a particular food and saying, "I don't like that!" We instructed him to not say that anymore.

A while later we were in the home of a woman who seemed a bit nervous about entertaining. She served succotash, a mixture of corn and lima beans common in that Pennsylvania Dutch area.

Taking a look at it, Marc declared, "That makes me throw up!"

When his dad and I looked at him in horror, he said with a shrug, "Well, I didn't say "I don't like that."

We had to admit he had obeyed the letter of the law.

Traveling too much

By the last half of our year on North America Ministry, it was harder and harder to travel, especially for the children. At times I dreaded the next trip, and chided myself for not having more eagerness for adventure. Some trips were separated by only a few days. At times Marci said she wished she weren't a missionary child who traveled so much. But in general they seemed well adjusted, happy, and as reasonably behaved as normal children. They were amazingly flexible in their routines and appeared to adapt fairly well. Marci always had been an extrovert and didn't hesitate to join a group of new children. Our children may not have the same memories of those times as their parents have.

We learned that it is one thing to look at blank days on the calendar and make a commitment and another thing to carry it out when the time came. But in spite of it all, we found the interaction with people stimulating and encouraging. There weren't any encounters that left us feeling negative.

What do missionaries sacrifice?

Do missionaries sacrifice anything? Compared to missionaries of earlier generations, we sacrificed very little. Before we went to Brazil, we hadn't been living in proximity to our parents and siblings anyway. Letters went back and forth overseas by airmail in a few days' time, rather than taking months on a ship. We could resort to phone calls but rarely did. As our family grew, the "nesting instinct" also grew. In comments to my recently-married sister during the spring of 1981, I admitted to having "the itch to have a place of our own." For me one of the most keenly felt sacrifices about our life as missionaries was not being able to buy our own house. But upon further reflection, I told her, "After so many years now of not being permanent in one place, I'm not sure anymore how long I would want to stay in one place." We didn't mind moving to a new area; it was just the messiness of packing and resettling that was hard.

"When we get settled again in Brazil…" was a common comment as our year in North America was ending. We already had all the essentials in Brazil, just waiting there in storage to be put back into use.

I rather enjoyed the challenge of planning details of packing and travel, and especially the shopping for luggage – so much so that the children would try to steer me away from the luggage sections in stores. Some of the newer suitcases had small wheels and pull-straps, which made them easier to handle.

Becoming weary

The busy year of moving about the country and seemingly endless travel had left me weary. I wished for some vacation time before we headed back overseas. But there was no time for that.

In June 1981, a year after our arrival in Kansas, we departed from the Wichita airport again and headed back to Brazil. The flight from Wichita arrived late in Dallas, leaving little time to connect to the next flight. We didn't take time to check out the airport shuttle. We just grabbed our children and carry-on bags and scurried, breathless and sweaty, around the circular terminal to the gate for the American Airlines flight to Miami. Marc and Marci struggled to carry their small bags and 15-month-old Carla bounced along on my hip.

Farewells

How many ways are there to say goodbye? Farewells are awkward. When an airport is the portal through which the travelers leave, it becomes even more awkward. We first wait together, sometimes in long lines to check-in. Family or friends watch the small children roaming around. When we reach the check-in counter, the complicated international itinerary is looked through, identities and visas checked, and each bag weighed and tagged. In 1981 non-passengers were allowed to go through the security checkpoint. We would all wait together in the lounge by the departure gate. After pictures are taken, hugs and embraces held tightly, then what? How many times can we say goodbye? What does one talk about waiting for the flight to be called? By then we are all talked out, yet family and friends hesitate to leave until we board the plane.

It was actually a relief some years later when travelers had to say final goodbyes before going through the security checkpoint. Once through security, we could turn to give them all a final wave, then walk ahead and let go of what was behind. Unless we were behind schedule, we could finally relax and enjoy the in-between time before boarding the plane for whatever lay ahead.

Part Six
Gama Again from June 1981 to September 1982

On our overnight flight from Miami on the Brazilian airline, Varig, we enjoyed the Brazilian touches - especially the coffee! It was good to hear Portuguese spoken again.

Some of our friends from Gama got up at 5:30 a.m. and took two buses from that satellite city to meet us at the Brasília airport the morning of June 18, 1981. Our missionary colleagues also welcomed Erwin and me along with our three children, as we began what we anticipated being another four-year term.

In spite of the warm welcome, I noticed that things looked shabby, paint was faded, and trash littered the streets. The brownness of dry season didn't help appearances.

Finding our next house
When we closed our suitcases in Kansas, we never thought it would be nearly two months before we would empty them in Brazil. While we looked for a rental house in Gama, we stayed with our new mission colleagues, Gary and Ellie Loewen. They were the second couple the Commission on Overseas Mission sent to Brazil. The Loewens completed language study during our time in the U.S. Ellie was the daughter of COM missionaries Dan and Ella Peters, Canadians who served in Mexico. A few months later, the Daku family we'd met in the U.S. came to Brazil.

The Loewens and their two little girls lived in Taguatinga, another of Brasília's satellite cities, about fifteen miles from Gama. Our family stayed in the unusually large and comfortable "maid's house" in their backyard. We did most of our cooking with the Loewens. This "unintentional community" was a good way to get to know them.

The day after arriving in Brazil, we arranged to purchase our first "American" car – a small white Ford Corcel, made in Brazil. Finding a house to rent in Gama took longer than finding a car. We looked for a house that had three bedrooms plus space for Erwin's study. My impressions of the first house like that were negative. During the two weeks between seeing the house and getting its rental agreement signed, I kept praying that the Lord would close the door if it wasn't the house for us. One friend looked at it and said, "It has possibilities" – another way of saying it needed a lot of hard work, more than our previous house in Gama had needed.

In addition to cleaning and painting inside and out, we installed our big transformer again so that we could plug in all our 110-volt electrical items throughout the house. We purchased light fixtures, bought cup-

Rempels' car in garage at their second home in Gama, Brazil from 1981 to 1982.

boards and wardrobes, had grates installed over the windows and across two wide openings on the covered utility area in the back. We fixed the high concrete wall around the back yard, replaced flimsy wooden doors, put screening on the windows, and installed laundry tubs. We tamed the dirt and mud of the backyard with a layer of concrete. We used a three-room maid's house along the rear of the lot for Erwin's dark room to develop film, for storage, and eventually for an office for a woman who helped with church administration and activities.

The masonry house was built in the squarish style typical in the Federal District. Our daughters shared one of the two bedrooms in the front part of the house. Son Marc, age six by then, didn't like sleeping in a bedroom in the back part of the house. He always brought his pillow and blanket and slept on the living room sofa.

The main bathroom was so small that the showerhead extended over the toilet seat, a common arrangement in Brazilian bathrooms. The whole bathroom got wet anytime someone took a shower. Studying the layout of the house, I discovered there was an enclosed empty space adjacent to the bathroom that would be right size for a shower stall. A neighbor who did construction work opened that hidden space and made it into a nice shower stall. No more wet toilet seats.

Two of my dreams for our second term were realized at that house.

First, I had a completely furnished desk and typewriter of my own, plus a filing cabinet. For the first time in our fifteen years of marriage, I didn't have to wait for the rare moments when Erwin wasn't using the study. He bought a big IBM Selectric typewriter for his use and I used our smaller electric typewriter.

The other dream realized was to have a piano

Angela Rempel typing at her desk in Gama, 1982.

again so that Marci could continue piano lessons she began during our time in Elkhart, Indiana.

Too busy to settle in

Instead of returning to the ministry work in Brazil refreshed, full of new ideas and enthusiasm, I often felt as dry and barren as the surrounding Brazilian countryside in the midst of the dry season.

Settling in took a long time – both the physical aspects and the emotional. The things we had left stored for the year of our absence were now dusty, moldy, and corroded. We soon replaced the gas stove and automatic washing machine. Furniture needed to be reupholstered and refinished. However, when we heard other missionaries tell about finding their things damaged by mice and termites or stolen, we were grateful our damage was minor.

To the dismay of our church people, who mostly lived near the church on the far west side of Gama, our house was on the east side of town. Even though the house was close to a bus stop, it wasn't the same easy back and forth we had previously enjoyed.

After being away a year, I felt "out of it." Things weren't the same. Our Portuguese was a bit rusty.

Before we even moved into the house in August, the schedule for the rest of 1981 was filled with meetings, trips, conferences, visitors, a regional retreat, and a missionary gathering. Erwin was appointed as the Executive Secretary of the AEM – the association of twenty-six Mennonite churches scattered throughout Brazil. As is his manner, he plunged in wholeheartedly using his administrative gifts.

New house and school year

The house was ready for us to move into by August 1, just a few days before Marci and Marc started school. They returned to Compacto, the private school they previously attended.

Marc totally forgot Portuguese while we were in the U.S. He played with Brazilian children in the weeks after our return and we assumed he was picking it up again. The first day of school, though, he didn't even know yet how to say that he needed to go to the bathroom. He was in tears until his teacher discerned his problem. However, by the end of the first reporting period, he caught up and got good grades again.

Neither Marci or Marc got credit for the year they were in school in the U.S. At Compacto, they both had been in a class for children a year older. Losing a school year put them with children of their own age. Marci was sad about not being in the same class with her former classmates – until she came to her math lessons and realized she was not ready for a higher grade.

Resuming responsibilities

I gradually began to resume my former responsibilities with the women's Bible studies, youth work, and music. However, since Wilma did so well playing the little pump organ for the worship services, I needed to let her continue doing that. Even though I missed playing organ, it was satisfying to know that I had prepared someone else do that task.

By the end of that year in our *Rempel Update* newsletter, we wrote:

> Erwin quickly became swamped with all the tasks and expectations of him as a pastor, executive secretary, husband, father, and chief maintenance man. ... As Erwin's time has been taken up more with his administrative duties and travels, he has little time to spend in pastoring. The church has suffered and we are trying to work with them in finding stronger national leadership.

With all the activities and travel, it was taking a long time to reach the point of feeling settled again.

Without Erwin at night

We were glad to see improvements being made to the street in front of our house. However, our car needed to be parked on the street overnight so that the concrete could set along the curb and entrance to our driveway. Erwin was traveling, so I was home with the children. During the night, I was awakened by someone at our door. I cautiously looked through the grates of the locked door. It was a policeman. He asked me to get dressed and come outside. Our new white Ford car parked out on the street had been a visible and tempting target for a thief who had broken into the car. He tried unsuccessfully to break the lock on the steering wheel. Unable to start and steer the car, it just rolled to a stop against the curb a few houses down the street. The would-be thief ran away. There was only minimal damage to the car. I easily drove it back to our house, over the nearly firm concrete, through the gate, and parked it inside the garage.

One other night when Erwin was gone, I was awakened by the eerie sound of our unlatched front gate swinging back and forth on rusty hinges with each gust of wind. I didn't want to get up and go out in the dark to close it. I prayed that there would be a gust of wind strong enough to push the gate shut. And sure enough, that prayer was answered. I felt as though the breath of God had touched that gate.

Brazilian summer break

December and January are the summer holiday months in Brazil. But for us, that transition from 1981 to 1982 offered no break in our busy schedule.

Two youth from our church who had gone to Bible college were a big help with the vacation Bible school at our church in January. About seventy children attended and several non-Christian parents attended the closing program. It was rewarding to have four youth from our church preparing to enroll in Bible colleges for the next school year.

Erwin took Marci along in January on a trip north. Marci was eager to spend time again with Susannah Gerber, whose parents, Bob and Fran, had moved to that area. When Erwin and Marci got off the first bus, they learned that heavy rains had made the final stretch of 200 kilometers impassable. They arranged to fly with MAF in a six-passenger single-engine plane to their destination.

Our children played well with Brazilian children, but they shared a special bond with other MKs – missionary kids. Susannah was one of four girls in our Mennonite mission group who were about the same age. The other girls were Sylvia Penner, daughter of Teo and Susie, from Curitiba, Debbie Hochstetler from Brasília, and Marci.

Erwin and Marci took longer than expected to return home from the north. That left less than twenty-four hours at home before we left as a family on another trip, by car, to the southern areas. That meant less than twenty-four hours for me to wash and dry their clothes – in almost constant rain and without a clothes dryer!

Erwin had AEM work to do along the way, but it was also a family vacation. When we got all the way south to Curitiba and Palmeira, we debated whether we should drive a short way east to the beach or head west to the famous large waterfall Foz do Iguaçu. Affluent German Mennonites offered us the free use of their beach house for several days. That settled it. We would go to the beach. We thought we would have other opportunities to go to Foz do Iguaçu.

Beginning a new school year

By the end of February 1982, school began again. We anticipated finally getting into a routine. Marci could start piano lessons and take regular treatments for her asthma.

Because much of Erwin's time was involved with the AEM administration, he could be "pastor" of our Gama church only about one

Angela Rempel giving Marcia piano lessons in Gama, 1982.

Erwin Rempel prepares graphs for a presentation, 1982.

Sunday a month. That frustration made me wonder if it would be better for the church if we just moved away so they would find other consistent leadership. New people had come during our year away on furlough, so we knew the church could grow without leadership by a North American missionary.

Another life-changing unexpected invitation

On February 26, 1982, I was pondering these things. *"What is wrong with me? Why can't I feel settled and satisfied here? Why do I keep wanting to go back to the U.S.?"* During our first term I hadn't felt that way. Before our furlough, I wasn't sure I could readjust to life in the U.S. Now I knew I could readapt, too easily perhaps.

A bit later that day, Erwin brought in the mail – and everything changed! What an unexpected invitation there was in one of the letters! Erwin remembers it well and writes the following:

> I had made my way as usual to the post office in Gama. Among the letters was one from Harris Waltner, pastor of

244

Bethel Mennonite Church, Mountain Lake, Minnesota, who was also the chairperson of the Commission on Overseas Mission. I thought it strange that Harris would contact me.

When I opened the envelope and briefly read the contents, I was stunned. It was an invitation to serve as the executive secretary for COM following the departure of Howard Habegger later in the year. Harris even mentioned that my name had been the unanimous first choice of the COM staff and commission members. I wondered whether commission members even knew who we were other than that we were COM missionaries serving in Brazil. Furthermore, I had not applied for, nor had I been interviewed for, the position. But there it was in black and white, an invitation to serve in this role.

Returning home from the post office, I showed the letter to Angela and she was as stunned as I was. We had only been back in Brazil for about eight months following our first North American Ministry. To accept the invitation from COM seemed somewhat out of sync in terms of timing.

What would an acceptance of this invitation mean for us?

As Erwin wrote above, we were both stunned by this invitation. My first reaction was that he shouldn't accept it – at least not at this stage of our lives. We were too involved to leave Brazil and move to Newton, Kansas.

With prayer and much deliberation, by March 4, 1982, Erwin wrote to Harris Waltner accepting the invitation.

Explaining to family

"Do you think you could put up with your other daughter and her family living in Newton?" I wrote to my parents. My sister, LaRita, and her husband, Darrel Claassen, were living in Newton too. My folks responded positively, of course.

When Erwin and I talked to our children, they immediately liked the idea of going back to the U.S. They hadn't put down many roots again in Brazil nor formed many new friendships. However, they did remember all the fun of playing with their cousins in the U.S.

Perhaps my lack of contentment had been the way the Lord prepared me for this major change in our path.

Reactions

As we grew ever more excited about our move, we needed to downplay our feelings as other people certainly didn't share them – neither the Brazilians nor the mission colleagues as Erwin explains:

> When the missionary team in Brazil became aware of the invitation, there was considerable pushback and even anger toward COM. Why would the mission agency take relatively new mission workers from Brazil and put them in Newton when we were just becoming more fluent in the Portuguese language and were in the first stages of learning more about and appreciating the local Brazilian culture?
>
> In the congregation in Gama there was considerable polite but also heartfelt disappointment.

It was hard not to feel a bit guilty, as if we were deserting. Some thought we were just interested in getting a better position. We felt, however, that it was simply a step forward in responding to God's call. The task ahead was daunting. We knew this move would change us and our family.

Scheduling our departure

When we heard from our colleagues, we modified the schedule for our departure, as we had done when leaving Pennsylvania. Erwin's presence was needed at several important events, including the annual assembly of the AEM in July. Instead of going back to the U.S. by July 1, as first envisioned so that Erwin could take up his new responsibilities by August 1, we waited until mid-September to leave Brazil.

Finding Brazilian leadership

Erwin felt strongly that when he left, Brazilians needed to fill his roles in the local church and the national church organization. That took some doing, but it was accomplished. Osvaldo Freitas, the young pastor in nearby Goiania, was called to pastor the Gama church. He and his wife and small children moved into the same pleasant house we had lived in during our first term in Gama, close to the church.

Teo Penner, a Brazilian-born German Mennonite whose parents had immigrated from Russia, took on the role of executive secretary of the AEM. Teo had worked closely with Erwin already for a while on those matters.

By late July, Erwin was so stressed with the workload that he began seeing double. He couldn't see to drive. Injections of vitamin B12 stabilized his vision.

Selling our things

People soon asked about buying our things. We gave our church people the first opportunity to buy our major items. Then we had a yard sale. People came and bought everything. I gave each of the women in our church one of my potted plants. When I moved one of the large plants, I pulled something in my back. For years after that, I had some back pain.

We dispersed most everything that remained from our original shipment in barrels to Brazil. The few suitcases we took back to the U.S. mostly contained Brazilian artifacts, especially wall hangings. In Kansas, we would start over again in setting up a house.

Erwin and I knew we needed some rest before going back to the U.S. In early September we drove our family to Rio de Janeiro. Our small hotel room was near the beach. There we slept, and slept! We would enjoy a nice hotel breakfast, go back to our room, and take a long nap. After a time on the beach with the children, we slept some more. What the kids did all the time, I'm not sure, but Erwin and I got a lot of much-needed rest.

Saying farewell again

Then there was another farewell for us at the church. The printed program listed twenty-six items – many of them musical items including a duet by Erwin and me. Would we ever see these dear friends again? Somehow, I felt that we would.

247

Instead of a four-year term, our second term in Brazil lasted only fifteen months. September 13, 1982, we boarded a plane in Brasília, flew to Rio where we took another larger plane overnight to Miami, again – bringing to an end another chapter of our lives. Our Pennsylvania chapter had lasted exactly seven years; the Brazil chapter was also about seven years long. We were excited and at peace as we began what became our longest chapter in one location.

Rempel family in Gama, Brazil, 1982.

Marc, Marcia, Carla Rempel in Gama, May 1982.

Chapter Five
Kansas from 1982 to 1994

Part One
Starting Over in Kansas

Within seventy-two hours of landing in Wichita, Kansas, in mid-September of 1982, we arranged to buy a house in Newton and two cars. When staff in the office at the Commission on Overseas Mission heard about these major decisions in such a short time, they were justifiably leery about their new co-worker's decision-making style.

The realtor assigned to show Erwin and me some houses on our first day back in the U.S. greeted us in Portuguese, much to our surprise. He had spent time with Mennonite Central Committee in Brazil. He showed us a variety of houses that day: houses less than twenty-years old and in our price range of about $60,000.

Late in the afternoon, the realtor realized another house was also on the market, but he hadn't made advance preparations for our visit. However, he knew the woman who owned the house and boldly knocked on the door. She was giving a piano lesson, but graciously agreed to let us go through the house while she continued with the lesson.

Stepping inside the front door, I saw a vista of refreshing green in the carpet, the walls, and curtains. The green view continued through wide patio doors to an expanse of green lawn in the backyard and beyond. Verdant green nourishes me. I drank it in. This was the house for me. We went to get our children and they too liked the house done in green.

By the end of the next day, after looking at more houses, we negotiated a price of $62,500 for that green house on the corner of West Fourth Street and Beverly Avenue. Mortgage rates at the time were at historic highs – fourteen percent at a bank. We were pleased that Erwin's folks, the Eitzens, loaned us the money at ten percent. We registered the loan through a financial agency that handled the monthly money transfers. A few years later when interest rates began to fall, we arranged to pay eight percent interest, which we continued to pay as long as we owned the house.

And the purchase of two cars in those first couple of days? Aware of our three growing children, the car salesman first tried to convince us we needed a big old Chevy Suburban van he had on the lot. Not only was the thing old and ugly, there was no way, after driving only small cars, that I would drive such a monster. He likely scratched his head in amazement when we signed up to pay cash for two small cars – a 1980 Chevy Chevette and a 1980 Dodge Omni. Both cars had low mileage. The Omni became the family car and the one Erwin usually drove. I putted around in the Chevette, taxiing the kids to and from school many times. We were quite satisfied with our purchases and those cars lasted us many years. Both cars had manual shifting and nothing automated. Each car had AM/FM radio but no cassette or CD player and no cup holders. Safety belts for laps and shoulders were standard by then, but no airbags. Air conditioning was also standard by then, and we no longer had delusions that we could get by without it.

Our new home at 1701 West Fourth Street was built about 1966 – the year we were married. It was a ranch-style house with a rectangular footprint, built in much the same style as the other houses in what was known as the Koerner Heights addition on the west side of Newton. The front of the house, partially done in brick, faced north with a covered porch. The siding around the rest of the house was painted green, of course. The generous two-car garage sheltered our two cars and provided storage space. Central air conditioning in homes was also standard by then. The furnace and water heater used piped-in natural gas

The main floor had 1,428 square feet, with three bedrooms and one and a half baths. The partially finished basement essentially doubled the space, and eventually we had the equivalent of another three bedrooms and a bathroom downstairs, plus a family room. Kansas is in tornado alley, so we didn't even consider a house without a basement. Several times each tornado season we gathered in the family room in the basement watching TV reports of threatening weather. Sometimes the loud outdoor tornado sirens wailed, but we never had reason to seek further shelter under heavy furniture. In all our years living in tornado alley, we never personally saw a tornado funnel.

Settling in at 1701 West Fourth Street

To furnish our new home, we stuck with our pattern of buying new furniture for the living room and new major appliances, but most of the other furniture we acquired second hand from yard sales and second-hand shops. The house didn't need painting, which seemed strange after all the painting we'd done in most other places where we'd lived.

Within a few months, we finished more of the basement. Erwin never even thought about needing a permit to do that kind of work. With the do-it-yourself attitude of farm life, he tackled everything, including electrical wiring after consulting someone knowledgeable.

Rempel home in Newton, Kansas from 1982 to 1994.

Telephone service had just become competitive. Instead of renting a phone from the phone company, customers bought their own phones in different colors and styles. All phones were still connected to a landline, and cords connected handsets to the base. The phone in the kitchen had a very long cord so that I could keep busy while talking. Rotary dials soon gave way to phones with touch buttons.

We lived in that house for nearly twelve years, the longest Erwin or I had lived in any one house during our childhood and adult years. The house served us well as the children grew up.

Caring for creation

In the early 1980s, there was a significant emphasis on environmental concerns and energy efficiency. With our Mennonite values of stewardship and frugality, we resonated with those issues. To reduce the impact of the long hot Kansas summers, we installed three turbine vents on top of our house to ventilate the attic and added a thick layer of attic insulation. Most summers we cooled only the basement and we all slept down there. But I still had to cook in the hot kitchen on the main floor.

Recycling was new at the time, and we joined in right away. We took recyclables to a collection site set up monthly at a large grocery store in town. Then we signed up with a new local recycling business for curbside pickup at home.

Part Two
Erwin's Work Experiences

Erwin didn't officially begin his work as Executive Secretary of the Commission on Overseas Mission until October 15, 1982, a month after we arrived in Kansas. Yet, work-related events during that month kept him quite busy in addition to settling our family. Initially, he traversed a steep learning curve. Erwin writes the following about issues and events during his years as COM executive secretary.

252

Unanimous first choice?

Soon after arriving, I [Erwin] met with Vern Preheim who was the general secretary of the General Conference Mennonite Church. He wanted me to be aware that some General Board members were less-than-enthusiastic about me. That was in spite of me being the "unanimous first choice," affirmed by the COM staff and commission members, and by the General Board. Some General Board members were concerned, unsurprisingly, about the schools I attended and graduated from: Grace Bible Institute, Dallas Theological Seminary, Westminster Theological Seminary and Eastern Baptist Theological Seminary (now Palmer Theological Seminary). Why hadn't I attended the General Conference-related colleges? Why only two audited classes at Associated Mennonite Biblical Seminary? Another person's concerns related to what theological directions I might take.

I am still amazed that I was appointed to the leadership of the Commission on Overseas Mission. I am also grateful that these concerns did not appear to continue for very long, as I am unaware of further pushback.

The other dimension of my appointment that was unorthodox in terms of present day procedures is that I had not applied nor been interviewed for the position. I was invited – in what seemed like out of the blue – to serve in this role. Later, the General Conference put into place clear policies and procedures to select persons for leadership positions.

Orientation

As the outgoing executive secretary for COM, Howard J. Habegger overlapped with me for one week. He provided very helpful counsel, insights, and suggestions about general procedures and policies. He alerted me to an unwritten policy that an executive secretary serves not more than ten to twelve years. At the end of my tenure, Vern Preheim checked the records and reported at my farewell that I was the longest serving executive secretary, about eleven and a half years, only slightly longer than others had served.

Finances

One of my first tasks was to familiarize myself with the COM finances. When I calculated that COM needed an average of $9,000 in contributions a day, each day of the year, I nearly broke out in a cold sweat. COM was just as much a "faith mission" as the para-church mission agencies with which most of our Bible college friends served.

Several times during my first year in the office, Bill Snyder, executive secretary of Mennonite Central Committee, called me. He was also from the General Conference and eager to maintain good relationships between MCC and COM. He expressed appreciation that I showed ability in understanding and managing COM finances.

Tensions in the Newton offices

During my orientation, Howard Habegger only hinted at some tensions with the other commissions – the Commission on Home Ministries and the Commission on Education – especially when it came to finances. Howard's counsel to me went something like this, "It is your role as executive secretary of COM to make the case for COM's interests." I soon learned how important that was.

The General Conference Mennonite Church had a centralized

General Conference Mennonite Church headquarters office at 722 Main Street, Newton, Kan., 1990.

Erwin Rempel works in his office in Newton, Kan., as the Executive Secretary of the Commission on Overseas Mission of the General Conference Mennonite Church, 1982-1994.

budget. Some of the General Board members and other General Conference staff had negative feelings because COM received about two-thirds of the contributions from individuals and churches. The General Board determined the percentage of the "pie" that each commission received. That discussion – with much debate and dissension – was usually held on a Sunday night during the annual Council of Commission meetings. It was known as the "Sunday Night Massacre." Shortly after my arrival, that pattern changed to "slicing the pie" only every three years. It didn't take me long to learn how COM's percentage of the overall GCMC financial pie was diminishing over the years.

COM had asked delegates at the 1980 General Conference Triennial Sessions in Estes Park, Colorado, to vote on a proposal to send and fund 175 overseas missionaries by 1985. That was an increase from its current 150. The proposal received a strong affirmative vote by the delegates. From COM's viewpoint, it needed more funds to accomplish that goal. That posed a threat to the funding of the other commissions, I learned.

Traveling

My role involved significant travel in both the U.S. and Canada and internationally. Each year I visited one continent where COM missionaries served – Africa, Asia, or Latin America.

As I recall, after starting my work as COM executive secretary on October 15, 1982, I spent only ten days in the office during my first six weeks.

Later, I recorded the following for 1988:

- 40 churches visited with speaking engagements
- 50+ pastors in 19 individual or group meetings
- 4 presentations at General Conference-related schools
- 23 meetings (consultations, committee, board, study group, etc.)
- 142 days away traveling or 39 percent away from home

In a chapel on May 18, 1994, in a presentation entitled "Rempel Reflections: 1982-1994," I noted that I had spent about forty percent of my time traveling.

I generally enjoyed speaking in churches, relating to constituency, and participating in board meetings.

The official policy was that staff of the same gender would normally share bedrooms in order to limit travel costs. However, as one who is easily disturbed by snoring, this was a difficult policy for me. Sometimes I personally paid extra to have my own room.

On one administrative trip to Africa, I had reached my limit of having sleep interrupted by snoring. I sent a note ahead to Gary and Jean Isaac, long-time friends who by then were serving with COM and Africa Inter-Mennonite Mission. I requested of them that when my colleagues and I would be with them in the Transkei of South Africa, that they arrange for me to sleep in a separate location. They accommodated my request and I slept soundly for the first time in a couple of weeks.

I really welcomed the occasions when Angela traveled with me as that took care of the snoring issue. However, I must admit that as the years have passed, unfortunately I am also accused of snoring.

Trip around the world – first stop, India

My first international trip as executive secretary occurred in March and April 1983, about six months into my new job. It was an around-the-world trip with Peter Kehler, director for Asia. We visited COM missionaries in India, Hong Kong, Japan, Taiwan, and South Korea. The entire trip was six and a half weeks long. We flew first from Wichita to Zurich, Switzerland, where we took in some sightseeing for a few hours before our flight to Bombay, India. After only a week or so in India, the two soft-sided suitcases I brought along were falling apart and were held together with rope. Peter Kehler was surprised by my luggage naiveté.

It was difficult at that time for mission workers to obtain visas to serve in India. The only missionaries I recall who were still in India at the time were Helen Kornelsen at Yeotmal, teaching at the Union Biblical Seminary, and Ed and Ramoth Burkhalter in Jagdeeshpur. India had been the first location for General Conference overseas mission work beginning in 1900. Many missionaries served in India over the decades, engaging in evangelism, church planting, leprosy work, schools, bookstores, reading rooms, and in establishing three large hospitals.

At the time of my visit in 1983, Peter Kehler and I still dealt with fall-out from a contentious delegation visit from COM staff and commission members in the 1970s. The context and explanations of that are in the book, *A People of Mission* by James C. Juhnke. Peter and I met with various people who were still dissatisfied.

Peter and I visited the campus of Union Biblical Seminary (UBS) in Yeotmal, where some of the English-speaking Mennonite pastors attended. We met and had dinner with the seminary principal, Saphir Athyal. UBS was in the process of moving its campus to Pune, India. We visited the Pune campus also, which was in the throes of construction. We met there with S. Paul Miller and his wife, who were from Mennonite Board of Missions. S. Paul Miller was overseeing the construction of the new seminary campus. Mennonites, including the Mennonite Church and General Conference Mennonite Church, contributed significant sums of money for the construction of the new campus in Pune.

Toward the end of our India visit, Peter Kehler and I went to Calcutta. There we stayed at a guesthouse operated by MCC and met with Pete Peters, MCC Country Representative. I was surprised when Peters explained that the Indian people preferred soft wheat to the donated hard red winter wheat shipped to India from Kansas. Peters had to sell the Kansas wheat and purchase locally grown soft wheat.

I learned later that MCC was encouraging North American farmers to "monetize" donated commodities so that the money could be used overseas to purchase locally grown wheat and beef. That saved on shipping costs as well as the inevitable decrease in the value of the commodity when traded for what people wanted. From my experience with raising wheat in Montana, I understood how satisfying it is for a farmer to haul a truckload of his wheat to the elevator and have it shipped to hungry people in India. It is a delicate task to balance the perceptions of North American donors and the realities.

While in Calcutta, I visited an orphanage operated by Mother Teresa and the Sisters of Charity. It was a very moving experience to view rooms filled with cribs of very small children who had been abandoned on the streets of Calcutta.

One of the tension points within the Mennonite church of India related to Mennonite World Conference. People jockeyed for the privilege of serving as a member of the MWC executive committee. In India and other countries, the pursuit of this privilege resulted in bribes, power plays, influence peddling, and even divisions in the church. I became reluctant to have COM bring church leaders from Asia, Africa, and Latin America to the U.S. for our triennial sessions of the General Conference Mennonite Church.

Later I had the opportunity to share my concerns with Paul N. Kraybil, then executive director of Mennonite World Conference. Paul quickly assured me that while sometimes there are negative experiences, overall it was important to nurture the meeting of church leaders in the global Mennonite fellowship and that I was remiss in my reluctance.

Visiting in the Far East
From India, Peter Kehler and I traveled to Japan, Taiwan, Hong Kong and South Korea. I had not yet met all of the mission workers

258

in those countries, so Peter had asked them to each write about themselves and their work. On the flight from India to Japan, it was only about a half hour before we landed in Tokyo that I finished reading what the Japan missionaries had written. I burst out laughing when I read at the end of Bernard Thiessen's report something of the following, "...and if you will actually read this account of who I am and what I do, I will buy you a bottle of Coca-Cola." Guess who met us when our plane landed? It was Bernard. He was surprised when I asked him for the Coke. There was Japanese writing all over the Coke bottle he got for me.

Peter Kehler's walking gait was faster than mine. Many times Peter sort of bit his tongue as I, walking as rapidly as I thought reasonable, caught up with him. In Hong Kong, missionary Hugh David Sprunger walked even faster. I wondered if there was a competition between these two men. They served together in Asia for many years before Peter began administrative work in the Newton office.

Length of international trips

I learned never again to take a six-and-a-half-week trip. I was so exhausted that I could hardly think. Angela joined me in Japan on this trip and together we also visited Taiwan and Hong Kong. Angela and I stopped in Hawaii for two days at our own cost to unwind before returning home. We went to a hotel near the beach and basically slept the entire time we were there. We spent only a couple of hours walking along the beach.

Back in the Newton office, I advocated for travel policies that would limit international trips to not more than three weeks. For the most part, I was able to follow that on most international trips from then on.

Writing trip reports

After that first long trip around the world, I needed to write a comprehensive report for staff and the commission. However, this was a new experience for me and, furthermore, I was completely overwhelmed by the stack of issues to be dealt with after the trip.

Peter Kehler occasionally inquired about my trip report, as he wanted to include my report along with his for the commission. Eventually, I did prepare a one or two-page report of impressions I had of the trip.

On future international trips, I kept detailed accounts as I was traveling and then prepared a written report on the way back home. On several occasions, prior to my return home from Africa, I stayed an extra day in Brussels and spent the entire day writing my report – handwritten in the days before I could travel with a laptop computer.

Technology in the office

From 1982 until about 1990 I used a Dictaphone for writing letters. My secretary listened to my recorded words and typed the letters. At times I typed out a letter and gave that to my secretary to redo and format on the proper letterhead.

Sometime in the late 1980s, I observed that the Mennonite Brethren Missions/Services International had fax machines they used to communicate between their offices in Hillsboro, Kansas, and Winnipeg, Manitoba. A document could be sent by fax (facsimile) immediately via a landline telephone connection. Since the Commission on Overseas Mission also had a staff person, Jake Harms, serving in Winnipeg, I thought it would be great to communicate with Jake using this kind of technology. When I mentioned this to Division of Administration staff who worked in the two offices, they were quite sure they would not need a fax machine.

However, the COM staff decided to purchase and install fax machines in our Newton and Winnipeg offices. The fax machines soon demonstrated the functionality of instantly sending documents without need for postage. Before long, staff in the other commissions wanted to use the fax machines too. Even the Menno Travel Service staff came across the street to use COM's fax machine.

One time, probably in the mid-1980s, I recall that Ted Stuckey of the Division of Administration explained that Larry Becker, who worked with the office's large mainframe computer, would install some desktop computer workstations. There would be only one computer per commission and one printer on each of the two floors. A computer would be used, it was assumed, only for big projects that required computing capacity.

Before that, back in 1983, Angela and I had personally purchased a computer for our use at home. It was a Franklin Ace 2E with 64 kilobytes of RAM memory, but no hard drive. I had to load the software program (First Choice-integrated software with word processing, spreadsheet, and graphics capability) from floppy disks each time I used the computer. Then I had to store the work on another floppy disk. We spent about $3,500 to purchase the computer and two printers (dot-matrix and daisy-wheel), along with all the cables to connect everything. I built a small computer desk on wheels so Angela and I could move it back and forth between our desks in the home office.

I had been impatient enough to personally purchase a laptop for my work use in the COM office – a Radio Shack Tandy 1400 laptop computer, which cost about $1,500 or more, and a dot-matrix printer.

After beginning with only one computer per commission, by the late 1980s computers were made available to all the staff and I could have COM pay for my laptop computer. On one occasion in the 1980s, a sales person advised me with considerable conviction that a twenty-megabyte hard-drive storage capacity on a computer would be more than anyone would ever need.

In the early 1990s, Larry Becker began conversations about email. Only a limited number of persons used that new communication method, so I told him I didn't think I would use email.

It was Sheldon Sawatzky, then a mission worker serving in Taiwan, who pushed me into the email age. Sheldon was computer savvy and eager to communicate with the Newton office and others by means of email. Before my next trip to Taiwan, I tried to learn what was involved in the use of email so that I could avoid embarrassment when I met with Sheldon.

Selling COM property in Asia

In Japan, Bernard and Ruby Thiessen lived in a Japanese-style house that COM had purchased for about US$30,000. After the Thiessens retired, COM decided to sell the house. I was astonished at the inflated value of that relatively small house and property. It sold for approximately $1,000,000, yes, one million dollars! Then the issue became how to utilize the million dollars.

Japanese law did not allow capital gains to leave Japan. Some missionaries in Japan thought the entire amount should be spent by the Mennonite churches in Japan. At that time, COM experienced a decline in contributions. The missionaries in Japan were the most expensive to maintain because the cost of living in Japan was about one hundred percent more than in North America. The policy of COM was to compensate missionaries so that they neither gained nor lost purchasing power because of their overseas location.

After considerable correspondence between Japan and the Newton office, it was decided to give fifty percent to the Mennonite church organization in Japan and for COM to use the other fifty percent to pay for the cost-of-living differential added to Japan missionaries' salaries. The money, thus, all stayed in Japan.

Request from Donald McGavran.

The well-known missiologist Donald McGavran, who had retired from teaching at Fuller Theological Seminary in Pasadena, California, sent me an unusual request.

McGavran's eyesight was deteriorating, and his wife couldn't read to him anymore. In looking for someone to help him with reading, he recalled his days as a missionary in India. He had been positively impressed with the Mennonite missionaries he met in India. His request to COM was for a retired Mennonite single woman missionary to come live with him and his wife in California and read to him.

Discussing this request with the COM staff and a few retired mission workers living nearby, we settled on suggesting a woman who had retired a few years earlier after serving many years as a single woman in the Congo. I contacted her about the request from Donald McGavran. She thought about it and responded that I could send a letter to McGavran mentioning her name for consideration. I wrote to McGavran and he contacted her. She flew to Pasadena and met with Donald and his wife. They mutually agreed not to pursue the arrangement.

Angela's reflections

Angela recalls additional aspects of Erwin's work as Executive Secretary of the Commission on Overseas Mission in Newton, Kansas, from 1982 to 1994 as follows:

Erwin and I both came from within the framework of the General Conference Mennonite Church, and always felt connected to it, although at a distance. Now, we found ourselves in the very hub of the denominational life. What a privilege!

Erwin took only one simple bookkeeping class in high school, but he enjoyed numbers. He took a special interest in overseeing COM's three-million-dollar budget. When the first spreadsheet computer program came out, he learned how to use it and appreciated that new tool for financial oversight.

Overall, Erwin's administrative gifts of attention to detail, careful financial planning and accounting, and willingness to work many long hours were well employed on behalf of God's mission in the world through COM. His easy laugh was a plus in relating to people. When he took the Myers Briggs Personality Test, it was a surprise to learn that he was actually an introvert.

Contrasting salary structures

Even though Erwin's position and salary were at the top of the office structure of COM, we initially concluded that financially we were better off living overseas on a missionary salary. We had saved money regularly during our time in Brazil. We dipped deep into those savings to resettle in Newton – and that didn't include anything toward the purchase price of our house, because the Eitzens provided us with a hundred- percent financing. To establish a typical American Mennonite house and two-car lifestyle, we spent about $25,000. Our experience motivated Erwin to set up a system whereby the missionaries could accumulate a resettlement fund for themselves.

Shortly before we began our overseas service in Brazil in 1975, COM had adopted a new salary structure and system. All missionaries were paid the same base salary and benefits. The only exception was an increase of one percent of base salary for each year of continuous service, up to fifteen years. It didn't matter whether a missionary was a plastic surgeon, a seminary professor, or didn't have an advanced degree.

The cost of living overseas was adjusted according to researched data supplied by the Organization Research Counselors (ORC). At times in Brazil it was deemed that our cost of living was less than in the U.S., so the portion of our salary expected to be spent in Brazil was reduced. Sometimes it was increased. That experience was most helpful for Erwin when he explained the ORC system to other overseas workers, often when they were unhappy about the system.

When we lived overseas, in addition to the basic salary, COM paid for the children's school costs including school uniforms, our medical expenses, housing expenses, any taxes, and a portion of our transportation costs. COM continued the practice, previously established for General Conference pastors and staff, of contributing a generous ten percent of salary into a retirement plan without requiring any matching contribution.

Except for that pension plan, the salary structure was different for General Conference home office staff. Staff salaries were determined by levels of responsibility. As the executive secretary in 1982, Erwin received about $1,000 to $2,000 more than the other COM office staff.

Family health insurance was provided with only a small deductible for us to pay. Otherwise, COM staff persons in the U.S. paid for their housing, local transportation, children's schooling, income tax, etc.

The Kansas climate had harsh extremes of cold and heat compared to the mild year-round climate in Brazil where we had doors and windows open much of the year. In Kansas we seldom opened up because it was either too hot or too cold – or too windy. That meant higher costs for heating and cooling. Buying clothing for growing children in changing seasons was another additional cost.

Unlike overseas where a missionary couple was paid one salary and both spouses were expected to be working as missionaries, in the U.S. the spouse of a staff person had no restrictions on obtaining other employment. However, until Carla went to school, I didn't seek another job. We were grateful that we could manage on one income, something that average middle-class families a few decades later were unable to do. Once Carla went to school, I began a variety of low-paying jobs that were part-time, allowing me to be available to transport the kids to and from school – there being no school bus service within city limits. For a while, we had children in three different schools. I was home after school with the children and prepared evening meals that we all ate together at the table.

Changing times for overseas mission

The initial optimism in 1980 about expanding COM mission work was soon challenged when the North American economy struggled and contributions declined in the mid-'80s. Instead of increasing the number of overseas workers, COM couldn't always support the ones it had. However, maturing Christians overseas were taking up church leadership and fewer foreign missionaries were needed.

In the legacy mission fields of the Congo and India, by the end of the 1980s the traditional mission compounds were mostly in the hands of local Mennonite believers. Generally, the maintenance of the systems for water and electricity and for the buildings – churches, hospitals, schools, houses – was more than local people could afford or knew how to manage.

The COM mission workers in countries other than India and Congo didn't build mission compounds. Instead, they lived among the people in the same style of houses or apartments that were typical for their area – ranging from simple tin-roofed African dwellings to small, but expensive, apartments in high-rise buildings in Asia.

Each year applicants and new mission workers met with the COM staff. Some people came well prepared with all the right kind of education, training, and experience in North America. Others were young and inexperienced. We observed some of the former who fell apart when something traumatic occurred and soon returned to North America. Some of the inexperienced people went on to become well-known leaders. We learned it isn't possible to predict who would serve effectively.

Several times Erwin and the COM staff went through the difficult experience of terminating an overseas worker. That was extremely painful for everyone involved.

Erwin's travel

Erwin endured many hours of work-related travel, especially by plane, although some by car or train. Usually the flights went as scheduled, and his luggage arrived when and where he did. He also experienced delays, tight connections, and misplaced luggage, which always eventually came through. Often it was cost effective for him to fly from Kansas City instead of from nearby Wichita, even with the cost of nearly four hours of driving each way and parking in Kansas City. The following stories relate some of his more unusual travel experiences.

Wichita or Saginaw?

Erwin was sitting in the O'Hare Airport in Chicago waiting for a flight back to Wichita. He probably had his laptop computer open, trying to keep up with his work. He heard the Wichita flight called, picked up his things, and headed toward the gate. He presented his boarding pass and settled into the plane for the trip of more than an hour between Chicago and Wichita. To his great surprise, less than half an hour into the flight, the captain announced that the plane was beginning its descent for landing. He checked his watch, then said something to the passenger next to him about how short the flight was, wondering if they needed to land somewhere else. Then he discovered that the flight was going to Saginaw, and not to Wichita. Both flights were boarding at the same time from side-by-side gates in the O'Hare terminal. A casual listener could misunderstand the two somewhat similar names.

When the flight attendants realized they hadn't noticed that Erwin's boarding pass was for a different flight, they were quite embarrassed. They helped him book a flight from Saginaw, which is in Michigan, back to Chicago and then on to Wichita later. When he deplaned in Saginaw, as a compensatory gesture, they gave him a bottle of wine. As a lifelong teetotaler, what was he to do? He couldn't offend the flight attendant's kind gesture. He took the wine bottle, which didn't fit into his computer case, and headed back to Chicago. He was concerned because often in the Chicago airport he encountered people he knew making their own treks from one Mennonite event to another. He didn't dare be seen carrying a bottle of wine! As soon as he deplaned in Chicago, he looked for the closest trashcan, slipped the wine bottle into it, and went on his way greatly relieved.

Stormy arrival

One late afternoon, the children and I went to meet Erwin's flight in Wichita. By the time we entered the airport, a storm had moved in. It was getting dark, lightning flashed and thunder roared. Strong winds flung heavy rain against the large windows of the lounge by Gate 10, where United Airlines flights came and went. (We could still all go out on the concourse to the gate in those days.) We soon heard that the plane was diverted and would land in Kansas City – about two hundred miles away. Tina Block Ediger, a friend and former COM mission worker and staff person, had arrived on a different flight and she kindly took our children home while I waited at the airport.

When Erwin arrived several hours later, he said the plane was already descending into Wichita when it experienced a great deal of turbulence due to the storm. They were close enough to catch a glimpse of the runway lights when suddenly the plane pulled up with a burst of power and headed back up into the stormy sky. It was too dangerous to land in Wichita during the storm, so the best option was to fly to Kansas City. Some other passengers were so unnerved by the experience that they opted to spend the night in Kansas City or take a bus to Wichita rather than get on a plane again.

Traveling internationally

International trips usually provided Erwin with some interesting travel stories. Whenever international mission workers get together, they have so many funny stories to share that everyone gets a good dose of laughter.

On one memorable trip to the Congo, Erwin and the delegation of other mission administrators traveling with him from North America spent a long day traveling from one site to another. Local church people showed them church-run medical facilities with shabby, broken equipment. The visitors saw mission schools with barren and bleak classrooms where children sat on rough wooden benches, or on the floor, trying to memorize information the teacher wrote on ragged chalkboards. The delegation met with local church leaders in various types of meeting places, ranging from simple structures with thatched roofs to large buildings. At each place, the delegation was warmly welcomed and also presented with a list of requests.

At many stops, they were served tea and peanuts, but they weren't offered the use of a bathroom. The hot sun beat on them as they rode in the back of an open pickup, which diminished somewhat their need to use a bathroom. By the end of the day, however, that duty could wait no longer. Arriving at the final stop of the day, Erwin inquired about a toilet. This produced a bit of consternation on the part of their hosts. He heard them consulting in the next room, in their own local language. After several minutes, a young person came to show him the way.

He followed his guide some distance from the house to a primitive latrine. It was a low structure, a bit more than three-feet high, formed by slim tree branches or twigs bowed or curved from one side to the other. Pieces of old gunnysacks laid over the branches provided scant coverage. At the entrance, there hung another skimpy flap of gunnysack. Inside, suspended over the pit, was a "floor" made of more tree branches. An opening to squat over yawned between the branches.

The whole thing appeared extremely fragile to Erwin. Equally traumatic to him as the thought of falling through into the pit below was that it faced a busy wide main road about hundred feet or less away. People walking past on the dirt road stopped in astonishment. They gawked as Erwin gingerly bent down to enter under the loosely affixed gunnysacks. He ended up thoroughly unnerved by that experience, the worst one of all his bad bathroom experiences.

Erwin had no trouble eating anything put before him, including high-protein dried caterpillars in Africa. He usually spent a day dealing with the effects of strange food and water on most of his long overseas trips.

In Japan, he was served squid, which reminded him of white dried Elmer's glue, with not much flavor until eaten with highly spiced hot sauce. One time at a food stand in Tokyo, he bought a mini hamburger. He squirted a generous dose of mustard-colored sauce on it. His first bite set not only his mouth on fire but also his nasal passages. It was a strong horseradish mixture and not the mustard he expected.

Erwin and I learned to travel with fewer but better quality suitcases. Whenever mission administrators planned a trip, people overseas sent them requests for items from America. Mission workers' families and supporting churches in North America also wanted to send them things with the traveling administrators. It was hard to limit the amount of luggage. Managing even one suitcase plus a handbag is cumbersome in small quarters, on public transportation, and in the small vehicles usually encountered overseas.

Mennonite connections

Mennonites are diverse and divided. Erwin somehow managed to navigate among them. He met regularly with what is now called the Council of International Anabaptist Ministries, the administrators and leaders of different groups of Anabaptists who work in international locations. The General Conference and the Mennonite Church worked together extensively, especially as the move for a merger gathered momentum. That put him into contact with leaders in the Mennonite Church. As a board member of Africa Inter-Mennonite Mission, Erwin learned to know people from the four or five other Mennonite groups that were part of AIMM.

Continuing education

For his continuing education, Erwin took courses from Fuller Theological Seminary in Pasadena, California – as if four seminaries weren't already enough (Dallas, Westminster, Eastern Baptist, Associated Mennonite Biblical). He took some of the Fuller courses by correspondence. Several summers he spent a couple of weeks in Pasadena for an intensive course.

The most memorable summer class he took at Fuller was on urban ministry. Along with others in his class, he went to a rescue mission where they sat through a sermon by a fiery preacher, went through the soup line, and spent the night sitting in a chair because the beds were full. He and his classmates also spent a night on the street with the homeless in downtown Los Angeles. Sleep was hard to come by on a piece of cardboard out in the open. When asked if that situation felt frightening to him, he said it wasn't. He doesn't scare easily.

More unexpected invitations

During the nearly twelve years we spent in Newton, more unexpected invitations came our way. Several medium and large-sized Mennonite churches in the U.S. approached Erwin about serving as their pastor. However, the mission administration work was a good fit for Erwin's gifts, and overseas mission was our calling. We didn't hear God's voice in those opportunities.

Part Three
Family Life during the Newton years

Because we had taken some much-needed rest in Rio de Janeiro before leaving Brazil in September 1982, we arrived in Newton, Kansas, after the school year began. In hindsight, we should have tried harder to schedule our transition so that the children could begin the new school year with their classmates. Only later did we realize how hard it was for Marci to make the transition into sixth grade at Santa Fe Middle School. Marc more easily slipped into second grade at Sunset Elementary School. Carla stayed at home three more years until she began kindergarten.

Most of our children's childhood memories are from the twelve years we lived in Newton. Even though the house was large enough so that each child had a separate bedroom, at first they didn't actually sleep in their own rooms much. Marci, at age eleven, thought she was ready to sleep in the basement bedroom. Sometime during her first night down there, she came screaming up the stairs, terrified by the new sounds of a basement, such as the water heater and furnace. Something apparently also scared Carla, age two and a half, about her designated room across the hall from our bedroom. She didn't want to sleep in it. One of his sisters often slept in the bunk bed in seven-year-old Marc's room next to ours.

Family living

We made mealtime together a priority – we ate together and the TV was off. When the children were small, we developed a short mealtime prayer that covered the basics: "Dear, Jesus, thank you for the food. Amen." We never got beyond that and have used it ever since then. Even on school days, we sat down together to eat breakfast, complete with a devotional time. We used *Rejoice*, a Mennonite devotional publication that had a child-friendly version at the time.

Going to Sunday school and church each Sunday morning was something we always did with rare exceptions for sickness. If possible, we avoided traveling on Sunday mornings so that we could attend church somewhere with people we knew.

Frugal living was a lifestyle we inherited. Erwin's do-it-yourself attitude was evidence of that. When our son was fourteen, Erwin employed him to help put new shingles on our roof. About six o'clock on those mornings, a big thump woke me as Erwin plunked packets of shingles onto the roof. It was during the heat of August, so by midmorning, he and Marc wrapped it up for the day. It took a long time to get the job done at that rate.

During those years in Kansas, several new technologies became available to average consumers. Beginning with personal computers, new technology expanded rapidly. Our older two children might remember when we introduced some of these items into our home, but as the youngest, Carla doesn't remember not having a computer, microwave, or video recorder for TV programs. We often were the first among our acquaintances and siblings to embrace new technologies.

As mentioned elsewhere, Erwin's work required extensive and prolonged travel. Since I had to take the lead in the home whenever he was gone, there was always some adjustment when he came home again. He realized that my relationship with the children was closer than his was, and he respected my insights. He called home every few days but only once a week when he traveled overseas. Not only were international calls very expensive, he wasn't always in a place where phone service was available.

The children looked forward to their dad's return – especially because he brought them something. Sometimes it was just a candy bar that he bought at the Wichita airport on his way home. If he had forgotten that, they were equally satisfied with a dollar bill to spend at the nearby convenience store.

I felt something in common with single mothers, but I had the blessing of having a good husband that I trusted, who always came home, and who earned a decent salary. As long as I had a reliable car, enough money for basic expenses, and knew when he was coming home again, I couldn't complain. I learned that our lives are all in God's hands whether we are at home or traveling far away.

Much of the guiding and disciplining of the children fell on me. I did a lot of praying. We are very grateful for the wonderful Sunday school teachers and youth sponsors who patiently nurtured and mentored our children as they each made their own decisions about the Christian faith and joined the church. I feel that God truly answered prayer as the children have all become responsible adults, and even are participating in our own Mennonite denomination.

Children growing up

During those years, Marci moved through the awkward years of middle school. By her second year in Newton, at the beginning of her seventh-grade year, she wanted to be called Marcia – but family could still call her Marci – and she developed a new circle of good friends. When prom time approached during Marcia's high school years, I inquired about what alternative plans the numerous churches in Newton might have for that night, as had been the case when I was in high school. I was surprised to learn that the Christian kids went to the high school prom. With hesitation, we allowed the children to attend the school dances. One year I sewed a complicated prom dress for Marcia that she had designed based on a wedding dress pattern.

Marcia became a lovely teenager, giving leadership to the church youth group. She played volleyball during her years in high school. Asthma and its complications plagued her, resulting in several trips to an emergency room. She graduated from Newton High School in 1989.

Marc moved from second grade at Sunset Elementary School and through the obnoxious years of middle school. With his Brazil background, for Marc his sport had to be soccer. He dabbled a bit in basketball, though. Before getting him contact lenses, he often dashed over to where I watched at the sidelines of a game, to give me his broken eyeglasses. We went to his home games but never even contemplated going to games out of town. Newton High School began a soccer program Marc's freshman year. He was salutatorian when he graduated from high school in 1993.

Carla was a thoughtful child and asked some good questions about spiritual things even before she went to school. She began kindergarten at Sunset School, and moved calmly through to middle school, completing eighth grade in 1994. She was quiet and content to be at home. She never wanted a big birthday party – maybe just with one friend.

The girls both took piano lessons. During their middle school years, Marc played trombone and Carla played flute, plus piccolo.

Making a bad choice

After their eighth grade recognition program at Santa Fe Middle School, Marc and some friends went to a party at the Newton Recreation Center. But they didn't stay there. Walking over to a nearby supermarket, Marc made a foolish decision. He tried to take some soda pop and candy without paying. He was caught and taken to the police station. Erwin was traveling, and I had already gone to bed when I got the kind of phone call every parent dreads. I quickly dressed and went to the police station, where Marc was released to me. We didn't talk much that night. But the next morning, he told me that it was a good thing he had been caught the first time he tried that silly stunt, or else he might have tried to do it again. He, and we as his parents, attended a series of meetings with counselors. That pivotal event set him on a course that eventually led him to working for about ten years as a counselor for juvenile offenders, and, we hope, preventing other kids from going on to commit more crimes.

Teaching money management

Erwin has always carefully planned and set up an annual family budget. We got the children involved in annual family meetings to go over the next year's budget. They mainly wanted to know what their allowance would be! In their high school years, we combined their allowance with anticipated costs for their clothing, school lunches, and other activities and gave them that in a monthly sum. They needed to learn how to manage it so that they still had lunch money at the end of the month. To encourage their participation in the church youth group activities, we paid the full amount for their service trips and other activities. As teens, Marcia and Marc began earning their own money. Before they left home, we made sure they managed their own bank accounts and did their own laundry.

Preparing for college

With two generations of college graduates in the family, it was a given that our children would also go to college. None of them seriously considered any school other than the Mennonite-affiliated colleges. Marcia was interested in youth ministry, which limited her choice, at the time, to Eastern Mennonite College (now University) in Harrisonburg, Virginia. EMC paid her plane ticket for a campus visit in fall 1988, an investment that really paid off for the school over the years. I flew with her using the first ticket we arranged with Erwin's frequent flier miles. It had taken about five or six years of slowly accumulating miles to reach that point.

After Marcia decided to go to EMC, her youth sponsors, who were Bethel College alumni, tried to change her mind. That was a real test for her in determining God's will. Her decision to enroll at EMC eventually impacted the rest of our family in unanticipated ways, even to our retirement.

At one point during his senior high school year, Marc told Marcia he didn't want to go to Eastern Mennonite because she went there.

Her insightful retort was, "So you let *me* make *your* decision?" He didn't say much after that. With his high grade point average, he received mailings from many schools, including the military. Finally, we asked him where he was planning to go.

"Eastern Mennonite," was his short response. Three of his Kansas friends set off with him for EMU in the fall of 1993.

Relating to extended family

Neither Erwin nor I lived near our grandparents when we grew up. It was a new experience for us in Kansas to live near our kids' grandparents, uncles, aunts and cousins. My parents, Erwin and Magdalene Albrecht, lived close by us at 912 Central Avenue, near our chil-

Erwin and Magdalene Albrecht celebrate Christmas 1984.

Angela's sister's family: Darrel and LaRita Claassen, front, with Brittany, Marisa, and Taylor, 1994.

dren's elementary school. Occasionally Marc or Carla spent some time with the grandparents either before or after school. We didn't expect nor need much child care since I didn't have other employment while Carla was small. Later my part-time jobs provided me with flexibility.

275

Erwin's sister's family: Barbara and Elwyn Busenitz, center, with Brian and Kyle, 1994.

For the first time, my sister, LaRita, and I had some things in common – we were both adults, married, had children, and lived within a few blocks of each other and our aging parents. The twelve years' difference in our ages didn't matter much anymore. LaRita and Darrel went to the Methodist church where he grew up, so she and I had different church experiences and acquaintances.

Erwin's sister, Barb, and her husband, Elwyn Busenitz, farmed about fifteen miles east of Newton. At times Erwin indulged his love of farming by helping Elwyn on the farm. Elwyn's farming practices reflected bigger trends in Kansas as he discontinued planting wheat and raised corn and soybeans instead. Barb and Elwyn attended Emmaus Mennonite Church, which withdrew from the General Conference during those years.

Going to mission seminar

The children often heard us talk about COM, the Commission on Overseas Mission. At church when a teacher asked the children, "What is the Great Commission?" one of our kids answered, "COM."

No summer was complete without our family attending COM's

annual mission seminar. Our kids interacted well with the missionary children. The location varied from the usual site of the nearby Bethel College campus to some place close to wherever the triennial sessions of the General Conference were being held – Pennsylvania, Saskatchewan, Illinois, and South Dakota – to cut down on travel costs and time. Mission workers and staff were expected to attend both the seminar and the conference sessions. Erwin and his COM staff put in much time and effort planning for presentations and displays. Each commission was responsible for a major presentation to the whole assembly. Erwin tired of going to all those conferences.

Hush money trip

By 1987, Erwin qualified for some study leave in addition to vacation time. We arranged to go as a family to Ventnor, New Jersey, where he would study at the Overseas Mission Study Center, located near the beach. Erwin and I realized that our growing children made the small Dodge Omni a tight fit.

We offered the children seventy-five dollars each if they refrained from complaining and fussing as we traveled – hush money, we called it. They gladly accepted the offer!

Carla was seven, Marc was twelve, and Marcia would turn sixteen during our trip. How we managed to get all we did into that small vehicle still amazes me. Our first day went fine and we got to our motel in Indianapolis. Just as we were ready to leave the next morning, there was a terrible sound when Erwin started the car. It was the compressor for the air conditioner. The car ran fine, though. We continued our trip during a very hot summer without air conditioning in the car. Maybe we should have added a premium to the hush money amount!

On weekdays in New Jersey, while Erwin studied missions, the children and I enjoyed the beach. On weekends, Erwin and I took our children to various places in the east that were only a few hours' driving distance from the Jersey shore. We visited the Pennsylvania churches we had previously worked with north of Philadelphia and the historic places around there, New York City, and Washington, D.C. Limousines caught Marc's attention. We didn't see those in Kansas!

He counted about a hundred of them, mostly around Atlantic City and the big casinos.

The hush money worked! All three of the kids refrained from complaining and bickering and they each collected.

That fall, Marcia had a driver's license and could drive to school. She drove the Omni and we bought a larger car for family use – a used Chevrolet Celebrity. We should have done that before the summer trip!

Using free air miles

One of the benefits of Erwin's travel was that the General Conference allowed staff to use airline mileage points for personal travel. Erwin flew on a variety of airlines at first. He didn't think it would be useful to join all of their frequent-flyer programs because it would take too long to accumulate enough miles for a free flight – 20,000 miles at the time. When some airlines offered triple mileage points, they accumulated quickly. We got a credit card with United Airlines Mileage Plus frequent flyer program that added one mile per dollar charged. The miles accumulated even more rapidly.

Our family benefited immensely from this perk over the years. At one point, Erwin had enough miles so that our family could have flown almost anywhere in the world, including to Australia. We didn't know anyone in Australia then, and didn't seriously consider going there.

The furthest we went as a family with air miles was to the West Coast in 1991 with Marc and Carla. We flew to Fresno, rented a car, and began a long road trip northward through California, Oregon, Washington, and into British Columbia before returning to Fresno to visit Erwin's brother Norm and his family. Scenic shorelines and mountains were quite a contrast to flat Kansas! That trip made a bigger impression on sixteen-year-old Marc than he let on at the time. Right after college he moved to the Pacific Northwest and has made that area his home ever since.

Angela's aging parents

My mom's cancer had recurred already by the time we moved to Newton in 1982. She struggled with various treatments and died only four years after we had come. However, she was very helpful in the beginning in arranging for our temporary housing and helping us get established. She and my Dad interacted with our children, although only our older two remember their grandmother.

My childhood memories of my mother are all positive. During the later years, that wasn't always the case. It has been said that the mother-daughter relationship is always complex, and ours was no exception. Even though in many ways she was my role model, I felt that I didn't meet her expectations.

On one shopping trip, Mom and I went together to get some basic small household items for our new home in Newton. She made a critical comment about each item I put into my shopping cart. She only meant the best for me, of course. Realizing that in many ways I am like she was, I try to relate differently to my daughters. It is likely that I succeed less in that than I hope to do.

"Do I give up and die?" Mom asked when a scan revealed that radiation and chemo hadn't stopped the growth of the cancer spreading through her bones.

She bravely hosted the Easter family meal in 1985 in spite of considerable pain. After that, she soon became bedfast. Hospice, a relatively new organization at the time, provided some help for more than a year before she died. Hospice arranged for a hospital bed that reigned in the middle of the living room for many months. For the day-to-day hands-on care, it was my dad who cared for Mom at home. Her sisters, Hilda and Dorothy, each came from out-of-town for several weeks at a time to help.

I'm sorry to admit that I didn't have a better understanding of what my parents were going through. Our children were young and I had gotten deeply involved in church activities. My husband traveled a great deal, so I was often the sole parent. I visited my parents regularly, but I don't recall ever telling Dad that I would stay with Mom while he took a break and tended to his own things, nor did I take them some prepared meals. My sister, LaRita, had a toddler plus another baby on the way. Since she had been a nurse, I left anything medical up to her. I felt squeamish about providing any hands-on personal care.

Mom never brought up the subject of her impending death, so we didn't bring it up either. Nor did we talk about her getting well. Surely she and Dad discussed it. Mom took strong painkillers that caused side effects that required still more medications to bring a measure of comfort. The medications clouded her mind much of the time during the last year of her life.

In the fall of 1985, Mom took a turn for the worse. An ambulance took her to the hospital. Dad prayed desperately that her life be spared. God answered that prayer, and Mom improved enough to go home again. She lived about another year after that – a year of pain and suffering. That experience has given me much pause about efforts to extend life – or prolong dying – especially in view of our faith in a better and eternal existence with God.

A year later, October of 1986, Aunt Hilda was there again to help. Even with her help, Mom's care was too much to handle at home. Abruptly, without consulting hospice, Dad arranged to have Mom moved to nursing care when a place became available at a Methodist nursing home.

Family members took turns staying with Mom at the nursing home. The morning of October 15 was my shift with her. Not yet understanding signs of the dying process, when I said goodbye, I kissed her on the forehead, and whispered, "I love you" – something I rarely said. I drove home so that Aunt Hilda could drive back over to the nursing home and spend the afternoon with Mom.

By the time Hilda arrived at her bedside, Mom had slipped away from her pain and suffering – as though she needed to be alone for that final breath. Or perhaps she had needed to hear me say that I loved her. It was just before noon when someone from the nursing home phoned to say that Mom had died. I quickly called Erwin at his office. Had I called him a few minutes later, he would have been on the road to the airport to catch a flight for a meeting. It would then have been difficult to contact him in those pre-cell phone days. Mom had lived only about a week at the nursing home.

We plunged into the whirl of contacting people and making plans for the funeral. Church people brought us prepared food – casseroles and desserts in particular. Eleven-year-old Marc was wide-eyed and delighted by all the food arriving.

"Just let us know if there is anything we can do," the church people said. Apparently they were startled when I took them literally and mentioned the need to get our house clean. My mom's four sisters were coming – all of them as diligent in their housekeeping as Mom had been. After two or three church women helped clean our house, later I heard that they figured I was used to having maids in Brazil. No one else, apparently, had the nerve to suggest that kind of help.

Dad Albrecht starts over at age 80

"She was so young," my grieving dad said of his wife. He was only days away from his eightieth birthday when she died. Her passing at seventy years and four months felt so young to him. Being only in my forties at the time, it didn't seem young to me. When I approached age seventy, I understood.

Dad bravely carried on alone. He baked bread and pies. He canned and froze the garden produce he continued to cultivate as he and Mom had done together wherever they lived after leaving Chicago in 1946.

LaRita and I regularly visited Dad and invited him for meals in our homes. He took an interest in two different women, but no relationship developed with either of them. Apparently one of them found him to be too old, and he found her to be too fat.

Several years later, 1990, Dad was among the first ten people to move into a new apartment building at Kidron-Bethel Village in North Newton, designed for independent living in retirement. To our surprise, Dad didn't want to take any of his garden tools to use in a garden plot he could have had at Kidron-Bethel. At age eighty-four, he was done with gardening. He did make use of the workshop there. However, without Mom's "quality control," his wooden craft items weren't quite square and the finish was uneven. Yet each piece he handcrafted that graces my home has special meaning to us.

A world-changing event

"Mom, Dad, come look at this!" Marc called from the family room downstairs where he was watching TV. It was November 9, 1989. The regular programming was interrupted for live coverage of an event in Germany. To our amazement, people clambered over and through the Berlin Wall, chipping away at it, and dancing on top of it. All my

Rempel family in Newton, Kan., 1989.

life that wall epitomized the stark division between us and the hidden, godless, nuclear-armed world behind the Iron Curtain. Now before our eyes, the wall came down. The world order we had grown up with changed dramatically. The fall of the Berlin wall became the iconic marker of the end of the Cold War between Western countries and what we referred to as Russia or the Soviet Union.

Part Four
Angela's Experiences During the Newton Years

Newton, Kansas, was the right size town for us, as far as I was concerned. With a population of about 17,000, all the basics were available there. If not, we could zip down the wide lanes of the Interstate to nearby Wichita, a much-larger city.

Bland, however, is the word that comes to mind to describe how I felt about the nearly twelve years we lived in Newton, from 1982 to

1994. That was in contrast to our years overseas where nearly every day brought something unusual, unexpected, and totally new to us. Once we were settled in Newton, life was usually fairly calm and predictable. The flat open fields that surrounded Newton and the big sky stretched overhead contributed to that blandness. Most everyone around us in Newton shared our skin color. Our children seldom saw people of other races except for some of our houseguests from abroad. We rarely encountered immigrants from other countries.

Whenever my life went on autopilot and got too bland, something occurred to stretch my comfort zone. That kept me growing in understanding and Christian faith.

Home life

In many ways, those were very good and eventful years for our family – even if they felt bland to me. It is the only major chapter in our married life when I was not regularly involved working together with Erwin. Instead, my days filled with bringing up the children. I taxied them to and from school, church activities, and other places. It was a new experience for us to live close to my parents and to our married sisters and their young children. I had other relatives in the area as well.

Erwin and I continued to enjoy offering hospitality. Our guest room had frequent use and our drop-leaf dining room table was extended even more frequently. As one of the Mennonite centers, Newton attracts a variety of people. Most of our guests were connected in some way to overseas mission work. One time a few hours before overnight guests arrived, we discovered that our kittens had pooped on the carpet beside the bed in the guestroom. A thorough cleaning and generous application of baking soda hid that fact from the guests, we hoped.

Not being averse to trying new technology, Erwin and I were eager to buy a personal computer for home use. I took an evening class at Bethel College where I first learned how to turn on a computer and load the software. Erwin has already described our first computer we bought in 1983, but I'll add that it had no mouse, no internal hard drive, no color, no modem and no touchpad. The internet wasn't in use yet. It took great quantities of patience and persistence to accomplish anything in those early days of personal computers. Several times

Erwin prints a document from first home computer, 1983.

after I typed an important document, it would all be lost because it was larger than 256 kilobytes available on a floppy disk.

Employment in Newton

I'm grateful we managed without me working outside the home while the children were small. Involvements outside the home, especially church activities, kept me from feeling house bound during those years.

My knowledge of worldwide missions grew, especially as I met more missionaries and traveled overseas. During the first years in Newton, I volunteered to help Erwin make a new monthly in-house newsletter, *The COMmunicator*, with excerpts from letters that mission workers wrote. Years later that publication continues as the monthly *News from Around the World* sent to mission workers and prayer partners.

"Standing in the gap," best describes the part-time temporary jobs I did after Carla began school in 1985. I've never considered myself a "career woman," and I didn't work fulltime. All the jobs I took were within the Mennonite world, arranged through "networking," although we didn't use that term then.

Working for COM

My previous experience of writing and making sound-slide sets based on our own Brazil work now opened the door to other communication-type projects. Under the direction of Jeannie Zehr at COM, I wrote and produced more sound-slide sets. I also made banners and displays that churches borrowed. Some of that work I could do at home.

Erwin purchased a video camera for COM – another new technology at the time. The camera was big and rested on the users' shoulder while attached to a heavy recording device in a shoulder bag. Erwin took the camera equipment along when he went to the Congo in late 1984. He videotaped interesting and colorful events. After his trip, I set up two VHS recorders in COM's small library. There I tediously and imprecisely copied bits and pieces from the original VHS cassette from one recorder to a blank cassette in the other recorder. Any time the office heating and cooling system turned on and off, a line of undeletable electrical static showed up on the video tape. To prevent that, I turned off the air system when I did the dubbing. To make titles, I put lettering on poster board and videoed it. Primitive, indeed.

Production studios began to make videos – for about a thousand dollars per minute of finished video. For ten thousand dollars, COM purchased a set of video editing equipment. Carefully following the instruction manual, I learned how to operate it. The video editing work was still very tedious, but it was a huge improvement over the simplistic earlier attempts. I learned how to do separate tracks for visual, narration, and background music. Over the years, I made numerous four- to ten-minute videos about COM ministries in various countries.

The COM offices provided a pleasant work environment. Jeannie Zehr was my supervisor because office policy didn't allow a staff person to supervise his or her spouse.

Working at First Mennonite

One year the church secretary at First Mennonite Church, Grace Yoder, asked me to work during her two-week annual vacation. She thus introduced me to a fill-in job that wove in and out of my life for more than twenty years.

The church doors at First Mennonite were unlocked in those days, so we never knew who might enter. Being a large stately brick church prominently located along a major street entering Newton from the nearby Interstate highway, the church attracted people who needed financial help.

One day I was alone in the church, busily running a noisy machine that put address labels on the church bulletins that we mailed prior to each week's worship service. I was startled to turn around and discover a stranger had entered the small office. The tall dark man claimed to have been a professional basketball player who now needed financial help. I felt very vulnerable. He was, however, mild-mannered and low-key. He quietly waited in the church foyer for someone to come and tend to his situation. Eventually, the church doors were kept locked during office hours.

Working with publications

Ever since my childhood, the mail brought to our household two Mennonite publications that informed us and kept us in touch with the larger Mennonite world. During our years in Newton, I worked a year

Angela first uses an Apple computer while working for The Mennonite, *1989. Photo used by permission.*

for each of those publications. It was good to experience some of what took place before they showed up in our mailbox.

Mid-1989 to mid-1990 I filled in for an assistant at *The Mennonite*, published twice a month at that time. An Apple computer with a mouse was then the new state-of-the-art in desktop publishing. Proofreading and record keeping filled my days there as I worked with the editor, Muriel Thiessen Stackley, and Gordon Houser, the assistant editor.

The *Mennonite Weekly Review* (now *Mennonite World Review*) also hired me for a year. The *Review* staff developed its own photos from film and had a printing press on-site. During my year there, they also began to use Apple computers with desktop publishing. In addition to proofreading and editing short news items and church news, Robert Schrag, editor, assigned me to write a front-page feature article. It was about two growing Mennonite churches in Taiwan that had each built multi-story structures. They rented out the lower levels under their top-floor sanctuaries. That was an enjoyable writing assignment, especially because I had been able to visit Taiwan earlier.

Working at Prairie View

The last job I had during those years in Newton was as half-time secretary in the chaplain's office suite at Prairie View, a Mennonite-founded mental health facility. Each morning I inserted several floppy discs in succession to boot up the computer with software for the day's work. That is where I first used email, limited to communicating within the Prairie View office system. The Prairie View chaplain was a pleasant man and easy to work with.

Prairie View then hired a marriage counselor to work alongside the chaplain. The marriage counselor insisted that he needed a car phone – a new technology featuring a brick-sized box with a cord attached to a full-size phone handset, plus exterior antenna. He frequently called me from the car to let me know he was going to be late. He was also late in giving me material to type for record keeping.

After we moved away from Newton, I was surprised at what happened to both of those men. The chaplain came out as gay and left his wife and little boy. The marriage counselor and his wife separated. He eventually attacked and wounded her and then committed suicide.

Keeping connected internationally

Even though I was busy with parenting, church activities, and other jobs, I was still in touch with global mission. Going overseas again remained in the back of my mind.

"I can leave all the advantages of living in the U.S. and move to another country again," was my mantra. That assumption was tested, however, when we got our first microwave – that would be hard to do without.

Erwin kept me informed about his work, both the ups and the downs. I made sure to keep his trust and not "leak" anything he shared in confidence.

During the annual Council of Commissions meetings in Newton, whenever the COM sessions were open to the public, I made sure to sit in the gallery. I enjoyed hearing the commission members discuss and make decisions about issues encountered in working internationally. Applicants for overseas mission service publically shared their inspiring stories of God's call during those sessions.

Traveling overseas with Erwin

Each year Erwin traveled to one of the three continents where COM mission workers lived. A generous spouse-travel policy and eventually Erwin's accumulation of frequent flier miles helped make it possible for me to accompany him. I went with him once to each continent and to most of the countries where COM had missionaries. Those trips were amazing highlights during our time in Newton.

As related in an earlier chapter about my childhood, I grew up meeting missionaries and hearing about overseas mission work. I am humbled by the unusual privilege I had of going to those same distant places, visiting mission workers in their homes, and worshipping together with believers in various styles of worship and languages. We accepted the accommodations offered us in homes or simple guesthouses. We slept on beds that ranged from comfortable to just thin mattresses on the floor. Tourists staying in nice hotels and going on staged tours would find it hard to duplicate the richness of the meaningful encounters we had.

Thanks to my enjoyment of photography, I set off on each overseas trip with a camera bag and rolls of film in a special lead-lined bag. The lead bag protected undeveloped film from the X-rays at airport screeners. The experiences and photos from those trips provided me with information for writing and making visual projects for COM.

Flying alone overseas

"Alone I shall not wander one single day," were the comforting words from a familiar hymn that encouraged me in 1983 as I set off on my first solo international flight. Friends from college days met me at the airport in Tokyo and helped me connect with the bullet train that took me to where I joined Erwin and Peter Kehler for part of their around-the-world Asia trip Erwin wrote about above. It felt a bit awkward that my relatively young husband was the administrator for veteran missionaries we visited, including Verney and Belva Unruh from my home church in Montana. Compared to South America, the religions, cultures, and spoken and written languages of Japan, Taiwan, and Hong Kong made Asia feel exotic to me. On Easter Sunday, we joined a Japanese church for a sunrise service in a cemetery.

Erwin and I felt honored to travel together the following year with Jim Bertsche and his wife, Jenny, veteran Africa administrator and mission workers. I joined the Bertsches and Erwin in Paris after they attended the 1984 Mennonite World Conference in Strasburg, France. We traveled together for five weeks in five African countries where COM, through Africa Inter-Mennonite Mission, supported mission workers.

First, in Burkina Faso in West Africa we saw how mission workers adopted the lifestyles of the Africans around them, living in rugged conditions. Living conditions for missionaries in Botswana, Lesotho and the Transkei in southern Africa were similar to what we experienced in Brazil. However, due to the struggle with apartheid, tensions were high in that region. We heard stories of oppression and close escapes from bombings.

The last two weeks of our Africa trip, we spent in Congo, called Zaire at the time. The president of the Congo Mennonite churches accompanied us on a small Missionary Aviation Fellowship plane as we visited several locations "up country." We visited some of the mission stations I'd heard of as a child. Established in the early 1900s, the mission station compounds included large stone churches built in Western styles, houses for missionaries and Congolese staff, medical facilities, and schools ranging from elementary grades to a Bible training institute. Missionaries had developed infrastructure for water and electricity on the mission compounds. About forty missionaries served in Congo at the time we visited. The dysfunctional government depended on church organizations to provide services we typically expect government and private business to provide, including education, health care, transportation, and financial services.

The trips to Asia and Africa that Erwin and I took together during his first two years on the job reduced my anxiety when he needed to travel overseas again, especially to Africa. We were grateful to our extended family who helped care for our children during those long trips.

Returning to South America

Life was too busy and complicated with growing children and aging parents for me to consider going with Erwin on another overseas trip until six years later. In September 1990, we went to five countries in South America: Brazil, Uruguay, Paraguay, Bolivia and Colombia. We traveled with Glendon Klaassen, the COM director for Latin America. By then Marcia was in college and Marc could drive himself to high school and other activities. Carla, age ten, was in middle school with a simple schedule that my sister, LaRita, was able to accommodate.

We arrived in Brazil on our first stop in South America in time to witness a sunrise baptism at the beach in Recife. We joyfully reconnected with the Gama congregation we had served earlier in Brazil. A colorful sunset marked the conclusion of our South America trip. On our final day of that trip, we visited Cachipay, a mission location in Colombia I'd heard about all my life. It was fitting to observe a beautiful sunset as we drove the curving mountain road back to the city where we would catch our flight back home.

Going to India

In January 1991, I went with Erwin to the exotic land of India for about three weeks. My sister, LaRita, again helped with the children. En route, our layover in Bangkok was long enough to take a city tour on a flimsy rickshaw that competed with heavy traffic. We switched to a taxicab, which felt safer.

Our previous international trips had been arranged and guided by the staff person serving as the area director. However, in India we, along with Vern Preheim, executive director of the General Conference, were on our own. No missionaries from North American were still serving in the established mission churches, hospitals, schools, or seminary. It was quite an adventure finding our way around! Many times I marveled at God's care and provision for us.

Once again, Erwin and I had the privilege of visiting places we had heard about since childhood. In India we saw traditional large mission compounds built years earlier in a pattern similar to what we'd seen in Congo. We visited Champa where doctors Harvey and Ella Bauman had worked. She was the one who God first used to speak to me as a child about being a missionary.

Like a bonus, in early 1994, I accompanied Erwin on a two-week trip to Spain, where he helped evaluate the mission work of the Mennonite Brethren mission agency. Our Portuguese helped us understand some of their Spanish, but we missed a lot.

With these travels, we had been on five continents. It seemed unlikely that we would ever go to Australia.

Part Five
Church Experiences

Which church should our family join? We seldom faced that question when we moved because the church was part of the equation in the job we accepted. Moving to Newton, Kansas, in 1982, there were many Mennonite churches nearby from which to make a choice.

My parents and others at First Mennonite Church urged us to join them there. As its name indicates, First Mennonite Church was the first one begun in Newton and it was located on First Street. Started by immigrants from Prussia in the 1870s, it was among the largest Mennonite churches in the area and offered a wide range of programs and activities for children and youth. That was what we wanted for our children ranging then from age two to eleven. The church had a long history of supporting and sending missionaries and short-term workers. It was known as more theologically conservative than the other General Conference Mennonite churches in Newton. The stately, European-style sanctuary lined with large stained-glass windows was constructed during the Great Depression. The external pipes of a pipe organ graced each side of the choir loft. Over the years, several building additions kept up with the congregation's growth, which peaked in 1981 slightly above a thousand members. Even if weekly attendance was about half of the membership number, to us it was a very large church.

Checking out First Mennonite

Greeters warmly welcomed us at the door. They showed the children to their appropriate Sunday school classes. Erwin and I were directed to an adult class with couples about our age.

The next evening, we enjoyed a meal at the home of Delora and Jerry Decker, along with Betty and Dewayne Pauls, and another family whose children were about the ages of ours. They were all from the Sunday school class we attended the day before. Within the week, Pastor Floyd Bartel visited us. With all that welcoming, of course, we would go to First Mennonite! We began a thirty-year journey with the church through various highs and lows.

After the small intimate fellowship of the congregation in Gama, Brazil, it was hard for me to adjust to such a large church. I missed the Brazilian exuberance, lively music, and contemporary songs. I missed being one of the musicians. One Sunday morning months later, while I walked toward the sanctuary as the pipe organ prelude played, I realized I had begun to appreciate and anticipate worship there too.

Nurturing our children

The congregation nurtured, supported, and encouraged our children. The youth group was an important experience for the children, especially as the dedicated youth sponsors mentored them. Each of the children made a public confession of faith in Christ and was baptized there. Erwin and I also found fellowship and friendship.

Getting involved

"How can I get to know more people at church?" I wondered after we had attended First Mennonite for about a year. God knew how to take care of that! I was asked to be part of what they then called the Board of Christian Education. I quickly began to know more people – essentially most of the large congregation. For several years, I was the superintendent for the children's Sunday school classes.

I enjoyed teaching a mission class during summer vacation Bible school. From my travels with Erwin to the various continents, I had a personal supply of inexpensive artifacts to use with the class. The Commission on Overseas Mission had developed mission curriculum for children that featured countries I had visited.

Erwin usually had limited involvement at First Mennonite due to his heavy workload and travel as Executive Secretary of the Commission on Overseas Mission.

My limited musical abilities didn't get much use during the years at First Mennonite. I took some lessons on the pipe organ and played it a few times. But as a short person, it was a struggle to play accurately when I was fighting just to keep my balance and not slide off the bench onto the foot pedals. The monthly church newsletter, *FMC Connections*, which I initiated, continues with a digital format on-line.

Changes impacting church life

We observed how, during the 1980s, the congregation tried to maintain programs and activities that started during its first hundred years of existence. Many of the church members back then were farmers and most women worked at home. Now only a few members at First Mennonite were still traditional farmers with a measure of discretionary time. Many of the women had jobs outside of the home. Those factors made it difficult to maintain the traditional programs of the church.

Family life came under more and more stress in those years with both parents having employment and children becoming involved in an exploding number of extra-curricular activities. The old-timers couldn't understand why families preferred to stay home together on Sunday evenings rather than attend another service at church. Older church members were greatly distressed when Sunday evening services were discontinued.

There weren't enough people to continue a two-week daytime summer vacation Bible school program. Even a one-week, evening Bible school was a challenge. Eventually, only one women's group continued to meet instead of thirteen different circles, as had been the case when my mother served as overall coordinator.

The membership and attendance fell at First Mennonite, in part, because families had fewer children and more of them moved away when they grew up. Several newer Mennonite churches nearby competed for members. However, First Mennonite attracted a good number of missionaries and pastors, such as my parents, who moved to the Newton area for retirement. The congregation had something like more than 250 people over the age of sixty-five.

Attempting outreach

New ways of outreach were needed. In the early 1990s, Mennonite churches developed a program called LIFE (Living in Faithful Evangelism written by Ed Bontrager, who entered our lives later). Delora Decker and I were co-chairs of the LIFE process in our congregation. After attending a LIFE orientation, we wondered if our church could do what some other churches did on Wednesday nights – fellowship meals and activities for all ages. We tried that, and it was well accepted. With some alterations, Wednesday evening meals and activities continue to draw people more than twenty-five years later.

Experiencing discord

All congregations seem to have a measure of divisions and First Mennonite was no exception. About the time I felt a connection with someone in the church, often she and her family left for a more theologically conservative church. Those divisions surfaced intensely in the mid-1980s. The youth group had raised money and purchased new songbooks, *Sing and Rejoice*, and placed them in the sanctuary hymnal racks. Some deacons took offense at songs in that book that spoke to the radical aspect of Jesus' life and teaching and referred to Jesus as the Lord of the dance. The concerned deacons went through each book and stamped each of those songs with something such as, "This song is unworthy of our Lord." Marcia remembers that the pages for one of those songs were actually glued shut. In response, other deacons made another label they placed inside each book with a different explanation. The songbooks were soon removed from use entirely, leaving the youth bewildered.

A significant group of people eventually left First Mennonite to form another church that affiliated with a more theologically conservative group of Mennonites. It was painful, personally, to feel rejected. That new church became the largest church in Newton with multiple services. Our church also prospered as we enjoyed a new sense of unity.

Processing a painful episode

One Sunday morning before church in the early 1990s, the chair of the deacon board came to our house to talk privately with Erwin who at the time was a deacon. Erwin learned that a number of years earlier our pastor had an inappropriate relationship with a woman. The pastor was well liked and the congregation was shocked. The pastor was immediately removed from his position. People took different views on how to handle the matter. At a congregational meeting, Erwin had the task of attempting to explain the dynamics involved in what the pastor admitted he had done. People who strongly supported the pastor then directed their ire at Erwin. During that turmoil, I dreaded going to church at times. A highly respected church member, Verney Unruh, a retired missionary and pastor, filled an important interim pastoral role by helping the congregation in that difficult time.

Larger church circles

On the broader church scene, Erwin and I were deeply involved at the denominational level in North America and with the global church as it related to the Commission on Overseas Mission. We had little time or energy to be involved in the regional Western District Conference. Several "Old" Mennonite congregations flourished in nearby Hesston, along with Hesston College, but that was another world away for us. It didn't help that phone calls to the Hesston area were toll calls. Erwin's work, however, often was alongside Mennonite Church people and organizations at the denominational level where he personally knew many of their staff and board members. Yet at that time, there was little joint activity between our local congregations or between our Western District and their South Central Conference other than in MCC projects.

In other parts of North America, however, some General Conference and Mennonite Church area conferences not only worked together but merged. Some congregations belonged to both denominations. Those were significant factors driving a denominational merger.

Part Six
Anticipating a New Chapter

Our years in Kansas passed quickly. Erwin's role as executive secretary of the Commission on Overseas Mission was approaching the ten- to twelve-year limit drilled into him by his predecessor, Howard Habegger. We felt that it is better to leave when things are going well than to stay too long. We began to think and pray about what the next chapter of our life together would be.

After 1990, the church leaders moved toward merging our General Conference Mennonites with the (Old) Mennonite Church. That was all fine, but Erwin wasn't interested in working with the complexities of integrating into one entity. By taking another overseas assignment, the merger would be completed by the time we returned to the U.S. – or so we thought.

Exploring another international ministry

We explored options for overseas ministry again. Because I had traveled with Erwin to most of the places where COM had mission work, we both had some firsthand knowledge about the overseas locations we considered.

Carla would complete eighth grade in May 1994 and be ready for high school, a good time to make a change. We hoped to serve in some place where she wouldn't have to go to boarding school.

Deciding on Botswana

Eric and Kathy Fast, the country administrators at Mennonite Ministries in Gaborone, Botswana, were completing their term and returning to Canada. We applied for that position and were approved as co-country administrators for a team of both Mennonite Central Committee workers and people serving with Africa Inter-Mennonite Mission. Our term would begin in June 1994. Erwin was well acquainted with AIMM having served on its board for twelve years. AIMM administered all the COM mission workers in Africa. Although we had heard of MCC all our lives, this would be our first experience serving with MCC overseas.

The political climate in southern Africa had changed greatly since the tension-filled days of a visit Erwin and I made there ten years earlier, in 1984. Apartheid in South Africa had officially ended, people of every race had voted, and Nelson Mandela was elected the new president of the so-called "rainbow nation." From our earlier visit, we knew that living conditions in Gaborone, Botswana, provided electricity and running water – enough for us to set up housekeeping.

Gaborone also had a fine private international secondary school so that Carla wouldn't need to go to a boarding school. By the fall of 1994, Marc would start his second year at Eastern Mennonite University and Marcia would have completed her second major at EMU and be ready to find employment. We were grateful at how the Lord led in bringing all the pieces together.

An unsettling experience

A few days before Easter in 1994, we experienced our own personal Gethsemane and resurrection. I felt a lump in my breast and underwent a biopsy. Because of my mother's history of breast cancer, that was a scary time for me. My mind is good at imagining all sorts of scenarios. What joyous relief just before Easter Sunday when we learned it was benign. We could move ahead with preparing for Botswana.

Anticipating our move

When we announced our plans to go to Botswana, some of the people in our Sunday school class couldn't figure out how we could uproot

Angela, Erwin, and Carla Rempel, 1994.

at age 50 and move to Africa. More than one person asked if we were taking fourteen-year-old Carla along to Africa. But, of course!

While initially Marcia and Marc were supportive of our going overseas again, when the reality of what that meant for them sank in, it turned out to be harder than expected.

"Are you going to sell the house?" Marcia asked anxiously about the place that had provided the security of home for nearly twelve years. It wasn't financially viable for us to keep the house, plus we didn't know how long we would be overseas nor where we might be called to after that. We wanted to be open to wherever God might call us.

Typically, young adults leave home – parents don't. Again we felt we needed to downplay our enthusiasm about beginning a new chapter of life.

Selling our house

When a realtor looked at our house, she told us we needed to replace its various styles and colors of carpet with uniform "Mennonite beige" carpet. We made some repairs and painted the walls a neutral color, but replacing the carpet seemed like too much. People looked at the house,

298

but it hadn't sold yet when we moved out in late May. We relented and ordered "Mennonite beige" carpet. In mid- June, while we attended a leader's orientation session at Mennonite Central Committee offices in Akron, Pennsylvania, we finally got an offer on our house – right after the new carpet was installed.

Packing, dispersing, and storing

For Botswana, I knew we wouldn't need more than what fit into the standard airline baggage allowance of two checked bags each. Erwin's books, however, we packed and sent by ship again. I made a detailed inventory of our possessions indicating what to take, what to store, and what to get rid of. Most things fell into the latter category.

Even though Erwin and I didn't usually go to auctions, we realized that an auction would be the best way to dispose of our furniture, appliances, and many other things. Erwin's sister and her husband let us store some small basic items and memorabilia in their nearby farmhouse attic.

At our auction on May 21, 1994, people actually paid us to haul our things away. As we saw the last of our stuff riding off down the street, we felt light and free!

For our final days in Newton, we got a taste of life in a retirement community. We appreciated living in Lois and Pete Voran's fully furnished house at Kidron-Bethel Village during the three-week gap between moving out of our house and leaving for Botswana.

Leaving for Botswana on June 26, 1994

By the last Sunday of June, everything was ready. Marc had moved in with friends for the summer while he worked on Dwight and Janet Regiers' farm as he had done previously. Marcia was a candidate for youth pastor at our church, First Mennonite. Later that same day, after our departure, a congregational vote affirmed her for that position.

On Sunday morning June 26, First Mennonite Church commissioned us for our new chapter of life in Botswana. It was a very moving service. We had chosen several poignant songs including *Here I am, Lord* and Patty Shelly's song, *The Lord Lift You Up*. This transition time, especially the final day, was another occasion when I deliberately put my emotions into a figurative box in order to function. That works for everything except the music. During transition times, songs are more meaningful to me and tears flow.

That same afternoon we headed to the Wichita airport. At first, the check-in agent interpreted the baggage limit differently than how we had so carefully packed and weighed each bag. She was going to charge us something like $1,200 in excess fees. What relief when she was convinced to see it the way we understood and didn't charge any extra.

We bid farewell to my father, Erwin A. Albrecht, then age 87 and in good health. I expected I'd see him again. Tearfully we bid farewell to Marcia and Marc. Somberly we walked down the jet-way to the United Airlines plane for the first leg of our long journey to southern Africa and to the next chapter of our lives. It is good we didn't realize how challenging it would be for all of us.

Chapter Six

Botswana from 1994 to 2000

Part One
Life and Ministry in Southern Africa

After working through the pain of saying goodbyes at the Wichita airport on June 26, 1994, Erwin, Carla, and I allowed ourselves to feel the excitement of our new venture to Africa. At O'Hare Airport in Chicago, we boarded an over-night British Airways flight to London. We were surprised at how tight and close the plane seats were, even for someone as short as I am. A ten-hour layover in London provided time for us to check into a day room, stretch out, and get some sleep.

Walking down the jet-way in London to board a big Boeing 747 for a long overnight flight to southern Africa, I was stopped and my carry-on weighed. It was overweight. I quickly tried to grab some items I needed during the long flight before the bag was sent down below with checked luggage.

That carry-on bag didn't show up when we arrived in Gaborone, the capital city of Botswana, the next morning, June 27, about eleven o'clock. That bag had all the important things one is supposed to put into a carry-on. It had been taken off the plane during our short stopover in Johannesburg, South Africa. My imagination went into overdrive thinking of the worst. When my carry-on arrived the next day in Gaborone with all its contents intact, I was relieved and grateful for God's protecting hand.

Introduction to Botswana

Since the time Erwin and I visited Botswana in 1984, not only had the tense political climate changed dramatically, but Mennonite Ministries' office and guesthouse had downsized and relocated in a smaller facility.

As we arrived, the Mennonite Ministries (MM) team of about eighteen adults and nearly as many children converged on Gaborone from their assignment locations scattered around Botswana. They gathered for their annual planning meeting, led by outgoing country representatives Kathy and Eric Fast. We were immediately impressed with the qualified, capable, and delightful people who formed the MM team we'd work with.

Mennonite Ministries used facilities on Pudomo Road that were owned by the Botswana Christian Council. What originally was a simple house had been enlarged to accommodate the MM office, library, bedrooms for guests, a lounge, dining area, and kitchen. Erwin, Carla, and I stayed at the guesthouse during our first week in Botswana. We slept on bunk beds in the two small rooms of a concrete block building behind the main building.

Within a short time after our arrival, we began the process of getting residency documents. Thanks to the Technical Service Agreement that MCC had negotiated years earlier, that was easily accomplished.

The three of us embarked on a steep learning curve in all aspects of our work and life.

Living in an African village

After the planning meeting, our next important task was to learn the Setswana language and culture. Botswana had no structured full-time language school, so MM team members learned the local Setswana language using the Brewster method. Brewster advocated self-guided language learning while living among local people. Learning imitated the way a young child learns – listen and try to speak. New MM workers went to live in a village right after arriving in the country. We did that too.

The thought of living in an African village for nearly two months may sound very exotic and difficult. In many aspects, it was just that!

The Fasts took the three of us to the village of Metsimotlhabe about fifteen miles from Gaborone.

Harriet, our village host, waited for us. Her spacious yard, kept free of vegetation, was swept clean. We drove up with the MM van and a small pickup carrying some basic furniture and simple items for our use.

Metsimotlhabe wasn't an untouched traditional African village but rather a village very much in transition, which helped us understand the realities of life in a fast-changing society. Harriet's husband, along with many other villagers, commuted daily to Gaborone, riding in overloaded VW vans that served as public buses. His job with the water department paid enough for his family to have a nice house with electricity. They anticipated having piped-in water soon and a landline phone. Three of their children went to private schools. Their house was nicely furnished, including a color TV. But they had no vehicle.

A short distance behind their nice house, we set up our temporary home in one of the other buildings in their yard – a plaster-covered concrete block, two-room structure without electricity or water. A small propane-powered refrigerator and two-burner camp-style stove functioned adequately in our kitchen corner of one room. Several shelf units and a table with a dishpan for a sink made a small convenient kitchen area. In the other room, we arranged three single beds and a small desk.

After experimenting, I figured out a system of doing our laundry by hand, outside, using several plastic tubs. Three teenage girls looked on in amusement as this white woman clumsily scrubbed and wrung out things by hand. I asked one of them to show me how to do the scrubbing on a washboard, and she did so. In hindsight, instead of being a frugal, do-it-yourselfer, I should have thought in terms of "job creation," and paid the girls to do the washing.

The cold air and dust of dry season filtered inside through the loosely fitted windows and the gaps between the top of the walls and the tin roof. We used an outhouse, which was an unpleasant cold experience – especially in the dark at bedtime and early morning when the temperatures dropped to nearly freezing. A flashlight revealed spiders and bugs in the outhouse. It was easy to imagine other invisible creatures.

During the daytime, the sun provided welcome warmth. Away from bright city lights, the star-filled night sky looked like the Montana skies

I'd seen in my teenage years. Candles and a gas lantern illuminated our small quarters at night. A movable heater with a small propane tank kept us warm. We tuned in to BBC World Service on a shortwave radio to keep up with world events.

Long before dawn, roosters' crowing announced the coming day. Baby goats' cries sounded eerily like a human child. Other sounds we heard in the village ranged from the sound of donkeys' death-defying braying to piercing car alarms. The place where we stayed was on the edge of the village, next to a busy paved highway where cars zipped past and noisy trucks and buses roared and rumbled along. A work crew accompanied a big Caterpillar machine digging a trench alongside the highway. They laid fiber-optic cable for a new landline phone system that eventually circled all of Botswana.

Every day Erwin, often Carla with him, took plastic containers in a wheelbarrow for a ten-minute walk to get water from a public water tap. Maneuvering the wheelbarrow with heavy full water containers over the uneven dirt paths was strenuous. We marveled at how slender girls of about twelve years of age appeared to manage doing that quite easily. Women carried large water containers on their heads with graceful ease.

Angela and Erwin wash dishes during village live-in, Botswana, 1994.

Carla and Erwin take a wheelbarrow to fetch water during village live-in, Botswana, 1994.

Our host's oldest son, about age twenty, was a language tutor for Erwin. My tutor was a young woman who attended the University of Botswana. She, her three-year-old daughter, and the child's father lived in another building on the same yard.

The Brewster language-learning method probably works fine for extroverts. We found it hard to overcome our shyness and actually try to talk to people using the new Setswana words. Villagers were startled that white people would try to say more than the basic greeting, *Dumela*. Their mumbled responses didn't resemble what the books said they were supposed to say in return. One of several Bantu languages, Setswana is very different from English, other than using the same ABCs for writing.

Our host, Harriet, took us to meet and greet some village people. One day we walked with Harriet out to "the lands," visiting people at homesteads along the way. This gave us a valuable glimpse of rural life and an opportunity to try out some Setswana. Each homestead consisted of several small buildings, often round thatched huts. Some type of fence edged each yard – a single wire strung between posts, perhaps a barrier of tightly packed thorn-tree branches, or low concrete block walls. A traditional family often had two or three locations – "the lands" where they grew crops, the "cattle post" for their prized cattle, and a house in a village or city.

We white people living in the village caused quite a stir. People asked us for things – jobs, scholarships, and, of course, money. I was flabbergasted when one woman boldly asked me for the skirt I was wearing. I had just bought a couple of skirts in the U.S. that I hoped would last me for several years in that culture where women, at that time, only wore skirts. If being asked for things is a flattering sign that one has attained a position of status and wealth, it didn't feel that way to us. Responding to begging had been difficult for us in Brazil, and we still hadn't learned how to deal with it very well.

Harriet was a lovely woman, a "congregational worker" in the Lutheran church, where she took turns preaching. She wore a black and white uniform to church, as did other Lutheran women. In contrast, red, black, and white uniforms identified Methodists. Harriet's husband was a quiet man we seldom saw. In addition to the oldest son who tutored Erwin, we met the other five delightful children, mostly girls, ages 18, 16, 14, 12 and 10. Their ages confirmed for Carla what I had told her about the typical natural spacing of children when no birth control was used.

Even though our host's house was nicely furnished, they lived outdoors much of the time. The unheated masonry house remained uncomfortably cool during the day. But outdoor living was also a traditional year-round lifestyle.

Harriet had a hand-cranked sewing machine. To sew, she sat down flat on the ground beside the sewing machine with her legs stretched out straight. Wrapped in a blanket from head to toe, people took naps on the ground alongside the house where the warm sun shone. The family cooked and ate outside much of the time. When visitors came, they enjoyed tea together seated on the ground. Sometimes they sat on a wooden bench or used their attractive white metal patio table and chairs. Some evenings a group gathered around an outdoor fire before their early bedtime. Had we known the language and been invited, it would have been most interesting to join the fireside group. The older boys slept in a shed rather than in the main house.

Early in the cold mornings, while we shivered even in coats and sweaters, the younger girls stood outside in a large basin, undressed, taking a bath before putting on uniforms to head off to school. The older women washed up in an outbuilding, sometimes appearing bare-breasted.

A wire fence marked the edge of our hosts' lot and kept out the goats that ate anything, including trash. One of the girls proudly told us the hen and her fluffy little chicks were "free-range." In spite of the care of the hen and the elegant rooster, those free-range youngsters made an easy meal for keen-eyed hawks. Only a few chicks remained by the time we left the village. Chickens made themselves useful by hopping up on an outdoor table to peck off scraps of food from the dirty dishes waiting to be washed.

A new batch of puppies provided us entertainment. We even mixed up some cereal for them just so we could watch them gobbling it down. Village dogs led a rough life, having to scrounge for food.

"Why feed the dogs?" people would say. "We don't eat them."

Plunging into new work

Eric and Kathy Fast and their three children left Botswana right after getting us settled in the village. Several times during our village live-in, Erwin and I needed to go into Gaborone for business. Sometimes we took the local public vans. Sometimes we drove the MM van to the village. On Erwin's birthday, August 8, we took our first Flying Mission flight across the Kalahari Desert because a young MCC couple was finishing their term there.

By the end of our village live-in later in August, we had learned the common complicated Setswana greetings and acquired a list of words we knew. The Brewster method, we concluded, worked better for people who learn primarily by listening, such as young children, than for those of us who learned by the written word. When we moved into Gaborone, where many people spoke some level of English, we used little Setswana other than the greetings. Schools were taught in English from at least seventh grade on up. Setswana was the national language, but English was the official language for business and legal work. That was a legacy from Botswana's time as a British protectorate. We didn't need to use Setswana very often in contrast to when we were in Brazil where hardly anyone spoke English. We took some additional Setswana lessons, but without more need to speak it, that may have been a waste of time.

Carla at times was a bit bored in the village, but she learned some language and helped with household tasks. She kept a positive attitude. By the end of August, we learned there was an opening for her at Maru-a-Pula Secondary School beginning in September. That was a joyful relief. We had wondered what Carla would do if she couldn't start classes until the next academic year the following January.

Living in an African city

We survived the challenges and frustrations of the village live-in. It was a valuable experience and we're glad we did it.

On August 20 we eagerly moved from the village to Gaborone – Botswana's planned capital city. With only a few multi-story buildings, Gaborone felt like a big village, as symbolized by its design of semi-cir-

Angela in front of Rempels' house in Gaborone, Botswana, 1994 to 2000.

cular roads around the "chief's" dwelling. By then, the weather was warmer and quite pleasant, but still very dry.

After living in a village, we had a new appreciation for electricity and running water, both hot and cold. We moved into an AIMM-owned house recently vacated by Jonathan and Mary Kay Larson who had completed fourteen years of fruitful mission work in Botswana. The three-bedroom house was small, but it was satisfying to figure out how to arrange things conveniently.

With fresh paint, new floor tiles in the kitchen and bath, upgraded faucets, ceiling fans, and attractive sheer curtains that let in the bright tropical light, the house became our delightful home. In that section of the city, the streets were lined by government-built identical houses, considered medium-cost. The original kitchens were very tiny, as it was assumed a maid would do the cooking and her convenience wasn't considered. Gradually those houses were modified. We were glad for the extended kitchen added to our house when Fremont and Sara Regier served as the Botswana country directors about fifteen years earlier. The bathroom was in two sections – the toilet in one closet-size room beside a slightly larger room with the sink and a combination tub and shower. One of the three small bedrooms served us as a multi-purpose room with two desks, a file cabinet, short sofa, and our TV. On the hottest of days, we basically lived in that room as it was the only one with an air conditioner.

After using a very small fridge in the village, I had a new appreciation for a full-size refrigerator even if it needed manual defrosting. We soon replaced the finicky gas stove for an electric one with four burners and an oven. No microwave, though, as that felt like it would be too luxurious in that setting at that time. Dishwashers were nearly unheard of, but Erwin and Carla helped wash dishes, even if they fussed a lot about doing it.

We reorganized the small laundry area to fit in a full-size automatic washing machine. Laundry usually dried quickly outside in the heat and low humidity, so we didn't need a clothes dryer. Once again, I got in the habit of shaking the dust out of each piece of laundry when taking it down from the clotheslines as I had done in Brazil.

Backyard living

Our neighbors watched amazed at all the projects Erwin and I worked at in the backyard. We expanded the patio area and dug up the all-dirt backyard to put in rock-outlined areas for decorative foliage, flowers, and edible plants.

Erwin dug huge holes for new fruit trees – plum, peach, apricot, mango, plus grape vines. He obtained eight sacks of horse manure – ninety percent wood shavings and ten percent manure – from a stable and soon had a highly enriched soil for the trees. Too highly enriched, he discovered when the fruit trees began dying. Their roots were cooked by the strong mixture! Eventually, the grape vines produced generously, along with the lemon tree, mulberry, banana, and papaya already established in the backyard. Erwin's attempt at growing strawberries didn't fare any better than his fruit trees. If a little fertilizer is good, more must be better, he figured.

We eventually really liked that house on Leruo Road. We enjoyed many meals on the patio under shade cloth and overhead vines. Flowerpots, large ferns, and hanging plants added to the charm. We entertained guests from all over the world. Without a guest room in our house, it was convenient for overnight guests to stay at the nearby MM guesthouse, a short walk away through a simple park.

The arrival of this new white family in the neighborhood prompted people to stop by and inquire if we had a maid. People were desperate for work. To do our own manual labor rather than hiring someone was considered being selfish. I was glad that prior to our coming, the Fasts had arranged for a maid to help in our household, as well as at the guesthouse.

We had previous experience with house help in Brazil, but it still felt awkward to have someone cleaning and working in my house and kitchen, doing things I could do. One or two days a week was all the house help I needed – on Fridays to prepare for the weekend and again on Mondays to clean up after the weekend. Before I went to the office on the days the maid would come, I started a crockpot with a traditional combination of dried beans and corn, *samp*, so it would be ready for us to eat at noon. The maid ate at the table together with us. In most other households, maids did not eat with the family.

We usually ate much like we had in the U.S. Supermarkets catered to the large expatriate community in Gaborone. Botswana produced or manufactured very few products. Stores in land-locked Botswana were well supplied with items either made in South Africa, or imported from various countries, including China.

Because we were strongly encouraged to keep a dog for security purposes, we brought one of the puppies along from the village to our house in the city. Carla referred to the dog as the little brother she never wanted. But we all wanted a cat again. Carla's morning routine usually included a little "cat spat" with the growing kitten we had.

Buying a car

Although we were jointly supported by both MCC and AIMM, we followed AIMM's policies and financial structures. We had our joint salary credited to Erwin as we had done when we were in Brazil rather than divided between us. That practice wasn't considered politically correct by then, but doing so provided a higher base for Social Security.

Under AIMM's vehicle policy, mission workers purchased their own vehicle. We began looking for a car. Erwin writes about that.

> At first, we thought we would need to pay at least $10,000 to purchase a vehicle. The previous country representatives counseled us that the MCC vehicle, a brown Toyota Corolla station wagon, was too old and with well over 100,000 miles (160,000 kilometers) could not be trusted for the kind of driving we would need to do. I did some calculating and decided it would be wiser to purchase that old Toyota Corolla for $2,400. Neither Angela nor Carla was impressed with that old vehicle. I think it was a 1987 model but it was still quite usable for us.
>
> That car kept going for our entire time in Botswana, racking up more than 200,000 miles and surviving more than one break-in.

Adjusting to dry season

After several months without rain during the cooler dry season of May to July, temperatures warmed up. The heat sometimes went above forty degrees centigrade – more than one hundred degrees Fahrenheit. Humidity was low and dust blew. Even so, some trees and vines bloomed, a promise and hope that rain would come sometime. The heat and dryness generally peaked in October before any rain fell, making October a bad month for anyone susceptible to depression – it was even called the suicide month.

I too began to feel as dry on the inside as the weather was. "Is this what I left our children for and gave up a nice house in Newton?" I asked myself as we tried to cope with the mess of minor house improvements and with how things did and didn't happen in the culture there.

A refreshing trip to South Africa

In less than four months after our arrival in Botswana we made the first of what would be many a drive into South Africa. That trip in October was a welcome break during our challenging adjustment.

The South Africa border was less than ten miles from Gaborone. We went early enough to be the first car at the border when it opened at seven in the morning. To our surprise, when the gates opened, people jumped out of cars behind us and ran to the office building, forming a long queue ahead of us. We soon caught on to the process. We filed through the office on the Botswana side to fill out duplicate forms by hand and get our passports stamped. Then it was back to the car to drive the short distance to the South Africa side. We got out of the car again, stood in line again, and filled out more forms before entering South Africa.

What an interesting drive it was into South Africa. Gradually the nearly flat landscape dotted with thorn trees gave way to hills, rising to a point from where we could see for miles across fertile farmland. As in Botswana, two-lane paved highways had a speed limit of about seventy-five miles per hour– way too fast for safe driving. However, hitting a cow or other animal in South Africa wasn't as likely as in Botswana, thanks to better fences. In either country, other drivers were a bigger threat than animals.

We drove through South African towns and villages with names we couldn't pronounce. We saw mostly white people on nice streets lined with trim houses surrounded by green grass. It took a sharp eye to spot the shabby townships in the distance where, until the end of apartheid, non-white Africans had to live. Temples or mosques that rose above low-lying houses pinpointed the areas designated for people from India.

Tall grain elevators in the small towns of farming areas reminded us of Kansas towns. Reaching South Africa's largest city, Johannesburg, we took a multi-lane bypass only glimpsing the tall skyscrapers that lay in a distant haze in the city center. Several "townships" lay along the by-pass, a continuing reminder of the racial separation apartheid had demanded. Later we learned that the high barren piles of dirt around Jo-burg were the tailings from gold mines that tunneled far below the city. The first-world infrastructure of Johannesburg was made possible because of the dirty, dangerous labor in the mines done by dark-skinned men from all over southern Africa, including from Botswana.

After skirting Johannesburg, we took a nice toll-road, comparable to the Interstate highways in the U.S. Heading southeast, we passed through a dry landscape much like that of Montana or Texas, with wide-open gently rolling brown ranchland still awaiting the first rains. Rugged, high rocky formations of the Drakensberg Mountains appeared on the horizon. And then we saw green! As the highway wound through those mountains and down over the Escarpment toward the coast, what a welcome sight it was to see green foliage all around.

Our destination was a Catholic retreat center in the green hills above the coastal port city of Durban along the Indian Ocean where the semi-annual meeting of the Southern Africa Coordinating Group was held. We were greeted by leaders of MCC and Africa Inter-Mennonite Mission work. They were all North Americans working in five or six nearby countries. It was good to connect there with two couples we'd known for many years: Fremont and Sara Regier doing MCC work in Mozambique, and Gary and Jean Isaac doing AIMM work in the Eastern Cape Province of South Africa, called the Transkei during apartheid. We met others from Zambia, Lesotho, Swaziland, and South Africa. We appreciated the worship times together. Good storytellers in the group provided us with hearty laughter. Erwin and I so much appreciated having a bedroom with a view of the green hills.

"He makes me lie down in green pastures. ...He restores my soul." Psalm 23 took on new meaning for me. I soaked in the green and my inner dryness began to recede.

Administering Mennonite Ministries

The administration of the Mennonite Ministries program was a smaller version of what Erwin had done the previous twelve years as executive secretary of the Commission on Overseas Mission. He quickly assessed the various tasks, and he and I worked out our individual responsibilities. Erwin, of course, did the finances, including the day-to-day details of accounting. Relating to both Mennonite Central Committee and Africa Inter-Mennonite Mission meant two different accounting systems. The MCCers received only a small monthly stipend for personal use and MCC paid all their other costs. This required MCCers to carefully record what they spent, keep receipts, and turn in monthly detailed reports regarding costs for their housing, food, transportation, and health care. Some MCCers did a good job of keeping receipts and turning in their reports. Others hated the system. One young woman, whose final financial report at the end of her term wasn't satisfactory for Erwin, left in tears declaring she would never again in her life ever keep detailed financial budgets and accounts.

In his tasks, Erwin encountered many a long line of people waiting – at the bank, the utility companies, the post office. Erwin tended to the repairing and maintaining of the Mennonite Ministries' vehicles and buildings. He tended to legal work. His work was often stressful. Periodically some utility was shut off without notice. He had to chase down the reason, which often was because an office worker hadn't yet posted payments. Sometimes we thought it was just the inefficiency of a developing country, but we discovered that back in the U.S. not everything always goes smoothly either.

It felt as though all the facets of my previous life experiences came together in my work in Botswana. In addition to managing the guesthouse and library, the tasks of a human resources department were on my plate. That was a new challenge for me.

Mennonite Ministries team members seemed to constantly be either coming or going from Botswana. My responsibility included arranging

314

a village live-in for all new workers. Others on our team and local partner agencies provided valuable help with arranging the village live-ins.

Mennonite Ministries's facilities in Gaborone, Botswana, 1995.

Erwin and Angela Rempel share an office as co-country representatives of Mennonite Ministries in Botswana, 1999.

Working with changes

Over the years, there were changes in our team and the assignments. The greater turnover was with the MCCers. Their terms were only three years, whereas the AIMMers came for multiple and longer terms. Both MCC and AIMM required periodic evaluations of workers. Most of the MCCers were Mennonites, but not all of them. They hailed from the U.S., Canada, Switzerland, Paraguay, and England. In contrast, the AIMMers all were Mennonites, coming from several of the different Mennonite groups in North America that worked together in AIMM. Several of our AIMM workers were the grown children of missionaries, thus coming with a wealth of international experience. AIMMers were, on average at the beginning of our time there, in their upper thirties, most of them married with children. MCCers ranged in age from early twenties to upper fifties, single and married, with and without children.

A number of years prior to our coming, MCC and AIMM joined organizationally as Mennonite Ministries. The MM team members interacted daily with the local people; called Batswana in the plural and Motswana in the singular. They formed close and meaningful relationships. However, Erwin and I worked mostly with our team and didn't have as many opportunities to become directly acquainted with the Batswana.

Things were changing in Botswana. After years of placing many teachers in schools, we bid farewell to the last MCC public school teacher in the country. Some specialty teaching positions continued for MCCers in church-related private schools, such as carpentry classes for young men and pre-school education for children of the traditional Koi-San (or Bushmen, as they supposedly preferred to be called). All MCCers were seconded to serve with another agency, a local partner that also provided guidance and supervision. Throughout an MCCer's term, Erwin and I became well-acquainted with those local partners.

Relating to African churches

The AIMMers primarily worked with more than twenty different AICs – African independent churches, African-initiated churches, or African indigenous churches, depending on who was interpreting the

"I" of AIC. Begun by visionary, charismatic African leaders with minimal biblical knowledge, AIC congregations drew people who usually had little education or use of the English language. They could identify easily with the Old Testament accounts of the patriarchs and life in the wilderness. They often practiced animal sacrifices, kept some of the Mosaic laws, and used ceremonial robes for worship. Each group had its own distinctive system of colorful church uniforms. Their traditional animistic beliefs and practices blended into that mix, along with some high-church practices of the Anglicans. The AICs ranged in size from a single congregation to denominations of many congregations in other African countries. Their beliefs ranged from orthodox Christianity to a blend with traditional animism. Their worship services were long, loud, and active. Those descriptive words applied to their prayer times, offerings, sermons, and dancing. Other churches, first established by foreign missionaries, considered the AIC churches with suspicion, even persecuting them at times.

Mennonite work with AICs began when some AIC leaders saw the variety of development work MCC did in Botswana. They asked if Mennonites could send Bible teachers too. Reportedly, one influential AIC leader had a vision of someone coming to help him and his people learn more about the Bible. Jim and Anna Juhnke were the MCC country representatives at the time, in the 1970s, and relayed the request to the North American Mennonite mission agencies.

Africa Inter-Mennonite Mission responded. First, AIMM sent veteran missionaries, Irene and Ed Weaver of Mennonite Board of Missions, to live in Botswana, make contacts, and explore possibilities. After years of experience in India, and then working with AICs in West Africa, the retirement-aged Weavers took on this new task. They lived in a house on Leruo Street, which turned out to be the same house AIMM purchased and we moved into in 1994. Often we gave thanks to the foresight of Ed Weaver in planting shade trees around the house. Typical African houses bake in the hot sun because people are concerned that trees and other foliage might harbor poisonous snakes and scorpions.

Encouraged by the Weavers, AIMM sent more mission workers, most of whom taught Bible to the AICs. Missionary spouses often worked with other projects. AIMM was committed to working with the existing churches in southern Africa rather than starting Mennonite congregations. In that role, AIMMers could work among various different church groups, serving as bridges between various AIC groups and with other churches and institutions. AIMM also began work with AICs in Lesotho and the Transkei, a "homeland" for the Xhosa people of South Africa. The Bible teachers were pleased when, as a group studying the Bible, passages such as in Hebrews brought new understanding about sacrifices – that Christ's death was the final sacrifice for sin. They didn't need to continue animal sacrifices.

Learning Setswana and forming relationships was essential for the AIMM Bible teachers and that takes time – a commitment for several terms. AIMMers with families lived in the cities and larger towns in Botswana where their children had access to good schools. This created some significant lifestyle differences between MM team members. A young single person, or a young couple without children, can more easily spend three years living in a small rustic traditional African dwelling in a remote village. Most of the time the lifestyle disparities among our MM team members wasn't an issue.

Worshipping with AICs

Erwin and I periodically worshiped with AIC congregations, even though we couldn't understand much of the Setswana they spoke. They gave special honor to visitors, especially white foreigners, which we found uncomfortable. Early in our time in Botswana, we attended the large Spiritual Healing Church in Gaborone, one of the main AIC groups Mennonites worked with. Their venerable old Archbishop Motswasele asked us to sit at the front. At one point he called us forward, including fourteen-year-old Carla, to bless our work in Botswana. We three knelt, a large prayer cloth was spread over us, and various people prayed for us. Then Erwin and I, along with Carla, were to stand and participate in praying for people who filed past. It was an uncomfortable and confusing experience for us. After that, we didn't usually take Carla along to AIC churches. As a family, we settled into worshipping with an international Baptist church where English was the common language.

Tim Bertsche presents certificates to African church leaders who completed Bible training program, 1999.

Living in Botswana

First impressions are hard to rewrite. It was the brown dusty dry season back in 1984 when Erwin and I first visited Botswana. It was also dry season when we moved there in June 1994. So I tend to think of Botswana in that framework, even though nearly half of the year doesn't fit that idea. Rains usually began with sporadic showers in November or December, increasing in intensity and frequency for several months. It only took a small shower to trigger the growth mechanism in dormant plants. A pale green hue quickly spread over the landscape. After the first heavy rain, we experienced the phenomena of the flying ants rising from the ground for a brief fling before losing their wings and their lives. As the rains increased so did lush green growth and bright flowers.

The rains didn't always arrive on schedule or in sufficient amounts. Botswana's farmers could only count on getting a harvest one year out of three. The government established policies and structures to provide food commodities during the lean years. Corn (maize) was the staple crop, ground into mealie meal for a white mush served with most meals. The mush resembled mashed potatoes only in appearance. Pumpkins, squash, and beans were usually planted among the cornstalks in hopes the spotty rains would benefit at least something. Sorghum was another staple, often made into a soured mush that I couldn't manage to eat.

The main agricultural product was beef. A family's wealth was comprised of its cattle. Cattle were their savings account and investment used to pay a bride price and feed people who came to a funeral. Cattle pulled plows and provided milk. We learned that Botswana had more cattle than people. They exported beef to Europe. To control cattle diseases, strong fences cordoned off grazing land. Passing from one large section to another, every vehicle needed to stop at checkpoints to be sure it wasn't transporting any beef. Those fences, unfortunately, blocked natural migration routes for wild animals. A cattle lung disease spread widely one year. To contain it, the government destroyed the cattle. The meat was still edible by humans, so the farmer could keep the meat of three of his cattle. The other cattle were herded into large trenches, shot, and buried. Farmers received $150 per head of cattle. That gave them temporarily a significant boost in their income. Many of them built houses of bricks and blocks to replace their mud brick huts.

Except for a few rocky hills protruding out of the plains, much of the country is flat, averaging an altitude of about 3,000 feet. About the same size and shape as the state of Texas, Botswana largely consists of the Kalahari Desert. The highest rainfall is along the eastern side of the desert, where most of the country's one and a half million inhabitants live. By the time we lived there, a paved two-lane highway paralleled the railroad that was built in the 1800s to link South Africa with Rhodesia, now called Zimbabwe. With a speed limit equal to seventy-five miles per hour and lacking good roadside shoulders, the stretch between Gaborone and Francistown, the two largest cities, was a dangerous road to drive day or night. When the first Mennonites began work in Botswana, there were only a few miles of paved roads in the entire country. When we arrived, all but about two hundred miles of a highway that circled the whole country weren't yet paved. Half of that unpaved stretch was very rough.

Many vehicles sported sturdy bars in the front to minimize damage when hitting a cow or other animal. We soon learned that a motionless donkey along the road stays that way and drivers didn't need to slow down. Herds of goats could suddenly follow a lead goat and temporarily shut down the highway as they all crossed over. Cows' movements were unpredictable. We avoided night driving outside of the city.

Traveling around Botswana

About two years after we arrived in Botswana, the three of us, Erwin, Carla, and I, ventured on our first road trip around the country on an administrative visit to our MM workers. Until then, we traveled with Flying Mission on small one-engine planes to visit MM workers in the remote areas. We began a ten-day trip headed westward to the more primitive locations.

"The first two nights we were in a *rondavel* (round hut) made of mud-bricks and dung plaster, but with a tin roof. Then it was five nights under thatched roofs, without a ceiling, but walls of concrete blocks plastered over," I wrote to family about the trip.

There was no electricity at several places. For warm showers, someone had to start a fire under the "donkey boiler."

The nighttime noises we heard at the beginning of the trip were the rural sounds of donkeys braying, baby goats bleating, chickens, crickets, a goose, and ducks. When we were in the bigger towns, the sounds included loud drunks hollering, vehicle traffic, passing trains, alarms going off, and noisy machinery operating at nearby mines.

"Botswana has many, many miles of the same thing!" I wrote to our family after that trip of about 1,500 miles. "It was basically all covered with thick golden grass since rains were good this year. The density and height of the thorn trees and shrubs varies, but there was little truly open area without vegetation. There was a refreshing sense of cleanness and calm compared to the litter and bustle we have here in the city." We saw wild animals, especially varieties of the antelope family, plus ostriches, large vultures, and other birds.

"There are few gas stations in the rural areas. We weren't sure how far we could go on one tank of gas, so we had an extra can of gas along for one stretch where we drove for five and half hours between gas stations. We just made it!"

We planned a day off during the trip, reserving a furnished tent near a bird sanctuary. However, all three of us had picked up something that impacted our digestive systems. Carla fared the worst. We were glad to upgrade from a tent to a chalet with electricity and a "normal" bathroom for a couple of nights. We didn't see the bird sanctuary.

"The next visits to some of those areas we will do by Flying Mission again," I reported. "But it was good to drive it once as one gets a different feel."

Difficult endings

With the changing times, new technologies, and downsizing of the Mennonite Ministries' work, our office assistant, Tshgang, didn't have enough work to do. As was typical in Botswana, she was an unmarried mother. She was thirty-something with two teenage children. Once Erwin and I had settled into our work, we couldn't justify keeping her on. She didn't like helping with the tasks of running the guesthouse, which were probably considered below her position as an office assistant. She spent a lot of time just staring at the clock above her desk. She had taken driving classes, but still couldn't drive. Thus she couldn't relieve Erwin of trips to the post office or of standing in long lines to pay utility bills. With computers, Erwin and I did our own typing. Faxes, and increasingly email, nearly eliminated even having to put addresses and stamps on envelopes. We could see ways in which Tshgang could have made herself so useful to us that we couldn't have managed without her. But that wasn't the case. Difficult as it was, we dismissed her making sure to follow Botswana's rigid labor laws. She had talked about setting up a little covered trailer, a caravan, to sell take-out food. We provided her a substantial termination package and a nice set of pots and pans so that she could have done that. But apparently she didn't take that opportunity either. She died of AIDS a few years later.

Early termination of a team members' assignment was a painful situation for all involved. We took that difficult journey several times during our nearly six years in Botswana. As administrators, we tried to provide as much support as we could for our workers. We struggled with balancing pastoral and administrative roles. When difficult decisions had to be made, no matter how carefully we attempted to work through it, the "process" usually became the focus rather than the particular issues involved. After one particularly painful experience, we didn't have the courage to do more than gloss over the difficulties another team member experienced. Our successors had to deal later with that situation. It was uncomfortable to feel as though we were a tool in a surgeon's hands, causing pain.

About a third or more of our team members were singles – ranging in age from early twenties to middle-aged. While some of the unmarried team workers did well, others struggled. We admired the amazing work of the Catholic nuns, but they lived together in a supportive convent arrangement. In contrast, we had several single women living alone, even in remote locations where their work colleagues were from various other countries and Christian denominations. When the availability of email advanced rapidly, one single woman remained in such frequent contact with her family back in North America that she gave up trying to establish new relationships in Botswana and soon headed back home.

Several team members struggled with mental health issues, especially depression. We had no mental health resource professionals in Botswana other than one who visited periodically from Zimbabwe. We could only consult long distance with MCC or AIMM about those situations.

A couple of early terminations were due to physical health. Kathleen Rempel Boschman, an energetic, active young mother on our team, suffered a back injury. To speed up the healing, she was given an injection directly into her spine. She immediately felt something was wrong and suffered excruciating pain. The orthopedic doctor in Gaborone referred her to another doctor and hospital in Johannesburg for a MRI. I was designated to drive her to Jo-burg in the Mennonite Ministries' van, which allowed her to lie down. I hadn't driven the van much, so it was quite a stretch for me to drive it all the way to Johannesburg and find the way through city traffic to the big hospital in those days before GPS and cell phones.

After several unsuccessful efforts, we realized that Kathleen and her family should return to Canada. Needing to lie flat for the long trip, we purchased about five plane seats side-by-side to accommodate her on a stretcher laid over them. Even the first class cabin didn't have seats that could lay flat at that time. Her husband, Don, and she had done well in Botswana, and they were keenly missed. The medical care Kathleen received in Canada couldn't relieve her pain entirely either.

Such difficulties were the exceptions rather than the rule. Overall, we had many good experiences and enjoyed working with our team. For example, a young single woman, Rebecca Sack, met the challenges of her assignment in Botswana, eventually married and served with her husband as MCC co-representatives in Burundi and Rwanda before going on to pastor a Mennonite church in the U.S.

Another example was tall, blonde Sarah Adams who couldn't avoid attracting attention wherever she went, especially in the village where she lived. It wasn't long before Sarah reported that local men harassed, propositioned, and followed her, even onto the chief's yard where she stayed. With HIV/AIDS being rampant in Botswana, and sexual assault not uncommon, we immediately moved her into safer quarters in the city. She was a resilient person. After successfully completing her term in Botswana, she worked in the MCC office in Akron, Pa., giving leadership to MCC's global work with AIDS. She also served as a country representative in the Middle East.

Never a dull moment

Life in Botswana never lacked for variety and encounters with interesting people. The cliché, "never a dull moment," certainly applied. People from various countries and continents crossed our path. Some just passed through; some lived there, and, of course, many were the local Africans. My correspondence to family in the U.S. served as a record from which to share some samples of such experiences. As when we were in Brazil, I wrote about the events and experiences the most different from our typical life in the U.S.

Our modest guesthouse offered lodging for a variety of people connected in some way with our work or the local partner agencies we worked with, including AIC leaders. Other traveling Mennonites also came by.

False Ebola scare

Mennonite missionaries in the Congo, Rick and Marilyn Derksen and their three children, scheduled a vacation trip in southern Africa, stopping to see us in Botswana. I had supper waiting for them on the designated day. About 7:00 p.m., they phoned us from the nearby border crossing from South Africa. They were detained at the border because the border agents hadn't gotten word that a small outbreak of Ebola in the Congo was no longer a threat. Derksens had to leave their vehicle and luggage at the border and be taken by ambulance to the large government hospital in Gaborone, only a few blocks from our house. Derksens waited at the hospital for a doctor to certify that they weren't sick with Ebola. It was after 9:00 p.m. when someone at the hospital phoned us to pick up the Derksens. Erwin and I hurried over. Marilyn and the children came to our place while Erwin and Rick hurried back to the border to get their car and luggage. The border had closed at 10:00 p.m., but they managed to get through and pick up the car.

Interesting guests

A group of lanky blonde white young women with a Scandinavian aid agency stayed for a while at our guesthouse. They enjoyed sunbathing in the front yard – quite a show for passersby! They changed their sunbathing location to the back yard.

When British Commonwealth meetings were held in Gaborone, hotels were full. A man from Zimbabwe stayed at our guesthouse as recommended by someone he knew in the Brethren in Christ church in Zimbabwe. Apparently he was actually a highly placed government official. He soon found our rudimentary accommodations inadequate and located another place to stay.

Over the years we enjoyed meeting our team members' parents and families when they came to visit. The guesthouse was a convenient way station for them. When team member Andrea's parents, Ed and Edie Bontrager, came to see Andrea and her husband, Tom Unsicker, we surely didn't realize the Bontragers would someday be our next-door neighbors in the U.S.

We continued to enjoy inviting people for meals at our house. Some dinner guests from Scandinavia commented on the good strawberry jam,

325

as they generously spooned it over their mashed potatoes! When AIMM administrator Jim Bertsche was at our place, the barking and pacing of our dog, Oliver, led Jim to say, "That dog takes his work very seriously!"

More about life in Botswana

The majority of people in any shop or public venue had the dark skin and hair one would expect in Africa. They mostly dressed in western-style clothing: skirts and dresses for women and suits or shirts and slacks for the men. Younger women and girls wore jeans or slacks. Babies were tied to their mother's back with a plaid blanket. Women frequently wore a small headscarf.

We heard that southern Africans hadn't worn much if any clothing until Europeans arrived. Thus, they adopted European clothing styles. Occasionally we saw women wearing the elaborate and colorful dresses common in West Africa.

The variety of people we encountered in Botswana fascinated me. People from India operated many of the shops and largest businesses. The Indian women wore colorful saris or two-piece Punjabi suits. There were a few Chinese men in Botswana working on construction projects such as schools.

Whites in Botswana were a minority. Some of us whites were recent arrivals staying for a limited time. We found ourselves among Europeans, Canadians, Australians, New Zealanders and whites born in nearby countries such as Zimbabwe and South Africa.

However, many of the white people living in Africa were descendants of people who migrated from Europe in the 1700 and 1800s to settle in Africa. They were a part of Africa just as we are a part of North America. In some European families, one brother may have gone to America while another settled in Africa. When wagon trains headed into the western parts of the U.S., similar wagon trains of Dutch descendants, the Afrikaners, headed into the interior of South Africa. Some of the "white tribes" of Africa were originally from England, settling first in Kenya, fleeing to Zimbabwe (the former Rhodesia), and then to South Africa. With the end of apartheid in South Africa, some whites fearfully left for Australia, New Zealand, or other countries in the British Commonwealth.

Going about our daily routines, I could forget that my skin was quite a contrast to most of the people around me. I didn't see them as brown or black, and thus hoped they weren't seeing me as white. We didn't feel particularly unsafe.

We seemed to receive undue respect and attention. It was hard to know if that was because of their culture of hospitality, of historic relationships between whites and blacks, our job title, or an attempt to gain something.

Sometimes it was obvious that a beggar singled us out because we were white. Once when we were traveling with some local Batswana, a young fellow begged something from us whites. A mature black African woman in our group actually laughed in his face. She saw right through his ruse and would have none of his nonsense. Her example made it easier to turn down beggars. As in Brazil, we tried to help people we knew.

One of those was Gibson. He was a good worker and we hired him to do "piece work" for us, such as laying patio blocks. Gibson always needed loans and handouts. He somehow fell into one calamity after another – if his stories were believed. Whenever he was paid, he claimed to be robbed. Back in his tribal home area, he told us lions scared the donkeys pulling a cart in which his wife and infant rode. The frightened donkeys bolted, smashed the cart into a tree, killing the driver and the infant. His wife suffered a broken arm. He asked us for help with funeral and other expenses.

Mishak worked regularly for us cleaning the yard and trimming bushes. He claimed that his father was a Motswana, but his mother was from just over the border in Zimbabwe. He had no documents to prove his existence. Periodically he was picked up and deported to Zimbabwe. He always found his way back. When we first knew him, he said he was eighteen and had a five-year-old daughter. Once when he was sick, we took him to a doctor. When the diagnosis was pneumonia, we understood that to be a euphemism for AIDS. However, Mishak remained active and healthy as long as we knew him. He worked for several of the Mennonite households in Gaborone and seldom asked for extra money.

Classmates, church, Christmas

Carla's friends and classmates practiced various religions – Hindu, Islam, Jain, and Sheik. A couple of her friends were post-Christian Europeans. She confronted questions about the Christian faith in ways that her peers back in the U.S. didn't. She attended the Baptist church youth group, when it functioned. Sometimes she played flute with the worship music team.

The growing Baptist church we frequently attended was international, interdenominational, and inter-racial. The worship music was contemporary. The English language united the attendees from as many as thirty countries, including other African countries. Worshipping together felt like a preview of the heavenly scene in Revelation with people of every tribe, tongue, and nation. We appreciated the messages by the pastor, Denzel Tryon, a white South African. We participated in one of the congregations' small groups.

Our spiritual life was also nourished by listening to the cassette tapes of worship services at First Mennonite in Newton, Kansas. We learned to know their new pastor, Clarence Rempel, by his voice. We appreciated his carefully crafted and well-presented challenging sermons. During the two years that Marcia served at First Mennonite as youth pastor, we frequently heard her voice as well on the recordings. Clarence Rempel isn't related to Erwin's line of Rempels.

Although Christmas was commercialized in Botswana, it was a low-key event in the church we attended. Except for a well-attended special service on Christmas Day, very little was said or done at church for Christmas.

"You could lie down in the street and not get run over," people said about the streets of Gaborone at Christmastime. Many people who lived in Gaborone had moved there from their traditional homes in the villages or other towns. For the Christmas break, which came during the long summer school break, they returned home leaving Gaborone very quiet. Being in the southern hemisphere meant it was hot then. Forget about baking Christmas cookies! We've celebrated Christmas in the southern hemisphere ten times, but never quite got used to having it in hot weather.

For our final Christmas in Botswana, I wrote about our planned menu featuring items purchased locally: a frozen turkey from Brazil, pumpkin pie made from butternut squash, and imported cranberry sauce. We had a British woman on our team that year and she prepared mincemeat pie. Going to a hotel to swim in its pool was a common activity on Christmas day.

Neighbors on our street

Gaborone was a multinational town, and our neighborhood reflected that. A succession of mission-related people lived next door in a house also owned by Africa Inter-Mennonite Mission. When a Swedish family lived there, we learned that Sweden's taxes supported the mission work of the Lutheran state church with which they served. From Ethiopian refugee neighbors, we learned to appreciate Ethiopian food and their elaborate coffee ceremony. One time they had a goat tied up in the backyard before they slaughtered it for Easter.

Most of the time, our neighbors in that AIMM-owned house were other Mennonite Ministries workers and their children, first Don and Kathleen Rempel Boschman then Rudy and Sharon Dirks. Both of those families were from Canada. Cute little red-haired Lisa Boschman often came to our fence calling out for "Grampel." The Dirks oldest child, Nathan, eventually returned to Botswana with his wife to serve with AIMM and live in that same house.

Then there was the house on the other side of us. We weren't sure who owned it. It was rented to a variety of people including two women for a while, one American and one British. But the most interesting neighbors in that house were Sarah and Javid.

Saga of Sarah and Javid

We watched with interest the activity of someone moving into the house beside ours after it had been vacant for several months. After the hubbub of moving subsided, one day I saw the face of a young woman timidly peeking through the curtains of a bedroom window. My first perception that she was shy was soon dispelled.

Whether it was she or I who made the first overture, isn't clear. I recorded that it was on June 26, 1995, exactly a year after we had left the U.S., that she first invited me to come over.

Sarah was only nineteen years old at the time, a new bride married to Javid, a few years older than she was. They were Muslims from the island of Mauritius in the Indian Ocean. By their features, it appeared their ancestors were from India. Javid had previously worked in Botswana at the small Superette convenience store near us. Then he went back to Mauritius and brought back a bride to a land where she didn't know anyone other than her husband. He worked long days in a shop with his relatives in Gaborone leaving Sarah with many lonely hours. She had only met Javid briefly prior to their arranged marriage. However, she said she could have said no to the marriage. She showed us a long video of their elaborate marriage ceremony.

After my first visit in her home, Sarah felt free to come to the fence near our kitchen and call to me. She was always afraid of our dog, so I needed to hold him while she came around to our front gate. She would scurry to our front door, keeping as far away from the dog as possible. Whether it was fear of the dog or repulsion of dogs as taught by Islam, I wasn't sure. They had no phone of their own, so nearly every day she came over to use our phone for short local calls. They had no vehicle, so she didn't hesitate to ask us for rides, which I tried to provide, if possible. She tried to sell expensive gaudy T-shirts and cheap earrings. She "borrowed" cooking oil and gave us mutton and pudding in return. But she wasn't sure if she could eat any of the food items I offered her – they weren't *halal*, the way Islam proscribed. She wore a nice long headscarf, but as time went on, she was more casual about actually pulling it up over her head.

Even though Sarah clearly didn't have enough to keep her busy, they hired a maid. Then she would just watch the maid doing the work. Maids didn't last long working for her.

Sarah always came up with something interesting. When at one point they talked briefly about moving to a larger house, I realized I would miss her and all the unusual elements she introduced into my life. They were good neighbors – no loud parties or barking dogs.

Once at four o'clock in the morning, Sarah was outside our bedroom window calling us. Javid had a high temperature. She wanted to use our phone to call someone to take him to the hospital emergency room.

One day at our place, Sarah asked for a drink. I used a red plastic tumbler to offer her some water. She gingerly sipped a little.

"Did your maid drink from this one?" she asked. "I keep separate the things for my maid."

I didn't know if our cleaning woman had used that particular tumbler. "We treat everyone equally in our house. Why do you keep things separate?"

She was concerned about "diseases." I told her we wash with soap and hot water. For a while after that, she didn't come over as much and left right away after making her phone calls.

One time I drove Javid and Sarah to a medical appointment. As I navigated the big traffic circle by the Anglican church, Javid asked if that was our church. No. Then he asked what they believe. My mind raced to figure out how to explain a few basics of Christianity rather than the details of how Mennonites differ from Anglicans. Next, we went around the traffic circle near the Moslem mosque. He mentioned he doesn't go there much but was trying to become more firm in the Islamic faith. When we needed to stop for the traffic light near the Baptist church we attended, I pointed that out to them as our church. Then he said he did a lot of reading and searching of religions. He considered himself an "orthodox Christian," he said, much to my surprise. He explained that he accepts everything as leading to God: Old Testament prophets, the Prophet Mohammed, and Jesus. He asked about getting a New Testament. We gave them a Bible and trusted the Lord would point Javid to helpful Scripture passages. We didn't have other conversations about religious faith, but our hope and prayer was that they experienced the love of Jesus through our relationship with them.

Sarah "fell pregnant," as they would say in Botswana. Before giving birth, the couple returned to Mauritius. We never saw them again.

Going to the ends of the earth

Two locations where we had MCC workers felt like the "ends of the earth." It was comforting to recall Jesus' promise to be with us even there.

To visit our workers in those remote locations, we usually phoned Flying Mission and arranged to charter a single engine Cessna for the trip. A missionary doctor, Malcom McArthur, began the flying service about 1980 when most of Botswana's roads were rough dirt tracks. Flying Mission's rates were affordable for mission workers, subsidized by medical flights paid by the government. Flying Mission was very accommodating and it almost felt as though we had access to our own private airline. At that time, all their pilots were white men from Europe or America. When planning a flight to visit for several days in remote areas, we needed to arrange for the pilot's meals and lodging, because he usually stayed with us. The pilots never complained about the rustic, primitive places where we stayed. Several Mennonite pilots had served with Flying Mission.

Over the Okavango Delta

The little village of Etsha, located in the far northwest corner of Botswana was one of those "ends of the earth" locations. MCCers served there directed by Cristo and Annete Wiejs, from the Netherlands. Wiejses gave leadership to a community development and church-planting project sponsored by the Botswana Christian Council. They and their four sons seemed to have boundless energy, initiative, intelligence, and no lack of adventures living in Botswana.

Etsha lay just to the west of the inland Okavango Delta. The Okavango River flows southward from the highlands of nearby Angola into the Kalahari Desert of Botswana. There the waters spread out and around many small knolls in the delta. The water eventually either evaporates or soaks into the ground, never reaching any ocean.

Approaching Etsha, the Flying Mission pilot usually flew the plane low above the Delta. That gave us a fantastic aerial view of elephants, giraffes, wildebeests, hippos, and other large animals. What a treat – something we realized tourists paid thousands of dollars to do. Before landing, the pilot buzzed the grassy airstrip making sure no goats, donkeys, or other animals were on the runway. Flying Mission arranged for local people to cut the long grass on the runway and to drag a log over it to knock down any protruding hard termite hills. A ragged windsock provided the pilot with information about the wind. From the Etsha landing strip, it was only a short bumpy ride in a four-wheel drive Toyota extended-cab pickup to where the MCCers lived in a round, thatched roof dwelling. A tall reed fence enclosed their small yard. An outdoor fire pit, solar-powered lights, or flashlights were their sources for light at night.

The women around Etsha specialized in making baskets. Their patterned, tightly woven baskets could hold liquid. MCCer Andrea Bontrager Unzicker worked with the women to market their baskets. The exchange rate made Botswana baskets too expensive to sell in the MCC Self-Help stores (now Ten Thousand Villages). Tom Unzicker taught pottery skills and other useful tasks.

A women makes a basket in Etsha, Botswana, 1996.

To make a basket required not only a lot of time but also a good measure of courage. The women waded out into the hippo and crocodile-infested waters of the Delta to look for special plants to weave baskets. An encounter with a hippo could be deadly. From a safari website, we learn that the hippo is responsible for more human fatalities in Africa than any other large animal.

One time the pilot dropped us off in Etsha and responded to a request for a mercy flight from a nearby village. Two men had been attacked by crocodiles. The pilot replaced the plane seats with stretchers. He flew the men to a hospital where they each had part of an arm amputated.

Annete and Cristo Weijs homeschooled their boys in Etsha. On a visit back to their homeland in the Netherlands, she purchased a variety of school supplies and mailed them back to Botswana. Shortly after the Wiejses returned to Botswana, we were surprised to hear that Cristo was arrested for drug smuggling. When the package of school supplies from the Netherlands reached the custom agents in Gaborone, they checked it and found a two-kilo packet of white powder. Without testing it in a lab, they assumed it was drugs. They put it in the mailbag to Etsha. Agents from the Criminal Investigation Division went to Etsha to watch at the post office. When Cristo picked up the package, they arrested him and took him to jail in the larger town of Maun several hours' distant. Cristo had driven an MCC vehicle to the post office, so that was impounded for a while. The Botswana Christian Council worked with lawyers, and after several days, Cristo was released on bail. And the results of a lab test on the white powder? Plaster of Paris for use in the children's craft projects!

In the Kalahari Desert

If you've seen the 1980s movie, *The Gods Must Be Crazy,* you were introduced to the traditional hunter-gatherer people of Southern Africa. Over the years, MCC placed a number of people in development assignments among the Koi-San or Bushmen. The Botswana government was frequently at odds with the Bushmen, whose traditional lifestyle depended on hunting game and gathering edible plants in the Kalahari Desert. The government's reasons for resettling the Bushmen outside of the Kalahari were questioned.

To visit our MCCers who worked with the Bushmen on the western side of the Kalahari Desert also felt like going to the end of the earth. Among the leaders of the mission work among the Bushmen, we met Braam and Willimien. They were Afrikaners and career mission workers from the Dutch Reformed Church. They helped establish a school and church among the Bushmen in D'Kar, a small desert village near the small town of Ghanzi on the far western side of Botswana. The area was just as brown and dry as expected of a desert location, although not totally devoid of vegetation. Deep dry sand made walking difficult there.

Because of these longstanding connections with the Bushmen, our Mennonite Ministries' office received a most unusual request. A former MCCer doing research on viruses in different ethnic groups asked for our help. He wanted to acquire urine samples from the Bushmen for his research. He would provide the collection containers and pay for shipping to the U.S. We declined.

Matt and Sylvia Hofer, along with infant Meagan, came from Switzerland in January 1995 as MCCers assigned to work with Braam and

Matt Hofer and his little daughter chat with pre-school children in D'Kar, Botswana, 1995.

Willimien. They would resource a preschool where the Bushmen children learned basics before going to a public school. When we took Hofers on their introductory trip to that area, the house they were to live in had been vacant for several months after the departure of the previous MCC couple. Even though someone cleaned out dust and critters before our visit, the house didn't look very good. However, Matt and Sylvia cheerfully moved in, cleaned, and repaired the house. They made it into a comfortable home. It seems the worse some place is initially, and the more work its new inhabitants put into it, the more they eventually appreciate it.

A vehicle accident

Sylvia Hofer phoned us, collect, from Namibia, before eight o'clock in the morning on Tuesday, July 23, 1996. They were vacationing in Namibia, the country just west of Botswana, and had a vehicle accident the night before. She and Matt were in a hospital.

We had known that week would be busy. Tuesday was also the day a new family arrived: Rudy and Sharon Dirks and their three school-aged children, sent by Africa Inter-Mennonite Mission. Greeting the Dirks at the airport, orienting them, providing meals, getting them out to their village live-in would be all we could handle. Or so we thought until Sylvia's unexpected phone call.

Matt and Sylvia, who by then had two small daughters, plus Matt's visiting younger brother and a friend from Switzerland, were riding in an extended-cab Toyota four-wheel drive MCC vehicle. They had taken a wrong turn. Darkness fell before they could arrive at a rest camp for the night. What caused the accident isn't clear – did a tire blow out and cause the vehicle to roll over or did a sudden curve in a very sandy road cause loss of control. At any rate, the little girls and the two fellows from Switzerland weren't injured. However, Sylvia suffered severe whiplash and she needed stitches for a cut on her head. Matt experienced a lot of back pain.

Erwin arranged with Flying Mission to fly him out to Windhoek, Namibia, where Hofers were in a Catholic hospital. Before Erwin left, he managed to meet the Dirks family, take them to the immigration office to work on their residency documents, and to orient them to our financial system. I stayed in Gaborone to work with the Dirks family. Our son Marc was visiting with us in Botswana at the time for several weeks during his summer break from EMU studies. In Erwin's absence, Marc helped a great deal with driving vehicles, plus loading and unloading the furnishings for Dirks' village live-in.

When Erwin arrived at the hospital in Namibia, he saw Matt and Sylvia on side-by-side hospital beds. Sylvia's head was immobilized by a big neck brace. Matt had to stay flat on his back. The two little girls were clambering all over them. Soon Willimien and another co-worker from D'Kar drove over to help with childcare. The doctor in Namibia recommended that Sylvia undergo surgery to fuse some of the vertebrae in her neck. After consulting with MCC's medical people, that surgery was performed. Matt's back condition would heal in time – a lot of time. He was to lie flat for six weeks. Then he wasn't to drive for another six weeks.

Erwin had plenty to do in Namibia dealing with the hospital, the wrecked vehicle, and arranging for other details. The Swiss government medical plan eventually reimbursed Mennonite Ministries for the medical costs incurred by the Hofers. Insurance paid most of the cost of a replacement vehicle.

The Hofers returned to their home in D'Kar from Namibia via a Flying Mission plane. Matt, more than six feet tall, traveled on a stretcher. In spite of their injuries and limitations, they didn't complain. They commented on the difference between visits from their Bushmen friends and other people. The Bushmen just came, accepted what they saw, and sat with them. People of European descent asked about details of the accident, looking for cause and effect, perhaps in a subconscious effort to somehow avoid a similar incident happening to them.

The accident didn't keep Matt from participating in a teacher-training workshop. The teachers trekked over to his bedroom for his input. For music night, he played guitar while lying in bed. Matt's parents came from Switzerland for four weeks to help.

For Hofer's medical follow-up, we arranged to fly them to Gaborone. They spent several weeks in the Mennonite Ministries guesthouse. There we provided them support with meals and childcare.

They returned to their work in D'Kar as soon as they could. Swimming was recommended for Matt as therapy for his on-going back pains. The only swimming pool was at a hotel that didn't allow non-guests to use it. So God provided another swimming pool. A road crew blasting for gravel set off dynamite once too often. Water gushed up from underground and filled a large stone quarry, turning it into a nice community swimming pool.

MCC's policy against using alcoholic drinks didn't correspond with European Mennonite's practice. But Hofers' agreed to abstain. They couldn't help but comment, though, on how nice a glass of wine would be with the Christmas meal we celebrated one year with some of our team members. Even though Hofers experienced a serious vehicle accident and two pregnancies during their three-year term, they did well.

Visiting Hofers in Switzerland

When the Hofers' assignment ended, they returned to Switzerland. Erwin and I stopped to see them there en route back to the U.S. in August 1998. We enjoyed seeing them again – with four children by

337

then – and to attend their Swiss Mennonite church. It was an opportunity to ponder what my life could have been like had my Bixel ancestors not emigrated from Switzerland to America in the early 1800s. We marveled at the summertime beauty of flowers adorning window boxes, streets, and gardens. Modern buildings nestled close to charming structures hundreds of years old.

What an unexpected privilege it was to visit the historic Swiss locations most important to Erwin and me. We walked on the grounds of the St. Chrischona Theological Seminary in the Canton of Basel where Erwin's grandfather was studying the year when Erwin's father was born.

Matt's parents drove Erwin and me through the beautiful Swiss landscape to the Emmental area where my maternal Bixel ancestors, and other early Anabaptists, or Mennonites, had lived and suffered. Ulrich Bichsel (Bixel) was the fifteenth Anabaptist in Bern put to death because of his beliefs. The highlight of the tour for me was stopping at Trachselwald Castle, a large, old castle in the area where my Bixel ancestors had lived. Early Anabaptists were imprisoned there in inhumane conditions because of their beliefs. Could some of my ancestors have lain on those crude wooden beds with a round hole cut in the middle for disposing of human waste? It was a holy moment there for me, and a recommitment to Anabaptist understanding of our Christian faith. Out-of-character for me, I reverently added my name to others already written on a rough wooden wall. It felt as though I was joining in "the great crowd of witnesses" spoken of in Hebrews, chapter 12.

The Hofers also took us up a mountain in the Swiss Alps. An enclosed cable car lifted us up, close to the ragged edges of a cliff. After looking at that cliff awhile, I turned around and was startled to discover a fantastic view of snowcapped mountains behind us. It made me realize how we often just look at the close-up immediate issues of life without seeing the bigger beautiful picture.

That visit satisfied my desires to travel to Europe.

Botswana Christian Council

The Botswana Christian Council was a significant partner with Mennonite Ministries. Erwin became a part of their board, and thus interacted with a wide variety of people and projects in Botswana. The BCC was comprised of "mainline" churches. Funding for BCC projects came from international organizations.

One day Erwin and I had lunch with one of the BCC officials, a Motswana, at a restaurant. We each ordered a portion of chicken, with bones. In our American fashion, Erwin and I picked up the chicken pieces with our fingers and ate the meat off the bones. Meanwhile, the African man, well-educated with British manners, carefully used his knife and fork to politely cut the meat from the bones.

The Khama family and Botswana's history

One woman serving on a BCC committee with Erwin was Muriel Sanderson, a most interesting British woman. To explain who she was and why she lived in Botswana requires a brief history of the country. Her sister Ruth had married the man who became Botswana's first democratically elected president, Seretse Khama.

Khama had been in line to become the chief of Botswana's largest and most influential tribal group. When he went to England to study law, he met a white woman, Ruth Williams. They married in 1948 just as neighboring South Africa made apartheid into law. Their marriage became an international incident, as recorded in a book and movie, *An Inconvenient Marriage*. After a time of exile, the couple took up residence in Botswana. During Botswana's peaceful transition from a British protectorate to an independent country, Khama was elected president in 1966. As president he greatly influenced the founding of a stable democracy.

Botswana was one of the world's poorest countries at its independence. Khama began an economic program based on exporting beef and minerals. Only a year after independence, high quality gem diamonds were discovered in Botswana. These new riches were used to build infrastructure, such as schools and health care facilities, in all parts of the country. This sets Botswana apart from some other African countries where such riches end up in politicians' pockets and private Swiss bank accounts. Corruption was seldom an issue in Botswana. By the time we lived there, Botswana had moved from being one of the poorest countries to a much higher ranking on the economic scales. Botswana didn't have foreign debt; it had savings with international agencies. Therefore, international aid agencies, including mission and non-profits, reduced their funding. Some of the Scandinavian state-church missions pulled out of Botswana, as did the Peace Corps, during our time there.

Meanwhile, Ruth Khama's sister Muriel was also in Africa, serving with mission-related endeavors in Zambia. Eventually, Muriel relocated to Botswana, where she became active in projects sponsored by the Botswana Christian Council. She was a fascinating, outspoken person. Once she invited us to her modest home for a meal. Lady Ruth Khama, by then a widow and grandmother, was often seen around town. More than once I saw her by herself shopping in the children's section of the GAME store – somewhat of a regional type of nice big-box store that sold a bit of everything including the best selection of children's toys. After we left Botswana, her son Ian Khama became president of Botswana.

Robert Moffat's descendants

Through working with the BCC, we also met the wife of Doctor Howard Moffat, a descendant of the famous Scottish missionary Robert Moffat sent to South Africa in 1816 by the London Missionary Society. One of Moffat's daughters married David Livingstone, the well-known missionary explorer. The Moffats and Livingstones were instrumental in introducing Christianity to southern Africa, where it gradually spread. We visited the ruins of the Livingstones' dwelling in Botswana, not far from Gaborone. Botswana considers itself a Christian nation. When we were in Botswana, Dr. Howard Moffat was the head physician at the largest hospital in the country and the physician to the country's president.

The popular *#1 Ladies Detective Agency* series of novels about life in Botswana names real people we knew, such as Dr. and Mrs. Moffat, along with actual places we had been to.

Smoking issues

A lot of people smoked cigarettes, especially Europeans. Restaurants didn't have sections for non-smokers. However, I usually asked for a non-smoking section so they would realize some people wanted that.

"You don't have to smoke," one puzzled young waiter said as he led us to a table.

Botswana in the news

Botswana seldom made international news. Historically, its various tribes were known for being peaceful. Botswana was a peaceful democracy since independence. But there was one small riot reported internationally while we were there. Carla witnessed some of it. Erwin and I were out of town, so our mission colleague Don Boschman picked her up at school. As they drove around a big traffic circle near the entrance to the University of Botswana, they saw people with stones in their hands and a big stone and broken glass on the road. Branches burned in the road. Don quickly found another way home, and no one we knew personally was hurt.

What set off this event? A couple of months earlier, a fourteen-year-old girl, Segametsi Mogomotsi, was murdered in the large nearby village of Mochudi. The rumor mill indicated that the suspects, well-known businessmen with political connections, had done it as a ritual murder to obtain body parts as "medicine" to gain business success. That set off a chain of events among students, eventually including students at the University of Botswana, where Carla had seen some of the protesting. Peaceful protesters marched to the city center and wanted to enter the parliament building. Tear gas and rubber bullets were used against the marchers. Injuries and property damage occurred. A twenty-two-year-old man, related to our office assistant, was killed resisting arrest. The University and some other schools closed for a while. The main political parties jumped into the fray. Scotland Yard from England was called in to investigate, but their report wasn't released. The whole country was quite shaken because rioting was rare in Botswana. That incident revealed some underlying values and practices we hadn't known before.

Working with Lesotho, a mountain kingdom

Erwin had the position of regional counselor for Africa Inter-Mennonite Mission, which included workers in Lesotho and South Africa. That gave us a reason to periodically visit our friends Gary and Jean Isaac in Umtata in the Eastern Cape Province in South Africa.

341

As if life in Botswana didn't have enough unexpected events to banish dull moments, events in Lesotho were frequently dumped on our plate too. We, especially Erwin, often went to that small mountain country, an eight-to ten-hour drive from our home in Gaborone. South Africa completely surrounds Lesotho and influences many aspects of life there.

During the apartheid era, dissidents from South Africa sought refuge in Lesotho, as well as in other neighboring countries such as Botswana. When Erwin and I had visited Lesotho in 1984, things were very tense. With the end of apartheid, those tensions weren't an issue, but the country still had significant challenges. Millions of dollars of aid money flowed into Lesotho, but the country remained poor.

The capital city, Maseru, lay in the valley formed by a small river that is the boundary between Lesotho and South Africa. From there, the mountains rose to heights of more than 10,000 feet, with the highest one more than 11,400 feet. Winter snows covered the higher elevations.

About a year after we arrived in Botswana, Bill and Betty Enns from Manitoba, Canada, arrived in Lesotho to give leadership to Mennonite work there. Bill and Betty were about our age. This was their first overseas assignment after years of farming and pastoral work. We related to them through several traumatic events.

One evening a man with an AK 47 burst through their front door. Bill and Betty, along with two young men who had recently arrived to serve in Lesotho with MCC, took refuge in a small room in the back part of the building. They braced a small refrigerator against the door and hoped it would help keep out the thieves. Twice the thieves tried to enter, but the door held. Things crashed as the thieves ransacked the house. Betty later told how she felt the peace of God's presence as they waited about ninety minutes in that back room. Providentially, the regional MCC representatives in nearby South Africa were trained as counselors and went to Lesotho the next day to help them deal with the trauma. The two young men had been ready to get on the next plane home after that scary night, but after counseling, they went on to serve their terms as teachers in remote mountain villages.

Driving in African mountains

When our son Marc spent several weeks with us in 1996, our travels with him included a stop in Lesotho. Bill Enns drove our family in a Toyota 4x4 out to where Katze Dam was under construction up in the mountains. The large dam mainly served the needs of neighboring South Africa for electricity and water. That visit was helpful. One of Marc's college housemates soon began an MCC assignment there working with issues people faced when rising water in the dam's reservoir drove them from their homes and land. Our return trip down the mountains was memorably frightening as the vehicle careened down and around the curves. Views of deep valleys flashed by too close for comfort below drop-offs without guardrails. We heard that on the next trip Bill took into the mountains, with a North American administrator on board, the brakes had failed.

After hearing gunshots during one of our Lesotho visits, Carla wouldn't go along again. Several violent episodes occurred in Lesotho and details blur in my memory. One time there was major rioting contesting the results of a political election. The downtown area was looted and fires set. Troops from South Africa and Botswana went in to restore order. For their safety, the Mennonite workers left the country for a time.

Thieves were always a threat in Lesotho. One time white foreigners were targeted. Bill Enns successfully drove away from an attempt to take his vehicle. Some whites were killed. Betty Enns phoned us during one episode. We felt helpless trying to provide moral support over the phone as she reported the sounds of turmoil coming closer. Later that day, someone helped Bill and Betty sneak out of the country, scrunched down and hiding under blankets on the floor of a vehicle. The Ennses soon needed an extended home leave to deal with the stress. That meant yet more involvement for Erwin and me – at one point we were designated the interim country reps for Lesotho.

That interim role included relating to several newly arrived MCCers, one of whom was our son Marc's college friend. Erwin went to Maseru, planning to drive from the city into the mountains to visit the recent arrivals, located near Katze dam. The evening prior to Erwin's planned mountain excursion, he ate with a Mennonite family working in Lesotho with mission aviation. They told Erwin that because of snow melting then refreezing at nights, there were icy spots on the highway. Erwin remembered the highway's sharp curves alongside steep drop-offs. Erwin was also advised that the MCC 4x4 pickup he planned to drive was a prime target by hijackers. The pickup would be especially vulnerable at slow speeds going up the mountains in low gear. Travel into the mountains wasn't recommended except in a convoy with the dam's construction crew. The convoy schedule didn't fit into Erwin's schedule. He decided visiting the new workers would have to wait.

The next attempt to make the mountain visit was in connection with a vacation trip Erwin and I took to South Africa. Before heading up the mountain road, we bought a bucket of KFC chicken and some other things for lunch with the MCC fellows. The MCC 4x4 vehicle wouldn't start. So Erwin and I drove our little ten-year-old, ugly Toyota Corolla station wagon with about 186,000 miles on it. To our delight, it worked well on the grueling eight hours of mostly mountain driving. We felt much safer in it than in the 4x4 because we were familiar with how it handled; its low center of gravity made it more stable than a 4x4 pickup; and hijackers had no use for that kind of vehicle.

The final kilometer we drove couldn't be called a road. Light rain fell as Erwin carefully maneuvered our little old car around big rocks and through rough ruts. Something I'd eaten wasn't agreeing with me. I desperately needed a bathroom by the time we arrived at the MCCers' picturesque dwelling flanked with magnificent views. Our host pointed me up the bare mountainside to a small, narrow outhouse made from upright sheets of corrugated tin roofing. Lightning spiked down from the skies nearby. That little metal outhouse was the highest object around. I tried not to think about being fried in there by a lightning strike!

We had a nice visit with the MCC fellows and they enjoyed the KFC meal. That was the second time Erwin was prevented from driving the 4x4 up the mountains – there must have been a reason.

Changes in communication technology

Before we went to Botswana, Erwin was among the few people using email in the General Conference office in Newton. When we arrived in

Botswana in 1994, we wanted to keep in touch with our children, Marcia and Marc, in the U.S. by email. Only the University of Botswana had email at the time. We went to the office of a congenial university professor to send and receive email through his account. Within a few months, CompuServe opened a dial-up server in nearby South Africa. We signed up right away. To use email, we plugged our computer into the connector for our landline telephone and dialed the phone number for CompuServe. When we heard a loud screeching sound, we knew it was connected. Then we sent out our prepared email and received incoming email – all the while incurring long-distance international phone charges of about one dollar per call. We checked email only once a day.

Would our sending agencies pay email expenses as a utility? An AIMM board member suggested that email was only for emergencies or perhaps checked just once a week.

We first sent email messages to Marcia in Kansas via someone working in the General Conference office in Newton who would print it out and give it to her at church. One time in 1995, from an email we sent her, Marcia read about Botswana to her youth Sunday school class. That was their first exposure to email. Marc had an account as a student at EMU. It took several years before there was a dial-up internet service provider in Gaborone. That eliminated the long-distance phone charges.

Toward the end of our time in Botswana, we could check our financial accounts by the Internet. Erwin was pleased. Prior to that, we waited weeks for printed statements to come in the postal mail. He kept his own accounting, but couldn't verify what exactly was in the bank account until weeks later. He couldn't complete our annual financial records until February or later.

We experimented with Net2Phone, an early voice over internet protocol (VOIP). From our computer in Botswana we called the children's landline phones in the U.S. via the Internet, at ten cents per minute. That compared to $1.50 a minute when we called from our landline phone. However, it didn't work well. Calling was complicated with plug-in microphones and headsets, plus poor reception, time lags, echoing, and broken connections. We gave up on that.

Landline phone service in Botswana used a state-of-the-art fiber optic system – for the few phones there were. Not all our MM workers had phones when we first went there. We learned about living with the uncertainty of not knowing, and that no news usually meant things were OK. We eventually devised a system of contacts through other people for urgent messages.

Email service improved rapidly, making it possible for us to stay connected to distant family and friends much faster than by written letters. By the time we ended our service in Botswana, we could contact our entire MM team by email.

Prior to email, fax machines were the quickest way to communicate with the home offices. Arriving in our office some mornings, we saw a long tangled pile of curling fax paper that came in overnight. It was best to cut the pages apart and photocopy them right away because faxes faded.

Introduction to mobile phones

We first saw mobile phones in South Africa. People chatted loudly on their phones in restaurants, dressing room stalls in clothing shops, and other public places. Those first cell phones were quite simple – they only made and received phone calls.

It took the visit of U.S. President Bill Clinton to bring cell phone service to Botswana in 1998 because his security team needed it. After that, several stores opened in Gaborone to sell mobile phones and calling services. Their parking lots overflowed with cars because cell phone users went in person to purchase more minutes for the SIM card in their phones. They didn't have contract plans as in the U.S.

It felt like mobile phones were flaunted as a status symbol. We heard stories about "sugar daddies" who gave teenaged girls cell phones to make arrangements for trysts. Mobile phones, however, allowed many people to have phone service without the lengthy, complicated and expensive process of getting a landline phone.

As mission workers, we were just glad to have email and we didn't even think about getting a mobile phone. When we traveled, we prepared contact information in case someone needed to reach us. It was cumbersome to look up every place along the way and find that information. With aging parents and children in the U.S., we wanted to be sure they could reach us in an emergency – which never happened.

Using computers

In Botswana, Erwin used a laptop computer – something his fingers were attached to ever since 1983. I used an older desktop computer in the MM office. Would our sending agencies pay for a replacement computer for my use? Wasn't one computer enough for us to use, they asked? Erwin and I had enough experience with the home offices in North America to know that by then every staff person there had a computer to use. I successfully appealed for each of us to have a computer.

Erwin's laptop was a Toshiba, which MCC recommended at the time. Late afternoon on a Tuesday in June 1998, the laptop started making strange noises. In somewhat of a panic, instead of heading to Lesotho as planned the next morning, Erwin packed up and dashed off to Durban, South Africa, the closest place to repair Toshiba computers under warranty. It was a boring ten-hour drive for him. He arrived in Durban after office hours, and stayed overnight at a missionary guesthouse. First thing in the morning on Thursday, he went to the Toshiba place. It had moved – to Johannesburg, which he had passed on his way to Durban. He headed back to Jo-burg, arriving at the Toshiba place only about 15 minutes before closing time. About four o'clock the next morning, on Friday, he headed to Lesotho to work with tensions between church leaders there. Erwin picked up the repaired computer on Monday as he returned to Gaborone from Lesotho. Fortunately, he had regularly backed up his documents and the complicated accounting files. He had driven many miles to repair the computer - quite a wild goose chase, it seemed.

Watching television

We had a small black and white TV. Initially, we watched CNN, BBC, and a South African channel. We saw several broadcasts of the fascinating Truth and Reconciliation hearings. However, we had that television service only because someone illegally rebroadcast signals from South Africa into Botswana. When that was discovered and turned off, we were left with limited broadcasts from the only TV station in Gaborone. Before the next major sporting event, satellite dishes sprouted like mushrooms all over Gaborone. In remote areas, we saw thatch-roofed huts with satellite dishes connected to solar-powered television sets.

Security systems and thieves

We had lived with walls around the yard, metal grates over windows and doors, and car alarm systems in Brazil. In Botswana we tried to adapt to living with interior alarm services. What a nuisance that was.

So how often did the alarm system "catch" a thief? Never. The alarms were easily set off, unfortunately – by a cat in the storage shed, a bird in the guesthouse lounge, and accidentally by people with legitimate access to the premises. From our house on the next street, we heard the alarms at the MM office building. One of us would scurry through the small park to intercept the private-company security guards who came promptly to check out each alarm.

When a thief actually came, the alarm didn't go off. A smart thief managed to steal an old bicycle from the storage shed. We had small things stolen from outside at times. Some visiting Americans once left windows open in the back guest cottage. Some kids climbed over the back fence, reached through the grate of the open window and "went fishing," using long-handled mops we kept outside. They grabbed some money and personal items including shaving cream that they sprayed all around outside.

Most black Africans were frightened by our dog. He was a gentle dog and the worst thing he did once was to pee onto the foot of a visiting African church leader. That was embarrassing!

Soon after we settled in, the Mennonite Ministries' van was stolen from the yard at the office. Insurance money helped replace it. New mission worker Rudy Dirks had several personal encounters with thieves within the first three months that he and his family lived in the house next to ours. Once when he went out to see why their dog was barking, he saw a man by their van. When Rudy asked what he wanted, the man pulled a knife and started toward Rudy. Rudy called for the dog and the man slowly turned, climbed over the padlocked wire gate and left, sauntering down the street.

Sometimes people asked for money. We tried to find some work so they could earn it. I asked one man to clean the yard at the office. It didn't take him very long, though. Shortly after he left, the woman next door complained that he reached across a low wire fence and grabbed a nice tablecloth she had drying on the clothesline. That didn't help generate a generous spirit within me.

One late afternoon as I drove away from the MM office building, I got out of my car to shut the wire gate. A young fellow, a kid about my height, tried to grab my purse. Fearlessly I hung on tightly and managed to pull out a hundred Pula bill, worth about twenty U.S. dollars. He took that and left me with my purse and all its documents intact.

Thievery in South Africa went to a higher level. The Baptist mission guesthouse, where we often stayed in Johannesburg, had high walls and an electrically operated gate. They had some big steel cages around and over their vehicles. Thieves actually managed to steal vehicles out of such a cage. Thieves once held up the Baptist business manager coming back from the bank and relieved him of a considerable amount of money at gunpoint. We were grateful to not experience more than some petty thievery.

On one trip to South Africa for a regional retreat attended by all our workers and their families, would-be thieves targeted four of our MM families' vehicles. One vehicle was stolen.

Car trouble

Rudy and Sharon Dirks and their three children were living in a village about an hours' drive away from Gaborone to learn language and culture. There was no phone contact available and some message needed to be relayed to them. Carla and I set off in our old Toyota Corolla to go see them and deliver the message in person. About two-thirds of the way there, I noticed the car engine beginning to sputter. It had been serviced just the day before, of all things. The sputtering came and went, but was getting worse. When I slowed to turn off the paved highway to take the road to the Dirks' village location, the motor died. I coasted onto a narrow paved shoulder. With Carla's help, we managed to push the car just a bit farther away from the fast-moving traffic. Knowing it was futile for me to look under the bonnet (hood), I raised it anyway, hoping it would, at least, signal our distress.

It didn't take long until two men in a pickup pulled up and stopped to see if they could help. They were a father and son from Zimbabwe. The older man said he was the headmaster at the local primary school. I could hardly believe my ears when he said his son taught auto mechanics. The younger man quickly discovered that a screw had fallen out of the distributor cap – the rarest of screws, he said. Carla and I rode along with the men in their pickup to an auto parts shop. After the shop clerk said they didn't have any of that kind of screw, the store owner asked the clerk to get a particular box with a bunch of old distributors. He found an old screw, removed it, and gave it to us.

The two men took Carla and me back to our disabled car, still sitting forlornly beside the highway. The mechanic put in the screw but didn't have the tool needed to tighten it. Our car did start, though, so I followed them to a nearby location where the older man was building a house. There he found pliers to tighten the screw. As we talked, I learned that the man had met Rudy Dirks just that morning as Rudy was walking in the village to get water.

"So often we take God's care for granted, so every once in a while, He clearly shows us that He truly is involved in the details of our lives." *From September 1, 1996, letter to our children.*

Experiencing God's care

God's care was also evident when in February 1999, I bravely set out with Judy Gingerich to drive the MM van across the Kalahari Desert. We went to retrieve her things as she ended her assignment working with the Bushmen children. By then, the road was paved all the way to the town of Ghanzi, more than 400 miles away and about a nine-hour drive. All went well. The sky was blue with white clouds and the desert was as green as I'd ever seen it. We left the paved road at Ghanzi and continued on unpaved road a bit farther to our destination in the village where she worked. By the time I realized it wasn't just the loose dirt and sand making the vehicle unstable, a flat tire had been thoroughly demolished. We were within sight of a gas station on the edge of the village. Judy walked toward it. Someone stopped and gave her a lift in the back of a pickup. Judy returned with a helper and in quick order, the tire was changed. However, I couldn't buy a replacement tire in that small village. They were sure we could find one back in Ghanzi the next day.

The farewells for Judy and packing the van went fine in the village. She and I headed to Ghanzi the next day. As we drove into a place that sold tires, before I even turned off the ignition, a worker stepped up and took down the ruined tire from the roof rack. With a new tire, Judy and I headed across the desert toward Gaborone, glad to be back on paved road.

The needle on the gas gauge was dropping too fast on that long stretch to the next gas station. We turned off the air conditioner and drove slower. When Judy and I exchanged places at the steering wheel, we noticed that another tire had small "cracks" radiating out from the rim. So for the next 150 kilometers, about 93 miles, I was quite concerned about running out of gas and having another flat tire. The gas gauge needle was on E as we drove into the gas station. Some other travelers at the gas station also noticed the cracks in our tire. They said it needed to be changed right away. No new tire was available, so the spare went on again. With prayer and hope, we resumed the rest of our trip across the desert without a spare tire. It was a great relief to arrive home in Gaborone safely just at dusk that day.

Traveling in southern Africa

It is a good thing Erwin and I didn't mind traveling because we had lots of work-related travel during our years in Botswana. Ever since the 1970s in Brazil, Erwin did a lot of travel. Now as co-country administrators in Botswana, we usually traveled together – most often by car or small plane, but at times by van, 4x4 pickup, train or bus.

Most months Erwin and I took one or more trips. We kept basic travel items ready to go. We learned to pack lightly because whenever we took a Flying Mission plane, everything was weighed – including us! We would meet our pilot at the main Gaborone airport. He weighed our bags and bodies on the luggage scale, and then escorted us to the little Cessna waiting on the tarmac. After we awkwardly clambered into the plane, the pilot prayed before starting the loud engine.

Flights were smooth during the colder dry season. During rainy times and season changes, I needed a small amount of Dramamine to keep my stomach controlled. The little plane bounced through the wind, updrafts, and downdrafts created by alternating sunshine and cloud shadows. Erwin didn't need to take anything.

Two funerals on one day

Saturday, September 6, 1997, was a day with two funerals. The first one was for the husband of a woman who led an African Independent Church group. Mennonites had worked closely with her for some years. The man was only fifty-two and had tuberculosis, a common complication with AIDS. As was the custom in Botswana, unembalmed bodies were kept in cold storage at the mortuary until a Friday evening. Then a hearse took the body to the family home where a big tent in the yard sheltered the mourners during an all-night wake. The funeral service took place first thing on Saturday morning under the tent, with attendees spreading out over the yard. From the home, a slow procession of vehicles drove to the cemetery, including pickup trucks packed with people standing in the open back.

At the busy cemetery, some people were leaving after a burial service, others were arriving, and other services were in progress. We saw a row of open graves. It appeared that families took their choice of graves to bury their loved one. Nearby a group of well-dressed Anglicans sang traditional funeral hymns in good harmony. On another side, a small group of poorly dressed people joined our group for singing. The same songs were sung for each burial, each group of mourners beginning at different times, sometimes overlapping, and in different keys. At the conclusion of the graveside service, men shoveled dirt into the grave. They placed a wrought iron cage on top, often filled with a pile of big stones so that wild animals wouldn't dig up the body. Then people went back to the deceased's home for a meal. Two cows were slaughtered for the event we attended. The traditional meal included well-cooked tasty beef, shredded into a tasty concoction and served with lightly cooked greens, white cornmeal mush, and other foods.

That Saturday we hurried back home to watch Princess Diana's elaborate ceremonial funeral broadcast on TV. We were at Westminster Abbey only a few months earlier that year during a layover in London, so it was especially interesting to watch the funeral ceremony broadcast from there. Outwardly the two funerals were quite different, yet there were similarities in that the deceased were both loved even though questions remained about the nature of their deaths.

HIV/AIDS

"Botswana is number one!" some students cheered when statistics indicated the country had the world's highest rate of HIV and AIDS infections. When we had first arrived in Botswana, large billboards proclaimed that one in four persons in Botswana had HIV/AIDS.

The disease touched all of society, rich and poor, educated and uneducated. Yet it wasn't talked about much – at least on the personal level. Some called it the "radio disease" because that is where they heard about it.

Almost all HIV transmission was through heterosexual sex or passed from mother to infant. Health care providers sometimes contracted it accidentally through contact with body fluids. Christian church teaching and traditional culture emphasized virginity. People were ashamed to openly admit being HIV positive. Yet people, especially young adults, were dying at unnaturally high rates. Often it was said they died after "a long illness" or of TB, malaria, pneumonia – diseases they could have overcome if it weren't for their compromised immune system. Some reports indicated that the HIV strain common in southern Africa was more virulent than in other places.

Official statistics released in mid-1999 indicated that the Selebi Phikwe area, where we had several of our MM workers, had the highest percentages of HIV-positive people: fifty percent of pregnant women and sixty percent of men who sought treatment for sexually transmitted diseases.

Some weeks there were too many funerals to hold them all on Saturday morning, as was the custom. Traditionally the extended family cared for orphans. The large number of needy children severely stressed the family structure and there was talk of organizing orphanages. We heard sad stories of grandmothers trying to raise several orphaned grandchildren on a small government pension, and of uncles favoring their own children at the expense of orphaned nieces and nephews in their care.

Some Africans' view of HIV/AIDS

Leaders, both in the government and in the churches, first said little about AIDS. But it couldn't be ignored. Some people claimed it was a plot by the United States to destroy black people. We became acquainted with Edward, hired by the Botswana government to address the AIDS pandemic in Botswana. Edward, an Anglican priest from Uganda, had worked with Uganda's successful effort to slow its rate of new infections. That was in part due to the ABC campaign: Abstain. Be faithful. Condomize. Most people in Botswana thought it was impossible for unmarried people to abstain, for married partners to be faithful, and to use condoms consistently correctly.

Most MM workers related to organizations working with some aspect of HIV/AIDS. Bible teachers incorporated AIDS-related issues into the Bible teaching ministry among African Independent Church leaders. People were overwhelmed with grief and the costs of funerals. Casket makers kept busy.

In traditional African worldview, everything has a spiritual component. Even active Christians would consult a traditional healer to find out who may have put a curse on someone and why. The scientific causes of disease weren't accepted, as illustrated by the following incident.

The woman hired for house help by our neighbors, Rudy and Sharon Dirks, showed symptoms typical of AIDS. Unmarried, she had one little boy who was also quite sick. Sharon took Maria (easier to use than her long Setswana name) to a private doctor and set up counseling for her. Maria refused to be tested. She also refused to accept any scientific explanations for her illness. No, she figured she had displeased the spirit of her deceased father and he was causing her to be sick. Or perhaps her sister had put a curse on her because she was jealous of Maria's good job working for white people.

Maria was quite interested in the material Rudy used in his Bible teaching classes. Maria eagerly devoured whatever material Rudy gave her.

When Maria died, we discovered that she had passed along the Bible teaching to others who gathered around her in her home village.

There were enough interested people in her village to form a new Bible class for Rudy to teach. Yet, in the messiness of real life, Maria died shortly after giving birth to a very premature stillborn infant. I worked closely with Maria a short time before her death and never suspected she was pregnant.

Health care issues

Except for mammograms, private healthcare providers met all our basic health care needs there in Gaborone. Costs were reasonable and paid by our supporting agencies. We are grateful that Erwin and I continued to enjoy good health throughout our time in Africa. Botswana had a public health care system at minimal cost for all its citizens. If needed, they were transferred to larger hospitals in South Africa at no extra cost.

Because mammography wasn't available in Gaborone, each year I went to a clinic in Johannesburg where results were ready in an hour. One year, to the amusement of some people, I organized a carload of several of us Mennonite Ministries' women to drive together to Jo-burg for mammograms! All of us got good results, so we could relax and take advantage of that occasion to shop at the large, nice shopping malls and have fun together.

We women stayed at the Baptist mission guesthouse, BIMS, close to health facilities and the airport. BIMS was a place of refuge for mission workers. Each suite offered a small kitchen, two bedrooms, and two bathrooms. Interestingly, the Baptist woman, an American, managing BIMS wanted the MCC *More with Less* cookbook for each of the kitchenettes.

Visiting Americans

Ironically, we had better opportunities to see top-level U.S. political figures when we were overseas than we've had in the U.S. Our overseas assignments happened to coincide with Democratic administrations. In Brazil, I saw President Jimmy Carter's wife, Rosalynn, as mentioned previously. When Vice-president Al Gore briefly stopped in Botswana, we Americans were invited to see him at the airport. He reached over a fence to shake hands with a small group of people.

It was a much more elaborate event when President Bill Clinton and his wife, Hillary, came to Botswana in March 1998. The news about them that filtered through to us was rather sordid at the time. Yet we were curious. Americans living in Botswana received a gold-edged invitation from Botswana's president to attend a reception for the Clintons at the Statehouse, Botswana's equivalent to our White House. The attire was to be a traditional dress for women and a "lounge suit" for men. We learned that meant a business suit and tie. Along with colorful diplomatic corps of other nations and business officials, we were among several thousand people waiting in the hot sun for the Clintons' late arrival. We helped ourselves from large platters of attractively arranged finger foods on tables under large white tents set in a U-shape around a spacious grassy area inside the high walls of the Statehouse.

Speeches and formalities were mercifully short. President Clinton had a bad cold and looked miserable. Soon the Clintons left to spend some time in the northern part of Botswana where big game is plentiful.

Concluding our Botswana chapter

Approaching the end of our five-year commitment to serve as MCC country representatives in Botswana, both MCC and AIMM asked us to continue. We agreed to stay in Botswana another year, until about July in 2000. When we told our children, they were happy that we would come back to the U.S. Not sensing a clear call otherwise, Erwin half-heartedly applied for a position in North America that someone had suggested he apply for. The application and interview process was a new experience for him. We were relieved when someone else was hired.

Once again, an unexpected invitation came along. Ron Flaming, then the Executive Secretary of the Commission on Overseas Mission in Newton, Kansas, the position Erwin had held for nearly twelve years, contacted Erwin. Ron was deeply involved in bringing about the merger of the mission agencies of the Mennonite Church and the General Conference Mennonite Church. COM needed someone to help promote its work. Income wasn't keeping up with costs. COM wanted to be fiscally responsible

Ron invited Erwin to take a new specially approved position with COM as Director for Development and Church Relations. Erwin had previously done extensive travel throughout the General Conference. He usually enjoyed preaching and visiting in churches, in both the U.S. and Canada. The church relations aspect of the job would be familiar – the fundraising focus not so much.

Sensing this as God's call, we accepted the invitation and wrote about it to our family in early September 1999. We made plans to move back to Newton, Kansas, and to work again at the Mennonite offices at 722 N. Main Street. Could we "go home" again? The uncertainties of the upcoming denominational integration would mean additional changes in less than two years.

Our departure from Botswana would be in February 2000 rather than in July of that year. Again there was dismay that we were leaving our work so soon. Several new people had just arrived for assignments with Mennonite Ministries in Botswana. By then Sara and Fremont Regier served as the MCC regional coordinators. They lived in neighboring Zimbabwe. They oversaw the work in Botswana until new country representatives arrived.

To prepare for his new work, Erwin made a trip to the U.S. for a month. He spent time in the Newton office. He learned that Jim and Anna Juhnke, Bethel College professors, were looking for someone to stay in their house in North Newton when they went to Elkhart, Indiana, for several months. The timing was just right for us to again have a furnished temporary home for our transition. Erwin also went to Indianapolis for a course that introduced him to fundraising.

Unusual farewell gift

Leaving in February rather than July squeezed our remaining time in Botswana. One of the important meetings we attended yet was the regional leaders' meeting in the Durban area. From Zimbabwe, the Regiers brought along a farewell gift for us – a carved wooden giraffe over six feet tall. What were we to do with it? The car we drove at the time had back seats that folded down. We threaded the long giraffe through from the trunk so it could ride along with us, its head reaching up between our elbows. At our next stop in Umtata to see Gary and Jean Isaac, the first thing Erwin did was ask Gary for a saw. Erwin cut the giraffe in two pieces to fit crosswise in the trunk. From there he and I drove the scenic Garden Route along the southern edge of South Africa. We made our second visit to the lovely Cape Town area, the only vacation break we would have for quite some time. When we left Botswana the next February, the giraffe's top and bottom parts were reattached, and he proudly graced the lounge area of the Mennonite Ministries guesthouse. What a surprise it was about a year later to discover the tall giraffe standing in the Newton office. The fun-loving Regiers had found some way to get the giraffe to the U.S.

An unsettling experience

In late 1999 before we left Botswana, I noticed a lump in one of my breasts. After some tests, I was scheduled for a biopsy in the Gaborone Private Hospital, complete with full anesthesia. December 7, about eleven o'clock in the morning, I checked in at the hospital. Garbed in a skimpy hospital gown, and not allowed to eat, I waited until about six o'clock in the evening to be taken to surgery. Later I woke up in a dimly lit room with several other patients. It was dark outside. I hadn't eaten all day, and asked for something to eat. It was well past the regular hospital mealtime, but someone kindly warmed a plate of food for me – goat stew. That seemed unusual fare for someone coming out of anesthesia!

We were relieved when the reports came saying that it was benign. This second time for a breast biopsy wasn't nearly as frightening as the first time was back in 1994.

Our last days in Botswana

We spent one last Christmas and New Year's Day in Gaborone. It was the much talked about Y2K event. Would the computers in Botswana and the rest of the world be ready to roll over from 1999 to 2000? Erwin and I usually begin a new year with a full night of sleep. But on the momentous occasion of a new millennium, we stayed up until after midnight. We played games and visited with our MM team. It wasn't until a few minutes after the fireworks and uproar began that I realized all the lights were still on. The only thing that wasn't Y2K compliant was our dog. He was so scared of all the fireworks he snuck into the house to hide.

During our final week in Botswana our AIMM administrator, Garry

Prieb, and his wife visited us. So did a stalled rain system that repeatedly dumped heavy rain across southern Africa. Roads and bridges flooded. Our maid couldn't come in to the city, and we had to leave a farewell note and severance pay for her to collect later from someone else. Flying Mission came to the rescue and flew several of our team members to Gaborone to participate in a farewell for Erwin and me. The team gave us a nice tapestry of an African village scene, woven by the local Oodi Weavers.

When the Air Botswana plane lifted off from Gaborone, we saw flooded streams, broad rivers, and the overflowing reservoir of the Gaborone dam. The totally green landscape below helped balance my first impressions of Botswana as a dry and brown place.

What an interesting chapter we had experienced for nearly six years in Botswana.

Part Two
Our Family – a Funeral and Two Weddings

Prologue: *Piles of family correspondence from the years in Botswana face me. My mind has a way of distilling the memories from fifteen to twenty years ago, leaving mainly the impressions of the positive, fascinating, and interesting aspects. The shadows floating underneath are barely seen or felt. However, it doesn't take much glancing through what we and our children wrote back and forth during those years to feel as though I'm picking at the corner of an old scab. The feelings and experiences that we walked through one by one, day by day, come back in an overwhelming rush that tugs at the heartstrings.*

For our family, those years were marked by a funeral and two weddings, which helped provide opportunities to see our U.S. - based children an average of once a year. That was a blessing and evidence of God's sustaining grace. Knowing now how things turned out for the children, helps temper the pain and some measure of guilt.

Trying to adjust
We didn't expect going to Botswana in 1994 to be so hard for us, or for our children. Erwin and I already had previous experience living in

another country and culture. Marcia and Marc were age twenty-three and nineteen, respectively – ages when, we too easily assumed, they would be eager to cut the apron strings and be exploring the world as adults. For Carla, age fourteen, this would essentially be her first international experience. She remembers nothing of her life as an infant in Brazil.

The same day we flew off to Africa, June 26, 1994, as previously noted, First Mennonite Church, in Newton, Kansas, voted to invite Marcia to serve as a full-time youth pastor. It was a heavy emotional day for her. She soon moved her things from Virginia to Newton. She shared a house with Christa Wiens, a church friend from her high school years in Newton. They lived across the street from retired missionaries Verney and Belva Unruh, whose presence flowed in and out of our lives over the years. To Erwin and me, this felt like a good situation for Marcia. She was in touch with her two aunts and their families living nearby; she connected with her grandfather, great aunts and a great uncle; and she had many friends and acquaintances from her years growing up in Newton.

Not having a typewriter or email at first, Marcia wrote us long letters by hand, full of questions about our experiences in Botswana, and sharing details of her new life. At her installation service, August 28, she said something about this opportunity being God's gracious providence and gift at a time when her own family was scattered all over the world.

"I've been given back to my church family," she said to the congregation.

Marcia was frequently reminded of us and our absence. She missed us a great deal, especially when she went through the scary process of having a second biopsy on a lump in her breast and facing the resulting uncovered medical bills. The salary that at first seemed so generous didn't go as far as she expected. She bravely drove our old Dodge Omni that rattled and kept falling apart.

From the beginning, Marcia was only committed to one two-year term, and, at times, she even wondered if she would stay that long. However, her work there was effective and appreciated. She helped start a new Sunday school class of young adults that brought in new people who became long-term members of the church. The same caring adults she'd known as her youth sponsors were still present in the church to guide and support her. She appreciated the new pastor, Clarence Rempel, and his wife, Amanda. Having the same last name at times caused confusion, even though she wasn't related to them.

Marc completed that summer of 1994 as planned, working for Dwight and Janet Regier on their farm near Newton. He had worked with them several times previously. At the end of the summer, Marc drove our old Celebrity Chevrolet out to Virginia to resume his college education at Eastern Mennonite University. He too missed us. For both Marc and Marcia, planning a trip to see us in Botswana in August the next year, 1995, gave them something to look forward to. They each wrestled with uncertainties in their romantic relationships.

Most parents provide the roots as their children test their wings. In our case, both parents and children were testing new wings at great distances from each other.

"We know God can take better care of you than we can, but sometimes it isn't easy for us to just let go and rest in that knowledge," I wrote Marcia at one point.

Just as the struggle of a butterfly to get out of its cocoon helps strengthen it, so it seems to be true for young adults. In God's own way and time, God did provide for our children.

A funeral in Kansas

November 18, 1994, a Friday night, the phone rang in our house in Gaborone, Botswana. It was my sister, LaRita, calling from Newton, Kansas.

"I have some sad news," she said. My heart nearly stopped, thinking something had happened to either Marcia or Marc back in the States. So I was actually relieved when she said that our dad, Erwin A. Albrecht, had died unexpectedly.

"But I can't go back the States now," I thought in distress as LaRita's voice on the phone poured out the details. Less than five months after arriving in Botswana, I was struggling with adapting to life there. I knew people back in Kansas would ask how things were going, and I couldn't honestly say that things were fine. Erwin and I had agreed that either one of us would travel back to the U.S. in the event of a parent's death.

361

"Can Carla come too?" Marcia and Marc asked. With some trepidation about the impact that might have on Carla at this stage of her adapting to life and school in Botswana, we decided that both she and I would go.

First thing the next morning, Saturday, we were at the Air Botswana office and purchased plane tickets for Carla and me to leave yet that day from Johannesburg, South Africa, to Kansas City. By noon on Saturday, after hurriedly packing, we began the five-hour drive to the airport in Johannesburg. That evening Carla and I were on a long direct flight to Washington, D.C. Marc joined us in the Dulles airport, and we three continued together on to Kansas.

Erwin's sister, Barb Busenitz, and her husband met us in Kansas City and drove us the remaining two-hundred miles to Newton. Marcia was only a few months into her work as a youth pastor at our church in Newton. By the time I arrived, she and LaRita had arranged things for the funeral at First Mennonite Church, where Dad had been a member for about twenty years. It was a traditional funeral, followed by burial alongside my mother in the Restlawn Gardens of Memory.

We never learned just how and when Dad died. Compared to my mother's long months of suffering from cancer prior to her death, it seems good that he passed on while calmly sitting in his favorite chair. He had just celebrated his eighty-eighth birthday a couple of weeks earlier on October 25. I had phoned him on his birthday and talked to him for what was the last time. He wrote his last letter to me just after the 1994 elections that returned control of both the Senate and House to Republicans. As a lifelong Republican, Dad was very happy about that. That letter arrived at our Botswana address after his death.

During the three weeks Carla and I were in Newton, LaRita and I kept busy cleaning out Dad's apartment and beginning the legal processes of distributing his estate. Amazingly, the poor country preacher still had a net worth of more than $100,000, some of which he designated for missions. But more important than the money was the spiritual legacy he left to us.

That trip back to the U.S. was a turning point for both Carla and me in adapting to life in Botswana. For her, it brought closure to her childhood in Kansas. She realized she had already changed and Kansas wasn't home anymore. I returned to Botswana with new energy.

An American teenager in Africa

Carla did fine during the village live-in, as described earlier. When we moved into the city, her bedroom in our house was so small that Erwin converted her bed into a loft high enough to fit a desk under it. During one of her first nights sleeping up on the loft, we were horrified to hear a thump in her room during the night. She had forgotten she couldn't just sit up and step away from her bed to head to the bathroom, and she had fallen to the floor. Erwin made a sturdy rail that same day!

In the southern hemisphere, the school year began in February and ended in December before Christmas. Maru-a-Pula, a private secondary school, was where other missionary kids had attended. We were pleased that they accepted Carla and had a place for her to start in September, the last term of their school year. The school was conveniently located about a five-minute drive from our house. Considered the best school in the country, Maru-a-Pula attracted children of diplomats and business people. Sixty percent of students were Batswana. Carla was astonished in 1999 when one of her former classmates at Maru-a-Pula, Mpule Kwelagobe, won the Miss Universe pageant.

School uniforms are so convenient! Carla needed only basic white shirts and navy pants or skirts. To endure the cold unheated classrooms in the cold months, she wore layers of clothing under her uniform. Adapting to the new school, the British-style educational system, and the diversity of students and teachers was stressful for Carla. She found it easier by the next school year. She always had lots of homework and frequent tests.

Our old, ugly brown Toyota Corolla station wagon was quite a contrast to the other vehicles entering the Maru-a-Pula school grounds to drop off or pick up students. What was even worse, whenever Erwin took our car out of town, I drove Carla to and from school in the Mennonite Ministries' rattletrap of an old little Toyota pickup that with its bright yellow color really stuck out among Mercedes and BMWs.

What a diversity of school friends Carla had in Botswana! Her contacts with kids from all sorts of religious backgrounds gave us opportunities to talk with her about the Christian faith and how it is different from other faiths. Most young people aren't faced with those questions until they go to college, if ever.

One of Carla's friends was from a Hindu family. Carla was rather startled when the friend talked about reincarnation, what she thought she had been in a former life, what her cat had been before, and what she herself might be in her next life. Another friend was of the Jain religion, which also originated in India. Carla's Muslim friends fasted during the daytime for about a month during Ramadan. A British girl was post-Christian, and a friend from a former communist country in Eastern Europe was an atheist. One time Carla invited this diverse group of friends to our place for pizza. With all their different dietary rules, that became quite a challenge.

There were a few Christian kids at her school, including the daughter of the American ambassor. The Baptist church we usually attended had a youth group, at times. Carla occasionally played her flute with the worship team at the church.

Carla Rempel, front left, with school friends, Gaborone, Botswana, 1997.

Youth had to be eighteen years old in order to get a Botswana driver's license. That meant we always needed to drive Carla to and from everything.

At that point, Carla was essentially like an only child. We spent a lot of time together. She lived a fairly protected life, but she didn't complain. My worst fear for her and the other young women on our team was they might be raped in that HIV-saturated country.

To prepare her for living in the U.S., we began teaching Carla to drive. Her first driving experiences were in our car that had the driver's seat on the right side and manual shifting. She experimented on dirt paths at the Gaborone city cemetery, next to a crematorium.

Carla was an asset to our Mennonite Ministries team. Prior to our coming, team members hoped the next country reps would have a teenager to help with childcare. And that she did, especially during the team meetings. Once she went along on a Flying Mission flight to help a mother returning to a remote area with a new baby and a toddler.

Marcia and Marc visiting in Botswana

We saw our young adult children about once a year. That came about through a combination of some frequent-flyer miles, personal resources, our own trips back to the U.S., and mission-sponsored trips for college students to visit their missionary parents once during the four years of college.

Marc and Marcia were on different flights when they came to visit us in August 1995. The long trip was made even longer for Marcia with extra-long layovers topped off by a hassle in customs in Johannesburg about a box of items she brought along for us. Customs officials charged her most of the money she had. By the time we finally saw her coming out of the arrivals area, she was more than ready to relax in our welcoming embraces.

Marcia and Marc stayed in our small house during the days we all spent in Gaborone. We introduced them to various aspects of life there. They were with us on Erwin's fifty-first birthday. We marked that by climbing Kgale Hill, a rugged hill rising nearly a thousand feet above Gaborone. The kids assured me they would help me climb, and they did. By the time we got to the top of Kgale Hill, I had serious doubts that I could manage going back down. An angel unaware appeared in the form of a rugged workman who had driven up the hill to check on communications towers. He offered to give us all a ride down in his four-wheel drive pickup. We gladly accepted his offer. As we bounced down the rough dirt road, we learned that he was British, but preferred living in warm sunny Botswana rather than in cool, cloudy, and rainy England.

We took Marcia, Marc, and Carla along on an administrative trip to visit our MM workers in the two "ends of the earth" locations. We did that with Flying Mission. Our family of five just fit into a small plane.

To visit some others on our team, we took the kids on a big road trip using the MM van. We drove on to Chobe, an unfenced game reserve in northern Botswana, where we enjoyed seeing some of Africa's largest animals, including elephants. From there it was only a short drive into Zimbabwe and the Victoria Falls that amazed missionary-explorer David Livingstone years earlier. We saw the bridge linking Zimbabwe to Zambia. The bridge is known for bungee jumping, but no one was jumping when we were there. Heading south and crossing from Zimbabwe into South Africa was like passing through a time warp, Marc said. Under the repressive government of Robert Mugabe, Zimbabwe was stuck in the 1950s and '60s. South Africa, though, was quickly moving into the contemporary world. A variety of fast food places and other conveniences greeted travelers entering South Africa. Facing another parting, our family spent a subdued final night together in the Baptist mission guesthouse in Johannesburg not far from the airport.

The following year, 1996, Marc spent several weeks with us in Botswana during his summer school break. He helped with some painting and other projects. As part of his student work, Marc had written a paper on Mozambique, formerly a Portuguese colony. So we took him along on a road trip, in our old Toyota Corolla, into Mozambique to visit our colleagues Fremont and Sarah Regier. They worked there with MCC. Armed soldiers placed regularly along the nearly deserted paved highway were both reassuring and frightening – they wouldn't have been there had no threat remained after the end of Mozambique's civil war. We saw Portuguese influence mixed with African customs in Mozambique.

From there we drove through the tiny country of Swaziland to the port city of Durban in South Africa. We stayed there at Concord House, a simple, inexpensive mission guesthouse. In earlier years it accommodated Western missionaries waiting for their ship to leave. Marc thought the dining room tables at Concord House had more British-style cutlery than food! After passing through Lesotho, Marc headed back to Virginia for another year of college at Eastern Mennonite University.

Two weddings in one year

Before we took a two-month home leave in the U.S. in December 1996 to January 1997, Marcia completed her two years as youth pastor at First Mennonite in Newton, Kansas. She moved back to Harrisonburg, Virginia to study at Eastern Mennonite Seminary. There, she reconnected with John Weaver, whom she had dated earlier.

During our brief home leave, Erwin, Carla, and I visited family and the five churches that were our Mission Partners. During several weeks in Newton, Kansas, we lived in the recently vacated and still-furnished home of the late Gertrude and Menno Schrag. Marcia and Marc came from Virginia to join us in Newton for Christmas. John Weaver came for New Years.

Marc, a senior at EMU at the time, mentioned that he had just begun dating Hannah Gascho, a classmate. We wanted to meet Hannah on our last stop in Virginia before returning to Botswana on January 26, 1997. Marc somewhat reluctantly invited her to a pizza supper he had arranged for us to meet his housemates at the "stone house" on College Avenue in Harrisonburg. We enjoyed talking with Hannah about her experiences when she attended the Mennonite World Conference in India. She grew up in Johnstown, Pennsylvania, where her father, Luke, was principal of a Mennonite school.

By August 1997, Marcia and John Weaver were officially engaged and planning a wedding on January 3, 1998. It would be in his home church, Maple Grove Mennonite in Hartville, Ohio, a member of the Conservative Mennonite Conference. John is the youngest of seven brothers. Both of John's parents were born into Amish families but they became Mennonites. John's father, Herman, Sr., was severely injured in a motorcycle accident as a young man before he was married.

He suffered a lifelong disability, and the family struggled financially. Herman, Sr. died when John was only twenty. John had served with MCC's SALT program in Brazil – a factor that initially connected him and Marcia. When we met John, his brother Herman Weaver, Jr., was teaching at Eastern Mennonite University. Several of his brothers did cabinetry finish work in expensive new houses in eastern Ohio.

Even before Marcia and John's January 1998 wedding, Marc and Hannah announced their engagement. They wanted to get married in August 1998. Two weddings in one year!

"You can't coordinate love!" Marc said when asked if the two weddings could have been scheduled so that Erwin and I only needed to make one trip from Botswana.

Carla finished her secondary school studies and Cambridge exams at Maru-a-Pula in December 1997. That was just in time for her to leave Botswana for Marcia's January wedding and then stay in the U.S. We had learned to appreciate Christmas in Botswana, so Carla and I scheduled our departure for the U.S. the day *after* Christmas. A few days before we left, our cat was hit on the street and died. That was timely. After all the years with cats, with our youngest child leaving home, Erwin and I didn't want any more cats.

From hot Botswana, Carla and I arrived in a cold and snowy Ohio a few days before Marcia's wedding. She and John had planned a lovely traditional church wedding. During Marcia's high school years, I sewed her several fancy dresses based on wedding dress patterns. Regretfully, I wasn't available to make her wedding dress.

Erwin arrived a few days later in Ohio – without his checked luggage. His suit for the wedding was in the missing suitcase. We phoned the airline. The suitcase was located and on its way, but time was getting short. Erwin rented a suit from a tuxedo shop. About an hour before we left for the church, Erwin's missing suitcase arrived with his thoroughly wrinkled suit. He wore the rented one to the wedding. Erwin read Scripture. At the end of the ceremony, Erwin presented the new couple – but what had they decided their married name would be? "John and Marcia Rempel…. Yoder!" He was embarrassed to have forgotten "Weaver." Others enjoyed a good laugh.

Hannah Gascho came to Marcia's wedding providing an opportu-

Marcia Rempel marries John Weaver, Jan. 3, 1998, Hartville, Ohio.

nity for us to get to know her. By then, her parents had moved to Goshen, Indiana. Luke and Becky drove to a restaurant near Cleveland where we met them and talked about plans for the next wedding.

After Marcia and John's wedding, Erwin, Carla, and I flew on to Kansas. During the few days Erwin spent in Kansas before returning to Botswana, we bought a small red Ford Escort for ourselves and to leave with Carla. She didn't have a drivers' license yet and only limited experience driving on side roads in Botswana. To practice driving, I took her on familiar Kansas roads and streets. She diligently studied the drivers' manual. The day before I left for Botswana a few weeks later, she and I went to the Kansas Department of Motor Vehicles' office to take the driver's test. The written part was easy, but how would she do with the driving part? The DMV officials knew our situation and gave her a passing grade. What a relief that she was able to drive to her work, church, and other activities.

Marcia and John began married life in Harrisonburg, Virginia. They rented one floor of a small house on South College Avenue for several months before purchasing a house on Chestnut Street.

Adapting to new lifestyles

By then, 1998, email worked well. The printed copies I made of our email shows how often we wrote back and forth to the children, especially Carla. She missed us a great deal, experienced typical adjustments, and had some health issues. She stayed with my sister LaRita and her family until beginning classes at Hesston College in late August. Carla had a temporary job with Dewayne and Betty Pauls in their accounting office in Newton during the busy tax season. After tax season, Carla inquired and applied at numerous other places for work, but wasn't able to get another job other than some childcare.

Carla went to First Mennonite and participated in youth group activities, including a summer service trip to Chicago. She was baptized at East Lake – an event Erwin and I were sad to miss. Marc, however, was in the area that Sunday because of taking orientation for Mennonite Voluntary Service. He and Carla's two Kansas aunts witnessed her baptism. We and our three children were then all members of First Mennonite but we were scattered and not able to attend there.

The Cambridge exams that Carla took in Botswana in December were graded in England and the results weren't released until March. Carla got the highest marks possible! However, the grading system was so different that no one around her in the U.S. fully understood that remarkable achievement.

Back in Botswana, Erwin and I gradually adapted to being empty nesters. Not having children at home made it easier to travel frequently. When Erwin went to Lesotho without me, I realized I hadn't spent a night at home alone since Marcia was born twenty-seven years earlier. The Mennonite Ministries library had a good selection of interesting books, especially about southern Africa. Having read few books during the years of raising children, I started reading voraciously again.

The second wedding

Soon it was August and time for another international trip for the second wedding of 1998. We took advantage of that opportunity to spend several days in Switzerland, as detailed earlier. From Zurich, we flew to Kansas where we helped Carla move her things from my sister's house in Newton to the dorm at Hesston College. We drove the

Ford Escort from Kansas to Goshen, Indiana, for Marc and Hannah's wedding. It was no traditional wedding for those two! At the Merry Lea Environmental Learning Center of Goshen, where Hannah's father, Luke Gascho, was director, festivities began on the hot afternoon of August 22 with playing yard games.

After a nice chicken meal served under a big tent near a barn, a hay wagon transported the wedding guests to a picturesque spot beside a small lake for the wedding ceremony. Erwin performed the marriage ceremony. It felt as

Marc Rempel marries Hannah Gascho, Aug. 22, 1998, Goshen, Ind.

though Marc changed from a boy to a man in front of my eyes as he solemnly made his pledge to Hannah. Mosquitos plagued that idyllic lakeside spot. Wedding guests appreciated the generous supply of mosquito repellent thoughtfully provided for them.

Early the next morning, Erwin, Carla, and I left to drive back to Kansas so that she could enter Hesston College yet that day.

Marc and Hannah settled in Seattle. The previous year they had both done a year of voluntary service there, he with Mennonite Voluntary Service and she with a Lutheran agency. Marc stayed on as a paid staff person for two more years working with juvenile offenders, an outgrowth of his own experience with shoplifting as a young teen.

Family reunion in Africa

Erwin and I began planning to bring all three of our children plus the two new spouses over to Botswana.

"When siblings live in Seattle, Kansas, and Virginia, where do they go to have a family get-together? Africa!" (*email dated June 15, 1999, reporting to extended family*)

We arranged to be together the last two weeks in May 1999 in southern Africa.

It was a weird feeling to think of them on three separate planes crossing the Atlantic Ocean to Heathrow Airport in London, at the same time during the night of May 15 – Marc and Hannah coming from Seattle, Carla from Kansas, and Marcia and John from Virginia. They eventually found each other in the big Heathrow airport. They had enough time to explore downtown London before boarding their long overnight flight to South Africa. What a joy it was the next morning for Erwin and me to see all five of them together coming out of the customs' area at the Johannesburg airport.

All seven of us piled into the Mennonite Ministries' Toyota Venture, a type of minivan. As we rode along, the siblings resumed the teasing and bantering of their younger years. John Weaver and Hannah Gascho got a good introduction to our family!

We spent the first couple of days together at a South African game reserve where they saw numerous African animals and birds. Then in Gaborone we introduced them to our life and work in Botswana. They couldn't all fit into our small house, so the two married couples stayed at the nearby MM guesthouse. We headed back into South Africa. En route to Cape Town, we stopped in Lesotho where Marc visited his college friend serving there with MCC. We went on to see the sights of the historical Cape Town area at the tip of the African continent. The nearly two weeks of their visit went by all too quickly. After the two married couples headed back to the U.S., Carla returned to Gaborone with Erwin and me for almost two more weeks. Gaborone was still home for her. She enjoyed reconnecting with her friends from school and church.

During that time with us in Gaborone, Carla kept up a lively email exchange with Micah Hurst, whom she had met soon after beginning studies at Hesston College. He was another TCK – third culture kid. His parents, Mark and Mary Hurst, had served in Australia with Eastern Mennonite Missions during some of his childhood. We drove Carla back to Jo-burg where she bravely boarded the first of three long flights back to Kansas. She stayed with her aunt LaRita, again, for the rest of the summer and provided childcare for a family in Hesston.

Ending our time in Botswana

One thing we discussed with our children while we were all together was how much longer Erwin and I would stay in Botswana. The middle of 2000 seemed like a good time for us to make a transition back to the U.S.

We had been willing to stay longer in Botswana, and we were open to moving any place in the U.S. Our children were quite happy, though, when through invitations and opening doors, we felt God leading us back to Newton, Kansas, their emotional home community.

Chapter Seven
Kansas Again from 2000 to 2010

Part One
A New Life in the Same Town

We made another transition to a new chapter, another stint of gratefully living in someone else's furnished house. It was mid-February 2000 when we moved from Botswana to Kansas and lived in Jim and Anna Juhnkes' comfortable home while they went to Elkhart, Indiana, for the spring semester. Living in their house in North Newton provided us a glimpse of life in that Mennonite-dominated small town just across the railroad tracks from the city of Newton where we had lived for nearly twelve years. In addition to my father's *alma mater*, Bethel College, North Newton had a large Mennonite church, the offices for MCC, Western District Conference, and Mennonite Mutual Aid (now Everence). Big old trees shaded the streets and muffled the prairie winds.

We were so accustomed to email and internet by then that our first purchase was a computer. We bought a Hewlett Packard set with a desktop personal computer, monitor, keyboard, mouse, large tower -style processing unit, and desk jet printer. It cost less than our first computer equipment in 1983 but had much more capacity. Next item? A good quality treadmill for Erwin.

Our younger daughter, Carla, was in her last semester at nearby Hesston College's two-year program. We saw her occasionally and got to know the Micah Hurst she had written about. They both graduated from Hesston College a few months after we arrived.

Finding a new house

The Juhnkes would need their house again in May. Erwin and I considered options for where to live. We considered renting until the denominational integration would clarify our future roles and location. Rental options weren't appealing. We didn't regret having sold our other house in Newton. It would have been too big for us as empty nesters.

One Saturday morning in mid-March, clutching a list of houses for sale, we began looking in the north end of town and drove past several houses. None had enough curb appeal for us to consider looking inside.

We kept on driving to the south side of town. The last place on my list was Stratford Place, a new and growing housing development across from the new Newton Medical Center. Carved out of recently-farmed fields, the development had a crisp, bright, open new look. The model house wasn't scheduled to be open until later in the day. Providentially another woman had arranged for the realtor to show it to her at the same time we drove up that morning. When we stepped inside the house, we were delighted with its fresh brightness and light, neutral-colored walls and carpet. Designed for contemporary living, the house had plenty of electrical outlets, several connections for landline phones and cable TVs, and a two-car garage. The main floor included two bedrooms and two baths plus laundry. Because it was a model house, it had some extra features including a fireplace. It also had a finished basement with another bedroom, bathroom, and family room. It fit all the criteria of what we needed.

The ReMax realtor, our former work colleague Gary Franz, mentioned that someone had a contract to buy that model house. However, his office wasn't able to contact them. If we were interested, he suggested we make a backup contract. Otherwise, to live in Stratford Place we would need to buy a lot and wait during several months of construction.

As Erwin and I drove away, we hadn't gone a block before I said to him, "Let's call Gary Franz and make a backup contract."

Erwin was a bit startled at my quick decision and insistence because I usually thoroughly research and compare before buying. But he agreed, and we did it yet that day.

We had mixed feelings a few weeks later when we learned that the couple who made the first contract on the house was going through a

376

messy divorce. They wouldn't be buying the house. We took possession of that new house at 342 Victoria Road on May 1. By that stage of life, I was tired of scouting out garage sales and using second-hand furniture. We found reasonably priced new things for our new house.

Rempels' home in Newton, Kan., from 2000 to 2010.

Stratford Place was still in early stages of construction. Our house was near the end of the paved street. A field stretched away to the west. Additional houses went up quickly. For a while, it felt as though we lived in a construction zone. Within a few years, the streets were extended and most lots were sold. Typical tract houses, they were all quite similar in style with shades of neutral colors and with garages sticking out in front. We gradually made the yard into our own private little Garden of Eden, planting trees, bushes, perennials, and raspberries. Erwin took the lead in planting and tending the "food for the body" while I did the "food for the soul" plants.

Rempels enjoy their backyard with patio and plants in Newton, 2008.

Compared to the previously homogeneous bland community we'd known in Newton earlier, the Stratford Place neighborhood was ethnically diverse. We had neighbors of all races and from Iran, Mexico, Vietnam, Canada, England, and the Philippines. Several Mennonites also lived in Stratford Place, including our friends Gary and Jean Isaac who left southern Africa shortly after we did. That south side of Newton, near the new medical center, kept on growing. It became the most convenient location in which we've lived. Our work, church, medical facilities, grocery stores, restaurants, and most other essentials were within an easy two-mile drive. Equipping a brand-new house required frequent trips to the nearby lumberyard and hardware store my sister and her husband operated.

Seeing our children

We saw all our children within a few months of returning to the U.S. With Carla close by at Hesston College, we saw her first, of course. In March, Erwin and I attended a mission consultation in Harrisonburg, Virginia, where we stayed with John and Marcia Rempel Weaver. They had bought an older two-story house. They were members at Ridgeway Mennonite Church. The mission consultation meetings we attended were held in Detweiler Auditorium of the Virginia Mennonite Retirement Community and at Eastern Mennonite Seminary. Compared to facilities in southern Africa, these places were very nice and extravagant. I was in culture shock!

Marc and Hannah lived in Seattle at the time. We flew out to see them in April. Later in 2000, they moved to Corvallis, Oregon, where Hannah began a master's degree horticulture program at Oregon State University. She did research on raspberries. She had access to all the berries they could use. Marc obtained a job with the local county working with juveniles as he had done in Seattle. They bought a cozy, neat little house, found friends in the area, and became part of Corvallis Mennonite Fellowship.

The fall of 2000, Carla and Micah transferred to Eastern Mennonite University in Harrisonburg, Virginia. They announced their engagement and made plans for a wedding in May 2001, after their junior year of college.

Weaving life together in Newton

The ten years we spent in Newton from 2000 to 2010, wove together strands of work, family, church, aging parents, and a most unusual unexpected invitation. The following sections of this chapter takes up these subjects one at a time.

Part Two
Working Again at 722 Main Street in Newton

The next business day after our arrival in Kansas in mid-February 2000, without a break, Erwin began work again at the headquarters for the General Conference Mennonite Church at 722 Main Street in Newton. For his new work with church relations and fundraising for the Commission on Overseas Mission, he used a small office in the COM department on the second floor. An administrative assistant was using the more spacious and brighter office he had occupied for nearly twelve years as the COM executive secretary. It didn't bother us that he was working in a smaller office and was in a lower position on the salary scale than earlier. We felt it was simply moving forward through life as God was leading.

About a month after our arrival in Newton, I also began working at 722 Main Street – as the assistant in the development office of the General Conference, part of the Division of General Services. My co-workers were Harold Thieszen and Leonard Wiebe, former pastors who worked part-time as development associates. Harold not only seemed to know everyone in the General Conference, he even knew their family tree. Leonard, too, was well known and respected. I enjoyed working there and felt at home with the other staff, most of whom I had met before.

A bit later, I started a second part-time job at the First Mennonite Church office again. Each job had its pros and cons, but I soon disliked juggling two part-time jobs.

Buying a second car

Our small Ford Escort Carla used as a student at Hesston College met our immediate transportation needs. It was just my size, which means it wasn't Erwin's size at all! With both Erwin and me working, we needed a second car. Erwin's brother-in-law, Elwyn Busenitz, encouraged us to consider something bigger than the small cars we'd been driving. To prove his point, Elwyn let Erwin drive his own larger Buick. We checked out Elwyn's recommendation. A white Buick LeSabre had just come in to the car dealership – a 1994 model with quite a few miles on it. Erwin found it a comfortable fit and we bought it.

Having recently come back from Botswana, a developing country, to Erwin and me the Buick felt excessively big and ostentatious. For our first several church contacts, we drove the smaller Ford Escort instead of the Buick. At one church, the only other car when we arrived was a similar white Buick. We discovered it belonged to the pastor. We soon realized that many people, including middle-class Kansas Mennonites, drove that kind of car. With the Buick, we first used power controls for seats, windows, steering, and brakes.

Erwin's expanding role

Soon Erwin was asked to be the overall director for development on behalf of the General Conference, not just for the Commission on Overseas Mission. Since an employee could not supervise his or her spouse, that issue was resolved by making me a co-director with him – at least on paper, but not at the pay level. I worked by the hour with an extra stipend in lieu of benefits. Erwin and I worked together on development planning: I did the office work, but he did most of the donor contacts by himself.

The church relations aspect of Erwin's job was a continuation of what he had done a great deal of during his nearly twelve years as COM executive secretary. He again enthusiastically prepared sermons and other presentations. After years of illustrating his presentations using overhead projectors, he quickly learned to use the new computerized PowerPoint software and equipment.

Jeannie Zehr in the COM office helped Erwin arrange his church contacts across the United States and Canada in locations near clusters of major donors. The stressful part for Erwin was to arrange his own visits with the individual donors. He didn't yet have a cell phone at the time or a GPS device to find their homes. He made phone calls from motels or public pay phones. He found the visits quite pleasant, actually. He learned to know people who already supported the General Conference and COM in particular.

Meanwhile, things were gearing up toward the "integration" of the General Conference Mennonite Church and the Mennonite Church. The task that we thought would be completed while we were overseas was actually in its most intense final stages. What would that mean for us?

Erwin remembers integration

Note: The following are personal reflections and memories of a very challenging time in the life of our denomination and for us personally. Other people have different perspectives and memories. The official church archives contain the historic details.

Erwin relates his experiences as follows.

Out of the blue one evening in early October 2000, I [Erwin] received a phone call from Tom Lehman. He was chair of the Commission on Overseas Mission and a member of the Mission Transition Steering Committee. Tom invited me to serve as transition director for the process of integrating three separate entities: Mennonite Board of Missions, the Commission on Home Ministries, and COM.

Apparently my nearly twelve years as executive secretary of COM, from 1982 to 1994, along with my absence from the internal politics among these mission agencies during the previous six years while we were in Botswana were perceived as useful for the transition director.

I was surprised by the invitation and somewhat apprehensive of taking on this role. However, after about eight months into the fundraising role, I felt some restlessness. I enjoyed visits with donors and presentations in churches, but there was too much "down time." After arriving at a destination, usually by air, there were usually several hours before the scheduled events. I tended to arrive too early for my visits. I filled time sitting in a rental car or motel room. I was ready for a change.

Another factor was my earlier lack of enthusiasm for the integration of the General Conference Mennonite Church and the Mennonite Church. This was not due to a reluctance to work together, which we already did extensively, but rather to the enormous amount of work needed to accomplish a full integration. I had hoped to escape from that while we were overseas. Accepting the invitation to be transition director would land me squarely in the middle of the integration process.

I wondered what the agency staff leaders would think of my appointment: Lois Barrett of Commission on Home Ministries, Ron Flaming of Commission on Overseas Mission, and Stanley Green of Mennonite Board of Missions.

I phoned Ron Flaming, my supervisor, to let him know about this invitation. He seemed somewhat surprised but encouraged me to accept, which I did.

A tense staff meeting in Kansas City

My appointment to the position was confidential until the end of an all-staff meeting near Kansas City in late October 2000.

That Kansas City staff meeting was a highly emotional and contentious event. One of the two transition consultants led the staff in a process that did not sit well with everyone. In addition, there was considerable discussion and anxiety about who could possibly accomplish the task of transition director, how much power that person would have, and how that person might abuse that power. I sat among the staff as they talked. I became more and more anxious about serving in the role. However, to withdraw at that point would have been disruptive. I kept quiet and hoped for the best. When the announcement was made, Kay Nussbaum, chair of the Mission Transition Steering Committee, presented me with a bright orange hard-hat. It was an apt symbol of my challenging new role.

Working with consultants

One of the consultants was very helpful. He helped me get up to speed in understanding what had been envisioned up to that point, November 1, 2000, and to manage the ongoing mission transition process.

The consultants and the staff-driven transition team had developed the framework and vision for the new mission structures before I became the mission transition director. There would be one mission agency for the U.S. and another one for Canada; the new mission agency in the U.S. would encompass both home and overseas mission; and the term "missional" would describe the renewed understandings of what it meant to be in mission in the 21ˢᵗ century. Instead of a "merger," we would build a new structure and talk of "integration." We would forge patterns unique to the new mission agency and not hold onto previous methods. This meant that neither Newton nor Elkhart staff would impose previous patterns of administration onto the new mission agency. There would be no office designated as "headquarters."

The politics of integration

The mission transition process was one of the most politicized projects I have experienced. By nature I am not political, according to Angela's assessment. I had considerable difficulty understanding and appreciating the dynamics among the mission agencies and their staff persons.

The mission staff leadership in Newton wanted to make sure that the Commission on Overseas Mission and the Commission on Home Ministries not be simply integrated into the Mennonite Board of Mission way of doing things. From my more neutral perspective, while sympathetic to the Newton concerns, I had a positive view of MBM mission structures and patterns. My earlier relationships with MBM staff were quite positive

One significant difference between the General Conference and Mennonite Church structures related to budget systems. The Mennonite Church operated with an autonomous budget system allowing its Mennonite Board of Missions to raise its own funds. In the General Conference, a system of unified finances and fundraising diminished the ability of its commissions to undertake new program initiatives.

Another important difference was that the Mennonite Church combined home ministries and overseas mission in one organization, MBM, while in the General Conference, separate commissions administered home ministries and overseas missions. I learned that at a practical level MBM experienced some of the same dynamics internally as COM and CHM did.

Both the General Conference Mennonite Church and the Mennonite Church were bi-national. In the GCMC, sixty percent of the membership was located in the U.S. and forty percent in Canada. The

Mennonite Church had ninety percent of its membership in the U.S. and only ten percent in Canada. When the decision was made for the integrated Mennonite church to divide into two entities along national boundaries, their finances had to be sorted out. Sixty percent of COM's international missionaries were from Canada. Percentages of MBM's mission workers more closely reflected its membership distribution. I worked with J. Robert (Jack) Suderman, my counterpart for the Canadian mission agency, to understand how the separation affected our respective country budgets and support of our international workers.

New executive director and new name

In March 2001, Stanley Green was selected as the new executive director of the as-yet unnamed new mission agency. Stanley had served as the head of the Mennonite Board of Missions for about six years. At that point, Stanley became the transition director, and my title changed to transition manager. I continued to be deeply involved in the details of the transition process. There was no letup in the number of meetings and things to do.

Various names for the new mission agency were tested. Eventually, the descriptive name Mennonite Mission Network emerged.

The title for the highest-ranking administrator in the General Conference was General Secretary, the position then held by Jim Schrag. The title for the head of each of its commissions was Executive Secretary. The Mennonite Church used more corporate terminology, such as President and CEO. It was agreed that the head administrator of the new Mennonite Church USA would be Executive Director. Jim Schrag was appointed to that position. The new Mennonite Church USA had several agencies, which used the title Executive Director as well. The term "CEO" continued to be added to Stanley Green's title.

Newton-Elkhart dynamics in the new mission agency

As the new mission agency developed over the next eight years until 2009 when I finally went off the payroll, it seemed to many of us in the Newton office that the MBM way of doing things in Elkhart carried over into the new agency with some accommodations to Newton.

Angela remembers integration days
In addition to Erwin's recollections above, I'll add more details and note my personal involvement.

Meeting after meeting filled Erwin's calendar during transition. I spent many nights alone in our new home as he traveled. He frequently went to Kansas City and Chicago, major airline hubs that had nearby facilities with meeting rooms, lodging, and food service. Erwin also made many trips to Elkhart, Indiana. Some had suggested to Erwin that he apply for the position of executive director of the new mission agency. But he had no interest in that, and he did not apply. As noted above, Stanley Green was appointed to that position.

As transition director and later manager, Erwin gave overall coordination to eleven different teams that worked on eleven different aspects of integrating. I served on one of those teams, but most of my meetings were by teleconference. Those discussions weren't memorable enough for me to even recall what aspect our team addressed.

Erwin was involved in discussions the denominational leaders had about where and what kind of offices the new Mennonite Church USA would have. Should the existing offices be merged and moved to a new joint headquarters in a big city near a large airport? Or should offices be further dispersed in additional locations in dynamic cities, such as Los Angeles? Historically, rural-based Mennonites had developed large constituencies in and around the small cities and towns of Newton, Elkhart, and Harrisonburg. It was decided to keep the existing offices and not add more. However, a number of staff persons worked at remote locations.

The leaders of the newly forming denomination outlined a new funding structure they called First Fruits Giving. Working in the development office, I became involved in communicating the new funding structure to the congregations and donors of the General Conference. Our efforts weren't adequate. Many congregations, district conferences, and individuals were confused and didn't give as anticipated.

Nashville 2001

In the fairyland atmosphere of the Opryland Hotel in Nashville, Tennessee, in 2001, at the joint assembly of the two merging groups, both voted to complete the integration. When the results were announced, it was a holy moment complete with much rejoicing. About that time, Stanley Green asked Erwin to be one of the senior executives in the new Mennonite Mission Network. Erwin took the position of senior executive for Mission Network Services, a division that included the departments of finance, human resources, and information technology. Erwin was a member of the new executive cabinet that met monthly. The cabinet included James Krabill, Peter Graber, Marty Lehman, and Rachel Stoltzfus. Erwin continued in that role until he retired in 2008.

The MBM staff persons were proficient in cell phone use. They couldn't imagine how Erwin could function without one. So Erwin reluctantly ventured into the world of cell phones but never became a "real" cell phone user. His phone was often off or not with him. He didn't receive or make many calls on it. His cell phone did make it easier for Erwin to keep in touch with me when he traveled. He no longer made lists of locations and phone numbers where I could reach him.

Budgeting for Mennonite Mission Network

Erwin was especially interested in finances. He spent considerable time combing through the mission agencies' financial records in an effort to arrive at budget parameters for the new mission agency's initial budget. He came up with a figure of about $8,100,000 as a reasonable income/expenditure budget for the new Mennonite Mission Network. He was surprised by the optimism of his executive cabinet colleagues who advocated a higher figure of about $10,000,000, in expectation that the new structures would direct more funds to the new mission agency. The first expenditure budget was based on the more optimistic view of income. Staff was hired accordingly.

The new denomination officially began February 1, 2002. By mid-2002, Mission Network needed a considerable amount of belt-tightening. A special fund-raising appeal was made. At the end of the first year of the new mission agency, the actual income was about what Erwin predicted. He noticed that was about the same amount reported for 2015.

Angela's work

By August 2001, we knew that Erwin and several others had a job with the new mission agency. The rest of us employed by the merging denominations would have our employment terminated February 2002. We were encouraged to apply for positions in the new mission agency.

When the new "position descriptions" were posted, most of them contained corporate language unfamiliar to me. I wasn't sure there was any position for which I wanted to apply. Most of my previous jobs had come my way without a rigorous application process.

September 10, 2001, was memorable for me in part because of the following day's historic terrorist attacks. The 10th of September was the day I submitted my clumsy attempts at a resume with a letter of application to Mennonite Mission Network. I listed several positions in order of my preference, beginning with the international mission area.

Because Stanley Green and the rest of the executive cabinet members were in Newton on September 10, the development office where I worked tried something new for the General Conference. We invited Kansas donors to a meal at a restaurant. There Erwin, whom General Conference donors already knew, introduced the new mission agency plus Stanley Green and others from Elkhart. That evening event at the Old Mill Restaurant on September 10 went well, we thought. It would take much more than one meeting, however, for people who had given generously to the General Conference to feel a part of Mennonite Church USA and Mennonite Mission Network.

Experiencing September 11

The next morning, September 11, 2001, on my car radio as I drove to work, I heard something about a plane hitting a World Trade Center tower in New York City. Small planes had done that before, so it didn't seem too alarming. A bit later, word came that this wasn't just a small plane off its course. Two large passenger planes had apparently been flown deliberately into each of the two towers. One woman working in our office had a close relative who worked on an upper level in one of the towers. That brought the events closer home. She was relieved when word came that he had safely exited the building. Erwin and Larry Becker set up a TV in our staff chapel area. We watched stunned as the towers came down, and then mesmerized as the dramatic collapse replayed over and over. With all plane flights canceled, our out-of-town guests from Elkhart anxiously worked on other ways to return home.

By afternoon, we couldn't concentrate on our work and we went home to watch the unfolding drama. In central Kansas, it felt far away and of no personal threat to us. Marcia, John and little Rachel, along with Carla and Micah were in Virginia only about a hundred miles from the destruction at the Pentagon in Washington, D.C. Marc and Hannah were much farther away out in Oregon.

It took several days before planes were allowed to fly again. Erwin and I had plane tickets to go to a meeting in Elkhart shortly after flights resumed. Many people were afraid to fly then, so the planes and terminals were nearly deserted. We figured that security was tighter than it had ever been and it was actually the safest time to fly. That was about the last time we ever enjoyed nearly empty planes and terminals.

Angela accepts a new position

About two months later, Erwin and I were in the Elkhart office when decisions were made about job offers for Mission Network. To my surprise, and a bit of disappointment, the head of the communications department offered me a three-quarter time job: a fourth time each in communications, church relations, and alumni relations. Those jobs had been my lowest priority. I needed to choose between continuing part-time work at First Mennonite Church and taking this new job at Mission Network. Being tired of doing two part-time jobs, I decided to work with Mennonite Mission Network and give up the church office job. That was a good choice, in hindsight.

I struggled to figure out what I was supposed to do in those new roles. Several times, something I thought would be my task was already done by someone else in Elkhart. While officially there was no headquarters' office – Newton was supposed to be equal to Elkhart – that wasn't how it felt. At one point, I made a list of things we gave up in Newton to do the way Mennonite Board of Missions had done it. Fortunately, I've forgotten almost everything on that list. I figured it would take at least ten years to be truly integrated.

Because of my work in the communication department, I felt that I helped Mission Network use terminology appropriate to General Conference people. An example is the different usages of the word "conference" and "church." General Conference people referred to the denomination as "the conference." While for the Mennonite Church people, that term referred to their regional conferences. For them, "church" meant the denomination, while for us, "church" meant the local congregation. The term "area conference" was adopted in an attempt to make the distinctions clear to everyone.

Impacts of integrating

Some Mennonites in Kansas weren't even sure that the Newton office was still open. That impression was heightened by the sight of some boarded-up front office windows after a windstorm ripped off outdated blue tin siding on the building and broke some windows. A tasteful renovation eventually revealed the underlying brick front. There was a lot of skepticism among General Conference people about integration, as apparently, there also was among Mennonite Church people.

Erwin Rempel works again in same office in Newton, as Senior Executive for Mission Network Services, Mennonite Mission Network, 2002 to 2008.

When we hear of two companies merging, based on our experience, I wonder how that works for their employees. As a staff person, I felt as though we were squeezed between millstones. Some of us fared better than others. Things kept shifting, some people left, new people came.

389

Erwin moved back into his former larger office. My job description kept changing, as did my office space. I eventually did some aspects of work Jeannie Zehr had been doing before her retirement – work I once thought would interest me. I focused on the church relations aspects of arranging for staff persons and mission workers to speak in various churches. In a long-distance fashion, I became acquainted with most of the participating churches and their pastors. Previous extensive travel to churches in different parts of the country helped me understand and visualize the different places I dealt with. I especially enjoyed contacts with the international mission workers and working with them to arrange their speaking events. Our own experiences as international mission workers helped me understand and relate to them.

Changes in international mission

My Mission Network job put me in a position to note changes in how churches related to missionaries over the years. Even the term "missionary" had changed to "international mission worker." Compared to the days of my childhood when people would attend a mission presentation any weekday evening, now it was hard to schedule mission speakers for any time other than a Sunday morning; Sunday evening services had become rare. Some churches were even cutting back on summer Sunday school, eliminating a good opportunity for more informal interaction with mission workers. I was bewildered by how much our Mennonite churches had begun to follow the liturgical calendar. Those factors complicated scheduling church contacts for mission workers.

Instead of lifelong overseas careers, three years became the new long-term assignment. International mission workers often spent only a few weeks back in the U.S., usually during the summer or over Christmas when opportunities to speak in churches were quite limited. Mission workers barely had enough time to speak in the churches who were contributing to their support. It was hard to find speakers for churches who wanted international mission workers to speak at a fall mission Sunday.

Church people across the denomination no longer felt they knew the mission workers. Giving patterns and priorities changed. Churches were spending more on local programs and multiple pastoral staff. Churches and individuals directed their giving to support people they knew and contributed less to the general operating budget. Financially the new denomination and its agencies began to struggle.

In response to these trends, mission support teams were designed to provide prayer and financial support for missionary individuals and couples. However, some workers felt as though they themselves had to raise their own support. This new system troubled those of us from the previous era of missions. Erwin and I were grateful that we could depend on general contributions to the General Conference and Commission on Overseas Mission for our support when we were overseas. To strengthen relationships and prayer support, Jeannie Zehr had set up a Mission Partner Program that linked individual COM missionaries with congregations.

The number of international mission workers from North America kept dropping. The days were past when about 150 mission workers were fully supported by general contributions. New definitions of mission workers were applied. The prayer directory picturing mission workers was thinner with each printing cycle.

However, God wasn't depending only on North Americans to serve Him. We rejoiced in reports of new believers and growing churches in other countries. Local pastors and believers were effectively reaching people in their own country and beyond their borders. For example, the Brazilian Mennonites formed their own mission agency to send Brazilians to Mozambique and Albania. Partnerships and networks facilitated interconnected global mission. The work of North Americans overseas focused primarily on training leaders to train others.

Only a few, if any, North Americans continued to serve in countries such as Taiwan, India, Brazil, or the Congo. Years earlier in those countries, there were up to thirty, forty, or even about one hundred, in an earlier generation, in the Congo.

Working with other staff persons

Special staff events in the Newton office made work more enjoyable. Monday mornings the Mission Network staff gathered for a time of sharing and prayer; on Tuesdays the various staff in the offices had a joint coffee break; Wednesdays there was all-staff chapel; there wasn't anything special on Thursdays, but on Fridays some of us went out for a coffee break, usually at Prairie Harvest. Thus, the weeks passed very quickly.

As the only executive cabinet member based in Newton, Erwin went to Elkhart one or more times a month for cabinet meetings. It is difficult to be a lone voice on a conference call, unable to see the group gathered around a table on the other end. Video conferencing came into use, which helped. For some of the first video conference meetings I was involved in, the camera in Elkhart was placed in such a way that I could only see the backs of the people who were looking at my image on a monitor in front of them. With experience, techniques improved significantly.

Traveling continues

As in earlier years, often it was cost effective for Erwin to fly from Kansas City instead of from nearby Wichita. From Chicago he drove a rental car to Elkhart. When winter weather and construction delays made him too anxious about catching his flights in Chicago, he paid more to fly directly from Wichita to South Bend and back.

I also did work-related travel; at times with Erwin and at times by myself. Although I'm not an adventurous long-distance driver, several times I flew to South Bend where I rented a car and drove to Elkhart. Associated (Anabaptist) Mennonite Biblical Seminary in Elkhart had a guesthouse that became a home away from home numerous times for Erwin, for me, or both of us. Sometimes we stayed in nearby Goshen with our daughter-in-law's parents, Luke and Becky Gascho. We enjoyed visiting with them, as we do with all of our children's in-laws.

In his travels, Erwin endured tight connections, flight delays and cancelations, ever tighter plane seats, and crowded overhead baggage bins. One of his worst travel experiences happened on a winter trip to Elkhart. His connecting flight from Chicago to South Bend was delayed, so he arrived in South Bend after midnight. The car rental place was closed. His only option was to drag his suitcase and computer case across a big icy parking lot and over a snow-covered grassy area to a hotel, hoping it had an available room.

Erwin handled air turbulence calmly. On one memorable flight, when quite a few of the Newton staff were on the same plane going to a meeting, the turbulence was excessive. Most passengers were alarmed. Erwin continued working on his laptop until he couldn't hang on to it. A couple of women from the Newton staff who were on that flight were so frightened that they rarely ever flew again.

Erwin qualified for Premier status on United Airlines. That allowed him to sit in the economy-plus section with more legroom and to be among the first to board while there was still room overhead for his computer bag. Other rewards he could share with me when we traveled together were an occasional upgrade to first class or use of the nice Red Carpet airport lounges away from the hectic concourses.

Erwin's responsibilities

Erwin found well-qualified people to serve in the departments of the Mission Services division. As a senior executive, he went to denominational board meetings and met many other church leaders over the years. In my role with the communications department, sometimes I was assigned to report on Mission Network board meetings. In applying the Carver governance approach, they talked a lot about "polishing the ends." There wasn't much to report. What a contrast to the fascinating commission meetings I had enjoyed observing in previous times. Whenever executive director Stanley Green took his study leaves and sabbaticals, Erwin filled in for him.

Erwin and I were very busy during those years. Our conversations at home often related to Mission Network. Although at times we found our work stressful, we experienced many good times with our co-workers, good and capable people. At the official beginning of the new denomination in February 2002, our salaries increased to more-than-adequate. We did more charitable giving and saved more for retirement.

Planning to retire

By 2007, Erwin and I thought about retiring. We wanted to retire out of a positive situation. We certainly didn't want our coworkers to become more eager for our retirement than we were. Using spreadsheets, Erwin carefully calculated our finances. We decided to retire exactly forty years after beginning pastoral responsibilities at Indian Valley Mennonite Church in Harleysville, Pennsylvania, in 1968.

Erwin had essentially worked himself out of a job. Each department in his division had a capable director, all of them in Elkhart. However, no one else filled his intangible role of representing the Newton office on the executive cabinet. The most critical pieces of my work were parceled out to other staff persons. There were several special projects, however, that Stanley Green invited Erwin to work on part-time during retirement.

"Are you going to move?" several people asked when we announced our retirement. They had good reason to ask. Our previous transitions to new chapters of life were marked with geographical moves. Not moving would be different for us. However, we had relocated Erwin's mom, Lena Eitzen, from Minnesota to Newton in late 2006 so she would be near us and Erwin's sister and her husband. Mom Eitzen was receiving good care at the nearby Presbyterian Manor in her difficult and sad end-of-life decline into the mists of Alzheimer's disease. We were committed to remain in Newton and share that journey as a family. Dad Eitzen had died in December 2004.

Erwin and I were amazed as our co-workers, both in Newton and Elkhart, made a big occasion of our retirement. It felt as though we were present to hear nice things typically said at a funeral.

Ending a 40-year career

June 1, 2008, the two of us began retirement grateful for good health. We had no mortgage, and no debts. We had a wealth of positive experiences from our years of following God's call through various chapters of ministry.

We hadn't planned any big specific projects for retirement, which was just as well. We couldn't have foreseen the needs and opportunities that lay ahead.

Part Three
Our Family Grows, Moves around the World and Back

During the years from 2000 to 2010, while Erwin and I worked and lived in Newton, Kansas, our family kept changing.

First grandchild and third wedding

It was a very special moment at the small Shenandoah Valley Airport when Marcia and John Weaver placed little Rachel into my arms – our first grandchild. She was born in Harrisonburg, Virginia, in the first year of the new millennium. Nana was my preferred title to distinguish me from the grandchildren's other grandmother. It didn't make me feel quite as old either!

Carla and Micah Hurst were married between their junior and senior years of college at Eastern Mennonite University. On a bright May morning, they had a small, simple ceremony at Dyck Arboretum in Hesston, Kansas. They pledged their vows with only the closest relatives present, in keeping with Carla's private nature. En route to the reception at First Mennonite Church in Newton, Carla and Micah's car broke down along the Interstate highway. What a sight to see a bride in her wedding dress waiting alongside the road for a tow truck! By the end of the reception, their car was repaired.

New technology at Walmart made it possible for their photographer friend Damian Rowe to develop wedding ceremony photos in an hour. The photos were on display in the afternoon

Carla Rempel marries Micah Hurst, May 5, 2001, Hesston, Kan. Photo by Damian Rowe, used by permission.

395

at their reception for a larger group of friends at First Mennonite Church. With a reference to Carla's years in Botswana where a groom pays the bride's family a "bride-price" of several cows, at the reception they displayed a poster filled with pictures of cows.

In a bit more than a span of three years, all three of our children were married. That marked a change in our parenting role.

Arriving too early

Grandson Evan Henry Weaver's arrival caught everyone by surprise. He wasn't expected until October. But in late August he indicated it was time to get on with life. On a Sunday morning, Marcia was taken by helicopter "over the mountain" from Harrisonburg to the large hospital at the University of Virginia in Charlottesville. Their friends at Ridgeway Church prayed for them as they heard the chopper fly over. John hurried by car to the hospital. Evan weighed five pounds already at birth. By the time I could fly to Virginia, Evan had been moved to the hospital in Harrisonburg. I spent much of my time with little Rachel, nearly two years old, so that Marcia could be at the hospital with Evan. The last day of my visit, John and Marcia brought Evan home. Erwin was on a work trip in the eastern states and drove to Harrisonburg that day to see his first grandson.

Scattering to other countries

It wasn't long until we would be telling people that our closest child lived in Oregon. Closest? Yes, one was in Brazil and one was in Australia!

Carla and Micah both graduated from EMU in 2002. Then they were headed to Australia. Micah obtained a job at Camp Clayton, a Christian camp. He had attended that camp some years earlier when his parents lived and worked "down under." The camp was in Tasmania, an Australian island state south of the mainland.

Before they left for Tasmania, Carla and Micah came to Newton, along with the rest of our family, for Christmas and New Year's. It was a bittersweet time. Not only were Carla and Micah packed to leave for Australia within a few days, but Marcia and John and their two little ones were leaving for Brazil a few months later. When would we ever all be together again? As Marc crudely put it, this was the last Christmas we would be incontinent together!

Carla and Micah had tickets to fly from Wichita to Australia on January 6, 2003. But Carla didn't yet have her travel documents. She had submitted papers and passport to the proper consulate in Washington, D.C. with instructions to send it to her at our Kansas address. Micah was within days of his out-of-country limit for retaining his Australian residency. Would he have to go ahead of her?

On Friday, January 3, one of their friends, a neighbor in Harrisonburg, phoned to say that she saw a packet at the door of their old apartment. It was from the Australian consulate. We asked her to please take it to an overnight delivery service and send it. About noon the next day, Saturday, the UPS deliveryman was probably surprised when several of us joyfully accepted the delivery of Carla's passport. It was the last business day before their flight. First thing on Monday morning, we took them to the airport.

Now it was our turn to be the parents sending their child to serve overseas. It was even from the same airport in Wichita where our parents sent us off about twenty-eight years earlier. We accepted that the Lord was leading them to ministry. Camp Clayton hired them directly; no mission agency was involved. It was reassuring to know that Micah's parents, Mark and Mary Hurst, were also in Australia, although they lived near Sydney, more than 600 miles from Tasmania.

Erwin and I went to Harrisonburg, Virginia, in late May 2003 to bid farewell to John, Marcia, energetic little Rachel and cuddly baby Evan. They were taking an assignment in Recife, Brazil, with Mennonite Central Committee. I often wondered how my mother really felt when Erwin and I were about the age of Marcia and John and took her only grandchildren to Brazil. Just as our parents were supportive when Erwin and I followed God's call to a distant land, we sought to be supportive of our children. Feelings of sadness were entwined with a sense of satisfaction and excitement.

Visiting down under

It was still 2003, in November, when Erwin and I took the long flights to and from Australia to see Carla and Micah. It was good to see them and where they lived and worked. Their Tasmania acquaintances were of European descent and spoke English in Australia's unique way. Micah and Carla showed us several scenic spots, including a park where we walked in a meadow with various kinds of kangaroos and other marsupials roaming freely. The nocturnal Tasmanian devils were out of sight, although Micah tells the story of one attacking his foot as he rode a bike. Together with Carla and Micah, we flew to Sydney for several days where Mark and Mary Hurst enthusiastically showed us the sights, including the famous Harbor Bridge and Opera House. It was springtime there. Many beautiful flowers were blooming – even the lovely lavender jacaranda trees that I'd thought we would never see again. With that trip, Erwin and I had been on all six inhabitable continents.

Going back to Brazil

This grandmother was eager to see her grandchildren! I had no hesitations about flying by myself in August 2004 to see the Weavers in Recife, Brazil. My visit coincided with celebrating birthdays for Evan, two, and Rachel, four. I enjoyed being with Marcia and her family, seeing where they worked, and meeting their coworkers. Weavers lived in a third-floor walk-up apartment – above mosquito level. It was about a block away from the MCC unit house where I slept. I was pleasantly surprised by how much Portuguese I could still speak twenty-two years after we had left Brazil.

Erwin and I had dreamed about taking all our children back to Brazil as adults for them to see it with grown-up eyes. With Marcia's family living in Brazil, that was obviously the time to make such a trip. Getting our whole family to Brazil the last two weeks of March in 2005 was complicated. However, without a travel agent we managed to set up the whole trip with a number of different flights ranging from Australia, Oregon, Kansas, Chicago, and then several within Brazil.

Carla and Micah flew from Australia using Erwin's frequent flier miles on United Airlines. They needed to travel via the U.S. They made a stop in Portland so they could visit Marc and Hannah in Oregon and travel onward with them. Erwin and I met the four of them in Chicago's O'Hare airport. When I saw Carla nonchalantly walk off the plane in Chicago, I was so grateful because for a time it looked like that might not happen.

When Carla had applied at the Brazilian consulate in Australia for a tourist visa to Brazil, they insisted that because she was born in Brazil, she is a Brazilian citizen and didn't need a tourist visa; she needed a current Brazilian passport. In only a few weeks' time how could she prepare all the Portuguese documentation needed to get a Brazilian passport? I confess to being terribly anxious about that. What would we do if she didn't get it in time? Our mission colleague in Brasília, Betty Hochstetler, helped with some items. Once again, just in time Carla got her passport. When will I learn to trust the Lord and not be anxious?

After our long night on the plane from Chicago to São Paulo, Carla zipped through the line for Brazilian citizens. We Americans had to wait at the end of the line, be fingerprinted, and photographed – just as Brazilians need to do when entering the U.S.

Marcia, John, and their children flew from Recife to meet us in Brasília, where we all stayed in a hotel for several nights. Carla was only two years old when we left Brazil, so this was her reintroduction to the place of her birth. We made sure to point out the hospital where she was born.

The main purpose and highlight of our trip was visiting where we had lived in Gama when the children were small. The streets and houses had all changed so much that we could hardly find our former homes. Marcia and Marc enjoyed seeing where they had gone to school. We visited numerous people we knew before. We again shared a delightful meal in the home of MariaRosa and Manoel. The church building had been renovated and expanded. However, the same pulpit and benches Erwin helped make about twenty-five years earlier were still in use. Betty and Otis Hochstetler had retired in Brasília after serving in several other locations in Brazil. Betty did her usual excellent job as a tour guide showing us the unique aspects of Brasília.

The ten of us flew together from Brasília to Recife where Marcia and John gave us glimpses of their MCC work. We enjoyed family time at a simple beach resort and at an inland retreat center. We concluded the trip in Rio de Janeiro. Marcia flew with us to Rio while John and the children stayed in Recife. Carla and Micah both celebrated birthdays about then, so when we saw a beautiful cake in a Rio bakery, we bought it. In our hotel near Copacabana Beach, using dental floss to cut it (a clever suggestion from Hannah), we were dismayed to discover that the beautiful thing tasted terrible. And to add insult to injury for Micah and me, it was loaded with coconut, which neither of us like.

Rempel family of 10 visits in Gama, Brazil, 2005.

Had we not been able to use frequent flier miles for some of the flights, the whole event would have cost even more than the $15,000 we spent. It was a worthwhile investment in our family.

An Aussie granddaughter

Granddaughter Shawna Elisabeth Hurst was born in Australia. As our news media in the U.S. reported horrific Hurricane Katrina lashing New Orleans and the Gulf Coast, we thought of Carla in labor on the other side of the world. Of course, Shawna's other grandmother saw her before I could, as had been the case with both the Weaver grandchildren. Shawna was three weeks old when I arrived for about ten days. Australia has a good national health care system that covered them all. We were grateful for that because they didn't have a mission agency to cover their medical expenses as we always had when we served overseas. Baby Shawna thrived, but Carla struggled to recuperate. Carla could have used my help longer. It was hard to say goodbye and take the long flight back to the U.S.

Our children visit us in Kansas

Both the Weavers and Hursts visited the U.S. during those years they were overseas, for which we were grateful. Our family was all together over Labor Day weekend, September 2006. That turned out to be our last time together in Kansas. To celebrate our 40th wedding anniversary, our children prepared a special meal and elegantly served us at our Newton house.

Long-awaited grandchildren

After ten years of marriage, Madeleine blessed Marc and Hannah's home. In less than two years, her sister, Katherine, completed their family. Prior to having children, Marc and Hannah had purchased a larger, older house close to the campus of Oregon State University. Both of them had made career changes and worked at OSU: Hannah to library science and Marc to Geographic Information Systems work with the OSU library.

Our six grandchildren were born in the decade between 2000 and 2010. Some of them undoubtedly will live to usher in the next century in 2100. By then life may have changed for them even more than it has during my lifetime.

Dealing with cancer and a new grandson

Both the Weavers and Hursts returned to the U.S. and lived again in or near Harrisonburg, Virginia, after more than three and four years, respectively, overseas. Carla and Micah's second child was due in early February 2009. Erwin and I were retired by then, so I made plans to spend three weeks with her in Virginia. However, before that, another significant family event unfolded.

Our cell phone rang as Erwin and I drove from Kansas to Virginia where all of our family would spend Christmas 2008 together. Marcia called to let us know the results of a recent biopsy. Like me, she'd had several previous breast biopsies, so I hadn't given it much concern. But this time was different. At age thirty-seven she was diagnosed with breast cancer. Before I could even process that, she went on with more information than I could take in about what kind it was and what surgery and treatments she would have. The encouraging word was that the cancer was positive to respond well to the recently developed drug Herceptin. We know numerous women who are breast cancer survivors. I refused to let my mind consider anything other than that she would be among them.

It was good that Erwin and I were already en route to Virginia. Micah and Carla were working then as resident directors in the Roselawn dorm at Eastern Mennonite University. The dorm was empty during the Christmas break. We spread out as a family there and had plenty of space for sleeping, eating, visiting, and playing games. Marc and Hannah's six-month-old Madeleine was a big hit with her older cousins. We set up a Christmas tree to soften the institutional dormitory look and feel.

We didn't dwell on Marcia's situation. However, during the time there, at her doctor's request, Erwin submitted a sample for a DNA test to determine if Marcia's cancer came through his side of the family – his mother, his sister, and now his daughter were touched by it. The dreaded BRCA genes were not present, good news for the other females of the family. My mother had breast cancer too, but so far, none of her descendants had. *"I should have gotten breast cancer and not Marcia,"* I thought.

Erwin and I drove back to Kansas after the holidays. I already had a plane ticket to return to Virginia for three weeks in February when Carla's baby was due. I changed the ticket to fly out two weeks earlier to help Marcia after surgery in January. For such a time as this, it was so good to be retired.

John's mother, Rachel Weaver from Ohio, helped them the first week after Marcia's double mastectomy and reconstructive surgery. Marcia was still quite weak when I arrived. She needed help with the house, the children, and washing her hair. John was also immensely helpful. Rachel was eight and Evan was six at the time. The weather soon turned wintery. To be certain I would be available to take care of Shawna, age three and a half, if Carla needed to go to the hospital during the night, I set up my quarters in the Roselawn dorm with Hursts. As if it weren't enough that both my daughters needed me in Virginia, out in Oregon, son Marc underwent knee surgery during that time and they could have used some help as well.

Marcia started her chemo treatments during my time in Virginia. Her hair began to thin. I went along with her and her family when she had it cut off and replaced by an attractive wig. Her church friends held a hat shower for her.

One evening when Shawna was already asleep, Carla's labor began and Micah took her to the hospital. About midnight Micah called to say that Jeremiah (Jair) had arrived. The next morning, I took Shawna to see her new brother in the hospital. Jair is the only grandchild who I saw before the other grandmother did.

Carla had a rough time again after giving birth. When the doctor gave Jair a checkup about ten days after birth, Jair had a high fever. That caught the doctor's attention. He ordered a spinal tap to check for meningitis. He sent them directly to the hospital. They carried with them the vial of spinal fluid for testing. Carla needed to stay with Jair in the hospital while they waited for results of the test on the spinal fluid. With the stress of it all, she came down with a breast infection. At that point, she needed the hospital care more than Jair did. He was fine and had no further fever.

I'd been in Virginia for five weeks. It was time for me to return home to Kansas. Once again, it was terribly hard to leave Carla – she was in the hospital, no less! One of Micah's relatives from Pennsylvania came to help.

Several other times that year, I went back to Virginia, either flying by myself, or Erwin and I driving together. I timed visits with the bad days Marcia had after a round of chemo. She bravely went ahead with orientation for a new job at the Park View Federal Credit Union. The credit union's understanding and patience with her during those difficult times certainly turned out to be worthwhile – she eventually became manager of one of the credit union's branches.

As Marcia continued treatments that summer of 2009, she wrote Erwin and me a letter listing ten reasons for us to move to Virginia. Some reasons were expected, some were funny, but the one that touched our hearts most was, "We need you!"

"Let's try on the idea of moving to Virginia," I suggested to Erwin. We thought about the logistics of preparing the house for sale. We started painting the exterior of the house that fall.

Part Four
Back to First Mennonite Church in Newton

When we had moved back to Newton, Kansas, from Botswana in February 2000, we eagerly anticipated worshiping again at First Mennonite Church. We kept in touch with the congregation during our six years in Botswana by listening to the worship services recorded on cassette tapes. It was humbling and encouraging to hear ourselves prayed for regularly. Pastor Clarence Rempel began his pastorate there in 1994 when we left for Botswana, so we knew him only as a voice coming from our cassette player.

We found First Mennonite doing well. With new people attending, the sanctuary was essentially full. Church leaders commented on the unity in the church.

Serving on worship commission

I was soon invited to serve on the worship commission. The first big issues we dealt with was how to accommodate the growing number of attendees and diversity of worship styles. Careful thought and prayer led to beginning two worship services on Sunday mornings. The first service was traditional, followed by Sunday school, then a second service in contemporary style. We began two services in early 2003 with enthusiasm.

Sadly, having two services led to considerable discontent. The anticipated growth didn't occur. The large sanctuary looked empty.

We tried to serve coffee during a short fellowship time between services. When I bought some flavored coffee to serve, one of the women on the kitchen committee bluntly told me that was sinful.

Another new definition of sin also came out of that context. The sanctuary platform wasn't large enough for the musicians and other worship activities. People suggested various options, which led to a significant whole-sanctuary renovation project. As we considered the placement of pews, one suggestion was to shorten a couple of pews at the front to allow more space for the children's time and to maneuver a casket at funerals. One man in the church, quite skeptical about all of the changes, visited me in my office at work. He seriously told me that it was a sin to cut the church pews.

When the $100,000 renovation was complete, the functionality had been greatly improved. However, other than looking fresher and brighter, many people couldn't see what had changed. That was our architect's goal!

Sending a team to Brazil

"You're going to Brazil!" Linda Shelly told me before I was even over jet lag from my trip to Australia to see new granddaughter Shawna. Linda explained that at a congregational meeting the previous Sunday, in my absence, they talked about responding to overseas opportunities. Linda, a member of First Mennonite who worked at Mission Network as director for work in South America, shared a request she had received from Brazil for a work team. Spontaneously people expressed interest in being part of a work team to Brazil. To our amazement, the church asking was none other than the Gama Mennonite Church where Erwin and I had served from 1977 to 1982.

Even though I didn't have any special skills for renovating a former grocery store into a meeting place for the growing Gama congregation, I certainly wanted to go. If Erwin could have gotten away, he would have gone too. Ten of us went to Brazil in January 2006 for about two weeks. During a long layover in the São Paulo airport, it was fun to introduce my Kansas friends to Brazil's special soft drink, Guaraná, and *pão de queijo*, little rolls of cheese bread. Even better was introducing them to our Brazilian friends who were still involved in the growing congregation.

Without much effort, Portuguese still flowed off my tongue. The Brazilians graciously overlooked my errors and foreign accent. Dwight and Janet Regier were part of the work team. They knew Portuguese from their MCC assignment some years earlier and helped with translation.

The Gama people had already put much work and significant resources into renovating the dilapidated grocery store near their overflowing meeting place. Building relationships was more important than the work and painting our team did – and redid when the color scheme changed! We all stayed in Brazilian homes. Compared to the struggling poor people Erwin and I worked with earlier, our Brazilian friends had edged up solidly into middle-class lifestyles. They had cars, computers, mobile phones, and larger houses.

For me the best part was reconnecting with people we'd known, especially the family of Manoel and Maria Rosa. They hosted the Regiers and me quite comfortably in their greatly expanded house. What a privilege!

Seeing results from earlier ministry

It was humbling and affirming to see spiritual growth and maturity in people we had worked with earlier in Brazil. Our team worked alongside the children of individuals who had been in our youth group. Some people told me about life-changing experiences during our time with them. One woman expressed great appreciation for our approach to mission work. The Gama pastor was the daughter of a man we had known as a church leader. However, there were also sad stories of people who had not remained faithful.

The renovations were complete enough to hold a joyous dedication and celebration service before our team left. Music was played and sung with loud abandon in praise to God.

Over the following years, several visits back and forth took place between the Gama church and First Mennonite in Newton, strengthening the relationship.

Erwin serves as chair of church board

A few months into our retirement, Erwin was unexpectedly asked to become chair of the church board at First Mennonite in Newton. He accepted and began a two-year term beginning in January 2009.

The first day in that position, Pastor Clarence came to Erwin with a letter of resignation. Clarence had served about fifteen years by then. Erwin was immediately busy with finding an interim pastor and setting up a pastoral search committee. The tasks of the church board chair became almost a full-time job for Erwin. It was good to be retired!

Another big issue for the church board to deal with was the flags – an American flag and a Christian flag – that hung in the sanctuary since World War II. About every decade the flag issue came up. A significant number of men in the church served in the military during World War

II and wanted the national flag displayed. By 2009, most of them were no longer living, but their widows and family still wanted the flags in the sanctuary. Now the tide was turning. More people saw the disjuncture of worshipping a God who loves the whole world and flying the flag of the world's only superpower. One older woman phoned Erwin several times and harangued him on the importance of patriotism. With the help of a highly qualified interim pastor, the congregation discussed it and then voted to remove the flags. The festering issue of how to deal with two worship services was put on hold for the next pastor to work with.

Erwin and I journeyed with First Mennonite over a thirty-year span, through joys and difficulties. We are grateful for the spiritual nurture and fellowship we experienced there.

Part Five
Afghanistan Adventure

We had a wonderful "sabbatical summer" as an introduction to our retirement, which began June 1, 2008. No big trips, no big church conferences, no big family reunions. It was a calm, quiet time to enjoy a rare Kansas summer that didn't have extreme weather.

Retirement, however, didn't put an end to our getting unexpected invitations!

Introducing the situation

Erwin had arranged to return to Mennonite Mission Network the last week of August to work on some part-time special projects. On Saturday, August 23, 2008, a few days prior to his scheduled return to the office, we received an unusual email prayer request from Mission Network. It wasn't the typical special request from the prayer facilitator. It came, instead, from the director of communications and referred to a Crisis Management Team. Because I had worked in the communications department, I immediately noticed that difference and pointed it out to Erwin. The prayer request mentioned deteriorating conditions in Afghanistan and asked people to pray for the safety of Al and Gladys Geiser there.

407

The next day at church, I asked Linda Shelly, who worked in the Mission Network international department, about the unusual prayer request.

"Al has been taken," she quietly told me.

We were concerned, of course, but we didn't think that more than prayer would be required of us.

We had met the Geisers a few years earlier when they spoke to staff at the Newton office. Only a few years younger than we are, they told about Al's work setting up micro-hydroelectric plants in remote villages and Gladys' teaching in a school in Kabul.

On Monday, August 25, Erwin returned to the Mission Network office as planned. The Executive Cabinet was meeting in Newton that week. Stanley Green, executive director, and James Krabill, senior executive of global ministries, had come from Elkhart, Indiana. We hosted them in our home, as we had done previously.

Unexpected invitation

Stanley, James, and several others were part of the Crisis Management Team (CMT) that was dealing with Al's kidnapping. The CMT met daily by conference phone calls. Late afternoon on Wednesday, August 27, several of us were sitting outside the conference room in the Newton office where the CMT was meeting, waiting to go together to a restaurant for supper.

The director of human resources, Rachel Stoltzfus, was part of the CMT. She opened the door of the conference room, looked around, spotted Erwin, and called him to come in. Then seeing me there as well, she asked for me also. Curious, but without time to give it much thought, we joined the Crisis Management Team around the conference table. They briefly reviewed the situation.

"We're asking both of you to go to Kabul," someone on the Crisis Management Team said, probably Stanley. They asked us to serve as documentarists to record all actions and details regarding the situation.

We were stunned! This was the most amazing unexpected invitation ever! My eyes surely opened wide, my jaw dropped, and my breath nearly stopped. We had never been in a war zone before; we had never worked in a Muslim-context; we had never been involved in a hostage-taking situation; our extensive travels had never been to countries where Christians couldn't be open about their faith. We had absolutely no background for this kind of thing. But this wasn't the kind of request we could lightly dismiss.

Note: Due to on-going and increasing security concerns, some names and locations are obscured or changed. Many details are limited or omitted in this account of our brief involvement in the situation. Prior to publication, this was submitted to Mennonite Mission Network and others.

Learning more

We learned that on Wednesday, August 20, Al Geiser and Shukur, his Afghan business partner, rode a motorcycle out of Kabul, the large capital city, to an adjacent district to attend a funeral. Al had adopted the long beard and clothing worn by Afghan men. He blended in well. After the funeral, the two men headed back to Kabul on a back road probably thinking it would be more secure than the main highway. They were stopped by two men, one armed with an AK-47. They searched Shukur and then Al, discovering from his documents that he was an American. They kept Al and Shukur in the mountains. They demanded ransom for their release. Shukur's family learned about the kidnapping and they informed Al's wife, Gladys, who was in Kabul. She was probably wondering why it was taking so long for Al to return home.

Gladys served with the aid organization that Mission Network partnered with in Afghanistan. It was a non-governmental organization. However, Al worked independently as a businessman.

When Mission Network personnel in the Elkhart, Indiana, office heard about the kidnapping, they formed the Crisis Management Team. In addition to Stanley, James and Rachel, the team included John F. Lapp, director for West Asia; Deb Byler for worker care; staff from communications department and a clerical assistant. They immediately contacted Crisis Consulting International (CCI). Erwin recalled hearing CCI's director, Bob Klamser, speak a number of years earlier. CCI had dealt with mission agencies in sixty-five kidnapping incidents in the past twenty-some years. Bob Klamser's advice was to have a Crisis Management Team in Kabul and that the team include someone as documentarist.

John Lapp was already on his way to Kabul, as was Jerry (name changed), one of CCI's consultants. However, Jerry could stay only for one week. If Erwin and I went, our travel itinerary to Kabul would include a stop in Dubai where we could quickly obtain entry visas for Afghanistan.

Above all, this was considered highly classified and to be kept secret. Any notice in the press about Al's kidnapping could prove detrimental to his release. We shouldn't even tell our family where we were going and why.

Considering a response

James Krabill tried to reassure us that he had been in Kabul, it was quite safe there, and good medical care would be available.

If it had just been I, I'd have flatly rejected the request, but Erwin wasn't as hesitant. I knew we needed to keep the door open, trusting that God would direct us. Erwin, as is his style, moved ahead and plowed through the mountain of details in preparation for us to be gone for an indefinite length of time. The to-do list included making sure his sister, Barb Busenitz, could take care of the financial aspects for Mom Eitzen in a nursing home; getting documents so our son, Marc, could deal with our finances; working on our travel plans with a Menno Travel agent, and contacting neighbors to care for our yard. But, we couldn't tell people where and why we would be gone.

I hoped that God would close the doors! That the phone would ring and we'd learn we didn't need to go. I couldn't eat or sleep normally. For more information about what to take, I phoned Sheryl Martin in Pennsylvania. She and her family had completed fifteen years of service in Afghanistan only the year before. She was very helpful and encouraging.

We didn't tell anyone at church about our upcoming adventure. We arrived late for church and left early on Sunday, August 31, and skipped Sunday school – all out-of-character for us. We notified our pastor, Clarence Rempel, later by email.

Before we left home, we learned that Shukur had already been released for a ransom. Mission Network's policy, as it is for most mission agencies, is to not pay ransom. Paying ransom encourages additional kidnapping. The U.S. government doesn't pay ransom either. The American Embassy was informed about Mennonite values regarding armed intervention.

Flying to Dubai

We had plane tickets to leave Wichita on Tuesday, September 2. Up until the moment my sister came to drive us to the airport, I kept hoping for the phone to ring with word that we didn't need to go.

While waiting in the Wichita airport for our delayed United Airlines flight to Chicago, I read in *The Economist* magazine that security was deteriorating in and around Kabul. Rockets recently had been fired at the Kabul airport and several aid workers were killed within miles of the city. Not at all reassuring.

Due to the delay leaving Wichita, the connection in Chicago was tight to catch an overnight Lufthansa flight. We had an even tighter connection the next morning in Frankfurt, Germany. We rushed past the signs inviting us to "Relax in Frankfurt," turned one corner after another only to see yet another long corridor ahead, another security checkpoint, another long corridor, etc. We arrived panting at the check-in counter and were ushered right on board, probably the last ones to board the flight for Dubai.

Our last-minute ticket purchases meant our seats were in the crowded rear of the planes. The worst segment was on the long Chicago to Frankfurt overnight flight where Erwin and I had the two middle seats in a row of four seats across. It was very tight both sideways and lengthwise. For the connecting flight to Dubai, Erwin managed to exchange his seat for one on the aisle at the very back, but it wasn't a full-width seat. An overly solicitous Middle Eastern man sat next to me. I didn't want to answer questions, so I either buried my head in a book or tried to sleep.

Between Frankfurt and Dubai, the in-flight maps showed our plane flying over the Black Sea. We may have been passing over the route Erwin's father took leaving Russia via Constantinople in 1923. Later I was startled to see that we were flying across war-torn Iraq, right above Baghdad.

411

Stopping in Dubai

We'd heard about the amazing city of Dubai, but never imagined we would ever see it. It was dark as our big plane descended. We saw only the city lights as we landed. Hot, humid air enveloped us as we walked down the long stairway from the plane to a waiting air-conditioned shuttle bus that took us to the arrivals and customs building.

Most of the airport staff were men, wearing long white flowing robes and headgear we'd seen before only in photos. A few women worked at the passport control booths. They wore long black outfits, actually rather stylish, with black headscarves, but uncovered faces. A fully-veiled woman passenger in black waited by one of the few passport control booths staffed by a woman. The staff woman took the woman's passport and lifted the veil to see if her face matched the passport photo.

It didn't take long to clear customs. With our luggage, we went into the hot humid night. We had detailed directions for where to meet our driver. There were many people all around. How would we identify our driver?

"Mr. and Mrs. Rempel?" a young man quietly asked us. He was the driver for the people who hosted us in Dubai. He took us to a nice, comfortably furnished place. We slept well under blankets in the cooled facility.

In the morning, Thursday, September 4, our hostess, who knew the Geisers, drove Erwin and me to a nearby taxi stand. She gave us a map to the Afghan Embassy and loaned us her own cell phone. At the embassy, we submitted our papers, including a letter of invitation from the organization with which we'd be working. Then we sat in the waiting room for the two-hours it took to process our visas. A variety of interesting people came and went. Even in a family group, the Muslim women sat waiting separately from the men, with only their faces showing. In Dubai, foreign women weren't expected to wear headscarves. I wore slacks and a long-sleeved jacket.

At the end of two hours, Erwin approached the desk and sure enough, everything was ready. We obtained multi-entry visas in case we needed to return to the U.S. for some reason, such as a funeral, and then go back to Kabul. We used the borrowed cell phone to call the taxi driver for our return to the guesthouse.

We saw a bit of Dubai from the taxi windows. Green, well-watered, and nicely landscaped areas lined the highway. We saw tall construction cranes all around. The city was growing rapidly, a financial hub in the oil-rich Middle East region. Dubai is also a hub for all sorts of nefarious characters and schemes, we have learned. It is one of several small entities in the United Arab Emirates and has very little of its own oil. Desalinization provides water. We were intrigued with a water dispenser that drew water out of the humid air, filtered it, and then cooled or heated it for great-tasting drinking water.

We accessed email. We learned that Gladys Geiser met with John Lapp in the Dubai airport on August 28 while she was on her way back home to Kidron, Ohio, and John was en route to Kabul. She provided John with more details.

The second night in Dubai I could hardly sleep. We heard the constant low-flying planes landing and taking off at the nearby busy international airport. I had what must have been a panic attack. It took a lot of talking to the Lord before I got over that!

In the pre-dawn of Friday, September 5, the driver took us back to the airport for our flight to Kabul. What a relief to see so many other Westerners, including women and children, checking in for our flight. That helped me feel calmer. There were also big burly American men with shaved heads who we surmised were private contractors heading to Kabul. We flew on Kam Air, an Afghan airline.

We were served a generous breakfast on the plane. Most of the Middle Eastern people rejected the breakfast because it was Ramadan when Muslims fast during daylight hours. The man sitting next to me looked longingly at my breakfast.

What could be seen of the terrain below revealed a brown, sometimes rugged mountainous landscape, with very little vegetation. The flight was very smooth, and by noon we were descending in a spiral into the mountain valley where Kabul sits.

Each one of us involved in this situation has our own story to share. Based on my personal journal, this is an account of how I experienced our brief time there. It is not an account of the actual work we did there, nor an attempt to tell the Geisers' story.

413

Arriving in Kabul

We arrived in Kabul on a Friday, the Muslim day for prayers. That determines the business week for everyone.

My polyester headscarf kept slipping off my head as we walked from the plane to go through customs. We were now in territory where women should have heads covered, so I finally just tied the scarf under my chin. We went through all the procedures without any difficulty. I noticed a young blonde white woman in western-style clothing traveling with three small children. An Afghan man ushered her and the children around the passport control booth.

In the baggage claim area, an American woman with her uncovered hair in a ponytail was wearing a police-type uniform and carrying a walkie-talkie. She asked if we were with DynaCorp – one of the major private contractors for the military. Surely, we didn't look like their type!

We filled out forms to register with the local police. It wasn't until later that we realized Erwin's photo was attached to the card with my name on it, and my photo was on his card.

We followed the instructions we had for finding our way out of the terminal. What a relief it was to see tall, dignified John Lapp waiting for us. Jerry, the consultant from CCI, was with John. In the parking area, a big white Land Cruiser, with the aid organization's logo, awaited us. I sat in front with the driver who apparently didn't speak English. From there I had a better view of Kabul than Erwin did. The lack of military presence in this war zone was notable. We learned that the Afghan military and police controlled Kabul. The NATO or U.S. military forces were seldom seen in the city.

There would have been so many interesting things to photograph, but we were told not to take photos in public. It was the dry season and everything was dusty. Kabul looked bleak and dreary. Many low buildings of gray concrete or local earthen bricks were interspersed with bombed-out ruins left to crumble after previous conflicts. There was a sprinkling of newer and taller buildings, along with a couple of bright new mosques.

We drove across the city to where the aid organization was located, in several different facilities. That area had been quite nice back in the 1970s, but the Soviets heavily damaged it in the 1980s. That was followed by more destruction during the inter-tribal and Taliban conflicts. The area was now considered safe for foreigners. But we would need to follow basic security precautions in public, such as being in small quiet groups, women dressing modestly showing only their faces, and keeping off the streets from ten at night until morning.

Getting right to work

We went to the organization's team house and were shown to our bedroom on the second floor. Before further unpacking, we ate a late lunch of delicious soup and fresh bread. Then with John Lapp and Jerry we walked, carrying our laptop computers, about three blocks on uneven unpaved surfaces to the Geisers' house for our first work session. Geisers' good-sized dining room table was already set up with electric plug-ins for computers – but only two at a time. A technician came over to set up our laptops for secure communications. However, at times the internet connection operated painfully slow.

It felt strange to work in someone else's home. I could see that Geisers had enjoyed making the place homey, just as we had done in our overseas locations.

John Lapp and an American aid worker who knew Al well gave us new information. We were oriented to policies and guidelines. We learned that a taxi-driver was retained and on call by the Kabul Crisis Management Team, which now consisted of John, Jerry, Erwin, and me.

"Who took Al?" everyone wondered. There were many factions in Afghanistan. The eventual conclusion was that the captors were affiliated with Hisb-e-Islami, a faction headed by the notorious Gulbuddin Hekmatyar. There was relief that it wasn't the Taliban.

Another American aid worker and Shukur also came to Geisers' house. The aid worker knew the captors' Pashto language and spoke with the captors when they phoned. Jerry had set up a system to record all the calls on an iPod. What an unusual setting for Erwin and me to first be introduced to an iPod.

The captor's spokesman phoned that first afternoon. When the call was finished, it was played back and translated to English so Erwin and I could type a transcript.

415

Our accommodations

We didn't get back to the team house that day until after dark. The next day Erwin and I got a better look at our accommodations. We had a comfortable queen-sized bed. We removed some excess furniture and were able to make our bedroom a cozy private living space. The weather was hot enough to use a fan.

Remnants of faded Arabian elegance were visible in the two-story team house. Thick columns, ceramic tiles, and marble floors could be seen. But now it was a bit run down. The large rooms had been divided to make more bedrooms, heavy draperies designed to keep out the hot sun and cold winter winds now hung a bit askew, carpets were thin, and the furniture looked far nicer on photos than it really was. It reminded me of other guesthouses we've visited in various parts of the world. The fellowship there, however, was wonderful – as well as the food in the team house.

"A lot of testosterone is running around in the kitchen," the Australian woman who managed the team house told us. Two young men of different ethnic backgrounds had been trained to cook for Western tastes. Their competition resulted in really good food. Fresh grapes were in season along with some of the sweetest melons we've ever eaten. Products came from a variety of Asian countries. Cans and boxes had familiar logos and labels in English, Arabic, or Sanskrit.

The large team house was set inside a locked compound with tall walls all around. Thick rose bushes sent up thorny branches above the walls. That should deter anyone interested in climbing over the wall. A small green rectangle of grass behind the main building was ringed with a variety of small trees, a late-summer vegetable garden, and some rose bushes still blooming. Along one wall of the enclosed compound, a row of small rooms opened toward the main house. The gate guard stayed in one room. Other rooms could accommodate guests. The main entrance gate was only big enough for pedestrians to use. Vehicles passed through another tall, solid metal gate on a side street. Between the vehicle gate and the house sat a formidable row of shipping containers, some stacked double. In addition to providing storage for aid workers' furniture, the containers also provided privacy and a measure of security. A British woman who worked in the organization's office lived in a cottage at a back corner of the compound.

Electric power was sporadic, supplied in three different ways. The city provided several hours of power each day. During Ramadan (it was called Ramazan there), the power was on during the night when people were cooking and eating their main meals. City power was off during most of the daytime. The team house had a set of large batteries that could be charged either by solar panels or by a diesel-run generator. When one power source terminated, complicated switches were reset to draw upon another source.

Due to Erwin using a CPAP breathing machine at nights, we needed to sleep at the team house where electricity was reliable all night. There had been talk about us staying at the Geisers' house, but electricity wasn't constant there. For security reasons, I was uneasy about staying there anyway.

One spacious bathroom on the upper level at the team house provided for the occupants of five bedrooms. Even though silt had accumulated in the pipes allowing only a dribble of water through the showerhead, showers were refreshing. A large diesel-powered water heater sat in the corner of the bathroom. Periodically the gatekeeper carried up a container of diesel. He also did small errands and helped move heavy furniture.

Meeting new people

At the team house, we were well-provided for and felt secure. Already during the first week in Kabul we met a variety of interesting people staying at the team house. We were relieved when a family with four children completed the meetings they were attending and returned to their work location. They needed a lot of time in that one bathroom.

At the round dining table we enjoyed conversing with fascinating people. They ranged from new arrivals to others who had spent many years in Afghanistan, young and old, families and singles. European countries were most represented, especially Finland, along with Americans. Two British women kept things so lively they provided us with an equivalent of British TV sitcoms.

Being September, the temperature ranges and times for sunrise and sunset were much like back in Kansas. Day times could be hot, but nights generally cooled off.

The team house had a library, mostly paperback novels. Two books that interested me were written by Jean Sasson and Sultana – *Princess* and *Daughters of Arabia*. They were about Saudi Arabia. That was an eye-opening look behind the veils imposed on women there and the luxuries of the ruling royal family.

An interesting consultant

Jerry, the CCI consultant, spoke of having been in the Navy, in Vietnam, and in police and detective work. He told us that he and his wife contracted with the U.S. military to train Special Forces in covert operations. She wanted him to bring back padlocks from wherever he traveled so they could figure out how to pick them. His dry sense of humor ran to military terminology and comparisons – wearing camouflage underwear in a combat zone, was one of his phrases. These were not typical subjects in our Mennonite circles!

Jerry didn't feel safe in Kabul. His military friends had strongly advised him not to come to Afghanistan. They only traveled armed and in military convoys. Jerry was astounded to see faith-based aid workers and their families moving around freely without being armed. One European single woman who had spent many years in Afghanistan said she went all over by herself. She often rode public buses.

Using phones

Landline phones were few and didn't operate well. Therefore, as in other developing countries, for many people their first phone was a mobile one. Simple Nokia models with removable SIM cards and pre-paid minutes were used widely. In villages without electric power, enterprising shop owners set up solar recharging systems for mobile phones. Even small local shops sold cards with phone minutes in varying amounts. By scratching to reveal a number on the back of the card and typing that number into the phone, additional prepaid minutes were added. The revealed number could also be sent by text message to another phone for it to use those minutes.

We assumed calls to and from the cell phones the Crisis Management Team used were tracked.

The aid organization and security issues

We walked to the aid organization's office facilities nearby and learned more about their work. They had served for decades in Afghanistan, through several political changes, conflicts, and turmoil. They and other non-governmental organizations had developed a security network to inform each other about the constantly changing security situation. When we arrived in Kabul, the security alert was at "green," the lowest level of threat. Daily advisories were issued, sometimes with warnings about areas to avoid that day. Everyone was warned to always stay away from any street demonstrations or military convoys. At a set time each night, the aid agency called all its workers to be sure everyone was in and safe.

One day the security alert noted that more rockets had been fired at Kabul and other rockets disarmed. Hearing that those rockets were imprecise, I concluded that everyone other than the intended target was at risk.

Dynamic situation

Already by Sunday, September 7, Jerry was concerned that we were under surveillance at the Geisers' house. Jerry was trained to constantly look around and be suspicious. Tuesday afternoon we took our things from the Geisers' place and reorganized our work area in one of the larger bedrooms in the team house. The next day, someone reported seeing a man just sitting in a car along Geisers' street and looking through the rearview mirrors to watch all the comings and goings. We were glad we had moved out! An aid worker who lived in an apartment above the Geisers' place reluctantly moved to the team house for her own security.

The American aid worker who spoke with the captors by mobile phone needed to leave soon. The Crisis Management Team invited Bill (not his real name) to come from the U.S. and take that role, called a third-party intermediary. Bill had just finished work on his dissertation at Fuller Seminary in Pasadena, California, and didn't yet have a job. He immediately got on a plane and arrived in Kabul by noon on Tuesday, September 9. Bill and his wife had served in Pakistan for a number of years, as well as in Kabul. He was fluent in Pashto, the captors' language, and equally important, he knew the culture of that ethnic group. Bill was a valuable asset to the Crisis Management Team. He used an assumed name in his contacts with the captors.

Interacting with other foreigners

Other aid workers, from various organizations, lived nearby. We were invited for meals in their homes. While we couldn't talk about our work, we enjoyed those visits with interesting and dedicated people from different countries. We walked freely on the streets to and from those visits and to a nearby bazaar. The bazaar's tiny shops offered an amazing assortment of products – food, personal care items, electronics, clothing, and numerous other supplies.

Erwin and I were assigned a mentor couple, who were Americans. I asked the wife to check my wardrobe. To my amazement, she thought the clothing I had would serve just fine. In public, I wore my clothes in completely different and strange ways and layers: long pants to cover the legs and ankles, a tunic or skirt long enough to end below the knees, long sleeves, and a long headscarf. Such attire showed respect for the local culture. I didn't want to attract any negative attention, being uneasy about safety as it was.

Fears and hopes flowed back and forth regarding Al's situation. We knew that daily prayer groups were meeting in many places. I prayed trusting that the Spirit would intercede, as I didn't know what to pray. At critical times, I asked God to nudge people to pray. I knew we were praying for a miracle. We had regular phone conference calls with the Crisis Management Team members back in the U.S.

Completing our first week in Kabul

We learned so much in just our first week in Kabul. As our first week ended, some sounds had already become familiar – the Muslim calls to prayer loudly amplified and broadcast from numerous mosques five times a day, packs of barking wild dogs roaming the streets at night, donkeys braying, vehicles tearing at high speed along the nearby paved road during the night, the thumping sound of helicopters flying low overhead, as well as other aircraft circling to ascend or descend into Kabul's valley airport.

Large dumpsters on a nearby corner provided recycling opportunities for goats and people. More men than women were on the streets. Many men rode bicycles – some wearing traditional long flowing shirts and loose pants – sometimes two on a bike. Women dressed in a variety of ways but they all had something covering their hair. Even little school girls wore headscarves and long skirts or pants. Some women wore a bright blue burka that completely covered even their head and face. A burka-clad woman saw the world only through a patch of cutwork over her eyes. It was more common, however, to see women wearing long pants, long tunics, black long-sleeved tops, their faces visible but surrounded by a headscarf, often a white one. From the second-floor of the team house, I took photos of what we glimpsed on a busy nearby street.

The second week in Kabul

Due to our work, one evening we missed an invitation for supper and it was too late to eat at the team house. The four of us – John, Bill, Erwin and I – walked along a main street to a restaurant several blocks away. It was a much longer walk than anticipated. I had to keep my eyes fixed on the uneven sidewalk because in public I couldn't take Erwin's arm to steady myself. Little boys followed us trying to speak some English or beg for "one dollar." It was dusk. Busy small shops lined the sidewalk. My peripheral vision saw a bloodied head of a sheep on the ground by a shop door. At the restaurant, we ordered shish kabobs of beef and lamb, a rice mixture, and a couple of other dishes – some were quite tasty. By the time we walked back to the team house, it was dark, most of the shops were closed, and a few streetlights shed weak light on our path. I felt very uneasy, but the men didn't seem concerned.

Each day brought some new development regarding Al's situation. Hopes rose and fell.

"That is just the way it is here," Bill often told us. His knowledge and acquaintance with people in the area were helpful.

Settling into a flexible routine

Our days fell into a familiar routine – at least in the mornings. Erwin got up very early, as he always does. He went downstairs, made himself some coffee, and worked on his laptop at a table. About 5:30 a.m., I joined him, got some coffee, and had devotions in the sunroom as the sun rose over the mountains around Kabul. I clung to the Scriptures that speak of God's protection, power, and encouragement. By 6:30 a.m., other people were up and we'd go to the dining room for breakfast. From then on, the day could go in any direction!

A trip to the American Embassy

One day, John, Erwin, and I asked our taxi driver to take us to the U.S. Embassy. The drive took about an hour. What an amazing ride! The city appeared to be drowning in its own traffic. My senses were overloaded with all the intense new sights and sounds. Putting aside thoughts of roadside bombs, suicide bombers, and rocket attacks, I felt an amazing inner calm. With everything so totally out of my control, that was the only thing to do.

Traffic ranged from light to a choking standstill. Vehicles moved very close to each other, nudging over and merging with only inches to spare. Lane markings were irrelevant. Driving was an art. The streets were packed with big SUVs, many taxis, ordinary sedans, mini-vans with people hanging out the doors, police vehicles, United Nations vehicles, vehicles from other non-governmental organizations, and motorcycles. Bicycles, pedestrians, and hand-pushed carts mixed in with the vehicles. A big dark pickup with several armed guards in its open back closely followed an armored money truck.

Along the way to and from the Embassy, we passed:
- street bazaars with booths displaying a great variety and abundance of fresh produce and other items for sale
- crumbling hulks of large bombed buildings, including the former USSR embassy
- empty lots, strewn with rubble, tucked in between renovated or rebuilt buildings
- buildings with a minimal amount of visible war damage
- new buildings under construction

- steep hillsides with houses chiseled into and among large boulders
- traffic circles with police directing the traffic
- a traffic light with a countdown of the seconds until the light changed
  (We hadn't seen those in the U.S. at that time yet.)
- a woman and her little boy following a nice big trash truck, picking up what they could from the dumpsters
- men changing money on the sidewalk
- school children, including girls, amazingly unattended in the pandemonium
- nice buildings and shops
- some large, elegant three-story houses, villa-style, along the street just across from the high walls of the U.S. embassy compound
- a Yahoo training center, an airline office, parcel delivery offices, large buildings called wedding halls
- parks with roses bravely opening amidst the dust and smog

At the American Embassy

We arrived at the high outer wall that surrounded the large U.S. Embassy compound. We presented our passports to armed men who let us inside the gate. It was quiet and calm within the high walls as we walked some distance to the main building. Our contact person and two other men met us at the door. They were all very cordial. I noticed some men wearing flak jackets and helmets. Several women were also around.

We passed through a metal detector and walked a short distance to an office in a shipping container. The air-conditioned container was painted white inside and out. It had no windows. The Embassy compound had many such repurposed shipping containers.

Erwin and I mostly just listened as John talked with the men. Sitting there, I couldn't help but think, *"If fifty years ago, someone would have told me – the shy, country girl – that I'd ever be in this situation, I would never have believed them!"*

As we left the main embassy building and walked out toward the perimeter wall, a military convoy was entering the compound. Big tanks were draped in camouflage netting. We exited the compound, looked for our waiting taxi along the street, and saw another military convoy passing by. Traffic stalled and the convey stopped. Some of the armed military men jumped out of their vehicles. John wondered aloud, uneasily, if they were going to direct traffic or conduct some kind of operation. Remembering that convoys are targets for attacks, we were all a bit tense until that situation cleared up. Our return to the team house went without incident.

What a relief to safely enter the team house compound, which felt so refreshingly comfortable and calm after the heat of the stuffy taxi, the smell of exhaust fumes, and all the chaotic, intense sights.

Our daily tasks

Erwin and I needed to figure out a system for the documentation. We organized a structure of computer files and folders. There was a backlog of things to work on and it took days to get the documentation to the point where it needed only daily updating.

Lots of email, phone calls, meetings, and conversations took place most days, so there was plenty of action to keep track of and document. By the tenth day, after hours of work, Erwin and I completed the organization of the material and felt caught up. We wondered how much longer I needed to be there. Things seemed to be getting more tense. I struggled with feeling fearful.

I was particularly fearful that Erwin or I could be kidnapped and tortured. We had learned a great deal about the various dynamics and ethical issues at play in a hostage situation. I thought, *"I would rather be injured or killed in a roadside bombing or rocket attack than be kidnapped!"* I longed for the time when we could land safely in Dubai and go on back home. We hoped that a good resolution would happen soon.

The aid organization's staff was concerned about those of us on the crisis management team. They provided what they could. They arranged for us to meet with a counselor couple. That was a good opportunity for us as a team to reflect together on how we were faring and feeling in this situation and get to know each other better.

"We are doing what we can," was all the American Embassy contact person told Bill, John, and Shukur when they took the taxi to the embassy again several days later. The day after that visit, there were security alerts warning people not to go to the Embassy because there might be retaliation connected to bombing and deaths at the U.S. embassy in Yemen the previous day. We also heard that a gang in Kabul kidnapped foreigners and local people with any wealth, or their children. Certainly not reassuring.

One of the humanitarian workers was very helpful with Al's situation and provided a pastoral presence for us. He and his wife invited us to walk with them in the nearby community. They led us to the area where the Hazara ethnic people live. Their facial features show evidence of their Mongol ancestry. They have a low standing in Afghan society. The streets and houses in the Hazara section were different from where we stayed.

Using Skype for phoning, without video, we contacted our children. By then Erwin and I were allowed to let our family know where we were. We talked with granddaughter Rachel on her eighth birthday, September 17.

By the end of our second week in Kabul, the world's financial markets were crashing, taking our retirement accounts down with them. We were aware, but had too many other things to think about.

Beginning our third week in Kabul

On Friday, September 19, the whole situation began to change in new and surprising ways. New lines of communication opened.

This was an unexpected development. John sought the advice of Bob, the CCI consultant. By Sunday evening, different structures were in place to work toward Al's release.

Security concerns were growing. We were advised to not walk on the streets anymore, not use the special taxi, and to ride only in the aid organization's vehicles.

There didn't seem to be much reason for Erwin and me to stay in Kabul at that point. We began planning to travel home in a few days. The captors continued to phone, so Bill's language skills were still needed and he couldn't leave. Someone representing Mission Network also needed to remain in Kabul. John Lapp had plane tickets to take a two-week break back home in Indiana beginning October 10. Erwin agreed to remain in Kabul while John was gone. However, I could leave, so my plane ticket was booked. I arranged to stay in Dubai again until I could take a flight on back to Kansas.

Traveling home alone

I'd made numerous international trips by myself before, so I didn't think I would mind traveling alone, although we were disappointed Erwin and I wouldn't be going together. I knew that once the Lufthansa flight lifted off from Dubai, I would be fine. I began to be concerned about going alone through the unfamiliar airports in Kabul and Dubai where little English was used. I was especially concerned about the police registration cards with our names and photos mixed up. We decided it would be better if I took the card with my photo, as airport staff probably would check photos and not foreign names.

Shortly before I left Kabul on Friday, September 26, I noticed that in Philippians 4, the phrase I'd been clinging to, "Be anxious for nothing," was preceded by "The Lord is near." Of course, that is the reason we don't need to be anxious: because the Lord is near! That became my mantra.

It was reassuring to have Bill come along to the airport. Being a Friday, the day of prayers, traffic was light. It was heart wrenching to see several burka-clad women sitting at regular intervals in the middle of a street and begging as vehicles drove by on either side of them. Some women had infants with them.

Even before we entered the airport parking area, we had to get out of the vehicle and put my luggage through X-ray. I was body-searched in a small room by a woman official. We then drove into the parking area. Bill arranged with an older man working as a porter to haul my luggage from the parking lot to the terminal building. The old man was in quite a hurry once he got my bags on his cart. We could hardly keep up with him. All too soon, we reached the gate in a fence where I needed to say goodbye to Erwin. No public goodbye kiss was allowed there. I thought of Gladys and wondered what she thought and felt when she had passed through that gate about a month earlier. Did she wonder if she would ever see her husband again? She had great faith in his release.

Past that gate, trying to keep up with the old man with my luggage, I crossed a vast empty parking lot, which apparently is a safety perimeter around the terminal. At the terminal building, my luggage was hand searched and X-rayed several times. When I turned in the police registration card, the man took it without even looking at it. So all that anxiety was indeed for nothing. With that behind me, "The Lord is near. Be anxious for nothing," was easier to say. I kept repeating that in my mind.

Many people thronged the Kabul airport building and it was confusing to know which line was for what. After numerous checks and one more body search plus passing through a metal detector, I finally reached the departure lounge. I felt that I could begin to relax a bit, but the thought of periodic rockets aimed at the airport wasn't a comforting thought. There were several other Western women in the departure lounge too.

The plane's departure was delayed more than an hour. When we passengers finally walked across the tarmac to board the plane, all the checked luggage was on the ground below the plane. Only after passengers identified their bags did the baggage handlers put the bags onto the plane. I checked one small bag and carried on my wheeled computer case.

On the plane, I finally felt free to take off my headscarf. After takeoff, the plane circled, spiraling upward several times around the valley where Kabul nestled before heading over the mountains to Dubai. I wondered if we flew over the area where Al was being held. A generous meal was served, but it felt awkward eating beside a man who turned down any food or water because it was still Ramadan.

The landscape below was totally brown and treeless all the way to Dubai. As we crossed the Persian Gulf, I noticed a ship, probably an oil tanker. It was interesting to think that I was flying over the path that crude oil travels before refineries turn it into the gas I use in my car.

Feeling safe in Dubai

Flying into Dubai in the late afternoon provided an opportunity to see some of the skyline and housing below.

I was surprised by how nervous I felt at passport control in Dubai, more so than I had been when Erwin and I entered the country together. The man at passport control just glanced at my passport, stamped it, and handed it back to me. He did ask where I had come from but not where I was going in Dubai.

Because flights from Kabul seldom arrived as scheduled, I had instructions to use an airport phone to call the people hosting me. I was assured that their driver was already on the way.

My luggage was X-rayed once more when I left the baggage area. Then I followed another set of directions to where to wait for the driver.

"Since you are waiting here, we must be going to the same place," a British man said as he joined me. He was from the headquarters of another humanitarian aid organization. He made several trips a year to visit their projects in Afghanistan. He had been on the same flight from Kabul. He commented on the extended circling around Kabul before we headed over the mountains. Others talked about the extra levels of security. Perhaps that was because only a few days earlier the Marriot Hotel in Islamabad, Pakistan, was bombed. The director of the organization we worked with had been returning to Kabul from Europe and had breakfast at that hotel before the bombing.

It was dusk in Dubai as we waited for our driver. A call came from a mosque, at which the drivers in the nearby taxi line pulled out food and broke their daylong fast, eating off the hoods of their cars. Already what little I could see of Dubai looked clean and more developed than Kabul. Once safely inside the vehicle, I could relax still more.

A Mission Network couple was working in Dubai. Erwin and I had gotten to know them while they were on leave for a year in the U.S. They drove another visitor and me on a whirlwind tour of Dubai. What a privilege! I snapped photos furiously as we sped past tall skyscrapers lining the streets – each one designed in an attempt to outdo the others. One skyscraper under construction was becoming the world's tallest – the Burj Kalifa. We stopped at a luxurious shopping area where the shops were designed like a *souk*, a traditional marketplace. That was near a very expensive hotel, Burj Al Arab, said to charge $45 to just step inside, and $2000 and up for spending a night.

We drove out onto a set of man-made islands in the design of a palm tree. A recently completed road passed along the trunk of the "palm tree," which was lined with a monorail and look-alike apartment blocks. Large Arabian-style villas, which all looked the same, lined both sides of the "palm fronds." A luxurious Atlantis resort topped off the palm-tree shaped islands.

A highlight of the tour was a stop at the Mall of the Emirates with the world-famous indoor ski slope. In the midst of outdoor temperatures over 100 degrees, inside it was cold enough for snow in a winter park with a variety of winter sports. The rest of the mall looked like most any American mall with familiar store names including Starbucks and Gap. Most of the shoppers were Westerners dressed in shorts and T-shirts. A few local Muslim women were conspicuous in their long flowing black attire and veiled faces.

In plenty of time for my flight leaving at 1:30 a.m., on Sunday, September 28, the driver took me back to the airport. Check-in was uncomplicated. It didn't take long until I was through security and walking the long halls out to the gate area.

Big international airports fascinate me – seeing people from other races and many countries, conversing in numerous languages. At that point, I felt exhilarated and privileged to have experienced such an adventure and learning experience.

Right on time, we passengers boarded a bus that took us to the waiting Lufthansa plane. It was indeed with a sigh of relief that I saw the last of the lights of Dubai.

Returning home

Transiting through Frankfurt on the return home, I had plenty of time to take up their slogan "Relax in Frankfurt." After a long layover, I boarded a United Airlines flight to Chicago. Just as our plane was the next one to take off from Frankfurt, it pulled to the side. The pilot announced that a couple of backup computers were down. It took more than an hour to get going again. The Atlantic crossing felt very long – all in daylight, no movie shown, and I had little reading material left. The delay in Frankfurt meant a real rush in Chicago to clear customs, take the shuttle train over to the United terminal, go through security, and get to the gate for a flight to Wichita. I realized I could only go with the flow, do what I could, and see what happened. Finally, I wasn't particularly anxious. I barely made the Wichita flight. My suitcase didn't.

Elwyn and Barb Busenitz met me in Wichita. I could hardly stay awake on the drive to Newton as they explained about the mail they had picked up for us.

At home, I booted up the computer and sent Erwin word that I was home. He tried to phone by Skype, but the connection wasn't good enough to talk. We had turned off the water heater before going to Kabul, so there wasn't any hot water for a shower.

At 4:00 a.m. the doorbell rang. *"Who is here?"* I wondered, stumbling out of bed. I was home alone for my first night after being on the scariest adventure of my life.

"Who's there?" I called out, but no one answered. I peeked through a window in time to see a vehicle backing out of our driveway. About then our phone rang. It was the driver calling to say that he had dropped off my suitcase, which had arrived on the flight after mine. As if I needed it at four in the morning!

Erwin continuing in Kabul

Back in Kabul the ups and downs continued. What Erwin learned, he sent me by email, so I continued doing documentation work from home. John Lapp left Kabul on Oct 10 for his scheduled break. Erwin and Bill continued to accept invitations to meals with various people. At the end of Ramadan, the taxi driver invited Erwin and Bill to his home to celebrate Eid al-Fitr – an interesting cross-cultural experience.

The longed-for release

Five days after John Lapp left Kabul for his break in Indiana, early in the morning of October 15, it was Erwin and Bill who received an unexpected, yet eagerly longed-for phone call.

Al was free and resting at the U.S. Embassy!

Erwin phoned me at home with the good news. Apparently, a military special operations team rescued Al during the night. He woke to the sound of English voices calling him. He was airlifted by helicopter, checked over at the Baghram air base, and then taken to the

Embassy in Kabul. Erwin and Bill were invited to meet Al that evening at the Embassy, which they eagerly did. However, their conversation was limited.

There were many unanswered questions about what really happened. However, they soon realized that two people were killed, and possibly more, during and following the rescue. Bill knew how retaliation and revenge are engrained in that culture.

Erwin leaves Kabul

Bill and Erwin made immediate plans to leave Kabul. Erwin got a flight to Dubai on October 18. As they were leaving the team house to go to the airport, a cell phone rang. It was the same phone the captors always called. Bill didn't answer. It rang again. He asked Erwin to answer in English and quickly hang up. The aid organization's staff was quite concerned about Bill's safety. When Bill left the next day, they gave him a cell phone so he could let them know when he was safely on the plane. In Dubai, Erwin met the same Mennonite couple as I had and they took him on a similar quick tour of that unusual city. Erwin and Bill spent several days in Dubai waiting for their flights back to the U.S. At least they were safe there. Erwin arrived at the Wichita airport on Wednesday, October 22.

Al returns to Ohio

The embassy contact person accompanied Al back to Cleveland, Ohio, on October 20, two months after his capture. Al had spent fifty-six days in captivity, losing about twenty pounds, but otherwise he was in remarkably good health.

We listened to the recording of the church service at Kidron Mennonite Church when Al and Gladys shared about their ordeal. She had had amazing faith that he would be released. What a celebratory service that was in Geisers' home church!

Afghanistan Adventure Epilogue - 2013

It was hard to know how much and what to tell people about this most unexpected and unusual adventure. It took me five years to come to the point of sharing more of the details with our own children.

431

After being in Kabul, Erwin and I went back to our retirement in Kansas. In November we took a trip to meet our new granddaughter Madeleine in Oregon. Family situations occupied much of our time during the next several years.

My main conclusion is that life is messy. The brief glimpse of the dynamics of western Asian, Arab, and Muslim countries has significantly heightened my interest in news from that part of the world. Whenever another hostage taking is in the news, we understand what behind-the-scenes actions are probably taking place.

Mission Network discontinued work in Afghanistan.

Al felt such a strong call to his work and witness in Afghanistan that he returned to work there again in his business with Shukur. Gladys also returned eventually to Kabul and taught again. In July 2012, both Al and Shukur were shot and killed in a rural part of Afghanistan.[7] Al was buried in Kabul. Several other people we had encountered in Afghanistan, or knew of, were also killed in the following several years.

What an amazing adventure God had led us through!

Part Six
Erwin's Family Changes

Alvin and Lena Eitzen had lived close to the earth in the harsh climate of eastern Montana. To survive there in farming and ranching they had to be practical, flexible, and able to do what needed to be done. Those skills undoubtedly helped them, especially Lena, to cope with life's challenges.

One challenge was having their family double in size in 1957 after Alvin's sister had died in Los Angeles leaving three orphaned children – Erwin, Norman, and Barbara Rempel. Those difficult times and the children's transition from the big city to the wide-open spaces of Montana are detailed in this book's first chapter.

---

[7]Bearing Witness Stories Project, Gladys Geiser wrote their story, posted July 5, 2016. http://www.martyrstories.org/

Before the Eitzens took in the Rempel children, they dealt with the pain of childlessness by adopting a baby, Howard. Howard found it difficult to fit into the Eitzen family and accept the Christian and Mennonite values in which he was nurtured. Howard had the unusual experience of acquiring three older siblings when he was about eight years old. He struggled as a teenager and young adult. In contrast, the three Rempel children moved seamlessly from their biological home in California to the Eitzen home in Montana where they flourished in the Mennonite community known as Lustre.

On the farm, Howard learned to drive as a child. He enjoyed big equipment, especially big semi-trailer trucks. Following that passion, after high school he worked as a long-haul truck driver, traveling all over the country.

In 1981, as mentioned earlier, Howard informed the Eitzens that he no longer wished to be a part of the family. By then Howard was thirty-three years old.

Being estranged from their son was probably the most difficult thing the Eitzens experienced. They seldom knew where Howard was. It must have been painful for Howard as well. Eitzens followed the biblical example of the father who waited and watched for his prodigal son to return. They continued to pray regularly for Howard.

Adapting and planning

Clear-eyed and practical, the Eitzens retired from farming and ranching in Montana in 1981 before Alvin's health issues, at age 62, could have resulted in a crisis. They relocated in Mountain Lake, Minnesota, where they both had siblings and other relatives. Alvin was born and raised there. The Eitzens bought a relatively new bi-level house and became actively involved with relatives, church, and community. They joined the same church Alvin's father had pastored. They were disappointed when the church changed its name and dropped affiliation with the General Conference. However, they remained with the congregation.

When it became difficult for Alvin to manage the stairs in their bi-level Minnesota house, they knew it was time for another change. They sold the house, downsized, and moved a few blocks away to an apartment designed for senior living.

The Eitzens also dealt matter-of-factly with end-of-life issues, advance directives, wills, and funeral and burial arrangements. They even wrote their own brief obituaries. They lacked a power of attorney, however, which troubled Dad Eitzen.

Even before Erwin and I moved back to Kansas in 2000 after having been in Botswana, Mom Eitzen's ability to keep things organized was already beginning to slip at times. Physically, her health was average. As the new decade unfolded, Dad Eitzen increasingly battled his own issues with aging, hearing loss, chronic disease, and reduced mobility. He was frequently in pain and grumpy. Mom steadied him as he slowly made his way with a walker. He gave up driving, but she still drove. She fetched his wheelchair, rolled him to and from the car, folded the wheelchair, and lifted it into the trunk. When he fell in their apartment, she called the local rescue squad to help him up. He had his mind and she had her hearing. She carefully repeated things for him as he read her lips.

Taking care of business

Now Mom Eitzen's memory was slipping. Dad Eitzen couldn't understand what was happening to her. He was frustrated. He always took care of the finances. Who would keep the accounts and pay the bills when he couldn't?

"Mom can't remember anything," Dad Eitzen grumbled one time when we Rempels were visiting. "Who should be our power of attorney?"

"Erwin should be your power of attorney," the family said.

Dad couldn't understand how someone living five hundred miles away in Kansas could take care of financial matters in Minnesota. Fortunately, the internet and digital age had arrived for the rest of us. Alvin and Lena had provided for the three Rempel children when they were left orphans. Now Erwin, Norman, and Barbara were there for them, even if from a distance.

One day when visiting in Minnesota, Erwin and I drove the Eitzens to Windom, a larger town not far from tiny Mountain Lake. Dad struggled up the stairs to their lawyer's office to sign the documents naming Erwin as their Power of Attorney. Then Dad directed us around town.

Using a walker, Dad shuffled in and out of each office where they did business to introduce Erwin. That was very helpful.

Dad made sure we knew their wills indicated that if Howard couldn't be located within a year of their death, Howard's portion of the estate would be divided among the three Rempels. However, the rest of the family never doubted that Howard could be found within that generous timeframe.

Needing another change

Mom Eitzen's mental decline followed typical stages of Alzheimer's disease. On one visit to Mountain Lake, the conversation mentioned her forgetting things.

"I feel stupid," she said quietly. That was the only time we heard her say anything indicating her awareness of and feelings about what was happening to her.

When the Eitzens needed assisted-living care, they didn't have far to look. Just across the street from their apartment building sat Eventide Suites. It had been an institutional home for the elderly where numerous people they knew resided over the years. Eventide had recently been renovated with not only nice assisted-living suites but also a secured wing for residents needing memory care. It wasn't hard to persuade the Eitzens that was their next move. Earlier they had briefly contemplated and then rejected moving to Kansas to be closer to us.

With the help of Erwin's sister and her husband, in early spring of 2004 we moved the Eitzens across the street to a double room in the memory wing at Eventide. Mom's mind couldn't cope with making decisions about how to downsize. We had to do that for her. She didn't understand why their car should be sold.

The reversal of parent and child roles was well underway in the family's transition from one generation to the next.

By late November that year, Dad Eitzen was hospitalized in nearby Windom. Erwin, Barbara, and I drove from Kansas to Minnesota. We kept Norman, living in California, informed of Dad's condition. Norman went online and located Howard who was listed with a trucking company. Norm's message to Howard via the trucking company did get through. In his short response, Howard indicated he wasn't interested in the family.

Dad Eitzen improved to the point that the hospital could release him to a nursing home. He did not want to go to a nursing home. Mom's mind was clear enough at that moment to explain to him that it was the only option. He reluctantly agreed. We arranged for his admittance to Good Samaritan home in Mountain Lake. Some distant relatives plus their pastor helped Erwin move Dad Eitzen's things, including a big recliner and desk, into the nursing home in preparation for his transfer there the next morning.

Dad Eitzen must have been thinking, *"I'd rather die than go to a nursing home."* He took a turn for the worse the day before he was to leave the hospital. We reviewed his advance directives and his signed Do Not Resuscitate order. He died the next morning about the same time the transfer from the hospital to the nursing home had been scheduled. He was 86 years old. Howard didn't reply to the notice of Dad's death.

The same relatives graciously helped Erwin remove Dad's things from the nursing home only the day after they had moved them in.

Except for our two daughters who were then in Brazil and Australia, the rest of the Rempel family, including the grandchildren, gathered in Mountain Lake. After the funeral and burial, the entire family went to a restaurant with Mom Eitzen. She became talkative and asked questions – the same questions over and over and over. She was having a hard time figuring out who the grandchildren were – all young adults by then. They patiently repeated their answers to her repeated questions. By bedtime, Mom had forgotten that all of Norman's family from California had even been there.

Power of Attorney

Now the full responsibility of a power of attorney fell on Erwin, along with being executor of Dad Eitzen's will and trust. Whenever we visited Mom in Minnesota, Erwin checked the desk in her room to see if Eventide had overlooked some mail that should have been forwarded to him. One time he found something on her desk about a refund of about $2,000 from an old investment. The deadline to reply had just passed. Erwin learned that the money went to the state of Minnesota's unclaimed property account. Looking online at Minnesota's list of unclaimed properties, he noticed another item for the Eitzens from John Hancock Insurance Company. It simply indicated the amount would be more than $100. Erwin submitted the needed documents to reclaim that also.

One day a small folded postcard-size piece of mail arrived. It looked strange and we thought it was some kind of junk mail. Opening it, we saw it was a check from the state of Minnesota for more than $25,000. Could it be genuine? Erwin looked up the address, and it appeared legitimate. He called a phone number he found for the state of Minnesota and they said it was real. He sent the check to be deposited in Mom Eitzen's bank account, expressing his doubts about its validity. The bank was also dubious but processed it. It was genuine! John Hancock had gone through a complicated demutualization process that resulted in that unexpected money because of an old insurance policy the Eitzens' had with the company. Erwin's persistence paid off.

Moving Mom Eitzen to Kansas

Mom Eitzen received good care at Eventide in Minnesota for another couple of years after her husband's death. Her condition worsened to the point where more care was required than Eventide provided. The rest of us concluded that, in her confusion, it wouldn't matter if she moved only a few miles to another facility, or to a place in Kansas where we, along with Barb and Elwyn, could be more closely involved in her care.

Moving her from Minnesota to Kansas turned into quite an adventure. Eventide staff explained things to her but she didn't understand or remember. We essentially worked behind her back and kidnapped her! She willingly rode with us in a van to Kansas, but it turned into a long travel day with lots of repeated questions. The capable staff at Presbyterian Manor in Newton received her and provided good care. She maintained a good sense of humor, which again helped ease the situation.

Mom Eitzen fell several times at the Manor, breaking a hip one time. Erwin and I were glad we lived near Newton Medical Center and could meet her there whenever an ambulance brought her in for the required scans after a fall. By the summer of 2007, we agreed to her care team's recommendation that she be placed in hospice care. She remained at the Manor, but hospice oversaw her medical care at that point. That ended her trips to the emergency room. We appreciated the extra level of care hospice provided, especially when the three Rempel siblings and their spouses went on a cruise to Alaska. Norm was managing on the cruise with a scooter before his multiple sclerosis worsened. That cruise provided for good family time, sights of beautiful scenery, and for Erwin and me to have been in all fifty of the U.S. states. At each port the cruise ship visited, we disembarked, found a public phone, and called to ask about Mom Eitzen.

Looking back to the mid-1980s when my own mother was dying, I realized how little I had done for her and my dad even though we lived only a few blocks away. Relating to Mom Eitzen felt like an opportunity for me to do better. I loved her as much as my own mother.

By having Mom Eitzen in Newton, we visited her regularly. Prior to retiring, I often stopped by the Manor to see her on my way home from work. Together with Barb and Elwyn, we enjoyed singing familiar old hymns as Mom sang the alto part. When Erwin and I retired in 2008, we had flexibility and more time to be involved.

The light went out of Mom's eyes. She had a vacant look. She often walked to the end of the hall and wordlessly ran her hands over the wall. Was she looking for a way out? How much of her was still there deep down inside?

A brief clear moment

Alzheimer's patients sometimes briefly come out of their fog for a few moments of clarity. That happened once when Barb and I were visiting Mom toward the end of her life. Something reminded Barb of the absent Howard. Barb reminisced a bit about Howard. Mom made no response. Then Barb and I talked about other things for a while.

"Is he single?" Mom interjected.

"Who?" we asked her.

"Howard."

Quickly seizing the moment, I asked her, "Would you like to see him?"

"Of course!" she replied.

While Barb and I tried to digest that information, the window closed and Mom retreated into her vacant wordlessness. We wondered about again trying to locate Howard. Even if he came to see her, it was unlikely that Mom would know him. After talking with Erwin and Elwyn, we let it drop. With Interstate 135 passing within sight of the Manor, we wondered if Howard ever trucked past without knowing she was there.

The passing of a generation

By the end of April 2009, Mom was bedfast and it was obvious she would soon leave her tortured state. Hospice care had continued since the summer of 2007. The signs of active dying were obvious for a few days, but then her condition stabilized at a low level. Could there be some unfinished business in her befuddled mind?

Saturday, May 2, Erwin talked to Mom about Howard, not sure if she comprehended anything he said. He assured her that he would do all he could to find Howard. After that, the dying process resumed. During the early hours of Sunday, May 3, 2009, she slipped away quietly. She would have turned 86 the next month.

We made our final trip from Kansas to Mountain Lake, Minnesota, for Mom Eitzen's funeral. A smaller number of people attended her funeral than had been at Dad Eitzen's funeral about four and a half years earlier.

Another generation in our family had passed away. Erwin and I both became the oldest in each of our families.

Reconnecting

How long would it take to find Howard?

Erwin's sister, Barbara, phoned one of Mom Eitzen's nieces in Montana to notify her of the death. The niece offered to contact Howard, her cousin, with whom she had kept in touch over the years. So the very day Mom died, we were communicating by email with Howard.

To our surprise, Howard wrote that in 2005 he traded in the wheels of his big rig truck for the wheels of a wheelchair. The symptoms of his disease were almost identical to the symptoms Norman Rempel was experiencing with multiple sclerosis. Howard lived alone with his dog in Great Falls, Montana. Some of his children and his second ex-wife lived in that area as well. He could still use a computer. We received periodic communication from him, including some funny photos and videos.

As executor of the Eitzen estate, Erwin kept Howard informed of the progress in settling the estate and made sure that Howard received his one-fourth share.

A few months later, Barb and Elwyn took a long road trip and stopped to see Howard in Great Falls. They had a good visit with him. They marveled at Howard's ingenuity in adapting to his situation. Another time when Barb and Elwyn went to Montana, Erwin flew there to meet them and together they visited Howard. By then Howard had moved to a nursing home in Great Falls.

In the fall of 2013, Erwin and I both visited Howard. We had flown from Virginia to Oregon to visit our son and his family in Corvallis. From there we drove a rental car on a circular route across Montana. We saw Howard in Great Falls before driving to eastern Montana to visit the locations where Erwin and I each spent our teenage years. During our visit with Howard, one of his daughters stopped by on her way to work as a nurse in the nearby hospital. She was excited about an upcoming mission trip she was taking to Africa. However, Howard made it plain that talking about spiritual matters was off-limits. We respect that but continue to pray for him.

Howard easily keeps the conversation going when we visit or phone. He has repeatedly said that he holds nothing against the three Rempels who shared the Eitzen home with him. He had found it impossible to live with the Eitzens' standards and the community expectations. After twenty-eight years of estrangement, which we always knew would end somehow, we are all glad to be in communication with Howard.

Chapter Eight
Moving On as Retirees, 2010

Part One
Helping Family in California from April 2010 to August 2011

Multiple sclerosis advanced quickly after Erwin's younger brother, Norman, was diagnosed with it in his late fifties. Norm's always-inquisitive mind remained sharp while his body deteriorated. He was determined that his care could be managed at their home in Fresno, California. He didn't want to go to a nursing home. Norm's wife, Liz, retired from her nursing career.

Thanks to a generous long term care insurance policy, they hired a home health worker for several hours a day and purchased equipment that made his care feasible in their house. Norm's needs kept increasing. None of their three grown children lived nearby.

Erwin and I had been considering where to live during our retirement and declining years. After Mom Eitzen died in May 2009, we didn't need to stay in Newton, Kansas. We had observed some difficult situations of aging parents living far from their children. With our two married daughters and four grandchildren living in scenic Virginia, plus pleas from them for our presence there, we had decided to "try on the idea" of moving from Kansas to Virginia.

As we were contemplating leaving Newton, we went to a Rempel family reunion in California in November 2009. Erwin's siblings and their spouses, nieces, nephews and all our children and grandchildren were there. We were glad to see Marcia's strength and hair return-

441

ing after her cancer treatments. Carla and her husband, Micah Hurst, talked about leaving Virginia and going to Australia again. We also saw Norm's situation in California.

With these developments in our daughters' lives, the urgency for Erwin and me to move to Virginia diminished. He and I talked about perhaps spending a year or two in Fresno. Norm had suggested earlier, in somewhat of a joking manner, that we should move there.

The first Sunday of January 2010, we spoke with Norm and Liz by phone. Liz mentioned that Norm was getting weaker.

"So when are you going to move to Virginia?" Norm asked. That gave us an opening to explain that things were changing for our daughters and moving to Virginia didn't seem as urgent anymore.

"Why don't you move to Fresno?" Liz said.

"Well, we have actually thought about spending some time there for a while," I said. She assured us that we could be of help.

"You could live with us," Liz surprised us by saying! She repeated it again later in the conversation. She even offered us the use of their spacious master bedroom suite because they were renovating their den to better serve Norm's needs.

What an unexpected invitation that was! We had learned that when God calls through unexpected invitations, doors open and things move quickly.

Erwin and I bought plane tickets for an exploratory weeklong trip to Fresno yet that month. In the meantime, Erwin talked with the church leadership about the situation. Capable people agreed to take on Erwin's responsibilities at First Mennonite Church where he was chair of the church council. He was also on the pastoral search committee, which was at a critical point in the process that eventually led to the church calling its first woman lead pastor. The part-time work and special projects Erwin and I each had with Mennonite Mission Network were also ending.

Preparing to move

"We are moving to Virginia by way of California," is what we told people.

Our realtor, Gary Franz, wanted us to put our house on the market by March 1 to take full advantage of the spring house-selling season. We had gradually been repainting it inside and out. We knew the floor coverings needed to be replaced on the main floor. We were surprised when Gary Franz suggested we replace and update the shiny brass cabinet pulls and light fixtures. This time, we figured we'd better take our realtor's advice sooner rather than later.

Just before our exploratory trip to Fresno, we finished the painting. We were physically worn out and our fingers were cracking. The trip was a welcome break from the work of getting the house ready for sale.

As we drove to the Wichita airport on January 27 for our flight to Fresno, Marcia phoned from Virginia. She told us that her husband, John Weaver, a roofer, had fallen off a house and was in the hospital. His ladder had slipped and he fell about fifteen feet onto a concrete driveway. He had some broken ribs and other injuries. It could have been much worse. Once again, my heart was pulled in two directions – should I be heading east to help my daughter or going west to check out helping with Norm? With tickets in hand to go west, Erwin and I went on to Fresno, with mixed feelings.

In Fresno we got a taste of what life would be like there for us. Norm's personal care would be Erwin's task. And, yes, Erwin was fine with doing that, including the bathroom details. Soon a lift system on a ceiling track would join Norm's growing list of items that helped deal with his increasing limitations.

Liz made it clear she wanted us to live with them. We agreed to do that initially for three months. We recognized that negotiating the kitchen would be a challenge, as she and I would each do our own cooking.

Erwin and I returned to Newton with a sense of urgency to move to California. It was full steam ahead for us all through February to pack and prepare our house for sale.

Unlike our previous major moves, this time we stored basic furniture and household items. We didn't want the expense of starting all over again somewhere. However, most of Erwin's books, which we had shipped back and forth around the world, now made a final trip to Book Reviews, a used book store in Newton. He realized he hadn't even used some of them! With the advent of the Internet, Bible commentaries and other information was only a few clicks away.

Our realtor wanted houses decluttered before showing to prospective buyers – so much so that his office paid for a month of storage plus use of a moving van. We began moving things into a storage unit. After seeing rain drip in on our things, snow blowing in under the storage-unit door, and mouse turds, I paraphrased Matthew 6: 21 like this:

Don't hoard treasure down here where it gets eaten by moths (and mice) and corroded by rust, (mold, mildew or moisture from rain and snow; covered in dust, baked in Kansas summer heat, frozen in Kansas winter, or blown away by a Kansas tornado, burned by a wild grass fire, or stolen by burglars.)

With the Lord's help, I wasn't particularly anxious about our things. However, I could easily envision finding a nest of little mice in our sofa. Kind brother-in-law Elwyn agreed to periodically replenish bait for the mice while we were gone.

My digital piano needed climate-controlled conditions. My sister kept and used it in her house there in Newton. She was a pianist at her Methodist church and took advantage of practicing with headphones without disturbing her husband.

Selling our house and things

We worked hard to get our updated house ready to sell by Monday, March 1, 2010. That Monday, ReMax was posting photos of our house on their website and we were giving descriptions and final approvals for a glossy colored four-page brochure. We vacated our house for several showings. The listing price was $119,900.

Before noon the next day, Gary Franz phoned from ReMax. He asked us to come to his office that afternoon to consider contracts. Plural? Sure enough. A young man and a young woman were both interested. They had bid up the asking price. The top offer was from the fellow at $121,200. A brief window of tax incentives for first-time buyers played a role.

This felt like another of the Lord's confirmations that we were on the right track.

Whatever we didn't want to keep, we easily sold, either privately or at a garage sale. Things were hopping prior to our garage sale's opening time at three o'clock on the first Friday in March. A couple of women stopped about noon saying they were on their way to Wichita and could they please look now. They scooped up all sorts of our things. One of them seemed a bit daffy. She bought stuff she didn't even know what to do with. We were glad she bought our big analog TV because everyone was transitioning to digital high definition flat screen TVs at that time.

It was a madhouse! My sister, LaRita, was a big help. While Erwin and Gary Isaac carried out furniture for display, other early birds came. Erwin didn't have time to set up his cashier table before they were ready to pay for items. In the middle of that, the bank's appraiser came to do an appraisal of the house. He also bought some things.

By the official three o'clock opening time, some of the best things were already sold. We hadn't had time to move our car out of the driveway. A Kansas March wind was so strong that we kept our south-facing garage door shut. We directed people through a smaller side door.

Items Erwin was sure should just go into the trash, until I convinced him otherwise, actually sold right away. We had only a small load of unsold items that easily fit into our small car for one trip to the second-hand shop.

Finishing in Newton

I insisted that there was one more major item to do – buy another car. My small 1998 Ford Escort, even though it didn't have many miles on it, was aging. The larger Buick that Erwin had driven was totaled the previous year when he hit a black calf that strayed onto the country road he was driving after a nighttime meeting at a country church. We managed surprisingly well with only one car. Out of frugality, Erwin never complained about squeezing into that little car that fit me so well. I couldn't, however, imagine driving the little Escort, fully loaded, all the way over the mountains to California. It was time to get a newer and bigger car. We traded for a 2007 Honda Accord, which we both found to be a good car for us.

By March 21, with only a week left in Newton, notes in my journal read, "So many people express how much they have appreciated us, and comment on Erwin's leadership on the church board. While it is good to hear their affirmations, I still have a bit of a guilt feeling about 'running away.'"

It would have been easy to stay there in Kansas. We were letting go of lots of things – not just stuff, but also the security of a house paid for, a community where we knew our way around, and a support structure of family, friends, and church. We were nearly sixty-six years old; we had been married for about forty-four years; and we had spent twenty-two of those years living in Newton.

Sunday, March 28, everything was done. The car was packed and farewells said. That afternoon Erwin and I drove off toward the sunset and California. We felt light and free, ready for the next chapter of life. It was amazing how the timing of things large and small came together so well in the whole process. Surely God had been at work. We had questions about how it might work out, but no doubts about this being the right thing.

Settling in California

It was Good Friday when we arrived at Norm and Liz's place in Fresno. Their California-style ranch house, built in the 1970s, sat among other nice houses on a quiet street. Several redwood trees shaded the house from the intense heat of summer. It wasn't far from Fresno Pacific University where Norm had been registrar since 1988, along with other responsibilities, until his physical condition worsened.

The spacious master bedroom suite provided Erwin and me some private space. We fit in a desk for each of us. A French door opened from the bedroom to the patio. The fenced-in backyard included a swimming pool. We were surprised that in relatively balmy California we could enjoy the pool only in June, July, and August.

"You are going to need to buy another refrigerator," one of Liz's sisters-in-law had observed. At first neither Liz nor I thought that would be necessary. I kept our menus simple. Liz eventually did buy a small fridge, which was helpful.

Norm's condition varied from day to day. Erwin and Liz worked out a schedule between them to attend to Norm throughout the day and night. Norm needed repositioning every few hours. Several times a day Norm's surgically implanted catheter bag needed emptying. I marveled at how Erwin coped with it all.

We respected Liz's nature as a private person. We tried to simply provide a supportive, caring presence. We hoped that our being there lightened the load, even bringing a measure of joy and laughter to their home.

As the three-month trial period concluded, we realized it would be most helpful for Erwin and me to continue living in their house with them.

"Had you two been close?" people would ask Erwin and Norm. Not really. They had never lived near each other as adults. Norm had pursued academics and Erwin had pursued church ministries. Norm's bright, clear, curious mind and his positive, grateful atti- tude contributed a great deal to making our time together a good experience.

Being a bit older than Norm, Erwin remembered more than Norm did about their childhood and their parents. The brothers recalled both sad and humorous events of those long-ago days before their par- ents died. They enjoyed bantering with each other, each one trying to outdo the other with teasing and put-downs.

One morning, it was taking longer than usual for the two men to be ready for breakfast. Liz went to check on the situation.

"They are trying to solve the problem of evil in the world," she reported to me with a chuckle.

Adapting to MS

Norm embraced any technology that could assist him. When we arrived, he could still manage some movement. But left-handed Norm was soon reduced to using his right hand to push buttons on the remote control for his large-screen high definition TV, to click his computer mouse, or to peck out words on the keyboard. Velcro tape kept quite an array of gadgets close to Norm's one working hand. He got a TiVo and recorded interesting documentaries and programs. Most evenings Erwin and I watched the news with him and other programs he had recorded. Norm used a voice-recognition computer program until his voice became too weak for it to respond accurately.

Norm was a big man and difficult to transfer from bed to chair to bathroom, etc. A motorized lift system on a ceiling track made it possible for Norm to be cared for at home. To use the lift, Norm had to be carefully positioned in a sling. The motorized lift raised him high enough to be pushed manually along the track to his next location. There

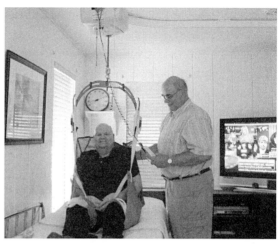

Erwin helps his brother Norman transfer in a sling on a motorized lift system, Fresno, Calif., 2010.

he was lowered into place. The lift extended from his bedroom into the bathroom.

In his powered wheelchair, Norm would motor himself to the family room, to the backyard, or outside to the handicap-adapted van. Liz was quite relieved when Erwin took over driving that van. More than once she had the frightening experience of the van malfunctioning.

A home health aide, Scotty, came daily to work with Norm. Scotty stayed overnight on Fridays so that Erwin didn't need to do the early Saturday morning bathroom routine. He and I took that opportunity to go out for breakfast, often to Panera Bread.

Typically, Norm spent a few hours in his recliner. There he ate and used his specially mounted Apple computer with an extra-large

Norm Rempel uses computer, Fresno, Calif., 2010.

monitor. When he couldn't manipulate spoons anymore, he could still tip out bite-size pieces into his mouth from a lightweight plastic cup. He looked forward to a daily treat of an ice cream bar on a stick.

Norm wanted to do as much as he could on his own. He had a list of "bucket" items to do. Sometimes on a "good" day, he motored out to the garage and instructed Erwin on sorting out his vast collection of tools and other handyman items he once used to maintain their house. As Norm's sixty-fifth birthday approached, Erwin helped him through the complicated Medicare enrollment process.

Sometimes Norm could still enjoy going to a restaurant. Liz's nearby sister, Evelyn Jean, and her husband, Richard Thiessen, usually joined us on those occasions. Norm's preferred place was Claim Jumper, an upscale restaurant that accommodated his power chair. His favorite menu item was onion rings! However, he needed help with eating.

Strong pain medications kept Norm's pain bearable – most of the time. He was susceptible to infections. The infections gradually became resistant to most antibiotics.

Norm saw a variety of medical specialists. His primary care physician was retiring. Thus when something serious came up, it meant calling 911, which inevitably meant Norm would be taken to the hospital. Liz, Erwin, and others took shifts at the hospital with him. It was difficult for Norm to reach and use the call button. Norm intensely disliked being hospitalized.

Could Norm really be cared for at home until the end? He never seemed to doubt that, but at times, the rest of us weren't so sure. After several painful hospitalizations, Norm agreed to hospice care in late June 2011. A hospice nurse, chaplain, and volunteers came to the house regularly. Hospice, however, only supplements the twenty-four-hour hands-on care given by family and others.

Worshiping in Fresno

Going to church worship services was no longer feasible for Norm by the time we arrived in Fresno. It would be too long with too many people wanting to talk. Erwin and Liz alternated staying home with Norm on Sunday mornings. Norm and Liz were members of Butler Church, a Mennonite Brethren congregation on the corner of the campus of Fresno Pacific University. Butler was the closest church and the worship time worked best with the schedule for Norm's care. We visited other churches, but Butler became our "home church" too. There we met Richard Kriegbaum, whose nephew was married to Norm's daughter. Richard later became president of Fresno Pacific University for a second time. The parents of the author of the hilarious book, *Mennonite in a Little Black Dress*, also attended Butler Church.

When we visited other Mennonite churches in the area, we were pleasantly surprised at how well we could connect with California Mennonites. Because of Erwin's work in our church-wide mission agency, we already knew some people in both Mennonite Church USA and Mennonite Brethren circles in California.

Some people, even at church, couldn't understand why Erwin and I would come to help Norm. To Erwin and me, this felt like our retirement Mennonite Voluntary Service assignment. We had the time and capacity to do it. And of course, family helps family.

Experiencing California

Erwin and I got California driver's licenses, license plates for the car, found medical doctors, registered to vote, got library cards, and changed our address to 1715 S. Caesar Avenue, Fresno – in other words, we became California citizens. For Erwin this was a return to the state of his birth and childhood. Now we could both say we'd lived not only in the central part of the U.S., but also in states in the north, south, east, and west of the country.

We enjoyed the mild climate in the San Joaquin Valley – especially in winter when the news reported bitter cold and heavy snow in other places. Palm trees and tropical plants grew contentedly beside tall redwoods and pine trees. Rows of ancient olive trees lined boulevards. Flowers bloomed year-round. Looking at all the green lawns and lush landscaping, one wouldn't know it was an arid climate.

The San Joaquin Valley itself is flat, lying between the coastal ranges to the west and the tall Sierra Nevada mountain range. We enjoyed seeing snow-covered tall mountains to the east on clear days. Unusually heavy snow fell in the mountains during the time we lived in California – only to be followed by a most severe drought after we left. When we were there, California was still suffering from the Great Recession of 2008. Many houses, shops, and offices were unoccupied. Abandoned construction projects deteriorated while waiting for better days.

Because of irrigation systems, many things grew in the valley. Erwin and I enjoyed taking drives into the country, driving past acres and acres of vineyards, nut trees, fruit orchards, and fields of produce. We were especially fascinated by large clusters of grapes drying on the ground between rows of grapevines. Any rainfall at that point would spoil them and the farmer would lose the crop of raisins. Erwin indulged his love of seeing things grow by planting edibles in Norm's backyard.

Periodically Norm and Liz's children came to visit – Evie from Phoenix, Michele from Chicago, and Ryan from San Luis Obispo, several hours' drive away. Vacating our bedroom space for them, Erwin and I traveled and saw more of California: the rocky central coastal area around Morro Bay, the historic Sacramento area, famous Lake Tahoe, and scenic Sequoia and Kings Canyon National Parks.

Marc and Hannah in Oregon weren't so far away either, less than 800 miles. We drove up to see them several times during the months we stayed in Fresno. It was always interesting to see their latest home improvement project. Once when Hannah went on a business trip, I took the Amtrak train from Fresno to Oregon to help Marc care for their two little girls. Other than a long uncomfortable nighttime layover in Sacramento, I enjoyed the train travel.

Hursts go and return from Australia

Within three months of our arrival in Fresno, Erwin and I flew back across the country to Virginia. We bid farewell to Carla and Micah, Shawna and little Jair, as they returned to Australia in June 2010. We supported their going, but it was still hard to see them disappear into the depths of Dulles International Airport. The job Micah had lined up in Australia, working with the Egyptian Coptic Church youth, didn't turn out very well. Their other efforts to find work weren't successful. They returned to Harrisonburg in less than a year. Carla began work as an assistant in the office at Eastern Mennonite High School. Micah took some seminary classes. Their second year back in Harrisonburg, Micah worked again as a resident director at Eastern Mennonite University. They moved back into the same apartment in the Cedarwood dorm where they lived earlier. Meanwhile, Marcia continued to do well health wise.

Considering our next location

Two big questions ran through our minds while we were in Fresno: how long would Erwin and I stay there and what would we do next? For a while, it looked unlikely that either of our daughters would be in Virginia. We considered other options, including moving to Oregon near Marc. Any retirement location for us needed to be close to family and our Mennonite church.

Once we knew Carla would be back in Harrisonburg, and Marcia indicated they would stay there as well, that settled for us that Virginia, indeed, was where we would settle.

We looked at houses for sale in Harrisonburg whenever we visited. However, we concluded that for the long run, it would be better for us to rent and eventually move into a cottage at Virginia Mennonite Retirement Community (VMRC). The costs and responsibilities of home ownership and someday preparing another house for sale was more than we felt up to. We were still in Fresno when we put our names on the waiting list at VMRC, potentially a five-year wait.

The days went by quickly in Fresno. My responsibilities were mainly to take care of cleaning and cooking for Erwin and me. I read numerous books from the public library. It seemed good to stay longer than the one year we had committed to.

Both my niece Marisa Claassen and Erwin's nephew Brian Busenitz were planning weddings in Kansas during early August 2011. As we discussed it with Liz and Norm, it seemed that would be an appropriate time for us to make a change and continue eastward to Virginia. Their daughter Michele arranged to take on the care-giving Erwin had been doing for her dad. She could do her computer-based work in Fresno and her husband traveled regularly back and forth from their house in the Chicago area.

As usual, once we made decisions, things moved quickly and the details came together. Via the internet, we checked out various rentals in Harrisonburg, and arranged to rent a two-story townhouse near the EMU campus.

The long drive from California all across the U.S. looked daunting. However, we would spend a week in Kansas between the weddings. That would provide a nice break and time to take our things out of storage and load a U-Haul rental truck. Son-in-law John Weaver bought a ticket to fly to Kansas and help us drive the rental truck and our car to Virginia.

On August 1, 2011, we had our car packed in Fresno. It was time to say a final farewell to Norm. At times, we hadn't thought he would live even that long. We left with heavy hearts, but glad that we had provided some assistance. While our sixteen months in California were often stressful and challenging, there were enough good and pleasant times so that in our memories the positives well outweigh any negatives.

In summary, we made it work. It was, overall, another good chapter of life.

California Chapter Epilogue

Only two and a half months after saying goodbye to Norm and Liz, he died on October 15, 2011. Norm had marked his sixty-fifth birthday in May of that year. He was the first in our family to be cremated, at his request.

Erwin, I, and our three children quickly arranged flights to Fresno for the memorial service. We were reminded that Norm believed "Happiness is a choice." He often expressed his gratitude for the many blessings he had – even with all the limitations and pain of MS. His life impacted many people.

Pastor Albert H. Epp, who in 1957 helped the three Rempel orphans transition to a new home, was able to attend the memorial service.

"All these years, we have followed them with interest and prayers," Dr. Epp shared at the service.

Liz continued living in their house in Fresno until the summer of 2013. Then she sold the house and bought a place for senior living in San Luis Obispo, California, where her son, Ryan, and his family live. When we saw her again in 2014 at a Rempel family reunion in Newton, she was doing well in her new location and situation. Amazingly, both of her daughters and their families were in the process of also moving to San Luis Obispo.

Part Two
Retirement in Virginia

Introduction to springtime in the Shenandoah Valley

The ethereal, almost mystical beauty of spring in the Shenandoah Valley of Virginia nearly overwhelmed me on a visit in 1993. We lived in Kansas at the time where we frugally planted small clumps of daffodils, and one or two blooming trees. In the Shenandoah Valley, extravagant large swaths and long rows of flowers and blooming trees were everywhere. The misty morning air enhanced the sun's rays that delicately backlit the gorgeous flowers of different shapes and colors. Dewdrop gems sparkled in the fresh green grass. What an awesome display of God's creative beauty.

We had flown to Virginia for daughter Marcia's graduation from Eastern Mennonite University in Harrisonburg the last weekend in April 1993. It was our first springtime visit to the area. For the commencement ceremony, blooming trees and flowers decorated the "outdoor auditorium" where prim rows of white chairs on the green EMU lawn faced iconic Massanutten Peak.

A prediction

After Marcia's graduation ceremony, we drove around sightseeing. Her younger siblings, Marc and Carla, and her Eitzen grandparents from Minnesota were with us. We stopped at the top of a hill north of the EMU campus on a portion of Park Road and College Avenue where infrastructure was going in for new houses. Getting out of our cars at that high point, we looked over the Shenandoah Valley and toward the distant ridges of the Allegheny Mountains. What a lovely view!

As we stood there drinking it all in, to our surprise Mom Eitzen said something about Erwin and me retiring there. What an unusual thing for her to say. Photos I took on that spring day in 1993 just missed another hilltop where new houses would be built and where we would eventually live.

Arriving in Harrisonburg

Eighteen years later, our two-vehicle caravan arrived at 955 Central

Avenue in Harrisonburg about two o'clock the afternoon of August 15, 2011. We were grateful for son-in-law John Weaver's help driving a U-Haul truck from Kansas. We eagerly explored our new home – a two-story townhouse in the middle of a three-unit building. It didn't take long to empty the U-Haul truck with the help of two sons-in-law and a couple of other fellows and some grandkids. During our first two weeks in Virginia, the weak outer bands of a hurricane passed over, and we felt the rumbling of a 5.9 earthquake. During our whole time in earthquake-prone California, we hadn't felt any shaking.

From that location on Central Avenue, it was just a few blocks to the Eastern Mennonite University campus where Carla and Micah, with Shawna and Jair, lived in a third-floor campus apartment. A knock at the door of our townhouse might be Shawna, then five, bicycling over ahead of her daddy who was dropping off compost at his brother Matt's place just a couple of houses up the street. John Weaver might stop by from a nearby roofing project to use the bathroom. Grandkids came and went at our place, and we went to care for them at their homes. When we invited all ten of our Virginia-based family for a meal, the extended table filled most of the small kitchen and dining area. The Hursts had recently returned from Australia and had no car yet at the time. We provided transportation for them when their bicycles weren't adequate.

Finding a church
In Virginia we again had a choice of churches to attend. Erwin and I had already visited several Mennonite churches on previous trips. The first several weeks after moving, we visited several more churches around Harrisonburg, all members of the Virginia Mennonite Conference of Mennonite Church USA. We discovered that they used our same hymnal and sang our same songs. These indeed were "our people." However, few people knew anything about the former General Conference that had framed our lives.

Visiting different churches is always a bit intimidating, even for those of us who have grown up in church and spent a lifetime working with churches. The important moments for me are how people greet us upon arrival and after the last "Amen." At one church the ushers asked me to move because I was sitting in someone's favorite pew. In contrast, at another church the greeter was a person we worked with years ago who welcomed us with hugs and introduced us to the congregation. At another church, no one interacted with us other than an usher handing us a bulletin. At yet another church, we were pleased that the pastor recognized us from our time in Kansas, even though no one else in the congregation greeted us.

Then Erwin and I went to Ridgeway Mennonite Church – and stayed! Marcia and John had gone there for more than a dozen years. We had visited Ridgeway with them before and knew several people already. Carla and Micah had decided to attend Ridgeway as well. There too, we were welcomed with hugs. We'd found our church home and transferred our membership from First Mennonite in Newton, Kansas.

Gradually Erwin and I both accepted leadership positions at Ridgeway – on the Outreach Commission and Worship Commission, respectively. The Ridgeway congregation began in the 1940s as an urban mission church in an economically depressed part of the city. By 2015, a renewed vision for ministry in the community around the church brought new vitality to the church.

Living in Harrisonburg

Harrisonburg, one of the Mennonite hubs, has been a good retirement location for Erwin and me. Thanks to our previous work at the denominational level, Erwin and I had already met quite a few people in the area. I was amazed when Erwin came back from an early morning walk and said that Ervin Stutzman, executive director of Mennonite Church USA, recognized him and greeted him by name. Myron Augsburger and others also remembered Erwin. We knew the staff at the Menno Media office in Harrisonburg because they had been our colleagues at one point as part of Mennonite Mission Network. It was nice that some people knew us based on our own past work and not only as the parents of our daughters.

We've learned to know other people, mostly within the Mennonite bubble here. More than enough opportunities abound to volunteer and attend events of interest, particularly in connection with either Virginia Mennonite Retirement Community or EMU. We have a nice balance between connecting with our busy daughters and their families and finding other activities and friends for ourselves.

We work at learning to know this community and region. We realize we have only scratched the surface of getting to know the Mennonite people and history here, let alone the extensive national history of this region. In general, we are outsiders here, and will always be to some extent. Because there were no General Conference churches in Virginia, some people here don't know what to think about us.

"Where are you from?" people ask us. That is a good question and has no simple answer. We've been "at home" in many places. For brevity, I indicate we've spent a significant time living in Kansas. Most Mennonites here know about tiny Hesston, Kansas, but their eyes go blank when we say we lived in Newton.

We live in the Parkview area of Harrisonburg. Parkview has even more and larger Mennonite institutions and agencies than there are in and around Newton, Kansas. When we lived in Newton, I was glad to live on the far south side of town away from the thick of the Mennonite world. Here, it feels right to be living amidst the Mennonites.

Virginia life and impressions

With each passing season, my appreciation deepens for the scenic beauty of Virginia. Shortly after our arrival, a drive at dusk with Ridgeway church-members Ray and Naomi Ressler in a vintage convertible felt ethereally beautiful. We rode along on narrow winding quiet back roads, passing lush green hills and trim neat farms.

Sometimes on those country roads one encounters very conservative Mennonites in horse-drawn buggies. Large semi-trucks barrel along the narrow roads, loaded high with crates of chickens or turkeys, headed to one of several large poultry-processing plants nearby. This area is the nation's second largest poultry producer.

Many of the Mennonites we know here are, like us, migrants from other areas, especially from Pennsylvania. We often draw upon our long-ago experiences in eastern Pennsylvania to make connections and to understand the broader world of Mennonites here in the eastern part of the country.

Local Virginians usually have strong southern accents, sometimes hard for us to understand. Erwin and I are learning about the lingering impact of the Civil War in this area – the war of aggression by the north, as they say here even yet. When my sister and her husband, LaRita and Darrel, were planning their visit here, they indicated they would be interested in seeing some of the Civil War historical sites and museums. So did our friends Gary and Jean Isaac, who moved from Newton to North Carolina shortly after we moved east. I had avoided thinking much about the Civil War and rather reluctantly scouted out places to take them.

There are indeed many historic Civil War places to see. Harrisonburg's current Main Street was the Valley Pike on which Civil War soldiers and military equipment passed back and forth. Civil War battles took place in this area. It is uncomfortable for us to hear the Confederacy and its leaders lauded and "Yankees" considered as the enemy. The Mennonites and Brethren living in this area suffered a great deal during the Civil War, including the burning of their barns, mills, and crops by Union soldiers from the north.

Beyond the university circles of EMU and the much-larger James Madison University here in Harrisonburg, politically most people lean Republican. Virginia recently became a "swing state," so our votes really do matter here, compared to in Kansas.

Harrisonburg feels like a big town to me, but with a population of about 50,000, plus more than 20,000 university students, it really is a city. Actually, it is a number of small towns that were amalgamated rather haphazardly into one city, making for a somewhat untidy look, especially in winter when bare branches reveal what summer foliage hides. Square blocks and streets are nearly non-existent here. Elegant old houses are generously sprinkled among smaller houses.

With everything we need close by, we gladly avoid the truck-packed, accident-prone Interstate 81 that passes through the city.

Wanting a different house

We tried to make the two-story townhouse on Central Avenue in Harrisonburg work for us. Yet we kept watching an EMU website with rental listings, hoping to find something with one-level living in the Park View section of Harrisonburg. I missed having a garage. Erwin missed having a yard.

We enjoyed becoming acquainted with our townhouse neighbors

– except that the people on one side of us were heavy smokers. Not allowed to smoke in their house, they stepped outside their door to smoke. If we had any window open, we'd close it quietly as soon as the smell of cigarette smoke wafted in. Learning to know the Iraqi refugee neighbors on the other side of us has helped us better understand the challenges Erwin's father faced as an immigrant. From the Iraqis, a brother and a sister who are Chaldean Christians and had worked with the American military, we also learned a great deal about the turmoil in Iraq and the Middle East.

One time Erwin helped Marcia mow her lawn when John was gone. That one time was enough to reawaken Erwin's "inner farmer." Except for several potted containers, there weren't any "farming" options at the townhouse. Rentals that would suit us seemed impossible to find. We wondered if we should change course and buy a house rather than rent until moving to VMRC. Perhaps God was chuckling a bit, leading us through the process of finding our next home.

Lake Terrace Drive

Erwin and I were introduced to the Lake Terrace housing development back in 2009. Orval and Dorothy Shank hosted each of us in their Lake Terrace duplex when we made trips from Kansas to help Marcia during her cancer treatments. That was when we thought we would buy a house. Whenever Erwin and I visited in Virginia, we checked out houses for sale all over Harrisonburg, including four houses on Lake Terrace Drive.

In late May 2012, on the EMU website I saw a duplex listed with "country views," renting for $1,200 a month. No specific location was given. Pricey, yes, but something made me phone right away rather than inquire by email. The duplex was on Lake Terrace Drive. It had one level, it had a garage, and it had a yard with options for gardening. Erwin did the spreadsheet numbers. We would have to dig substantially deeper into our retirement nest egg than we were comfortable doing. We let the homeowners know we didn't feel it was right for us.

We tried to reconcile ourselves to staying where we were at Central Avenue. I figured God had a mission for us in that neighborhood, especially relating to the Iraqi refugees next door.

A few days later, the duplex owners wrote back. They had investigated the rental market and realized they were asking too much. They lowered the rate to $985 a month.

"Lord, what are you trying to tell us?" I wondered in amazement.

We should at least look at the place, we decided. Erwin redid the spreadsheet. We could make this work. When we looked at 2203 Lake Terrace Drive, the spaciousness stunned us. But it was the country views of the valley toward the western and northern ridges and distant Allegheny Mountains that most impressed us. During all those years of living in flat areas, we had hoped to one day live somewhere on a hill with a view. As a bonus, from the front of the house, Massanutten Peak is seen in the distance. We moved in June 15, 2012. That was timely, because a few months later a knee injury temporarily made going up and down stairs impossible.

What a blessing and gift it is to live in this house. The views! The space! So many features to enjoy. Life feels "normal" again here after our sojourn in California and in a townhouse.

I struggled with feelings of guilt about the house being too much and too nice because I know there are many other Christians who don't enjoy such a lovely place. This house serves us, and our family, very well. The children hope we can live here a long time.

It is a nice neighborhood. About a dozen Mennonites live along this street, including Ed and Eddie Bontrager next door. We'd learned of Ed as an author some years earlier and then met them both when they visited their daughter and son-in-law serving on our team in Botswana. The woman who lives behind us, Jean Smucker Fisher, we also met when she and her family visited Botswana after having served there too.

From our front door, we can see the very hill, now covered with large, elegant houses, where we stood when Mom Eitzen predicted we would retire here. Also from our front door we can see the four other houses on Lake Terrace Drive that we looked at when they had been for sale. Behind our back fence is a rental about which we had inquired.

"Wait, just wait," God must have been whispering with amusement when we were considering each of those places. None would have offered the features we appreciate so much at 2203 Lake Terrace Drive.

Biblical references to sheep come alive as we watch sheep and lambs

Rempels' back yard view of Shenandoah Valley and sheep pasture, 2015.

munching grass on the steep hillside sloping down just beyond our back fencethat marks where the city ends and Rockingham County begins. Clouds, shadows, and light create a moving kaleidoscope vista of the sky, hills, trees, and fields, a calming reminder of God's presence in our lives.

Our crumbling denomination

During these years in Virginia, we are witnessing the unraveling of the denominational structures that have framed our journey through life. The congregations that formed our family heritage – churches attended by our grandparents, parents, siblings, and ourselves – have almost all chosen to disassociate from what was the General Conference and, more recently, Mennonite Church USA. The small country congregation of Erwin's teenage years in Montana dwindled, closed, and removed even the church building. With the divisive issue of same-gender relationships, by 2016 only three of the fourteen congregations in our heritage and personal experience remain with Mennonite Church USA, plus our current congregation in Virginia. Yet, I know that "My hope is built on nothing less than Jesus blood and righteousness. …On Christ the solid Rock I stand," as an old hymn reminds us.

Retirement Reflections

What a wonderful and delightful chapter this retirement is in Virginia. Erwin and I often look at each other and muse about how much we would have missed with our daughters and their families had we stayed in Kansas. We know there are no guarantees that our daughters will remain in this area, but for now, this is good.

Marcia's family outgrew their small house. They bought another house on a one-acre plot in the country, eight miles from where we live. They graciously allowed Erwin to tame an undeveloped strip of their acre and turn it into a berry patch, garden, and orchard.

Carla and Micah bought his brother's house on Central Avenue. After years of moving from place to place, it provides them with more stability and space for growing children.

The couple who owns the duplex we rent talk of living here again or selling it for their retirement. We are trusting that their timing will work well with our move to VMRC.

Erwin and I have traveled so extensively and seen so much of the world that we are content to stay home and avoid increasingly onerous travel conditions. Over the years we've adopted many new technologies and gadgets. Ever since Apple added a lower case "i" in front of their products' names, technology has advanced in an ever-faster confusing whirl that leaves us in the dust. We only somewhat reluctantly acquire things that are widely accepted and proven useful, and which our kids can help us use.

After so many years of needing to function as an extrovert, Erwin is content to indulge the introvert part of his nature. And this once-shy little girl seems to be more extroverted as the years go by.

Reflecting on life

Having attained age seventy, the biblical three score and ten years, there is more of life to look back upon than there is life to anticipate. We've seen tremendous changes in technologies and lifestyles. We cling to the basic beliefs of our Christian faith and the Mennonite perspective, even though at times there are more questions than answers.

Amazing is the word that best describes the cascading chapters that opened throughout the years. Had I set out to design my ideal life, I couldn't have imagined anything better than it has been. Life's joys have far outnumbered the sorrows. Enough challenges and new adventures kept pushing me for growth. After fifty years of marriage, Erwin and I still have each other and no serious health issues. Our financial needs have always been met. We enjoy these bonus years, this "jubilee-living" retirement. We are grateful for each day.

Why me? Why us? We're overwhelmed and give thanks to God.

Grandchildren: Katherine Rempel, Jeremiah Hurst, Madeleine Rempel, Shawna Hurst, Evan Weaver, Rachel Weaver, 2016.

Rempel family in 2016: Front: Shawna Hurst, Micah Hurst, Marcia Rempel Weaver. Second row: Carla (Rempel) Hurst, Katherine Gascho Rempel, Angela Rempel, Erwin Rempel, Jeremiah Hurst, Marc Gascho Rempel. Back: Madeleine Gascho Rempel, Rachel Weaver, John Weaver, Evan Weaver, Hannah Gascho Rempel.

Epilogue

Tents representing each continent we visited or lived in surrounded the Global Village exhibit area of the Mennonite World Conference assembly at Harrisburg, Pennsylvania, in July 2015. Inside each tent, interesting displays highlighted the Mennonite connections in that part of the world. People wearing colorful traditional clothing from their countries mingled with those of us dressed in Western attire.

The one and only day Erwin and I attended the Mennonite World Conference assembly happened to focus on Africa. Once again we enjoyed traditional African music enthusiastically played and sung by brightly garbed choirs. Singing together with a multi-national, multi-racial gathering of more than seven thousand people was a foretaste of the heavenly scene depicted in Revelation 7 of the great multitude from every nation, tribe, people, and language standing before God's throne.

Wherever we walked through the sprawling facility that day, or wherever we sat for the meetings, we encountered people we had met before – from other countries, other states, and even our next-door neighbors. These people helped reconnect us with the various chapters of our lives.

Attending Mennonite World Conference assembly reminded us that God is at work in the world, and that we've had the opportunity to participate in some small slice of that mission. What a privilege it has been!

Acknowledgements

Erwin and I want to acknowledge all those who trusted us with their unexpected invitations that changed our lives.

This writing project began first with our family in mind, especially the children and grandchildren. Erwin and I have wished for more information about how our parents and grandparents experienced life's events and changes. We wanted to avoid leaving such a gap for our family. Yet, even as I did most of the writing, I realized it might be for a wider audience. Laurie Oswald Robinson confirmed that for me when, as my writing coach of Tales of the Times, she read the material. Thus we offer to our church family, as well, some of how Erwin and I experienced changes in our lives, especially as we felt God leading us into various ministries of the General Conference Mennonite Church, then through the integration into what became Mennonite Church USA.

Perhaps the first inspiration for writing this came from my mother's youngest sister, Dorothy Bixel Killiam, who wrote about growing up in her generation. My cousins and I treasure her account of our parents' early years.

Of the many missionaries who inspired us and went before us, Lubin and Tillie Jantzens' lives not only served as role models but their book, *Guided Lives*, offered a pattern to emulate.

Ferne Lapp Bowman, a friend and writer in Harrisonburg, Virginia, introduced me to the Shenandoah Valley Christian Writers' Group. They have encouraged and motivated me to continue writing. Their insightful comments and questions about the excerpts I shared with them have been instructive. Ferne graciously read the whole manuscript, asking questions that other readers likely would ask as well.

Long-time friend Jean Isaac, currently retired in Winston-Salem, North Carolina, carefully pored over the manuscript, adding another pair of eyes to find typos, grammar issues, and other mistakes.

Lena Eitzen, who became Erwin's second mother, preserved family correspondence and copies of the letters and reports we wrote from our overseas locations.

My husband, Erwin Rempel, has lovingly encouraged and supported me all along the way of this project. He wrote about his experiences, supplied information, and read over the manuscript offering corrections and improvements. The publication of *Unexpected Invitations* in 2016 coincides with our celebration of 50 years of marriage.

About the author

Angela Rempel was born into a pastor's family in Chicago during World War II. Her parents soon left city life behind for rural pastorates, first in Missouri and then Montana. She and Erwin Rempel were married in 1966 after they graduated from Grace Bible Institute (now Grace University). A series of unexpected invitations led the couple into forty years of Mennonite ministries, beginning with a pastorate in Pennsylvania, followed by mission service in Brazil, mission administration based in  Newton, Kansas, an overseas assignment in Botswana, and culminated with another stint in Kansas as two Mennonite denominations became Mennonite Church USA.

Retirement in 2008 opened doors to yet other invitations to serve in different ways. In 2011 the couple moved to Harrisonburg, Virginia, where they are enjoying life near their two daughters and their families, while their son and his family live in Oregon. Erwin and Angela are members of Ridgeway Mennonite Church in Harrisonburg.